From the New Criticism to Deconstruction

From the New Criticism to Deconstruction

The Reception of Structuralism and Post-Structuralism

Art Berman

University of Illinois Press
Urbana and Chicago

©1988 by the Board of Trustees of the University of Illinois
Manufactured in the United States of America
1 2 3 4 5 C P 5 4 3 2

This book is printed on acid-free paper.

Library of Congress Cataloging-in-Publication Data

Berman, Art, 1938-
    From the new criticism to deconstruction : the reception of
structuralism and post-structuralism / Art Berman.
        p.   cm.
    Bibliography: p.
    Includes index.
    ISBN 0-252-01508-8 (cloth)
    ISBN 0-252-06002-4 (paper)
    1. Structuralism (Literary analysis).   2. Deconstruction.
I. Title.
PN98.S7B47   1988   87-27230
801'.95—dc 19   CIP

Contents

Acknowledgments

This book was written during a professional development leave generously awarded by Rochester Institute of Technology, through the College of Liberal Arts.

I would like to thank Perry Meisel, at New York University, for his encouragement, advice, and enthusiasm. The majority of the many scholarly works mentioned in this book are in the fine collection of the University of Rochester, to which it was the author's privilege to have access.

Bibliographical Note

Sources citations follow the format for parenthetical documentation recommended in the *MLA Handbook* (2nd ed., 1984). If the date of publication is an important piece of information, it is placed in parentheses following the mention of a title in the text, or in brackets if it is given as part of the parenthetical documentation. Quotations from the works of the seventeenth- and eighteenth-century empiricists are identififed by sections and subsections.

Introduction

This study examines the reception of structuralism and post-structuralism within the environment of American literary criticism. The central intention is to establish that while these movements at first seem to fulfill, from an American perspective, the basic criteria necessary for a valid critical theory, they ultimately prove to be based on underlying epistemological assumptions, particularly those concerning the self, that are incompatible with certain principal and fundamental influences on the temperaments and the predilections of American literary critics. The primary assumption is that the environment of modern American literary critical theory, like that of other disciplines of study, is—and historically has been—predominantly influenced by the suppositions of a philosophical empiricism, which within the Anglo-American setting simultaneously define the grounds of objective knowledge and the limitations of such knowledge. The early sections of the study identify the premises of empiricism and the effect of these premises on the development of the New Criticism; the later sections examine, in the same context, structuralism and post-structuralism.

The analysis begins by reviewing, in Chapter One, the empiricism of Locke and Hobbes, in which ideas in the mind are regarded as being derived from perception (sensation) and reflection (introspection). The duality yields philosophical contradictions, which eventually lead to the skepticism of Hume. The predominant theme is that the dynamic of this movement from empiricism to skepticism is repeated, cyclically, in the evolution of Anglo-American literary critical theory. After Hume, the first notable instance of this movement is the replacement of neo-classicism by Romanticism in the late eighteenth century. In the twentieth century, the pattern is repeated once again. The suppositions of a scientific methodology grounded in empiricism, especially beliefs about the self, are at first accepted and subsequently challenged. This dynamic occurs both in the development of the New Criticism and in the transition from structuralism to post-structuralism.

The second chapter begins with a discussion of the ways in which the New Criticism is founded on empiricist principles. First, I. A. Richards overtly allies critical theory with an empiricist psychology in his *Principles of Literary Criticism* (1925), drawing a distinction between scientific (propositional) truth and poetic statement. Criticism is purported to be a scientific-like knowledge of a content that is not itself such knowledge, a theme that has a number of variations in the New Critics, codified, for example, in René Wellek and Austin Warren's *Theory of Literature* (1942). Beginning with T. S. Eliot and including, from the 1930s to the 1950s, Cleanth Brooks, John Crowe Ransom, Allen Tate, and others, critics maintain the distinction between scientific knowledge and poetic assertion. It becomes important to establish the legitimacy of the status of poetry, and the poet, in a way not encompassed by the empiricist method, even though it requires an empiricist method to do so. The contradiction that follows is what generates the return, in this century, of the skepticism that traditionally follows the assertion of empiricism, much as Hobbes and Locke generated the skepticism of Hume.

Chapter Two subsequently considers how, over the years, the New Criticism gradually moves toward the incorporation of Romanticism into its theoretical assumptions. In particular, this involves an integration of the thought of Coleridge, who—at least from the point of view taken by Richards in the *Principles* and Brooks in *The Well Wrought Urn* (1947)—can be seen to have transformed a German Romantic philosophic idealism into an English psychology of creativity. The second chapter intends to show that this New Critical Romanticism is a reaction against the empiricism with which the New Criticism began. The reaction is provoked by an understanding that the consequences of empiricism are the elevation of scientific knowledge and technological practice and, for human behavior and the concept of self, a psychological determinism. Neither of these consequences proves compatible with the humanist perspective on self and creativity inherent in Anglo-American thought.

Chapters Three and Four demonstrate that four criteria for an ideal American critical theory emerge in the 1960s. First, an alliance with some form of empiricist science is demanded: such a legitimating science becomes, for a time, linguistics. Second, critical theory must allow for the maintenance of a free, autonomous, creative, Cartesian and Romantic entity of self, in opposition to the self of an empiricist scientific determinism. Third, theory must account not only for literary language, but for all language. Fourth, critical theory requires support on the political "left."

To understand this development in critical theory, a variety of American movements are addressed. The ambivalent response to the achievements and dominance of science and technology is evidenced by a study, in Chapter Three, of various writings of the 1950s and 1960s. During these years, furthermore, existentialism, particularly that of Jean-Paul Sartre, is imported from France, providing a counteraction to the same positivism against which the New Criticism reacts during its own history. Chapter Three also discusses the significance for literary critical theory of the history of psychology in America, especially the conflict between introspectionism and behaviorism. Finally, Chapter Four chronicles the rise of the study of linguistics, especially the work of Noam Chomsky. We find that American literary critics seek to reinforce the concept of the creative entity of self within an environment dominated by a science and philosophy that challenges and undermines such concepts. Critical theory does, however, retain the need for a scientific legitimation. Thomas Kuhn's The Structure of Scientific Revolutions (1962) offers a congenial model. Northrop Frye's Anatomy of Criticism (1957) combines empiricist investigation with a humanist outlook on self and freedom. The linguistics of Chomsky, similarly, provides a scientific format while preserving the same Cartesian self that Sartre defends.

In Chapter Five the focus shifts to the theory of structuralism. The underlying epistemology of structuralism and (as is demonstrated in later chapters) post-structuralism is a linguistic determinism: language itself becomes the causative constituent of selfhood and comes to replace the function of Marx's economic infrastructure in the analysis of social phenomena. Ferdinand de Saussure's Course in General Linguistics (1915) is used by Claude Lévi-Strauss and others to create a "semiology" based on a scientific empiricism. Language is viewed as the systematic integrity of a structure of phonetic differences, rather than as an aggregation of terms (words) each corresponding to a component of objective reality (things); language cannot be proven to be empirically referential, only differentially so. The linguistically constituted self of structuralism, which is maintained in post-structuralism, replaces the free, Cartesian self of existentialism, which had been derived from Edmund Husserl and Martin Heidegger.

I attempt to demonstrate—by discussing the work of Vladimir Propp, Claude Lévi-Strauss, A. J. Greimas, Claude Bremond, Roland Barthes, Tzvetan Todorov, the Russian Formalists, and Roman Jakobson—that when structuralism and, later on, post-structuralism come to America, they are received in an environment in which American literary critics seek to preserve the very notion of self that the French thinkers have been dismantling. Although French theory is well received—because of a purported scientific base, an ability to account for language, a political legitimacy, and, especially important, an elevation, even aggrandizement, of the status of language—theory in America, from the perspective of self, science, and empiricism, has in fact been moving in a direction contrary to European theory.

Thus, while the analytic techniques of structuralism at first appear useful, the underlying epistemological suppositions of structuralism are inharmonious with Anglo-American criticism. The reception of structuralism, discussed in Chapter Six, becomes an attempt to amalgamate it with other, less incompatible, movements or figures. Northrop Frye is for a time viewed as a proto-structuralist; some writers propose an interconnection between the work of Chomsky and structuralist theory. The effort to integrate structuralism into the Anglo-American environment becomes programmatic with, for example, Robert Scholes, Terence Hawkes, and Philip Pettit, despite the incompatibilities that arise in this effort. Jonathan Culler's *Structuralist Poetics* (1975) is the most significant attempt to create a synthesis, borrowing from reception theory in order to accomplish its end. In addition, we review the critique of structuralism that arises on the political left, notably in the work of Fredric Jameson and Terry Eagleton, which takes issue with the compatibility of structuralism and a Marxist historicism.

Chapters Seven and Eight show how post-structuralism is founded upon the recognition that the bonding of "signifier" and "signified" in Saussurian theory is a theoretical weakness. The "signified," which resembles Locke's "idea," can always be itself reduced, in a non-representational theory of language, to nothing but additional signifiers (more language). The bond, I will argue, is severed by Jacques Lacan, in the essays collected in *Ecrits* (1966); the severance is assisted by Michel Foucault's analysis of the separation of language and direct, or mimetic, referentiality in *The Order of Things* (1966). In the work of Jacques Derrida, especially *Of Grammatology* (1967), *Writing and Difference* (1967), and *Margins of Philosophy* (1972), the signified disappears entirely. For post-structuralism, Lacan and Louis Althusser provide the social psychology, Foucault the history, and Derrida—the focus of Chapter Eight—the full epistemology as well as the critical theory of "deconstruction." The "space" between signifier and signified, the fundamental post-structuralist metaphor, eventually opens an ontological chasm. The possibility of obtaining any kind of truth is eroded, which subverts both philosophical empiricism as well as the idealism of Kantian metaphysics. The self is constituted by language, beyond which there is nothing to know.

Central to the discussion of Derrida is the contention that a similarity exists between the movement from Locke's empiricism to Hume's skepticism and the movement from an empiricist structuralism to the Derridian skepticism of post-structuralism. Skepticism in the milieu of American literary criticism had opened an avenue of escape from empiricism as the New Critics began to incorporate Romanticism; likewise, Derridian skepticism oddly legitimates for American deconstructive critics the reinforcement of notions of self and creativity that are quite inharmonious with post-structuralist epistemology—a disharmony notable in the critiques of American deconstruction by Culler, Vincent Leitch, Frank Lentricchia, and Edward Said.

Deconstruction in America has come to be defined through the work of four critics, J. Hillis Miller, Paul de Man, Geoffrey Hartman, and Harold Bloom, each of whom is discussed in Chapter Nine. The attempt to integrate Derridian analysis, especially its ramifications for selfhood, is compromised in their writings. Beginning with a discussion of Miller's explication of late Romanticism in *The Disappearance of God* (1963) and then turning to his essays of the 1970s, I argue that the space left by the withdrawal of God becomes the "abyss" of linguistic indeterminacy in, for example, "Stevens' Rock," "The Critic as Host," and "Ariadne's Thread." While the signifiers of self in poetry (the poetic "I") undergo a deconstruction, there remains in Miller, nevertheless, the existential self, threatened though it may be by the subversion of the possibility of truth.

In *Blindness and Insight* (1971), de Man examines the structurally irresolvable self-contradictions of the discourse of normative literary criticism, basically through analyses of propositional prose. Some years later, in *Allegories of Reading* (1979), he makes an effort to integrate more fully the concepts of Derrida. The discussion of de Man considers how his theory of intention and of communication permits the preservation of the self of phenomenology and how his critical practice, in coming to terms with indeterminacy, incorporates the definition of the human dilemma in existentialism, which yields in de Man a mastery of the text that substitutes for the impossible mastery of time and mortality.

In the brief movement from *Criticism in the Wilderness* (1980) to *Saving The Text* (1981), Hartman, too, strives to incorporate Derrida into his critical theory. His need to sustain a belief in the critic as prophet and seer in a free creative act, a belief he inherits from Ro-

manticism and Emerson, is examined, especially in light of his "coun-
terstatement" to Derrida in *Saving The Text*, which reintroduces "representation" in language and a psychological poetic process resembling
that of Richards.

Bloom's criticism in *The Anxiety of Influence* (1973), *A Map of
Misreading* (1975), and *Kaballah and Criticism* (1975) proves to be a
rejection of the post-structuralist epistemology. Selfhood in Bloom—
derived from Freud, the Romantic poets, and Emerson—is paramount,
and only in his use of the idea of indeterminacy does he resemble the
deconstructionists.

Chapter Ten asks whether the interaction of post-structuralism
and American literary criticism does or does not provoke a severance
between the New Criticism and recent criticism. I attempt to show that
the critical methodology remains, in fact, the same, and that the issue
of empiricism and its alternatives comes to encompass an imported
post-structuralism of the kind adumbrated above. I believe there is a
continuity, not a conversion, even though the New Critical concepts
of objective knowledge and organic unity are subverted. This recuperation can be understood through, for example, an examination of
essays such as those collected by Jonathan Arac and by Robert Con
Davis and Ronald Schleifer. Chapter Ten also asks how, in the American setting, post-structuralism is modified by the influences of E. D.
Hirsch, reception theory, the speech-act theory of Austin and Searle,
and other disparate critical approaches.

As an encompassing theme, then, this volume examines the various
attempts to absorb, transform, and integrate structuralism and post-
structuralism, to make them applicable as critical methods within the
Anglo-American critical environment. I intend and expect to reveal
how each of these various approaches reflects the basic need of Anglo-
American theorists to legitimate criticism as a form of knowledge, to
understand the relationship between all language and literary language, and, above all, to maintain the creative entity of self.

CHAPTER ONE

Introduction to the Methods of Empiricism

The philosophy of empiricism has provided for English-speaking thinkers, including critics of literature, a clear and powerful methodology. In the physical and social sciences it has yielded so imposing an array of assertions about the world and its inhabitants that no discipline, from physics to theology, has been able to ignore its basic presuppositions. While Descartes had attempted to discard the systematic perplexities of an earlier scholasticism, its intricate embellishment of Christian revelation with elements of a subordinated Aristotelianism, he could achieve this only by assuming the autonomy of a rational entity of mentality—an immaterial mind, endowed with reason and certain innate ideas, which through its own powers could, it was proposed, begin with statements that appeared logically incontrovertible and deduce encompassing truths, an assuredness in epistemology and ethics. The British empiricists—Hobbes, Locke, Berkeley, and Hume—were rational, to be sure, but not, like Descartes, "rationalists." To them the human mind was not a demonstrably immaterial entity that could, through its own rational workings alone, yield the truths that it by its very nature itself contained: the mind was a capability for a methodology, based upon determinable psychological mechanisms, the capability of the human mind to generate knowledge through an organization of its *content*, a content solely derived from, caused by, "experience." An empiricist psychology was created from a preceding metaphysical "speculative" rationalism.

Empiricism

The empiricism of the seventeenth and early eighteenth centuries depends upon a basically aggregative or combinational theory of knowledge. Complex ideas result from the amalgamation of simple ones, which are themselves the immediate impress of experience upon the mind. It is "the most parsimonious model" to explain the operation of mentality on sense impression (Flanagan 122). It is for this reason that the empiricist approach was eventually, by the nineteenth century, found not especially helpful in investigating artistic *creativity*, which appears to demand more than a theory of the combination of ideas, although empiricism has long retained its applicability (even into the twentieth century, as in the methodology of the New Criticism) to the formal analysis of the esthetic *object*. The poetry of eighteenth-century England—of Pope, for example—has seemed to many critics in some measure unsatisfying or perhaps lacking in the full range of poetic inspiration when compared, depending on the critic's taste, with the poetry of those who preceded, whether the Elizabethans or the "metaphysical" poets, or those who followed, the Romantics. What now seem the limitations of much eighteenth-century English poetry (not that Pope, as G. Douglas Atkins demonstrates, is unresponsive to a deconstructive analysis) result in part from a reliance by the poets on a neoclassicism supported by empiricist doctrine. An elaborate philosophical esthetics, including theories of creativity, does not evolve as a distinct discipline until Kant replies to the empiricist tradition as it culminates in Hume. Subsequently this esthetics will find its way to England, transmogrified by Coleridge.

A philosophy founded on experience ultimately reveals the limitations of, and the constraints upon human knowledge: experience comes to serve as a boundary. What *form* experience will take cannot, in empiricism, itself be deduced, as Kant would later deduce it, from philosophical assumptions. Rather, the form of experience is given, is presented to perception (sensation), which receives it, and is the point at which analysis must commence. The content of the mind—as if the mind were an empty container that experience can fill or, in Locke's terms, a sheet of blank paper on which experience can write—is created by experience, an approach compatible with more recent theory that addresses the constitution and the construction of human consciousness, as does Marxism or a linguistic-based structuralism. The theories of Marxism and structuralism, I will argue, are themselves empiricisms, responding to the metaphysical systems of Kant and those who followed in somewhat the same way that the earlier British empiricists responded to a rationalist metaphysics.

Nevertheless, an empiricist view of the human self, of mind, cannot adequately explain what from a twentieth-century point of view—a point of view impermeated with an Anglo-fied Germanic Romanticism even when the critic purports to reject this—appears to be a creative act issuing in a *unique* form of truth, insight, or inspiration, contained in or communicated by an esthetic object. Since ideas, the content of the mind, are either the result of perception or of those molecular ideas aggregated or associated, not unlike the Lucretian model of atoms or of "particles and corpuscles" in physical nature (Robert Watson 193), it is not easy for those literary critics who believe that poetry contains a unique form of knowledge, not replicable in or reducible to other discourse, to account for the production of poetry in the classic empiricist way. Because this is, to a large extent, the project of the New Critics, they focus on the formal properties of the poem and the organization of experience.

Of course, it is possible to go around, or beyond, empiricism and to posit a distinct human faculty, an esthetic faculty that gains access to a special, even transcendental, realm of truth, or at least meaning, as in Kant or Schelling. Or one may posit a unique receptivity, usually inexplicable in its origins, of the poet, who becomes a conduit for truth, as in Plato's *Ion* or Shelley's *Defense*. Or perhaps one may believe there is a power to perceive experience in a way, perhaps "intuitional," available only to a limited few, as in Benedetto Croce. These options are obviously not available in a rigorous empiricism. The empiricist strategy—whether in Hobbes, the New Criticism, or Freud—is to identify a capability of the poet for the *organization* of experience, an ability that is not qualitatively different from customary psychological processes (it is not "mysterious"); rather, it is a very highly developed variant of these processes.

The problem can be identified in John Locke, for whom the human mind can come to know at first hand nothing but its own ideas. Consequently, it must be determined how ideas are gained. *How* the mind works can be discovered, but there is no metaphysical verification (if we interpret Locke along the lines taken by Berkeley and Hume) of the correspondence of the contents of the mind to an external material reality, which Locke assumes to exist (Leahey 103). This very problem is encountered by every subsequent generation of philosophers, including, two hundred years after Locke, the linguistic structuralists. Ideas come from "experience," in which "all our knowledge is founded, and from that it ultimately derives itself" (Locke, *An Essay Concerning Human Understanding* [1690] II.i.2): this is the "empiricist principle" (Copleston 78). "Our observation employed either about external, sensible objects, or about the internal Operations of our minds . . . is that which supplies our understandings with all the materials of thinking" (*Essay* II.i.2).

There are, then, two aspects of knowledge. Although Locke sees them as similar, they are likely not. That objects external to us leave impressions upon the mind supposes, of course, a mind capable of being impressed and an avenue into that mind. The senses provide, for Locke, these avenues, through which material "motions" can travel. This is a foundation of the scientific method, of data gathering. The position seems clear enough, even though it might be challenged. (It is not my purpose, either here or in what follows, to refute or rehabilitate any philosophical positions; I intend only to show their interaction with literary critical theory.) On the other hand, there is some difficulty with the notion that the operations of the mind, through "reflection," are also observed and are a source of ideas. First, to ask what (or who) performs this exploration raises the central issue of self and self-consciousness—an issue which, if it could be solved, might conclude the work of philosophy altogether. Locke cannot be blamed for assuming, as most everyone does, that the self exists and is active. Nevertheless, if humankind is capable of examining the operations of the mind (by which Locke means thinking, memory, willing, and perceiving), then one needs to assume that these operations of the mind are built in, so to speak, from the beginning: that is, the mind has innate properties. But if these innate properties are a source of ideas, then are they not, for a "self" conceived as having the potential to inspect its own operations, a pre-experiential source, even if the operations are activated by experience (Kendler 61)? Perhaps Locke has substituted an innate power of reflection for innate ideas (Watson 195). One does not simply observe memories or thoughts one at a time; rather, one gains as well an "idea" of memory, or of thinking, doubting, willing, and so on.

Since Locke, in Book I of the *Essay*, denies the existence of innate ideas, probably in response to certain theological conceptions of innate moral ideas (although the precept that all knowledge comes from experience itself resembles an innate idea), there may be a discrepancy here. This discrepancy will have some ramifications for the Anglo-American theory of literary criticism, as will be evidenced by a discussion of the New Critics. Once it is assumed that the operations of the mind are innate potentialities of the mind and that introspection reveals them, then more may be claimed to be found than what Locke had thought to authorize. Not that empiricism can be escaped by the New Criticism, which is a derivative of empiricism; but assertions will be made about whether the poet has special capabilities and whether, accordingly, poetry contains a unique truth or knowledge. If it does, what kind of knowledge is it, and in what manner is it perceived? How is it that this knowledge seems distinct from scientific knowledge, from "fact," which is itself—with Newton as the foremost example—the very, or perhaps the sole, knowledge that empiricism proposes to legitimate? The New Criticism, as it evolves, will attempt to demonstrate: the uniqueness of an inseparable poetic form and content, which makes the poem a self-contained and autonomous meaningful entity; the relationship of the poem to human experience in general, so that the "esthetic" need not be made a mysterious separate mental faculty; and the special mode of language that makes both this autonomy and this relationship simultaneously applicable. The New Critics will, in fact, come to separate scientific cognition and poetic cognition along lines resembling Locke's division between access to ideas through perception/sensation and through "reflection."

Before considering their proposals, however, a fuller acquaintance with Locke (to whom we will return in a subsequent section) and with the other British empiricists will be helpful.

Hobbes

Empiricism confines what can be known to human experience and reflections upon that experience. Consequently, it is situated between a pure skepticism on the one hand and an unverifiable metaphysics on the other, both of which it attempts to avoid (Scruton 83).

Objecting to Descartes' belief in the mind as a spiritual, immaterial substance, Thomas Hobbes presents a thoroughgoing materialistic rebuttal. Sense impressions are physical motions; ideas in the mind are motions in organic matter as well ("Objections," discussed in Stephen 33). All thoughts originate in experience, in sensation: "for there is no conception in a man's mind, which hath not first . . . been begotten upon the organs of sense" (*Leviathan* [1651] I.1). Since nothing more than materialistic motion and causation is posited, the theory is a determinism. The term "free subject" is without meaning. This approach will eventually issue in the psychological theory of behaviorism, a challenge to the relevance of mentality, over two hundred years later.

Language, for Hobbes, is arbitrary and conventional in the sense that it is "made" or devised by humans as an instrument. This is not to suggest that language somehow contributes to creating the world that is known to us; rather, the terms of language (words) are conventions standing for the ideas in our minds, the motions in the brain. "A name is a word taken at pleasure to serve for a mark" ("Concerning Body," *Works* I: 10). Since we can only experience "particulars," general terms denote collectively the members of a class, not abstract (Platonic) universal ideas.

Interestingly, Hobbes in his earliest writing seems to profess not only that speech (language) is necessary to understanding, but even that language and thinking are the same (Leahey 100). "What shall we say if reasoning is perhaps nothing else but the joining or stringing together of names . . . by the word *is*? In this case, reason gives no conclusions about the nature of things, but only about their names" ("Objections," IV; qtd. in Copleston 11). Although Hobbes is soon to turn in another direction, this early question seems provocative in the light of a modern linguistically based structuralism.

Desire, another foundation of empiricism in Hobbes, is basic to all humans. In his terms, motions in the brain cause motions in the heart ("Human Nature" [1650]). Humankind is motivated by desire, and the satisfaction of a desire is succeeded by the need to fulfill still another desire, interminably.

The literary criticism of Hobbes (who translated all of Homer) is consistent with his empiricist materialism. In his *Answer to Davenant's Preface to Gondibert* (1650) Hobbes states, "Time and education begets experience; experience begets memory; memory begets Judgment and Fancy" (214). The "strength and structure" of the poem come from judgment; the important quality of the poem is its "resemblance of truth." Fancy is responsible for the "ornaments" of a poem, and the beauties of imagery are derived from memory, in which the records of experience have been registered over time and linked together through a mechanical association, a natural process of the mind. The poet employs this process with dexterity, guided, if he is a good poet, "by the precepts of true philosophy." What the poet provides is his "experience and knowledge of nature"; and "resemblance of truth is the utmost limit of poetical liberty" (215). Robert Weimann has suggested that the neo-classicists found a metaphor appropriate if it was inherent in the "qualities of the subject," while for the Romantics metaphor was believed to characterize "self expression . . . achieved in the creation of character" ([1984] 201). A Platonic version of poetic creativity, in which the poet is receptive to transcendent truths that come to him, and not to others, in a special way, is dismissed by Hobbes as reflecting only the unreasonable position of poets in "heathen" times who were, erroneously, thought to be prophets of the divine. In Hobbes's *Answer*, then, poetic truth is measured by the criteria that philosophy applies to statements of other kinds. Judgment is paramount; the beauties of poetic language are ornamental, helpful to imitate "human life in delightful and measured lines, to avert men from vice and incline them to virtuous and honorable actions" (213).

Although the New Criticism will come to separate scientific knowledge and poetic meaning in a way quite unfamiliar to the early empiricists (because Romanticism will intervene), its approach will be based on empiricism's assumption that the primary origin of the content of the mind in experience is the key to understanding literary language. The New Criticism will maintain the belief that the *structure* of poetry corresponds, as a form of organization, to the particularly human experience of the world; this is distinctly different from a belief that the *ideas* in poetry are like those in philosophy or science. The New Critics will further maintain that analysis must proceed through an "objective" (even scientific) method, not from a critical impressionism or empathy.

Structuralism, too, will have an empiricist foundation, which in part accounts for its attentive reception in the United States. In addition, the transition from structuralism to post-structuralism resembles the movement from Hobbes and Locke to Berkeley and Hume.

Locke

John Locke, like his predecessor Hobbes, understood human knowledge, however complex, to derive from the basic knowledge originating in experience, in sensation. Since nothing can be known directly but "ideas" in the mind dependent upon sensation, truth cannot be achieved, as in Descartes, by the efforts of an immaterial mental substance (a soul, perhaps) exploring its own powers. Descartes' need to introduce an external authentication for truth, a non-deceptive deity, only generates a Cartesian impasse. That nothing but ideas can be known directly sets boundaries to knowledge: truths transcendent to experience cannot be obtained.

While it is not essential for our present purposes to pursue Locke's arguments along these lines fastidiously, it is important to understand the intellectual environment created by his work, for it is the environment in which Anglo-American literary critics write. The materialistic ideas of Hobbes met with some resistance, in Ralph Cudworth and Henry More (the Cambridge Platonists), for example. The publication of Locke's *Essay Concerning Human Understanding* in 1690, following upon the publication of Newton's *Principia* in 1687, assured the wide acceptance of empiricism. The philosophical method taken to support scientific inquiry, which in Newton's extraordinary work achieved influence and priority, has hardly diminished to this day.

As Newton had explored the material universe, so did Locke intend to explore the mind. But the mind seems known to each of us only through introspection, while the world outside appears available for public scrutiny. This situation caused Locke to propose two sources of knowledge: we can address either "external, sensible objects" or the "internal operations" of the mind. It might be argued that the techniques by which the external world can be explored cannot be those by which the mind is explored, that Locke illegitimately compares "reflection" on the workings of the mind with the way in which one examines what appears to be external to us, even granting that we can know nothing more about the external world than the ideas we have of it. For example, Locke sometimes uses the term "ideas" as if it refers to thoughts (mental items); at other times he uses the term as if it refers to the primary sense impressions themselves. (Kant will later criticize the empiricists for this application of a single term to separable notions.) Furthermore, when Locke discusses personal identity, he distinguishes between the organism, which can change radically over time, and the "person," whose identity is traced to a continuity of consciousness, memory of the past and anticipation of the future. Locke is responding to Descartes, for whom it is a self-evident truth that self, the thinking immaterial "substance," is enduring and indivisible (Descartes, *Meditations*, Sixth Meditation). For Locke, self-consciousness "constitutes the essence of personality," although as Hume will recognize, the notion of self-consciousness seems to presuppose the self, rather than to account for it (Allison 116). There appears, then, an internal/external duality that Locke's terminological bridge cannot span.

The problem, throughout the subsequent history of philosophy, does not disappear. We seem to know our "selves," the mind, directly (whether we are remembering or feeling a pain), and we seem to know the outside world indirectly, through sensation—unless we do not wish to assume that there is an external world.

Although the theory of language proposed by Locke would today have few proponents, it is of interest because of the very ways in which it is inadequate. In Locke's opinion, a word, which is a sound, signifies an idea in the mind: "so far as words are of use and signification, so far is there a constant connexion between the sound and the idea, and a designation that one stands for the other" (*Essay* III.ii.7). Words are "the instruments whereby men communicate their conceptions" (III.ii.6), "marks" for the ideas within the mind. It is "necessary that man should find out some external sensible signs, whereof those invisible ideas,

which his thoughts are made up of, might be made known to others"
(III.iii.1-2).

There are a number of difficulties here. Locke apparently assumes
that the ideas, having been caused by sensation, are already in the
mind regardless of language, and that language is a convenience for
transmitting these ideas to others. "The use of words is to be sensible
marks of ideas" (III.ii.1). What these "ideas" or "internal conceptions"
might in themselves be, preceding language as they do, is most obscure.
This obscurity again lends support Kant's criticism that the empiricists
use the term "idea" to encompass a sensation, its impression upon the
mind, a reference to external things themselves, and thought. For what
might it be, whether called concept or idea, that language can stand
for? Locke assumes thought in itself is distinct from the use of words;
the issue again becomes of central importance in the twentieth century.

Since, for Locke, the external object leaves an impression upon
the mind through a transmission of "motions," it may be that mental
ideas are conceived as images, pictures of the world, to which words
correspond: perhaps there is a word for each picture, with complex
words representing complex aggregations of pictorial ideas. It would,
however, be a challenge to describe how this accounts for the structure,
syntax, and vocabulary of an entire language. (How can one even
account for words like "but," or "is," or "not"?) It is important to note
as well that since, for Locke, the ideas in the mind—caused directly by
experience, by external sensible objects—are all that one can ultimately
know, one can argue that it is impossible to prove a clear relationship
either between the ideas and an external world or, consequently, between words and an external world (Robert Watson 191). Locke does
not himself proceed in this direction, as does Berkeley, who well recognizes the dilemma. Locke seems not to doubt that it is a very real
material world that impresses ideas upon the mind. Although ideas
are all we know, we are getting to know the world that actually exists—
in our own way, within our own limits. It is likely that, for Locke, the
"ideas" mediate between words and things themselves. (Words do refer
to ideas, but also through them, somehow, to an external reality.) Without such mediation, language would be unable to refer, indisputably,
to anything really existent, as Locke believed it did (Kretzmann 127).

Such a predisposition is what allows Locke's empiricism to un-
derwrite physical science. Consequently, his theory of language is a
"correspondence" or "referential" theory. There is a natural connection
between external objects and ideas and an equally natural, though
admittedly (as far as any specific word, as a sound, is concerned) con-

ventional, relation between words and ideas: language is partitioned like the external array of objects themselves.

Like Ferdinand de Saussure, Locke looked forward to a science of the "doctrine of signs" (*Essay* IV.xxi.4). Interestingly, Saussure, in the *Course in General Linguistics*, will define a sign as composed of a signifier (the sound) and a signified that is a "concept" in the mind, rather than an existing thing in the world (evidence that structuralism is a new empiricism); and the post-structuralist reformulation will focus upon the inadequacy of this notion of "concept" for the very reason that the notion of "idea" is perplexing in Locke. Unlike Locke, Saussure will lack the confidence to believe that language is partitioned the way the external world is, in itself. It will be Wittgenstein (in the *Philosophical Investigations*) who, for many, will refute the notion that words come into being through use as markers for our private inner thoughts and feelings, markers that then allow us to share what is on, or in, our minds.

Literary criticism is affected by this dilemma: the literary work is itself an object in the external world, yet the *meaning* of the work seems most comprehensible in terms of mental events that have occurred within the mind of the writer or do occur within the mind of the reader, unless we limit meaning in literature to either a straightforward theory of mimesis, usually based on Aristotle, or a naive realism like that found in the theories of some nineteenth-century novelists. But few critics can now tolerate such a restriction, because so much recent theory has attacked even the remote possibility that the world "as it really is" can be known and translated into a work of literature. Recent theory aside, the familiar esthetic theory and the poetry of Romanticism cannot simply be discarded from the critical milieu. Equally important, Westerners today hold ever-questing selfhood in greater esteem than the exterior world: much of modern literature is based on the distinction, at times quite painful, between what goes on inside us and what outside. No philosophy has brought a harmony. On the contrary, philosophy itself has likely diminished in importance because it has run out of comforting things to say on this matter, leaving the duality found in Locke to be divided between physical scientists on the one hand and psychologists on the other.

But the literary critic, again, has a stake in more than one claim. Insofar as the poem is a sensible external object, it must be available for an objective analysis of its structure and its formal procedures, as the New Critics declare. Insofar as the content of the poem, whether it can be separated from form or not, appears to be, in numerous poems, the "operations" of the mind, then it must be available for an analysis involving knowledge of mental operations, subjectivity, and a decision about whether or not such operations can yield "truths." The New Critics also declare that such truths may be evidently verifiable—not by a scientific objectivity such as physics professes, but by an objectivity nonetheless. Since the critic of literature needs to speak at once about an external object and an internal creative mentality, this position is somewhat challenging if the critic wishes to declare that literary criticism can achieve objective results in illuminating a poetic, non-propositional, truth: the critic is seeking to bring together what the history of empiricist thought has kept apart.

Literary critics no longer wish to retreat to positivism on the one hand or impressionism on the other. They need simultaneously an anatomy, an esthetics, and a psychology employing a single set of terms. In defining objective results, the critic hopes to reveal the poem as a structured object and, at the same time, to reveal the poem as *meaningful*, which is, in fact, the very concern (since it applies to language generally) that has led to the science of linguistics.

The unique problems that this circumstance poses may account for some striking developments in twentieth-century literary criticism. It has been recently asserted that since an analysis of language may be at the heart of epistemology, and consequently at the heart of every philosophical dispute, literary criticism—the investigation of the interaction of meaning and structure—may have the potential to become the paradigm for all philosophical analysis. In French structuralism and post-structuralism, the very duality found in Locke has resulted in theories of how the self is "constructed," a new empiricism (also created as a rebuttal to metaphysics and Cartesianisms), a language-based empiricism that we find in a Marxist analysis of "ideology" and in the most advanced work on psychoanalytic theory. It is not surprising, then, that such theories have been incorporated into the analysis of literature, for they promise to resolve through a linguistic model the internal/external dilemma as it applies to literary composition.

Berkeley

A quite remarkable development occurs in the philosophy of George Berkeley: If all that can be known are ideas in the mind, how is it possible to assert the existence of real objects at all? The logical consequence of accepting Locke's premises is a philosophical idealism. The "experiences" and the "ideas" are, in Berkeley, one and the same. When something is said to exist, this is equivalent to saying that it is perceived—*esse* is *percipi*, to exist is to be perceived. The existence of things "without any relation to their being perceived . . . seems perfectly unintelligible" (*A Treatise Concerning the Principles of Human Knowledge*, Paragraph 3). Berkeley, on this basis, defends the apparently extraordinary position that there is no real evidence that a material world, physical matter, exists at all. "In short, if there were external bodies, it is impossible we should ever come to know it" (Paragraph 20).

Berkeley proceeds in this direction, which might seem at first a clever conundrum, to undermine the determinate materialism of Hobbes and Locke, and to reintroduce the importance in philosophy of acknowledging the existence of God. Not that Locke denied spiritual reality (as Hobbes did) or even revelation, but he set such matters outside of philosophy altogether, "above" reason and not in conflict with it; and in this way no doubt saved himself many difficulties, since his philosophy, as Enlightenment thinkers understood, most naturally leads to a materialism (Copleston 141). For Berkeley, God becomes the philosophically demonstrable ground of all ideas about the world (Mourant 282).

There is some difficulty, again, in determining how we come to know the mind itself, even to know that there is a mind. It cannot be an "idea" since we do not perceive it directly. We perceive only its content, which is not the mind itself. Berkeley circumnavigates this issue by declaring that there is a "notion" of the mind (somewhat as Kant later invents the "transcendental unity of apperception") arising from individual awareness of volition and from the very fact that we each know ourselves to perceive. He subsequently demonstrates that God sustains a world of other minds, too (*Treatise*, Paragraphs 146-47).

It is not unwarranted to compare, in a preliminary way, the implications of Berkeley's proposals with those of the twentieth-century structuralists. It is, for example, possible to link Berkeley's philosophy ("to exist is to be perceived") to a reader-centered critical theory that makes "each reader responsible for constituting the text": "works of art do not exist, according to some current theories, until they have been perceived" (Lipking 80).

Moreover, if persons can obtain no knowledge beyond that of the contents of the mind, then they are, one might say, "locked into" the mind, which would lead to solipsism if God were not interjected into Berkeley's system (the maneuver taken by Descartes as well) to assure that there exists a world and a community of minds. The mind, to borrow Nietzsche's now familiar phrase, would become a "prison-house" from which there is no philosophical route of escape. The identical dilemma is faced by the structuralists, for in their view the structure of a person's language determines what his knowledge of the world can be. No transition from language to a reality can be known for what it really is, and language becomes, for some analysts at least, a "prison-house" (Jameson, *The Prison-House of Language* [1972]). Berkeley rejected Locke's assertion that we can distinguish between the primary qualities of an external sensible object (e.g., extension and other qualities that become the subject matter of the physical sciences) and secondary qualities that depend upon sensation alone, such as color or smell. To Berkeley, all of these qualities are alike ideas in the mind (*Treatise*, Paragraphs 9-15). It is not imprudent to identify this approach as a precursor to the post-structuralist rejection of the *immediate* presence of the Being posited by the phenomenologists.

Both systems, Berkeley's and structuralism, can lead logically toward a radical skepticism, or at least toward the recognition that radical skepticism cannot be dismissed. In the eighteenth century the notable skeptic is Hume; in the twentieth century it is Derrida.

This comparison will be helpful when discussing why post-structuralism was, in some quarters, well received by American literary critics; for it can be argued that structuralism and post-structuralism did not simply replace or displace the New Criticism. Quite the contrary, which is why a common ancestor of both the Anglo-American and the European criticism is often identified: Russian formalism. The fundamental empiricism of the New Critics was, for those who had the heart for it, pushed by the Europeans toward the recognition of some of the extreme implications of focusing on the formal properties of language itself as a key to meaning, just as Berkeley pushes empiricism. This is the direction of certain American critics, the deconstructivist critics. There is, of course, more to be said about this transition, during which some historians of literary criticism do, in fact, place what they identify as a moribund New Criticism in opposition to structuralism and post-structuralism.

Hume

Agreeing with his predecessors that what can be known are ideas in the mind, and that complex ideas are formed as an aggregation of simple ideas based on experience, David Hume does not retreat to Berkeley's position, which repudiates the substantiation of an external physical reality in order to introduce the presumption that God in some way assures the integrity and coherence of human knowledge. Ideas that are "facts," ideas that are "empirical" can come, for Hume, only through experience (*A Treatise of Human Nature* [1737]). Ideas are linked together in the mind by "association," that is, by resemblance and contiguity in time and place (*An Enquiry Concerning Human Understanding* [1751]). Consequently, there can be no proofs of God, or the assertions of religion, or of moral principles. Other ideas that seem intuitively or demonstrably certain, such as arithmetic, appear so because they are relational and definitional; they are not facts about the world (*Treatise*). Hume's stance is an absolute experience-based psychological science (Scruton 121): the experimental procedures of Newtonian science can be extended to a study of humankind, with the law of "association" as central a principle as that of "gravitation" in Newton (Robert Watson 205).

As for Berkeley, knowledge of a real, external, physical world is put in jeopardy by Hume, but he accepts the responsibility for an unyielding doubt and for this reason has been most frequently read as a consistent skeptic. While, for example, the existence of causes and effects may appear certain to us, nothing can be known but the frequent or constant conjunction of events, one following the other. That there is cause and effect cannot be demonstrated (*Treatise* I.ii.3).

Even the existence of a "self" is placed in doubt: reflection on the mind reveals not a Cartesian "I" but simply, at any moment, a bundle of sensations, memories, feelings, and so on (*Treatise* I.iv.6). What, then, beyond these, can the self be? That self-consciousness accompanies thought cannot, as for Locke, validate the existence of a continuing entity of self-identity. This problem is, of course, addressed in the twentieth century by theories that attempt to describe a self equivalent to its content; for by the mid-nineteenth century "the self could no longer be conceived of as a transparent unity acting as an originating intention upon a purely instrumental language or as the neutral locus of immediate perception" (Donato [1979] 40). Marxism and Freudianism avoid the assumption of an autonomous, indivisible, immaterial Cartesian self pre-existing experience, which Descartes derives from the concepts of the human soul in earlier theologically based philosophies.

Hume assumes that human beings are motivated by passions, not by reason, which corresponds to Hobbes's notion of human desire and Locke's belief that humankind's basic motive is to seek happiness and avoid pain.

Hume believed in deliberate action, that our volition can cause the outcome of an action. "The motion of our body follows upon the command of our will. Of this we are every moment conscious." At the same time, "the means by which this is effected . . . must forever escape our most diligent enquiry" (*Enquiry*, Section 52). Surely this avoids rather than resolves the issue, especially since Hume has already established that cause and effect of any kind cannot be proven. Even assuming cause and effect, this "will" need not be *"free* will"; it may be argued that the "command" given by the will is itself fully determined.

The point is of interest because such an approach to human action is incompatible with theories of creativity professed by Coleridge and other Romantics. Since writing is willed action, those who think like empiricists will, if they are like most literary critics, feel confined and discontented by Locke and Hume on these points and endeavor somehow to supplement them. In the twentieth century, a disillusionment in some circles (including literary ones) with the social consequences of a society in which science and technology predominate will provoke an attempt to interject Romantic notions into a fundamentally empiricist outlook, more because of the temper of the times than for reasons of philosophical rigor. In the 1950s the New Criticism participates in this attempt, and more recent innovations in literary criticism reflect it, especially those following the efflorescence of free will, self-discovery, and the quest for fulfillment in the 1960s. Accordingly, an overview of cultural change is essential to understanding modifications of critical theory.

With this admittedly scanty summary of Hume, one can nevertheless look ahead to the sequence of ideas that will ultimately lead to the linguistic structuralism based on Saussure and the post-structuralism that will follow. Kant responded to Hume, in the *Critique of Pure Reason* (1781), by stating that the recognition that we know nothing but the content of the mind, ideas, does not lead to skepticism; rather, it demonstrates that there is, in fact, subjectivity and therefore a subject. Since the subject is the sole basis of knowledge, it cannot itself be used as an argument to eliminate itself. Furthermore, some ideas that seem absolutely necessary are neither purely logical (like mathematical relations) nor facts that can come from experience (the idea that space is infinite, for example). Although Kant maintained that we only know what is in the mind and cannot, therefore, know things outside ourselves as they really are, in themselves, he also believed that the self, the material world, causality, and ethics could be derived from a thorough understanding of subjectivity. The linguistic structuralists, eager not to fall into idealism, will look to the processes of language as an explanation of how subjectivity or consciousness of self arises and how what seems to be knowledge is acquired. Language will be said to create, or to have a hand in creating, both the knowledge of the world and our minds. We find it declared, quite recently, that "the 'self' has . . . already been discredited among almost all philosophers" (Johnston [1983] 109). Since language is at once internal (a product of mentality) and external (an existent phenomenon, e.g., writing, sound, bodily movement), it will come to serve as the bridge between ideas of external, sensible objects and ideas of the operations of the mind. Language encompasses both.

In addition, the post-structuralists, relying on Nietzsche and Derrida, will argue that since what we know is nothing but language, any explanation of things, any organization of experience, Kant's included, will be nothing else than more language—a modern version of Hume's disclosing the ramifications of positing that knowledge is limited to Lockean ideas. The movement from Hobbes to Hume, via Locke, resembles the movement from Saussure to Derrida, via structuralists like Lévi-Strauss.

Hume on Taste

Hume wrote, in a biographical essay entitled "My Own Life," that he was "seized very early with a passion for literature." Some correspondences between the New Criticism and empiricism as it culminates in Hume are apparent in Hume's essay "Of the Standard of Taste." Admittedly, Hume, as Ralph Cohen notes, "does not have a systematic literary theory" (97).

"Though it be certain that beauty and deformity . . . are not qualities in objects, but belong entirely to the sentiment; . . . it must be allowed that there are certain qualities in objects, which are fitted by nature to produce those particular feelings" ("Standard of Taste" 481). One can make "general observations, concerning what has been universally found to please in all countries and in all ages" (479). Consequently, "there are certain general principles of approbation or blame, whose influence a careful eye may trace" (480). There are, in fact, universal "principles of taste." Hume understands that judgments of taste often differ from time to time or place to place, but this does not deter him from the support of universal principles. Errors of judgment, of taste, may be caused by prejudice or other "defective states" of a person, in the way that a person with jaundice is unable to properly judge colors (486).

The theory suggests the formalism of the New Criticism, presuming that that there are qualities in the poem itself about which persons of sound judgment can agree, even though Hume's "princi-

ples" are more evaluative criteria than structural ones. Although the
term *New Criticism* encompasses a variety of opinions rather than a
homogeneous system, the belief that the poem itself contains characteristics, properties (in particular, the organization and the structure
of language) that can be objectively identified by a competent critic,
an ideal reader, is central. Not that all persons have the capability to
make sound judgments in these matters. "Few are qualified," persons
"with good sense and a delicate imagination, free from prejudice"
(484). "There is just reason for approving one taste and condemning
another" (486).

Furthermore, the purpose of the poem is to please and the source
of pleasure involves "the general rules of art" as well as the receptivity
of the reader to this pleasure, to what Hume calls "beauty." This the
place where I. A. Richards begins. Like Hume, Richards separates what
is communicated by the poem from the facts of science. To Hume, in
fact, universal standards of taste are more dependable, more reliable,
than the conclusions of our understanding, since (in keeping with
Hume's criticism of human knowledge) the latter may easily be mistaken (485). The astronomy of Ptolemy may today have no adherents,
but the *Iliad* retains its devotees.

This distinction will be of utmost importance to the New Critics
because it can lend support (on shaky ground, to be sure) to a dual
theory of truth or, more precisely, of cognition—of scientific truth as
distinct from the truths of poetry, which are not propositional statements. Admittedly, for Hume, as for Hobbes (but likely for John Crowe
Ransom, too), the *truth* in a poem should be recognizable, perhaps
even substantiated, by reason, like philosophic truth, and is not the
same as the effects of *beauty* caused by the poem; but, after all, Romanticism had not yet intervened to link beauty, the esthetic experience, and the truth-bearing insights of the "imagination," a word that
the empiricists, unlike Coleridge, used for the associational or combinational function of mind. And the empiricists would, for obvious
reasons, disdain Platonism, even though it was available to them. In
Hume, "taste" is more a term designating a competent identification
of quality, an aptitude for judging value, and not a critical capacity for
meticulous close reading and structural diagnosis. Nevertheless, positing objective criteria and the possibility of critical consensus, with "a
due attention to the object," is an approach quite congenial to the New
Criticism.

While Hume does not excuse "vicious manners" described in a
poem of another age, he has some tolerance for outmoded or erroneous
views that might be found because of the time in which it was written.

"All the absurdities of the pagan system of theology must be over-looked" (488). One recalls that T. S. Eliot will ask only that the creed of the poet be mature and worthy of respect. The later New Critics will take the same precaution to discriminate between the apparent factual content of the poem, its truth or falsity, and the *function* within the poem of any such content.

In other essays as well, Hume's speculations are not dissimilar to the orientation of the New Criticism, especially to some of the earlier ideas of Richards, who attempts to place the function of poetry within a psychological science, rather than within a metaphysical idealism. "Poets in all ages," writes Hume, "have advanced a claim to inspiration. There is not, however, anything supernatural in the case" ("Progress of the Arts"). Hume persistently writes with a psychological vocabulary about the function and effects of art. In "Of Tragedy" he makes tragedy "conform to the principles governing normal human passions" (discussed in Cohen 105).

There is the sense in Hume that human experience is fundamentally fragmentary, disorganized, and sporadic, and that it is an important function of the mind to organize—by piecing together or patching up, if you will, or filling in gaps—a coherent, consistent view of reality. That poetry partakes in presenting a coherent vision of chaotic, diverse, perplexing experience is central to T. E. Hulme and to the later New Critics; and an esthetics of the formally satisfying completeness and organizational totality of the poem can be based on Hume (Piper [1983]).

Conclusion

With its secular methodology of analysis and its straightforward language; its looking toward "experience" to locate the origin of all mental content; its fundamental predisposition to see the human being as a biological creature, endowed with motivation and capabilities, most prominently passion and reason, who can be known objectively, as "natural" science comes to know the world through examination and a precision of deduction from ideas caused by primary perception and sensation rather than innate truth; the empiricism of Hobbes, Locke, Berkeley, and Hume reflects what may be seen as the strategy most basic, because most comfortable, to thinkers in nearly every intellectual discipline in England and the United States.

An analysis of the New Criticism will give specific attention to its pronounced empiricist leanings: an esthetics that rests upon a psychology, rather than a metaphysics; a poetics of form, structure, and organization, rather than of transcendent truths; a methodology presumably objective and consequently having the potential to yield agreement about the properties of an esthetic object; a clear and precise writing style avoiding abstruse philosophical concepts; and a theory of creativity founded in notions of the enhanced capacities and procedures of the author, rather than in mysterious esthetic powers.

Not surprisingly, the tactics of the New Criticism will be found to be influenced by the Romanticism that intervenes between the eighteenth century and the twentieth. This does not, however, change the basic empiricist outlook (yet it not infrequently muddles it), which pulls "Romanticism" in England away from the German metaphysics that so influenced Coleridge toward a practical literary criticism.

It is intriguing to note at this point what will need to be addressed further along: While Romanticism may be explained, in part, as a reaction against the science of the Enlightenment, and while the New Criticism may be explained, in part, as a reaction against the dominance of scientific thought and technology in the twentieth century, why is it that the New Critics were, nevertheless, no real allies of the Romantics? This occurs because the literary critics in England and America in the first half of the twentieth century were reacting not against empirical science and methodology itself, which they (being empiricists) must respect and emulate, but against the *social consequences* of science and technology and of an economy based upon them. This very problem—the interrelationship of culture, economics, and language—is addressed in a way quite unfamiliar to most Americans before the last two decades by many European thinkers. Influenced primarily by Marxist controversy, those Europeans will come to be read by literary critics in the 1960s and 1970s for a new empiricist methodology set upon linguistic theory.

CHAPTER TWO

The New Criticism

To link the New Criticism with empiricism is neither to present a unified history of philosophy and literary criticism nor to illustrate the direct influence of certain philosophers on critics. Rather, it is to recognize that both philosophers and critics work within a common, and continuous, intellectual environment in which ideas necessarily interact, regardless of, and in addition to, the specified intentions of any one theorist. That ideas and systems illuminate one another, becoming mutual sources of understanding and interpretation, is distinct from the tracing of direct lineage, even when this exists. To examine the concepts of the New Criticism from the point of view of an empiricist heritage is to clarify the context in which the New Criticism can be understood, which will lead, afterward, to a clarification of the American reception of structuralism and post-structuralism in the 1960s and 1970s.

The literary critics who are customarily gathered together in studies of the New Criticism, as if it were a "school" of criticism, in fact have different, at times contrary, opinions. They often, however, seem to share the assumption that they are all tilling the same, or at least adjoining, fields. A lengthy meticulousness on this point is not feasible here. Included in the discussion below, which pertains to poetry, are I. A. Richards, T. S. Eliot, T. E. Hulme, Cleanth Brooks, Yvor Winters, John Crowe Ransom, Allen Tate, Robert Penn Warren, and W. K. Wimsatt; whatever similarities can be perceived among them are emphasized, despite an acknowledgment of their dissimilarities and disagreements.

The New Criticism is based in empiricism, a philosophy given its fullest expression, as we have traced, in the late seventeenth and early eighteenth centuries. In empiricism, all ideas, the content of the mind, are grounded in "experience." Fundamental ideas come from perception (sensation) and reflection (introspection); complex ideas are compounds of these or organizations of them, which the human mind has the power to form. The methodology is itself "experiential," like that of the physical and social sciences, rather than that of a "speculative," "rational," "metaphysical," or "idealistic" philosophy.

While empiricism provides a philosophical ground for the scientific method, it is also a theory of self, consciousness, and epistemology not limited to the physical sciences. For example, empiricism can include skepticism. To place the New Criticism (and, later, structuralism) within empiricism will be to emphasize the philosophical basis that it shares with scientific investigation, the theoretical compatibilities between disciplines at the level of empiricist assumptions. Furthermore, while the critical method may be "scientific," the method should not be confused with the content of the poetry investigated by the method, which, as we will see, is said to be the opposite of scientific.

The New Criticism will find poetry to be about human experience, particularly about the poetic "organization" of such experience, whether obtained through perception or reflection. This type of organization of experience is poetic form, a use and configuration of language involving structure and pattern—together with certain rhetorical devices, such as metaphor, irony, and paradox—which serve to organize the complexity of human experience, often itself disparate and incongruous. The New Critics will seek, at first, these organizational qualities of the poem rather than metaphysical, transcendental, or revelational knowledge. The critic will often seem to be a scientific-like investigator of the phenomenon of the poetic object, neither an effusive impressionistic critic nor a seeker after arcane poetic mystery.

The New Criticism is, nevertheless, quite far from a coherent theory. Nor does it remain consistently empiricist: because the critics, as work progressed in the 1930s and 1940s, increasingly strove to accommodate (more for cultural than for theoretical reasons) a portion of the approach to poetry customarily subsumed under the concept of "Romanticism," with its elevation of a special poetic knowledge based in a Kantian esthetics inimical to empiricism, a poetic knowledge of "higher" realities, beyond science.

This accommodation occurs not because the New Critics are themselves Romantics attempting to expand upon the metaphysics of Coleridge and the German philosophers he admired—which is the position taken in *The New Romantics* (1962) by Richard Foster, who recognizes that, over time, the New Criticism had "a shift of critical emphasis from the idea of poetry-as-form to the idea," which he links to

Romanticism, "of poetry-as-meaning." Rather, the accommodation, which never becomes a synthesis, occurs because the empiricism inherited by the New Critics (even if blended, as Charles Altieri notes [311], with an Arnoldian humanism) cannot adequately account for poetry, at least not to most twentieth-century humanists. Modern critics attempt to stretch their empiricism to include Romantic notions (for example, poetry as "higher" knowledge, or "intuited" knowledge) because, in a scientific and technological age, they need a place to turn, a place that will provide a uniquely defined realm for poetry. Grounded in an empiricist tradition, the New Critics seek at the same time not to be dominated by the scientific worldview (a process traced by Graff in *Literature Against Itself* [1979]*) that originally provides them with their methodology. This leads not to a Romantic criticism but to an empiricist poetics filled with incongruities.

Since these incongruities are caused by an attempt to integrate a theoretically incompatible "Romanticism," they cannot serve to resolve any critical issues. Only a further development of empiricism may do that for empirical critics; and such a further development will come to depend, in the 1960s and 1970s, upon a theory of language and self unavailable to the New Criticism.

In the following sections, the discussion will review (1) what the poem communicates, (2) the role of the poet, (3) poetic language. A

---

*The belief that poetry contains, is defined by, a form of truth other than the propositional assertions of science is analyzed with exceptional insight by Gerald Graff, who rightly attributes the rejection of the claim for logical, rational, verifiable truth in poetry to "the warfare of literary intellectuals against technology, commerce, and utilitarianism" (*Poetic Statement* [1970] x). He argues that this exclusion of propositional assertion and logical idea from poetry is detrimental to literary criticism, that it is inapplicable to a large class of poetry, and that it is, in fact, a relinquishing to science, by default, of the very battlefield of truth for which the literary critics, with their alternative mysterious "truth" usually ill defined and vague, avow they are defending. Advancing this argument in *Literature Against Itself* (1979), Graff presents the New Criticism as a reaction *against* empiricism and modern science. Scientific rationalism is made to seem antagonistic to poetry (145), which is consequently left in "irrational" subjectivism, relying on a "talismanic use of the term 'experience,' " as if experience itself were opposed to "logical concepts about experience" (139). He sees an alliance between the New Critics and the more modern "radical skepticism" of Derrida and his American disciples.

Graff's argument is an admirable one; the only issue I take with it here (albeit a crucial one) is that it does not recognize that the confrontation occurs *within* empiricism (even skepticism is empiricist), rather than *against* empiricism. The New Critics are seeking an augmentation of empiricism, through formal analysis. The philosophical "opposition" is idealism and metaphysics. Scientific methodology and empiricism are not discarded by the literary critics; quite the contrary. The *social consequences* of science and technology, a far different affair, constitute the enemy.

concluding analysis of the New Criticism looks forward to the influence of structuralism on American literary criticism.

The Poem as Object

The scientific codification, categorization, and an unrelenting rationalism that appeared in the mid-seventeenth century, in part founded on Hobbes's concept of mind, unfortunately undermined, according to Cleanth Brooks, the Jacobean and Elizabethan poetic practices (*Modern Poetry and the Tradition* [1939] 33). As reason and emotion became separated, the former was given priority in the determination of truth, and the specific techniques by which poetry is able to present experience were designated as additions or ornaments to a truth recognizable by non-esthetic criteria. John Crowe Ransom believed that "what Bacon with his disparagement of poetry had begun in the cause of science and protestantism, Hobbes completed" (*World's Body* [1938] 134-35).

For Brooks, however, and for the New Critics generally, the meaning that poetry contains is different from that of science and is not to rival, parallel, or contain truths of the sort that, in science, are propositional and can be shown to be demonstrably true or false (*Modern Poetry* 45). That poetry has an important meaning but not a meaning with the truth values of science, while at the same time critical method is itself a scientific-like endeavor, is an essential assumption of the New Criticism. The particular project and contribution of the New Criticism is to attempt to incorporate a plausible theory of special poetic meaning within a structure of empiricist thought that, in its origins, seems unreceptive to such a theory.

The extraordinary success of the scientific method (of "positivism"), not only in its systematic descriptions of an orderly physical world but in its creation of a view of the world that is both materialistic and deterministic, jeopardized the truth value of whatever assertions could be made by poetry. Given enough time, it seemed, science would fully explain whatever there might be to know about the universe and humankind, and would bring, beside this knowledge, equitable government, prosperity, health, and general well-being. It has been argued, convincingly, that with science in command of exploring the world around us, poets more and more claimed subjectivity, the contents and potential of the individual mind, as their domain of interest: that they considered subjectivity, which within Romantic theory might be opposed to science as an alternative access to truth, as even a higher form of access to truth than science could attain. The distinction between

scientific truth and poetic truth can be found, for example, in Wordsworth's 1800 preface to the second edition of *Lyrical Ballads*. Whether
Romanticism is seen as a withdrawal to the interior by the poets (Peckham [1970]; Eagleton, *Literary Theory* [1983]), a transformation of earlier
theologically based concepts of salvation and redemption (Abrams,
Natural Supernaturalism [1971]), or a courageous focus on human capability and aspiration (Barzun [1961]) is a less important issue, at this
point, than recognizing that the meaning of poetry, once severed from
truth of a scientific kind, could no longer rest satisfied on a simple
theory of mimesis. Rather than holding up a "mirror" to the world,
poetry would have to establish its own territory and affirm the uniqueness and indispensability of its insights (Krieger, *New Apologists* [1956]
5). This proves especially true in the twentieth century, when science
and technology come to seem unchallengeable in their methods and
results (Pritchard [1956]). According to many of the most important
literary critics, the modern outcome was unforeseen in the enlightened
eighteenth century: a technological dehumanization of culture, a reduction of knowledge to fact, an eradication of belief (or faith) in what
cannot be scientifically placed in evidence, and an accompanying ero-
sion of the values most supportive of human community. Ransom, for
example, in *God Without Thunder*, saw science as power-knowledge
contributing to hubris, while poetry challenges this very hubris. Science
is not fully trustworthy (Goldsmith [1979] 103). Poetry, then, is essential to right the imbalance; what it has to say is of the utmost
importance.

But what does poetry communicate if not demonstrable truth
about the world? What does it mean? Before answering the question,
the New Critics assumed that the poem itself is a self-contained and
self-sustaining entity (Krieger, *New Apologists* 21). The relationships
among the words of the poem construct a linguistic milieu that contains
a meaning defined by that milieu. Meaning is not derived by evoking
direct factual correspondences between the poem and facts of the matter otherwise ascertainable, although the critics are obliged to ask how
the poem does relate to the external world. The poem is an object,
open to an analysis that can be confined (more in theory than in practice) to the poem itself. The procedure of close reading and a working
critical vocabulary evolve around this assumption.

Designating the poem as an autonomous object to be studied
entails rejecting critical methods that would understand the poem
through history, biography, sociology, or other non-literary disciplines,
a significant move that came at a time, the 1930s, when "most literary
study was understood to be a variety of history" (Adams 205). The

tactic has often been linked to Kant (as in Handy [1963]), who gives, in the *Critique of Judgment*, to all esthetic objects a special ontological status, although the New Critics for the most part do not seem extensively familiar with Kant. But, significantly, this tactic also gives the poem a special status understandable through the assumptions of empiricism. It has been emphasized that Locke believed knowledge to come from two sources: ideas in the mind resulting from experience, the impress of external objects on the mind; and reflection, the ability of a person to look at the workings of his own mind, such as memory, thinking, and willing, and to report accurately upon them. If the poem is thought of as an external sensible object, which can be objectively analyzed as such, and if at the same time the content of the poem concerns what is going on in the mind of the poet or the reader (an organizing function, for example), then the poem bridges both sources of knowledge, which is to become the crucial problem in the study of language. In effect, poetry maintains a mimetic function, embodying the results of reflection on the operations of the mind and portraying certain of these operations through poetic structure rather than through scientific description. Although one can recognize this bridge (between perceptual mentality and its reflection upon itself), it is, in fact, no more explicable in the theory of the New Criticism than it is in Locke, who without an adequate theory of language can only resolve the distinction between ideas of (about) the internal mind and ideas of the external world by saying that ultimately they both rely on "experience." As Berkeley saw, this assertion can have the logical consequence of denying material substance altogether: we can, after all, know nothing but these ideas, the existence of an external material world being insusceptible of proof.

The New Critics were able to identify an external *object* whose meaning has primarily internal import. This was the contribution of I. A. Richards and founds the New Criticism in the attempt to exercise a scientific procedure of analysis on an esthetic object, professing to fill a theoretical gap between an analysis of the (apparently) external world by the physical sciences and an analysis of the internal world by psychology, while moving toward an esthetics of cause and effect (how the poem works). Later, to anticipate, this theoretical gap will be filled, in structuralism, by a general model of language (not confined to poetry) in which *all* language will be—like the poem to the New Critics, a notable similarity—both an external and an internal phenomenon.

Again, the approach of the New Criticism does not resolve the issue, for how the external world and consciousness are linked remains perplexing despite the New Critics. But it emphasizes what might be the major task of modern literary criticism in English: to bind together (as an attempt, to be sure, not an achievement) the outlook, philosophical biases, and critical method of scientific theory—based on an empiricism in which man is an observer of objects and a formulator of publically testable abstractions (laws or general descriptions) about the physical world and mentality—with the invigorating committedness to the importance and significance of poetic meaning in English Romanticism, characterized by its ideas of the poet as a creative participant in the structuring of the world with access to unique knowledge, in that peculiar English version of a German idealism whose own critical method and philosophical underpinnings must, nevertheless, in the long run be rejected.

To isolate the poem is, then, to create an external object capable of scientific analysis, an object with a meaning whose significance is not itself dependent upon a demonstrable (experimentally verifiable) truth-bearing reference to that external reality in which it exists. And the New Criticism is, as an empiricism, a form of scientific analysis of unscientific meaning, which is a capsule definition of the movement. While science itself may be attacked, in general terms, as Allen Tate attacks the social sciences in *Reason in Madness* (1941), the techniques of the New Critics, insofar as they seek objective properties in a poem and believe these qualities are verifiable by a consensus of observation, are an applied science; Richards asserted this in his *Principles of Literary Criticism* (1925), and it is not unusual for historians of the movement during the 1950s and 1960s (before linguistic structuralists charged, ironically, the New Critics with a lack of scientific methodology) to see modern criticism, New Criticism included, as scientific criticism (Hyman, *Armed Vision* [1948]). That which describes "certain features in a contemplated object [the poem]," we shall, says Richards, "call the *technical* part" of literary criticism. And Wimsatt and Brooks see Richards as the source of a new "science of tropes" (631). "What is said about the poem is subject to the same scrutiny," writes W. K. Wimsatt, "as any statement in linguistics or in the general science of psychology" (*Verbal Icon* [1954] 5).

For René Wellek and Austin Warren—whose theory is supportive of the New Criticism, although they are not, strictly speaking, New Critics—literary study, while not in every way comparable to the physical sciences, involves "intellectual methods." Literary criticism is "a species of knowledge or of learning," requiring a "coherent scheme which must be rational," even if the literary work itself has "unrational elements" (*Theory of Literature* [1942] 15-16).

Poetry and Meaning

In attempting to define the type of meaning that the poem contains, or is, the New Critics are not always in agreement. Cleanth Brooks maintains that the meaning of the poem is equivalent to its organization of its own content and that this meaning is therefore unparaphrasable. On the other hand, Yvor Winters demands a paraphrasable "evaluative" component, and John Crowe Ransom seeks a "logical" one. For the early T. S. Eliot, the important concern is for the relationship between emotion and its causes.

What is shared, nevertheless, is a belief stated in the negative. The meaning of the poem is *not* scientific meaning. Poetry does not contain scientifically verifiable propositions (even though the *analysis* of poetry contains such statements), yet it communicates to the reader a form of cognition or insight or a desirable mental state, feeling, or outlook.

The early work of I. A. Richards, especially *Principles of Literary Criticism*, is influential. Richards cites a passage from Coleridge that is central not only to his own theory but also to that of the critics who follow him. "That synthetic and magical power, to which we have exclusively appropriated the name of imagination . . . reveals itself in the balance or reconciliation of opposites or discordant qualities . . . the power of reducing multitude into unity of effect" (*Biographia Literaria*, Chap. XXIV). In his earlier work, *The Foundations of Aesthetics*, written with C. K. Ogden and James Wood, Richards states that what causes us to identify beauty in a work of art is *synaesthesis*, a harmony or equilibrium of diverse impulses.

Continuing along these lines in *Principles*, Richards rejects Kant's notion of a special esthetic realm of mental activity. In reading a poem Richards invokes no unique psychic capabilities beyond those needed for other forms of normal human activity. Reading poetry is an experience; consequently, its effects can be described using concepts available through psychology, without resorting to a separable esthetic parlance. "The conduct of life is throughout an attempt to organize impulses so that success is obtained for the greater number or mass of them" (46). Value, whether moral or esthetic, is attributed to those experiences that satisfy as many of these appetencies as possible, or that satisfy one without frustrating another of greater importance. Coherence and organization, as a state of mind, is satisfying, hence valued; and most of us are assisted toward this organized state by "other minds." "Literature and the arts are the chief means by which these influences are diffused" (57). The talent of the artist is to take the diversity of impulses caused by experience and organize them coherently and harmoniously, which is the effect of the good poem on the reader. Dispelling "disorganization and confusion" is the major purpose of art.

Furthermore, "the mind is the nervous system, or rather a part of its activity" (83). Richards proposes, not unlike Freud, that the science of neurology will some day clear up many of the outstanding problems. The aggregation of our impulses, some in opposition, seek satisfaction, customarily a discharge in activity. Poetry and other art address experiences in which are involved large numbers of impulses requiring resolution. Although the poem cannot usually cause an action to resolve the satisfaction of impulses, it can create "attitudes," which are responses still in the "imaginal or incipient degree" (111). Richards admits that evidence for these attitudes is indirect, since no action occurs to verify them. Still, the "after-effects" of the poem, the attitudes brought about, remain of prominent value (132).

For the Richards of *Principles*, poetry does not contain verifiable factual statements, which are the business of science. (In his *Science and Poetry* [1926] Richards will refer to the poem's "pseudo-statements" and "pseudo-questions.") Still, he recognizes that it is not unusual for the reader to feel a form of "belief." These beliefs are "objectless," referring to nothing in the external world; they are supported for us by the poem because they bring about the adjustment or harmonization of impulses, which seems to us like a form of knowledge, of cognition. And in a way, it is a form of cognition—about our internal state, about how we are doing, how our life is going—that offers important "knowledge," despite the absence of a factual basis. "Pleasure . . . and emotion have . . . also a cognitive aspect. They give us knowledge; in the case of pleasure, of how our activities are going on, successfully or otherwise" (99). Richards notes the strain of living in an age in which people are disposed to orient themselves to scientific truth alone (280).

Richards's strategy is typical of the New Criticism: the movement from Coleridge to Richards's own theory is based upon reworking the specifically Romantic definition of the term *imagination* to fit a modern psychology, a procedure calling for not a little distortion in the effort to amalgamate scientific method with continental philosophy.

Physiologically based psychological theories, whether in Richards or Freud or Lévi-Strauss, are empiricisms compatible with the earlier, more rudimentary seventeenth- and eighteenth-century theories of the effect of "motions" on the mind. Their logical consequences are determinism, for it can be argued that consciousness, the feeling of satisfaction or balance of conflicting impulses, is a by-product of the causal chain between stimulus and response. Richards tends in this direction, and he refers favorably to behaviorism as a promising theory (*Principles* 83). Later critics, however, will try to integrate or respond to theories of creativity and language inherited from Romanticism. As noted earlier, classical empiricism does not account satisfactorily for creativity; empiricism relies on "association," which at best is, in the poet, a splendid ingenuity. For Hume, "imagination" is but a certain coherent linkage or combination of ideas, much like Coleridge's "fancy."

Later critics will reject Richards's physiological presuppositions while accepting a theory of poetry involving the reconciliation of opposites. As the specific vocabulary of literary criticism evolves in the 1930s, even Richards will abandon the lexicon of psychology and neurology for that of rhetoric (*Philosophy of Rhetoric* [1936]). By the 1940s, the Depression and World War II will add to the many demonstrations of the sad state of a technologically dominated world. The determinism of behaviorism itself will be discarded by literary critics and other humanists as a symptom of scientific limitation and confinement. While criticism will remain "scientific," maintaining the poem as an object to be objectively analyzed, there will be a turn first to a literary critical methodology employing a distinctive vocabulary so that criticism will no longer be subservient to other sciences. Then, by the 1960s, there will be a turn to language theory, which will seem a more amiable version of science, in contradistinction to the physical sciences.

In *Modern Poetry and the Tradition*, Cleanth Brooks, following Richards, quotes Coleridge's passage concerning the reconciliation of opposites. The metaphysical poet (John Donne, for example) "is constantly remaking his world by relating into an organic whole the amorphous and heterogeneous and contradictory. Insisting on imaginative unity, he refuses to depend upon non-imaginative classifications, those of logic or science" (43). Science "cannot tolerate the incongruous" (205). Brooks attributes belief in this mode of "organization of experience" to Richards, Tate, Ransom, and Eliot, whom he cites as agreeing that the poet's mind is constantly amalgamating disparate experience.

While Richards had concentrated on the poem's effect on the reader, the establishing of "attitudes," Brooks emphasizes the characteristics of the poem that bring about the essential poetic fusion. The poem is constructed so that the reconciliation is, through language, located *in* the poem; this is where it can be discovered. Richards would not have identified an effect in the reader with a real quality in the poem; Brooks seems to say the qualities of the poem exist regardless of particular readers. Once completed, the poem stands on its own. The difference is an important one, since in some theories the properties of the poem cause and in others (reader-centered theories) do not cause

the effects of the poem. Brooks will later use a distinctive terminology
(e.g., irony, paradox) that sounds like the attribution of mental states
to the poem itself, a most ingenious strategy to bind subjectivity into
an autonomous object.

The poem, for Brooks, does not communicate an idea that the
poet has had before writing the poem and then translated into verse
(*Well Wrought Urn* [1947] 74). What is communicated by the poem is
itself: relationships and assertions supportable within the poem, whose
statements have a "dramatic" propriety, not a propositional accuracy.
"A poem is to be judged, not by the truth or falsity as such, of the
idea which it incorporates, but rather by its character as drama—by its
coherence, sensitivity, depth, richness, and tough-mindedness" (256).
As for Richards, the poem has a cognitive function. It is a form of
"knowledge": not the knowledge of science, which separates and cate-
gorizes, but a knowledge of experience as unified and harmonized, "a
pattern of resolutions and balances" (203).

Other critics, both earlier and later, address the "meaning" of the poem
in various ways. Each attempts to analyze the poem as an autonomous
object, a formal construction, while at the same time proposing some
connection between the poem and experience of the world. This connection becomes mandatory if poetry is to be important, for only then
can poetry involve ideas instrumentally affecting the world about us
in some way. Such a viewpoint, inherited from Matthew Arnold's
"Function of Criticism at the Present Time" and reinforced by F. R.
Leavis, is a reaction against an "art for art's sake" stance, of which the
New Critics have also been sometimes accused.

John Crowe Ransom accepts the by now familiar thesis that "poetry treats an order of existence, a grade of objectivity, which cannot
be treated in scientific discourse" (*The New Criticism* [1941] 281). The
word "objectivity" should be noted.

In his extensive rebuttal of I. A. Richards, Ransom objects to
Richards's belief that the poem has no objective reference to reality
but serves a solely psychological purpose. For Ransom the poem is a
"cognitive object," more than merely the language of emotion. "I should
think there is generally, and ideally, no emotion at all until an object
has furnished the occasion for one" (*New Criticism* [1941] 20). Ransom
must know, of course, that Richards understands that the poem exists
as an object composed of language and that, as has been mentioned
earlier, it can have a (special kind of) cognitive function. What Ransom
is referring to is the cognitive *content* of the poem, for the mental
harmony created by the poem is, according to Richards, in the reader;

therefore it cannot be located in the poem itself. What, then, is there
in the poem itself to analyze? If we limit analysis to mental states,
emotional affect, we forsake the referential relationship between the
poem and the world, which Ransom is unwilling to do (perhaps because he is himself a poet). Such an approach segregates poetry from
the external world, leading to a theory, like Brooks's, of internal dramatic coherence alone. But since emotions, for Ransom, are produced
by something to which the poem refers, this content can be evaluated
in other than solely emotional terms. Such an outlook is clearly influenced by Eliot's "objective correlative." For example, it is unlikely,
Ransom continues, that an important emotional effect can be caused
in a reader who believes that the cognitive content of the poem is
nonsensical or false (40). It was Eliot's opinion that the worldview of
a great poet must be mature and coherent, even if the reader cannot
share it; this also presupposes cognitive content. Ransom does not deny
that a literary work can have the effect for the reader of bringing about
a harmony, perhaps even a reconciliation of opposites. To know this
effect is not, however, to explain what is in the poem; it is only to
describe what happens to the reader.

For Richards, the poem generates a level of "belief" independent
of external reference: that is, in fact, what poems *do*. But for Ransom,
the harmonizing of diversity is more than merely a resolution of the
needs of a human organism seeking the fulfillment of impulses. The
world is itself "not cleanly made"; it is full of "concrete" particulars,
more heterogeneous than the world of science can picture. "The confusion of our language is a testimony to the confusion of our world"
(*New Criticism* 79). The poet captures this state of affairs, performs
more than the creation of structures that may be fictions or falsehoods
with beneficial psychological consequences such as the formation of
attitudes helpful in coping with life. The poet pictures the world, addresses the "local detail" of the world. Consequently, poetry is a "more
'realistic' kind of cognition" than is science, with its abstractions, which
attempts to make the world "docile" (43).

The poem, for Ransom, must structure thought and references to
the world in addition to provoking feelings and emotions. In an important passage, he says that "a beautiful poem is one which proceeds
to the completion of a *logical* structure, but not without attention to
the local particularity of its components" (53; emphasis added). Furthermore, "a beautiful poem is an objective discourse which we ap-
prove, containing objective detail, which we like" (54). Ransom is not
defending detail as ornament; rather, he is distinguishing between two
components of the poem, neither of which can be thought of as sub-

ordinate—the logical progression of thought in the poem, which requires a resolution of its own, and the content upon which the thought
is exercised. Nor is he challenging the assumption that form and content are inseparable, though he is saying (as do most critics) that, inseparable or not, there is form and there is content. "We need only to
say that the poem develops its local particularities while it progresses
towards its functional completion" (58).

T. S. Eliot's early opinions on the subjects here under review are,
to a significant extent, compatible with Richards's. "A degree of heterogeneity of material compelled into unity by the operations of the
poet's mind is omnipresent in poetry" ("Metaphysical Poets" 243). Of
particular significance has been Eliot's early essay entitled "Hamlet
and His Problems" (1919), in which he defines an influential concept.
"The only way of expressing emotion in the form of art is by finding
an 'objective correlative' " (124), which is comprised of objects or events
that serve as an "objective" formula for the emotions that are to be
communicated. Since it is *emotion* that the poet is sending to the reader,
rather than an idea, principle, or moral message (which will eventually
be acknowledged as a purpose of poetry in some of Eliot's later criticism), the definition of "objective correlative" nicely supports a psychological focus distinct from a descriptive or referential one. Additionally, the passage is an early example of assuming that the poem
is an entity in its own right, an entity whose internal workings can be
analyzed.

Yvor Winters demanded that a poem possess paraphrasable moral
content: "the artistic process is one of moral evaluation of human experience," he writes in the *Anatomy of Nonsense*. Although Winters
uses the term *moral* in a number of ways, his emphasis is on the use
of understanding in the assessment of human values, which can be
stated in rational terms, accompanied by feelings, brought about by
the poem, appropriate to these values. He is inclined to value "the
logical, the definite, and the unequivocal" (Wimsatt and Brooks 673).
This is not to say that poetic cognition for Winters is equated with that
of science. His view is perhaps best understood by referring back to
Hume's positing of an innate moral faculty in humankind, a gratuitous
concept in Hume that creates more difficulties than it solves. Interestingly, as a comparison, when Richards addresses the matter of evaluation, of judgment as distinct from the analysis of the mental status
effected by the poem, he states that judgment "nearly always settles
itself; or rather our own inmost nature and the nature of the world in
which we live decide it for us" (*Practical Criticism* 284). This is also a
reversion to Hume—in this case, to his theory of "taste."

Lastly, to Allen Tate the poem is itself an action given as a totality: it is "the vision of the whole," grasped through an act of imagination, a vision that cannot be verified on external grounds (*On the Limits of Poetry* 105). This position is quite compatible with that of Brooks.

The basic dilemma of empiricism is apparent in the debate concerning the meaning, function, or import of the poem and the interpretations the poem generates among critics. If we assume that the human mind is empty at birth, free of innate ideas, and that all ideas must be derived from "experience," presumably the result of the impressions left upon the mind through interaction with an external world, then knowledge of any kind must consist of *connections* between these ideas, an *organization* of them. While this fundamental empiricism has been a basic constituent of the temperament of thinkers in England and the United States, the influence of Romanticism, with its roots in Kantian idealism, demands that the contribution to knowing of the human mind itself must be reevaluated. "Creativity" then assumes new proportions. The New Critics, with their characteristic limited use of philosophy, try to progress in this direction: this attempt is their contribution to criticism. They are, nevertheless, at best compelled to accommodate. The separation of a scientific, factually referential "truth" and a poetic non-referential "cognition" (or "truth") is not a coherent theory with two consequences; rather, it arises over time from an uneasy composite of two theories, empiricism (with its own ill-defined external/internal duality) and Romantic idealism.

Following empiricist presumptions, it is first assumed by the New Criticism that language is the vehicle, the instrument, by which a communication of some state of affairs, such as a specific emotion or the union of discordant elements, takes place from poet to reader. As the New Criticism evolves, the critics are led to recognize that in poetry language plays a role in some way independent of the *reporting* of experience or ideas. Early in the 1940s Ransom described poetic composition as a "contention" between the logical meaning intended to be conveyed and formal properties such as meter, yielding for the poet an "excess" of "indeterminate" meanings and sound patterns (*New Criticism* 299), with which the poet can subsequently experiment (324). Six years later, in *The Well Wrought Urn*, Brooks, as we have seen, says that the poet has no specific preexisting "idea" that is then translated into a poem; the poem is itself its meaning, a meaning created in the writing. But by then we have reached 1947, a long way from the early Richards. Nine years later Krieger writes that "the interaction between artist and material produces the art object; this object is not predictable

by the artist. . . . For this reason, the object's value can never be attributed to anything but the formal organization which is the object"
(*New Apologists* 117). Each of these critics, with a somewhat simplified
and inelegant theory, is attempting to account for meanings generated
by and *during* the process of creativity, meanings the poet does not
know he will produce until he is confronting the formal demands of
expression.

We are heading toward what will be the "linguistic model" of
the structuralists. Their non-referential theory of all language is meant
to resolve the external/internal paradox, to obviate any "dual" theory
of truth or cognition, and to explain the creativity of language through
the formal properties of its own structure. This will involve a theory
of language and a theory of the constitution of the "self" unavailable
to the New Criticism.

Before elucidating this matter further, we must review how the
New Critics describe the contribution of the "self" of the poet and,
afterward, how poetic language functions.

The Poet

The theory of the poetic "self" found in the New Criticism is, in large
measure, a reaction against what was thought to be the extremity of
personal emotive self-consciousness in Romanticism. It is also an attempt to explain how a "subject" need not merely be subjective but
can portray things in an objective way, even through an objectivity
that is somehow different from scientific objectivity. This coincides with
the "dual truth" theory of cognition, and leads to similar incongruities.

Coleridge, in the *Biographia Literaria*, specifies two faculties of the
mind, "distinct and widely different" although often "confused under
one and the same word" (50). *Fancy* is a "mode of memory"; its processes are within the "law of association," a familiar notion of the
empiricists. But Coleridge, influenced by the German philosophers,
especially by Kant's distinction between Understanding and Reason in
the *Critique of Pure Reason*, intends to go beyond what Owen Barfield,
in *What Coleridge Thought*, calls Coleridge's "empirically minded English contemporaries" (43). Coleridge defines *Imagination* as a "synthetic and magical power" (174), which takes two forms. "The primary
imagination I hold to be the living power and prime agent of all human
perception, and as a representation in the finite mind of the eternal act
of the creation in the infinite I AM." The secondary imagination, of
the poet, "dissolves, diffuses, dissipates, in order to re-create. . . . It
struggles to idealize and to unify" (167). Within these concepts of fancy

and imagination a number of discrete theories are insinuated. In these few sentences are encapsulated Locke, Hume, Kant, Schelling ("Relation of the Plastic Arts to Nature"), and the God of both Berkeley and Aquinas.

For the modern critics—following Coleridge by the hundred years during which a secular modernity becomes entrenched, quite uncongenial to philosophic idealism, not to mention the infinite I AM—the task will be to preserve, as best one can, in an objective and empirical mode, Coleridge's distinctions and relationships between perception in general and creativity as a mode of non-scientific knowing (which includes the union of disparates as one of its organizing potentials) by substituting a rational, scientific-like poetics for the metaphysical abstractions.

The rejection of what will be taken to be a perplexing metaphysics of subjectivity will be a rejection of Romanticism itself for Hulme, Eliot, and others. They will identify their own position as a return to "classicism," which may be interpreted, whatever it is named, as a reaction of steadfast English empiricism to German idealism (not unlike the structuralist reaction to phenomenology). The controversy between the classic and the Romantic, which cannot be addressed here, has generated much literature revolving around the determination of a fundamental human nature (Barzun; McGann; Wellek, *Concepts*). Some critics believe that Romanticism erroneously posits an almost unlimited potential for human capability, while classicism, like the Greek tragedians, more accurately recognizes human limitation: this is notable because the insistence on human limitation (in epistemology, admittedly) was precisely the stated project of the empiricists in their response to Cartesian rationalism. The New Criticism, in general, will contain disapproval of much of Romantic poetry. To Winters, for example, Romanticism is "obscurantism," "the development of the feeling in excess of the motive" (*Maule's Curse* 327).

"The Romantic," writes Hulme, "must always be talking about the infinite" ("Romanticism and Classicism" 768). For Hulme, the poet needs the faculties of mind both "to see things as they really are" and to have "the concentrated state of mind . . . which is necessary in the actual expression of what one sees" (772). Where the poet attains "the exact curve of the feeling or thing . . . there you . . . have the highest verse" (774). The role of the poet, then, is not as a transmitter of his subjective personality alone, but as a maker or craftsman of poems founded on an accurately perceived state of the world. Although Hulme discriminates between talking about the world in an intuitive language and in a scientific one, the "self" is for him, as for Hume, a receiver

of impressions, experience, and, whenever possible, a dependable or-
ganizer of these, even though the world may be "a flux of interpen-
etrated elements unseizable by the intellect" ("Bergson's Theory"
777).

In T. S. Eliot's "Tradition and the Individual Talent" (1919), poetry is "not the expression of personality, but an escape from personality." At the center of this brief essay is an analogy, not an argument.
As certain chemical reactions occur only in the presence of a catalyst
that is itself unaffected by the reaction, so the mind of the poet serves
as a catalyst to the reaction that yields the poem. "The more perfect
the artist, the more completely separate in him will be the man who
suffers and the mind which creates." The essay allows the poet to be
at once active and passive, genius and conduit; these inconsistencies
can be traced back through Shelley's *Defense of Poetry* to two incom-
mensurate views, both located in Plato—one in the *Ion* and the other
in the *Republic*. Eliot seems to mean that, although the poet has a
personality, this personality is not equivalent to the mind itself; at the
moment of creativity the mind functions to coalesce various elements,
which are "experiences" of the personality rather than attributes of it,
into a new entity, the poem. One can perhaps detect the influence of
Keats's "negative capability." In this way the poem is about the experiences of the poet, which are "objective" in the sense that others
can and do have similar experiences, rather than about the subjective
personality, unique to each individual, that undergoes the experience.
This approach is central to the New Criticism, which attempts to define
the poem as an independent object esthetically located *between* the
personality of the poet and the reader, without taking on (from the
aspect of critical relevance) the properties of either, as do the approaches of biographical criticism at one extreme and impressionistic
criticism at the other. Later, in the essay on Hamlet, Eliot will propose
the "objective correlative," a quasi-scientific term, in order that the
poem may stand independently by becoming a "formula" for emotion.
This is a further attempt to undermine any notions of *direct* contact
between the "personality" of the poet and the reader.

But the most remarkable sentence in "Tradition and the Individual Talent" is the following: "The point of view which I am struggling
to attack is perhaps related to the metaphysical theory of the substantial
unity of the soul." Nothing elsewhere in the essay, including the sentences that immediately follow, clarifies this. If we assume that Eliot
is here following Hume—who found, during reflection, only impressions, images, and so on, and no distinct and separate idea of the "self"
itself—then the sentence exemplifies a taking of sides with the empiri-

cists, rather than with Kant or Hegel. Years later the major rebuttal of the structuralists (a new empiricism, as we shall see) to the existentialists, phenomenologists, and preceding metaphysicians will also be based on attacking what Eliot calls "the substantial unity of the soul," an attack from which the structuralists' "linguistic model" is derived. Perhaps because the essay was written in 1919, and by so important a poet, it is tempting to call it precocious, although two dozen words do not make a philosophy.

Still, it is compelling to give Eliot all possible credit for foresight. His belief, expressed in the same essay, that "the whole of literature . . . has a simultaneous existence and composes a simultaneous order" is remarkably compatible with both Saussure's theory of language as a "synchronic" system and with even more modern theories of "intertextuality."

Significantly, Eliot does not concern himself, in these early writings, with "belief" in any factual matter contained in a poem. As we have noted, the New Critics all make this distinction, leaving facts to science. The Romantics had relied upon concepts of intuitive truth, so that the poem could be both true and believable. But this raises the idea of an intuited truth *preceding* the poem, which then contains it. In the New Criticism, the poet organizes the content of experience, rather than reproducing it. The poet structures the poem around the perplexing, often incompatible multiplicities of human experience, and/or concentrates on areas thought to be inaccessible to science—emotion, feelings, or judgment. Evaluated in an esthetic context, these domains may be seen as as appropriate, coherent, meaningful, or applicable to the human condition, rather than verifiable.

Although the New Criticism, like Romanticism, leads to a "dual" theory of "truth," the poetic variety of truth in the New Criticism is not the transcendental intuitional insight of the Romantics, although this is a major influence. Instead, it is more an organizational and evaluative function of the poet's mind, a theory trying to remain closer to a psychology than a metaphysics.

A psychological system will—like any science, including a scientific literary criticism—ultimately concern itself with the *how* of things rather than with some ultimate *why* of things, in which metaphysics delights. But since science deals with causality, any psychology followed to its logical conclusion will lead to a determinism—unless freedom is posited at the outset, which is to beg the question. Richards, for example, while basing his system on a psychology, writes that the poet "is distinguished . . . by the freedom in which all these impressions are held in suspension, and by the ease with which they form new relations between themselves" (*Principles* 181). The average person has little capacity for organizing disparate impulses, so he suppresses incongruities; the poet has a high "degree of organization of the impulses." The use of the word "freedom" does not help here; the most that can be said is that some people have, for whatever reason, a capability that others do not. Richards's way out is to admit, in a chapter on the "imagination," that "we do not yet know enough about the central nervous system" (251) to clear up all the difficulties.

The impact on the New Criticism is evident. The poet has a certain capability; this capability is not merely the setting into poetry of the poet's own subjectivity; it is not a revelation of verifiable "truth." It concerns the organization of experience, rather than a discovery of the fundamental facts of external reality on which the possibility of experience is itself supposed to rely. The New Critics persistently separate the poet from the completed poem, while simultaneously recognizing that the former creates the latter, which presumably involves freedom of some sort. This is done by assigning to the poet a productive function, an object-creating craftsmanship, rather than by viewing the poem as a revelation of the poet's "personality," as in a confession or a diary. When Richards comes to distinguish four types of meaning in *Practical Criticism* (1929), he does, however, include the "aim" of the author, "*conscious or unconscious*, the effect he is endeavoring to promote . . . what he is trying to do" (176). He further states, perhaps surprisingly, that "good poetry owes its value in a large measure to the closeness of its contact with reality" (238).

When Brooks discusses poetry, quoting Coleridge, as a "reconcilement of opposites," he adds that "such a definition of poetry places the emphasis directly on the poet as *maker*." The poet (and it is the seventeenth-century metaphysical poet who serves as his ideal) "is constantly remaking his world" by relating "the amorphous and heterogeneous and contradictory" (*Modern Poetry and the Tradition* 43). This idea is compatible with those of Hulme, Tate, and Ransom. It contains the assumption that external reality *itself* is complex, but that the poet can come to know it. The poet can then make something that informs the reader about it, not by giving specific facts, but by producing an object, the poem, organized as the poet's *experience* of reality is organized. In 1939 Brooks, like his predecessors, is still seeking a quasi-mimetic basis, a psychological one evidently, for the communicative function of the poet, in a continuing attempt to have the poem communicate what the world is like, at least to us. This approach is, for the New Critics, a predisposition.

But as time passes the theory is modified in Brooks. By 1947 the poem is not merely reflecting what the poet knows to be the case about complex reality, for this would suppose some preexisting "knowledge" that the poem is about. When we examine a poem (at least one of the type Brooks liked) we do not find "an idea or set of ideas which the poet has communicated" (*Well Wrought Urn* 74). "In fact, if we are to speak exactly, the poem itself" (as distinct from other forms of writing) "is the *only* medium that communicates the particular 'what' that is communicated" (74). Brooks is attempting to discard the theory that poetry is somehow about the world as it really is (a strict mimesis), replacing it with the theory that poetry is about the world as it *appears* to us or can be made to appear to us (a modified mimesis—Berkeley and Hume's problem again). He takes us, perhaps too far (the farthest that the New Criticism will go), to a point where the poem is primarily about the experience of itself. A page later Brooks says that the putting together of a poem is, "probably through a process akin to exploration," itself an experience, "which is the poem." Although the experience that is the poem is communicable because "we can come to know the poem," still, "the poet is most truthfully described as a *poietes* or maker, not as an expositor or communicator" (75).

That a philosopher would not write in this manner about this topic is beside the point. Brooks himself says, ingenuously, "I do not wish to split hairs" and goes on to other matters. The significance of the *Well Wrought Urn* is its move toward the description of a poem containing a meaning validated only by the context of the poem itself, not by meanings or information found elsewhere. For Brooks, Keats's line "Beauty is truth, truth beauty" is not to be evaluated as if it conveyed a truth ascertainable in other ways. We cannot ask if Keats was right or wrong: his statement should "drive us back to a consideration of the context in which the statement is set" (153). Brooks refers to the "dramatic propriety" of poetic statement (255). What is important is that, in the twenty years between Richards's *Principles* and Brooks's *Well Wrought Urn*, there is a continuous isolation of the poem as an object in its own right, explicable in a vocabulary of literary analysis dependent neither (at least in principle) upon psychology nor upon Romantic metaphysics. This increases the separation of the poem, for the purposes of literary analysis, from the specific personalities of the author and the reader. Close reading, "objective" reading, of the poem becomes, accordingly, a primary virtue. This is the characteristic for which the New Criticism is most popularly known.

But with an attentiveness, sometimes exclusive, to the poem, the role of the poet is either set aside or attributed to a power or capability not explicable in the terms of literary criticism. In both cases the critic has determined what a poem is and then either takes for granted or avows that the power of the poet is to be able to make one.

To set the matter of the poet aside (which is not, of course, to avoid paying homage to the poet) is to bequeath the area to other disciplines. In the United States, the Freudians will rush in to fill this freed-up space. In Wellek and Warren's *Theory of Literature* we learn that, whether we envision a psychology of the writer or the reader or the content of the poem, "we should disavow any attempt to evaluate literary works in terms of their origins" (81). The view of these two critics is compatible with that of Brooks, though more abstract: "the work of art . . . appears as an object *sui generis* which has," as it did for Kant, "a special ontological status" (156). In the well-known essay of Wimsatt and Beardsley on "The Intentional Fallacy," we are cautioned that "to insist on the designing intellect as a *cause* of a poem is not to grant the design or intention as a *standard* by which the critic is to judge the worth of the poet's performance" (*Verbal Icon* 4). The poem "is detached from the author at birth and goes about the world beyond his power to intend about it or control it" (5).

The critic might treat the reader similarly, as Wimsatt and Beardsley do in "The Affective Fallacy," where they reject deriving a "standard of criticism from the psychological effects of the poem" which "ends in impressionism and relativism" (21). (The essay includes a rejection of the Richards of the *Principles*.) Thirty years after the publication of his major works, Brooks is still answering the charge that the New Criticism gave insufficient attention to the reader. "No one in his right mind could forget the reader," Brooks writes. Nevertheless, it is important not to "reduce the study of literature to reader psychology" ("The New Criticism" [1979] 604). Theories concerning the reader will emerge years later, in the space undoubtedly left somewhat vacant by the New Critics, in the writing of Stanley Fish and of those influenced by the German theorists Wolfgang Iser and Hans Robert Jauss.

To attribute a special power to the poet is usually, for the New Critics, a reversion to Coleridge. We learn in Tate, for example, that there is "a power of seizing the inward meaning of experience, the power of sheer creation . . . the vision of the whole of life . . . *a quality of the imagination*" (*Reactionary Essays* [1936] 84). In Wimsatt's introduction to *The Verbal Icon* there is a chart that contains, as a characteristic of the poet, "genius" (xvii). Ransom writes that poetry "must be much more 'creative' than science is, or at least much more spiritedly, incessantly so." Much might be asked of his word *creativity*.

He continues, asserting that poetry is such "an eager cognitive impulse that it overreaches its object. . . . That is its glory." Poetry "makes its own version, a new and not clearly authorized one, of the world" (*World's Body* [1938] 165). When contemplating the world under the form of art, Ransom "is in such a marvelous state of innocence that I would know it for its own sake," which leads to "a knowledge so radical that the scientist as a scientist can scarcely understand it, and puzzles to see it rendered" (45).

These various, sometimes effusive assertions of the New Critics when they discuss what the *poet* does are sometimes very different from what is said about a *poem*. This is not intended as a philosophical critique. The New Critics were not systematic philosophers, nor did they mean to be; neither were they psychologists, estheticians, or epistemologists.

A philosophically systematic concept of the "self" was not, could not be, developed within the New Criticism. The critics inherited a belief in the fundamentally combinational or associational self, which organizes, aggregates, or synthesizes impressions (the empiricist's "ideas") received, by means of an organic biological process, through experience. In Hulme, Tate, and Brooks it is reality itself that is found to be complex, inextricable, diverse, and not capturable by the neat categories of science. Or, more precisely, such is the effect of reality *on us*. To the extent that poetry reflects these circumstances, it is, one would have to say (despite the protests), mimetic; its formulations can, as in science, be said to have reference to the world itelf. Unlike science, however, the cognition in poetry concerns the ideas that Locke attributes to reflection. Such cognition has to do with feeling, thinking, judging, willing, and synthesizing, rather than with propositions about the (presumably) material substance of the world. This "dual" theory of truth or cognition in the New Criticism is a consequence of empiricism's view of the self.

Not that duality theories of truth are lacking in other philosophical systems. There are such, whether in Aquinas, Descartes, Spinoza, Kant, the German Romantics, or Hegel. But these dualities have to do with the material vs. the spiritual; reason vs. revelation; the finite vs. the infinite; the transcendental vs. the mundane; or the real vs. the apparent. In the New Criticism these dualities do not apply: the duality is an empiricist one, having to do with the distinction between our impressions of external objects and our reflections on (our observation of) the workings of the mind. These two aspects apply to any science, such as psychology, without need of metaphysical categories, categories that are also avoided by the English philosophers of the time from Bertrand Russell and C. D. Broad through Gilbert Ryle and, more recently, John Wisdom, P. F. Strawson, Norman Malcolm, and others who (intend at least to) look to define self and mind without resorting any more than Hume to metaphysics or the invention of abstruse terminology. In this light Eliot's theories, Richards's psychologizing, and Tate's (and others') view of the poet as somehow disassembling and reassembling the elements of complex experience with some sort of fundamentally empiricist mental apparatus make the most sense.

Yet the New Criticism could not help but be influenced by Romanticism, particularly because Coleridge's "reconciliation of opposites" superficially bears a resemblance to the empiricist's concept of the formation of complex ideas through combination. Romanticism, however—with its notions of the self as a co-creator of the world, or a self participating in the very spirit that comprises the world, or of poetry as special knowledge—derived its concept of self from a tradition (Kant, Fichte, Hegel) that is itself a reaction *against* empiricism. This influence, whenever it appears, brings to the New Criticism a logical inconsistency regarding the concept of the poetic self.

Again, the point is not simply that the New Criticism at times left the creativity of the poet in a non-scientific, Romantic realm. This is, to be sure, the source of the ambivalence, which is why some commentators have seen the New Critics as classicists with a Romantic streak—especially the poets among them, who undoubtedly (regardless of theory) preferred the Romantic image of the poet as seer and prophet to the staid neoclassical image. Moreover, the influence of philosophical empiricism in the English-speaking countries led, in the New Criticism, to a purportedly objective, "scientific" reading of poems as external, sensible esthetic objects or entities. As the New Criticism developed, theories of the writer and reader were left behind, relegated either to an inherited Romanticism or to other disciplines, such as psychology and sociology. Consequently, the New Criticism is open to the attack that it was not sufficiently encompassing, that it resulted in a limited, admittedly valuable, technique of meticulous reading but could not envision a unified theory of language, literary composition, and literary analysis. Such a theory, as we shall see, was to be the project of structuralism; and the "science" that was to encompass these areas was to be linguistics. But by that time linguistic theory would also be a theory of how the "self" comes to be "constructed." It is an adequate theory of language—all language, poetic or not—and an accompanying theory of the self, poetic or otherwise, that the New Critics can be accused of lacking.

Language

Despite appearances, then, a systematic approach to language is not found in the New Criticism. The critics focus on certain aspects of language usage in poetry to provide evidence for their concepts of what a good poem is. Since much of this theory of poetry involves beliefs about the juxtaposition, union, or reconciliation of opposites or of the apparently incompatible, the descriptions of the use of language in poetry will support these beliefs. Any disagreements concerning poetic language (on the use of irony for example) can be traced to differences about what the poem, ideally, should do. Poetic language is seen as a means to achieve what the New Critics have previously defined (perhaps, some say, in a narrowly prescriptive manner) as the ends, the specific operations, of a good poem. In Wellek and Warren, for example, we find that "the literary man is a specialist in association ('wit'), dissociation ('judgement'), re-combination (making a new whole out of elements separately experienced)" (88).

Brooks's *Well Wrought Urn* is in these matters the most representative work. The harmonizing of the poem's diverse elements is achieved through the "pattern" of the poem (194). The pattern is described, with some inconsistency, either as a "balancing" (195) or a system of "resolved stresses" (203) or a pattern of imagery (46). The latter is of most interest here, for it leads to a valuable critical method: the demonstration of the "unity" of a poem through an analysis of the consistency and interrelatedness of images. In the most general sense, the "pattern" seems to mean the overall interconnections within the poem, from whatever direction approached; basically it entails the assumption, common to much modern criticism, that the poem must somehow be unified. To cite Wellek and Warren again, poetry organizes a "unique, unrepeatable pattern of words, each an object as well as a sign and used in a fashion unpredictable by any system outside of the poem" (186).

A poem is not poetry because there are special words or subjects that are themselves poetic (*Well Wrought Urn* 218)—the word "alas," say, or a sunset. "Things are not poetic per se" (*Modern Poetry* 11). Similar assertions are found much earlier in Hulme. As we have seen, it is the method of treatment, of organization, that makes a poem, together with its characteristically persistent use of certain formal capabilities of language (such as metaphor) and techniques (such as meter). "Poetry does not inhere in any particular element but depends upon the set of relationships, the structure," writes Robert Penn Warren. "Nothing that is available in human experience is to be legislated out of poetry" ("Pure and Impure Poetry" [1943] 991).

In discussing the language of poetry I. A. Richards defined a distinction which for many years was to influence literary criticism. A statement can be used for "the sake of the *reference*, true or false, which it causes. This is the *scientific* use of language." But language may also be used for the "sake of the effects in emotion and attitude produced by the reference it occasions. This is the *emotive* use of language" (*Principles* 267). In his *Practical Criticism* Richards asserts that poetry belongs to "the whole world . . . of abstract opinion and disputation about matters of feeling" (5). Poetry is meant to affect feelings and attitudes, not (like science) to communicate statements bearing "truth."

The distinction drawn by Richards was, for the New Criticism, as much a place to begin theorizing about language as it was for discussing the function of poetry, an approach to which Eliot's early views added support. Over the years, however, the distinction proved too simple for the analysis of poetic language. First, many critics came to demand a special cognitive role for poetry: the opposite of (scientific) "truth" is not necessarily "feeling" but truth of another sort, a different, perhaps even better or higher truth, the truth of imagination. This strategy, which entails a move away from the psychology of Richards, will require a changing evaluation of poetic language, especially of metaphor.

For Richards, feeling is enhanced by figurative language. "The poet's task is . . . that of finding ways and means of controlling feeling through metaphor" (*Practical Criticism* 212). At this point, metaphor is described as a practical tool for creating feeling, just as a cry may be a practical means for obtaining help. Later critics, drawing on the testimony of poets, will not be satisfied with such a limited approach to metaphor.

Although Eliot's "objective correlative" is a "formula" for feeling, Eliot and Richards, while in a number of places mutually reinforcing each other, do not uniformly share a common view. For Eliot "the essence of poetry is metaphor" (Wimsatt and Brooks 665). This view is comparable to that of Hulme, who wrote, "images in verse are not mere decoration, but the very essence of an intuitive language" (qtd. in Wimsatt and Brooks 661). Not, of course, that Richards would have believed metaphor to be but a decoration, as did Hobbes. But Richards's approach is less influenced by that unique type of poetic insight and cognition that, inherited from Romanticism, often goes under the name of "imagination" than are the approaches of Hulme, Eliot, and most of those who follow them, who must incorporate, though not in any coherent systematic way, the very Romantics they avow they are rejecting.

Brooks, in the late 1930s, is somewhere between Richards and Eliot. He, too, observes that metaphor is not a decoration but "is frequently the only means available" if the poet "is to write at all" (*Modern Poetry* 15). Like Richards, he recognizes "the immensely important function of metaphor in qualifying the poet's attitude" (28). "Qualifying" refers to the poet's ability to balance and harmonize conflicting and discordant elements.

But it is especially notable how Brooks writes of metaphor in the 1940s. The technique of modern poetry is "the rediscovery of metaphor and the full commitment to metaphor" ("Irony as a Principle of Structure" [1949] 1041). "Poetry is not merely emotive . . . but cognitive. It gives us *truth* and characteristically gives its truth through its metaphors" (*Well Wrought Urn* 259; emphasis added).

By this time, a duality theory of truth has become evident, at some remove from Richards's discrimination between truth and feeling. This duality theory substantiates the increased influence of a Romanticism upon a fundamentally empiricist criticism, the admixture we have repeatedly emphasized and to which we will need to return—perhaps even to explain as a reinvigoration of certain concepts of the self—in tracing the climate of the times during which the New Criticism flourished in American universities. At about the same time, Tate, who had called metaphor "the climactic figure" (*World's Body* 133), writes, "If a poem is a real creation, it is a kind of knowledge that we did not possess before" (*Limits of Poetry* 250). Poetry is called "this special kind of knowledge" in the well-known Brooks and Warren anthology of poetry entitled *Understanding Poetry* ([1938] xiii).

The variety of truth to which Brooks is referring straddles the two traditions. On the one hand, he seems to be speaking about what may be thought of as a *mimetic* truth in an empiricist mode; the organization of poetry is like the organization of the world as it appears to us. As an example of this, we can turn to Ransom, who writes (like Hulme on Bergson), in speaking of metaphor, "the density or connotativeness of poetic language reflects the world's density" (*New Criticism* 79). Or as it is expressed by Lee Lemon, a recent follower of Ransom, poetry gives us "a picture of the universe unavailable elsewhere." On the other hand, Brooks also seems to be referring to the "higher"truths of intuition and imagination, a species of truth discernible in poetry and nowhere else. Perhaps transcendent to, unavailable to, or at least preferable to scientific truth, poetic truth is as much created as reported by the poet, not severable from Romanticism. (There is, if we could have a third hand, also the Brooks for whom the poem has only a dramatic propriety, without a truth-bearing reference of *any* kind to the "real" world.) It is this very two-sidedness (or more), no doubt philosophically disreputable, that makes the New Criticism, at its height, so attractive: a rigorous, objective, scientific-like scrutiny of the subject matter (the poem), the content of which is, depending on where one opens the critical work, both objective and subjective, real and contextual, emotive and intellectual, referential and non-referential, down-to-earth and mystical.

Defining a symbol, Brooks states that "the metaphor becomes a symbol when by means of it we embody an ideal content not otherwise expressible" (*Well Wrought Urn* 259). This is much unlike Wellek and Warren's more pedestrian "an image may be invoked once as a metaphor, but if it persistently recurs, it becomes a symbol" (189). Nevertheless, the New Criticism, with Brooks as its most popular representative, is usually in both camps at once, firmly entrenched in empiricism yet courting a metaphysics to which it can never, in good conscience, fully yield. Bounded by science and both envious and contemptuous of those who do not respect those bounds, the New Critics find themselves in a circumstance paradigmatic of modern times: while the path to truth is defined by a scientific methodology, that path unfortunately ends short of where we wish to go.

The critical terms "paradox" and "irony" achieved such prominent status in the critical lexicon of American writers on poetry in the 1950s and even into the 1960s that much explication of the time may seem, looking back, the insertion of the same critical key into every poetical lock. In Brooks, who did most to give the terms their celebrity, both terms evolve from the underlying theory of a poetry reconciling opposites, fusing contraries, amalgamating diversity, and ordering complexity.

The first chapter of *The Well Wrought Urn* is entitled "The Language of Paradox," and paradox is said to be "the language appropriate and inevitable to poetry" (3). While scientists stabilize their terms through a consensus about the referentiality of those terms, in poems each term is defined by the context of the poem in which it appears. In this sense the poem is like a drama, where utterances are to be evaluated as speech assigned to fictional characters, not as verifiable assertions. "The poet must work by contradiction and qualification"; accordingly, he, "within limits, has to make up his language as he goes" (9). Paradox, then, reflects the nature of the poet's insight insofar as he finds the complex multiplicity of viewpoint and circumstance that we have stressed previously. Poetic paradox is not the puzzling antinomies of Kant (the irreconcilability of two deductions, both apparently necessary) or Russell (What does it mean when a Cretan says, "All Cretans are liars"?). Rather, poetic paradox is the technique by which multiplicity is given organization, a resolution that is a balance or harmony rather than either a solution or a despairing of one.

The term "irony" can be used like "paradox," for in a basic sense it means to suggest the opposite of what in fact appears to be stated. This is not sarcasm, although some writers give an example of sarcasm to illustrate irony, as when we say that someone is "a real charmer" to indicate his repulsiveness. One example of poetic irony cited by Brooks occurs in Gray's "Elegy," where he describes the "animated bust" on a tomb; "animated" is ironic because it is derived from the latin for "breath" or "soul." Mining the canon of English literature for examples of irony and paradox (perhaps in too predictable a manner, argued David Daiches) would become somewhat of an industry.

But "irony" is also used in a more important structural sense by some of the New Critics. The meaning of any term in a poem is determined not only by the common "denotation" of that term (its fundamental dictionary definition) but also by the context of the poem in which it is situated. The context structurally creates, or yields, the "connotative" meanings that adhere to each term, meanings quite unique to the specific poem. Any statement in the poem "bears the pressure of the context," Brooks writes, and this "may throw some light upon the importance of the term *irony* in modern criticism" ("Irony as a Principle of Structure" 1043). Irony is, then, structurally created in the tension between customary usage and constructed contextual meanings; criticism can point to, but not completely untangle, this process because meanings created by poetic structure cannot simply be translated into critical prose structure. That is why, for Brooks, the most important meanings of the poem are not paraphrasable.

For Warren, as for Brooks, the poet must "remain faithful to the complexities of the problems"; the poet's vision must have "reference to the complexities and contradictions of experience." These "contradictions" are embedded in the structural irony of the poem, at once a manifestation and a testing of the poet's vision. "The saint proves his vision by stepping cheerfully into the fires. The poet . . . proves his vision by submitting it to the fires of irony—to the drama of his structure—in the hope that the fires will refine it" ("Pure and Impure Poetry" 992).

It should be mentioned, as a qualifying view, that for critics like Ransom or Winters, who demand either a logical resolution or a clear moral evaluation within the poem, irony seems a less attractive device. "Opposites can never be said to be resolved," says Ransom. "If there is a resolution at all it must be a logical resolution," and if there is no such resolution the poem is "without structural unity." But "this is precisely the intention of irony, which is therefore something special, and ought to be occasional" (*New Criticism* 95). Winters says in *In Defense of Reason* that it is not the preferable poetic practice to take uncertainties or irreconcilables, bond these within a poem through irony, and then claim as justification that the situation itself (the world, life) is perplexing. When they use the term "irony," both Ransom and Winters, who likely are confusing irony as a structural device with irony as the actual poetic "message," are no doubt recalling what Tate called "the peculiar frustration of the poet known as romantic irony" (*Limits of Poetry* 87), an uncertainty, confusion, or disillusion that qualifies or undermines optimism or determination.

But Brooks is far more perceptive in this matter, and his elucidation of irony is his best and most original contribution to criticism. He posits irony not as merely one device among the many available but as an *essential* element of poetic structure. The function of a poem is to *create* meaning through structure (context), and such meaning must be forged in tension with other potential meanings, whether denotations, everyday language, other structures (other poems, for example), and inherent or contrived ambiguities (which Empson handles so well in *Seven Types of Ambiguity* [1930]).

Through these speculations Brooks is taking the New Criticism to its theoretical limits in addressing the issue of language. Not that Brooks or the other New Critics are philosophers of language—far from it. Although solidly grounded in empiricism, their theories are quite rudimentary, detached from linguistics (Wellek, *Concepts of Criticism* 310), and, from a theoretically systematic point of view, meagerly developed, since (as Americans) a practical application was their propensity. Brooks, interestingly, was attacked by R. S. Crane in 1948 for "reducing" the thought of Coleridge to the single principle of irony.

The idea that irony (assuredly the opposite of scientific truth) is a structural necessity in poetry allows Brooks to identify irony with *the* fundamental contextual operation of poetry, its "dramatic" structure. The poetic statement is "dramatically appropriate" (*Well Wrought Urn* 154). The meaning of the poem *is* the poem, not something it contains and that consequently can be extracted by, for example, rewording (a point analyzed by J. Timothy Bagwell*). The "truth" of the

---

*If interpretation is to take place at all, according to the recent analysis of J. Timothy Bagwell, it must be assumed that something can be said that is in some way equivalent to what the poem says. Yet to formalists, like the New Critics, the poem cannot be

poetic statement is what that statement is in its context and is demonstrable in no other way. It is notable that Warren seems to equate the "fires of irony" to the "drama of . . . structure" in his impassioned description. Meaning, therefore, at least in poetry, is determined by structure, not simply by the individual terms or sets of terms that are the units structured. Moreover, the meaning is paradoxical and complex, with a balance of irresolvables, limited neither to a formal denotation (as a scientific language) nor to an evident consensus (as in everyday language). In poetry, says the New Criticism at its most inspired, meaning and structure (content and form) are not two separate things but one thing that can be viewed in two ways.

If the model of the overall structural determination of the meaning of the units that comprise the structure is applied to *all* language, not just to poetic language, we find ourselves in the very linguistic structuralism that was eventually to be imported from France. Not that the New Criticism and structuralism are the same, or similar, or heading in the same direction, or compatible. That is not the point here. Rather, I intend to suggest, almost parenthetically here, one course of transition, of linkage, without forgetting that it may be a narrow one (and not the only one). This focus on the theoretical consequences of defining irony in a certain way is but a small part, and a late contribution, of the New Criticism, which begins and endures within the tradition of a fundamental British empiricism quite some distance from Paris. We might, as tentative evidence, point to Richards's belief in the 1930s that all language is metaphorical (*Philosophy of Rhetoric* [1936]) or to Brooks's admission that his critical terms will not "turn out to be anything more than metaphors" (*Well Wrought Urn* 203). But this complicated issue must be left for later.

Recognizing that the New Critics had no more comprehensive a theory of language and self than might be legitimated by the basic empiricism they inherited can lead us toward a better understanding of the confusion, ambivalence, and indecision when the critics write about the referential value of poetic statements, to what extent such statements refer (or do not refer) to the world, to "reality." We have seen that in the writings of these critics the "meaning" of the poem

---

referential in the sense that the poem points to some external circumstances (meanings, truths) to which the interpretation also points. An equivalent statement would then be to state what the poem is *talking about*, i.e., referring to. While interpretation, then, seems to be provoked by poetry, it fails to yield statements equivalent to it. At the same time, formalism behaves as if equivalent meaning *could* be generated, which legitimates interpretation (*American Formalism and the Problem of Interpretation* [1986]).

can refer (1) not to the external world but to inner human impulses (early Richards); (2) to shared human feelings and emotions (early Eliot); (3) to the real or apparent world in its real or apparent complexity (Hulme, Ransom); (4) to moral evaluations (Winters); (5) to a logical organization (Ransom); (6) to some portion of the external world captured in its immediacy and entirety (Tate); (7) to a self-validating structural or dramatic coherence (Brooks); and so on. The list is meant to be suggestive, not exhaustive, and most of the critics choose among these as they please. The critics sometimes take additional approaches, as when Wimsatt writes that verbal style itself "designates a level of meaning distinct from the substantial," a meaning "more like a shadow or echo or gesture" (*Verbal Icon* 202).

In all these cases the critics are resolutely searching for a "truth" or "meaning" or "cognition" in poetry, in any place whatsoever that they might find it, outside the descriptive, classificatory, propositional statements that "science" makes about external physical reality. Yet there is no coherent, systematically adequate theory of non-scientific knowledge for these empiricists to take hold of. They cannot help but understand the importance of the Romantic conception of poetic truth and being lured toward it, for they know that it is necessary to find some such poetic truth if poetry is to be important in a scientific and technological age. Yet they cannot, as empiricists, be comfortable with the metaphysical system, from Kant forward, on which this conception is based. They have nothing better; accordingly, while often disparaging the Romantics, they take certain statements of Coleridge and rework them (not simply following them, as William Van O'Connor states) into a system of psychology and empiricist critical technique. A distracting and uncongenial Germanic philosophy is left off to one side, but nothing is substituted for it save an assortment of admittedly powerful recommendations, none on sturdy philosophical ground, concerning the formal properties of poetry and the possible forms of referentiality (or lack of it) to the world, including the reader, outside the poem.

Conclusion

The review of the philosophy of seventeenth- and eighteenth- century English empiricism in Chapter One pointed to the basic premise that all ideas come from "experience." One can, ultimately, know only ideas, the content of the mind; therefore the relationship between "experience" (when defined as sensation or the perception of existent objects) and the "real" world becomes a problem. The recognition of the problem does not, however, subvert the system; it is, for the empiricists, a limitation of human knowledge, not a refutation of the empirical approach, which can consequently substantiate scientific procedures.

That there is knowledge both of external sensible objects and also, through reflection, of the workings of the mind itself has been shown to create a difficulty, even from the beginning of empiricism. This difficulty is applicable to the New Criticism, an empiricism based upon the positing of an esthetic "object" with formal properties. Specifically, feelings and emotions, long thought to be especially suitable for poetic expression, are not themselves objects in the world, nor do they seem to be "ideas" that represent objects. Yet, since there are names for these, they are clearly "experienced" by the subject. The relationship between the experiencing of what we come to understand occurs inside our minds and the real world (leaving the proof of its existence aside) is a dilemma. If poetry has meaning because, and only because, it refers to inner states, then it cannot be send to have reference to "truth," if truth is defined as propositional and verifiable statements, like scientific statements. But American critics (whose basic tradition, says Robert Con Davis, is "philosophical pragmatism and temperamental optimism" ["Error" 105]) will not rest satisfied with a poetry that does not talk about how things are in the real world. Theories of psychological equilibrium seem affiliated with therapy, not with poetry; and so it becomes necessary to modify or improve the theory, so that poetry can yield a form of "cognition." At first the cognition is said to be about an internal state of affairs, but this will not suffice. There must be a link between the content of poetry and a real external world.

This link in the New Criticism is found in Coleridge's theory of the reconciliation of opposites. This is a most important theoretical tactic because Coleridge's theory is based on a philosophical tradition which, founded in Kant, was itself an alternative to empiricism. The critics attempt to extract a psychology from the metaphysics by taking the reconciliation of opposites to refer to a mental organizational capability (rather than to what they saw as the mystical and magical powers of Romantic theory) to fuse disparate experience through poetic form. Since poetry, in this view, can accurately reflect how the world appears to us, poetry can retain its mimetic function, which is an empiricist value. And this organization can be opposed to that of science, which is said to classify in such a way that much of our reality is not accounted for. Poetry can then become a special form of "truth" and be placed in an equal, if not higher, status with science, whose extraordinary accomplishments have made it, in most circles, the sole vehicle of truth. And once poetry is determined to contain truth, new meaning is given to metaphor, irony, paradox, and other elements of poetry.

It has been argued, however, that empiricism does not contain or allow for a sophisticated theory of creativity, certainly not one of a "truth" unique to poetry alone. The theory of creativity remains within the boundaries of psychology. Yet poets themselves, since Plato, have contended that there is, or seems to be, more to creativity, something that cannot be deciphered by describing the customary mental mechanisms of perception and the formation of ideas based on perception. Romanticism provides the most alluring of theories of poetic creativity, even for (even *especially* for) Americans, despite its roots in an unacceptable speculative soil. Following nineteenth-century Romanticism, no poet or critic can ignore its compelling elevation of poetic power. The New Criticism leans toward Romanticism in the 1940s. This leaning accounts for its progression toward a duality theory of truth and for its more ardent statements about the poets' perception of the world.

But the theories of Romanticism cannot resolve, for these American critics, the shortcomings of empiricism. Those shortcomings will have to be resolved, if possible, within the empiricist tradition itself. The lure of Romanticism is that it makes the poet and poetry what critics and poets want them to be, among the most important people and things of all; it makes us all, in some sense, who we want to be. Yet Romantic theory, while quite compatible with the temperaments and the ambitions of the New Critics (at least by the mid-1930s), is not compatible with what must serve as the empirical foundation of the New Criticism. Nor is it compatible with any philosophical theory that would presently be acceptable to those in England and America with an influential voice in such matters, although it adds a certain fervor to a critical school that began with a rather down-to-earth and practical poetics.

One way forward will prove to be, for some, the recognition that an alternative to empiricism need not be metaphysical idealism but perhaps a different, more up-to-date formulation of empiricism. This new empiricism will also address the relationship between the self and the world, between what reflection shows us to be inside and what perception shows the world to be outside; and the link will be language. Since it will purport to rest upon linguistics, it will have the scientific underpinnings necessary for a modern disciplinary study. At the same time—a most satisfying discovery for the literary critic—it will place language, the critics' own territory, at the very center of epistemology and psychology.

American critics through the 1960s and 1970s continued to be in need of a theory compatible with empiricism. Such a theory had to be disdainful of metaphysics and capable of accounting for the distinction between scientific meaning and poetic meaning, for the function of language, and for a creativity (compatible with a modern psychology) of the human self. A similar need had also been felt by certain European thinkers, who were seeking an empirically based critical theory to succeed phenomenology and existentialism.

CHAPTER THREE

Cultural Influences on American Literary Criticism

Understanding the transition in American literary criticism from the New Criticism to structuralism and post-structuralism requires some knowledge of the cultural environment; for literary criticism is, at one level, always a product of social circumstances that determine the success or failure of any particular form of criticism among that small percentage of the general population who find a need to occupy themselves with it.

Examining the growth of structuralist literary criticism and its post-structuralist successor in the United States, it is often assumed that American literary critics read certain French critics and found in them ready-made, compelling theoretical truths, which were subsequently imported into the United States to be used in the applied procedures of literary criticism. Susceptibility to intellectual discovery is no doubt preceded by a predisposition motivated by a disaffection or discontent with current theory. Furthermore, it may be presumed that the discoverer is somehow attuned to what is discovered. It is, however, unlikely that literary critics in the United States were able in full measure to accept, as a satisfying view of the world, the implications of the European structuralism, which are incompatible in certain fundamental ways with American predilections. That is, Americans have been using structuralism and post-structuralism for purposes of their own; they have not been simply following European practices. Although the subject matter and the critical methods fit the needs of certain American critics, those critics are in fact doing, and intending to do, something quite different from what the French were doing. We may even find that they are heading in different directions.

At the heart of the matter is the concept of "self," its properties and components, especially as these involve disputes concerning freedom of will and determinism. Beliefs concerning the self will be found to underlie critical assumptions about language, creativity, and interpretation. To clarify the context of recent American literary criticism, it will be helpful to survey the intellectual setting from which literary analysis emanates, both before and after the New Criticism.

Science, Technology, Society

The response in American society to science and technology is of particular interest here. The New Criticism is founded upon a scientific methodology, itself grounded in empiricism, which attempts to account for the formulation, in literature, of a non-scientific cognition. The resultant theory is an inconsistent imposition of Romantic notions upon a purportedly scientific procedure, which occurs because there is, for the New Critics, no theory of language and self that can bring an encompassing coherence to their criticism. Literary critics will look for such a theory in structuralism. Some writers, like Frank Lentricchia and Gerald Graff, conclude that the New Critics failed to demonstrate any special poetic cognition, that the "dual" truth theory is no longer supportable. As we have seen, the importance of that theory had to do with poetic meaning being non-scientific, a negative definition. About what the content of poetic meaning *is*, as distinct from how it is structured or processed (as through the reconciliation of opposites or by metaphor), the New Critics are customarily vague. The attitude toward scientific knowledge motivates the primary definition.

The relationship of the New Critics to the technological industrial society has often, with some disagreement, been commented upon. They are said to view poetry as a "haven from the alienations of industrial capitalism" (Eagleton, *Literary Theory* 45), while following the "technocracy" in their methods (49). It is said both that they "had little to fear from any scientific method" (Norris, *Deconstruction* 8) and that they offered a "defense of literary studies against encroachment by various sciences" (Culler, *On Deconstruction* [1982] 20). The New Criticism is classified as a "scientific" criticism by Hyman in 1948 and is also said, by Louis Kampf, to be "fathered by advanced industrial capitalism" and its educational bureaucracy (638). Yet elsewhere the New Criticism is seen as a "traditional" reaction by southern agrarians longing for " 'rooted' organic community life in the face of the threat from the industrial north" (Hawkes, *Structuralism and Semiotics* 153).

But the issues are larger than literary criticism. They concern the attempt, in the society generally, to unite a system of humanistic values with a scientific technology that threatens to subvert those values, a central dilemma of modern times that is played out in the sciences and the humanities and in the political and economic systems. The ambivalent response to a technology that seems to promise the material wealth needed for the opportunity to be fully human, but at the possible price of humanity itself, has existed in one form or another throughout the history of the United States. It remains a major issue, perhaps *the* major issue, in the twentieth century.

Literary criticism in the United States, grounded in a pervasive empiricism, needs a scientific, or at least a quasi-scientific, legitimacy if it is to function in the universities as a peer among other disciplines. Yet it is among the writers and critics of "literature" that the most cogent warnings concerning the potential effects of technology are announced. This calls for an important distinction: there is a difference between science and technology. It is not science itself that has been the enemy for modern humanists, prophets, artists, or philosophers; rather, it is the uses to which science has been put, the dominance of scientific formulations in the modern worldview of what "reality" is, the psychic and physical effects of mechanization and of mass communication, of pollution, of the control of wealth by large corporations, of modern weaponry. The empiricist perspective, fundamental to American thought, undergoes a constant uneasiness when the prospects for modern humankind are analyzed. (The prominence in recent criticism of Rousseau, that "enemy" of the Enlightenment, is most germane here.) Although the empiricist perspective is never forsaken, even in a literary criticism that tries to supplement it, that perspective is intermixed with values and aspirations that seem, at times, incompatible with what the employment of modern science has done to us, or might do to us, if we are not careful. Yet being careful seems to require, ironically, the further application of the very technology that has caused the problem. This is the Enlightenment with a certain vengeance.

In the United States, much contemporary writing on the modern technological society conspires to combine a pessimistic analysis with optimistic hope. The accomplishments of technology are praised; the dangers and excesses are deplored. It is widely acknowledged that the achievements of technology have progressed faster than a coherent system of values, beliefs, and ideals that would allow society to deal with them. While enormous opportunities have been created by technology in the United States, the conflict between material and spiritual needs remains (Boorstin). Technical virtuosity has not brought with it a consensus "as to the quality and character of the industrial civilization we want" (Head 116). America "is a civilization founded on science"

(Lerner 209); yet, despite the sending of men to the Moon, there is a "huge disparity between our technical competence and our understanding of how the fruits of this competence affect human society" (Collingridge 15). We may assume, unfortunately, that technology is "an end in itself" and allow it to develop haphazardly, putting it in the hands of the wrong people, of government, the military, or big business (Muller). The abundance yielded by "Wayward Technology" (Braun) may be causing a displacement of "the original, more meaningful articulation of the American dream" (Woodward 5). A thriving technology is part of the promise of democracy, yet the fulfillment of the promise may eliminate democracy itself unless counteractive measures are taken (Mumford).

While there are those who are unremittingly pessimistic about technology, believing that the worst has already happened or is in any case unavoidable, it is notable that they are in the minority. Far more common are those, like Nigel Calder or Michel Benamou, who see technology promising society a happy future, who maintain their faith that even if things go amiss or astray from time to time, even if the present situation looks dire, with sufficient care and attention the best of human values will prevail and technology will serve humankind well and graciously. The ideal of a "democratic technic," an ideal we can still (according to Carroll Pursell) share with Jefferson, may still be preservable. Though we have entered the maze, we may have a hold on "Ariadne's thread" (Hardison). A positive outcome will not occur by itself, however: it requires human intervention, diligence, attentiveness, and planning, guided by a firm agreement—which we do not at present have—on ethics, government policy, social need, international competition, corporate behavior, and economic growth. Nearly all the books mentioned above conclude with some hope, calling on politicians, scientists, social scientists, scholars, planners, teachers, philosophers, artists, and sometimes even the clergy to collaborate in harnessing technology to a system of values, calling especially on those who are still young (some of the authors ask us to attend to the counterculture of the late 1960s), in whose hands rests the future.

In *The Machine in the Garden* (1964), Leo Marx focuses upon the "pastoral idea of America." First found in the writings of Shakespeare and his contemporaries, who "thought about the unspoiled terrain of the New World as a possible setting for a pastoral utopia," the idea emerges strongly during the eighteenth century (73). Although machines (the railroad, for example) soon entered the American landscape and were greeted at first with much enthusiasm, the nation continued to define its "purpose as the pursuit of rural happiness while devoting itself to productivity, wealth, and power" (226). This contradiction becomes the theme of our serious writers, who compel us "to recognize that the aspirations once represented by the symbol of an ideal landscape have not, and probably cannot, be embodied in our traditional institutions" (364). Technological innovation, Marx writes elsewhere, brought a new era, separating us from the past, "from the rest of human history"; it is the "suddenness and finality of change" that American writers persistently address" (Leo Marx, "Alienation and Technology" 122-24).

While it is possible to relate the conservative "agrarian" politics of the New Critics and their search for a non-scientific truth to the themes of science and technology, as well as to illustrate the ambivalence of American writers to technological achievement (see Slade), the entire issue can be viewed from a broader perspective, one that will make the theoretical issues involved in the importation of structuralism and post-structuralism into literary criticism more understandable. We need to ask the question what it is, exactly, that everyone fears to lose as technology gains power: What is at stake?

It is more than intriguing to note that much of the political thought that contributed to the founding of the United States came from Locke's *Two Treatises of Government* (1690). The Declaration of Independence has, in fact, been called a summary of Locke's views by Victor Ferkiss, in *The Future of Technological Civilization* (1974). Ferkiss also argues that Locke's empiricist epistemology reduces knowledge to scientific knowledge. "Natural" things have no inherent worth to Locke, in Ferkiss's opinion; they are only made valuable by man's industry. Consequently, technological progress has been promoted and the accompanying power relationships, particularly those of private property, have become entrenched, leading to "a ravaged continent and a discordant society" (31). Ferkiss's view of Locke and "liberalism" may be somewhat one sided, although from the viewpoint of a modern Marxism it can be argued (as Stanley Aronowitz illustrates) that the "discourses" of science and technology are currently used in "advanced industrial society" in the service of "conservatism and reaction." The major point of interest here is that a principal influence on the political environment comes from the very same source as the influences on the philosophical/theoretical environment of Anglo-American thought in general and literary criticism in particular: seventeenth- and eighteenth-century empiricism.

What is, for our purposes here, the most salient connection? Ferkiss writes in an earlier book that we are threatened with "enslavement to technology" (*Technological Man* [1969] 31); he fears the "spiritual dangers of an impoverished anthill world" (289). "Freedom and identity must take on new meaning," he continues. "Who is it that is doing the choosing?" (22).

The question concerning this *Who* is the important one. At the most significant level, the major issue is the concept of the "self" and its "freedom," the most indispensable concept of all—so I propose throughout this study—if we are to understand the temperament of American intellectuals, their political aspirations, their psychology, their analyses of culture, and their literary criticism. There is nothing more important to us than freedom; yet there is no philosophical evidence that man is "free," either in empiricism or in any other philosophy unless freedom is supposed as the outset (as in Sartre), which makes the argument circular, or posited as beyond the reach of philosophy fully to comprehend (as in Locke or Kant), or legitimated by the deity (as in Descartes or Berkeley). Despite this, freedom is what we—the vast majority of us, excluding those few scientists and philosophers who refuse to violate the intractable logic in which freedom is indefensible—cannot do without. Americans can take any system of thought and expand it to include freedom; if it does not yield to the expansion, we will subvert it.

Yet where, other than in yearning, is the justification for this freedom to be found? In one sense, a quite notable one, it is found in the "loophole" in empiricism. We have seen that empiricism can begin with a materialistic Hobbes and end, in some decades, with a skeptical Hume. Once Locke allows two sources of knowledge, the (presumably) external world and "reflection" upon what goes on in the mind, a dilemma arises, for it is not certain what it can mean to look into the mind. Who is doing the looking, if not the very mind that itself is being looked at? If the contents of that mind are not innate thoughts in an immaterial unified entity but are caused from without, by experience, then the self is constituted and the notion of a unified entity of self falls apart. This is what in fact has happened in modern philosophy. But Americans are not, except for a meager clan, philosophers. They are impatient with such speculation; they have a strong streak of anti-intellectualism, which, according to Richard Hofstader, "is founded in the democratic institutions and the egalitarian sentiments of this country" (407).

Another approach is available. If one concedes, as does Hume following Berkeley, that we can know nothing but the ideas that happen to be in the mind, and if thought is accordingly only combinations of these, then we cannot demonstrate, once and for all, that the world or other minds exist. We cannot prove any of our most aggrandized notions—"freedom," "self," "cause," "God," and so on—reflect anything real. But, Hume admits, we must conduct our affairs anyway, for such is our nature. We must act as if we were free selves surrounded by an orderly universe, even though if we stop to think about it we realize we do not have a philosophical leg to stand on. This is the saving "loophole" in empiricism—even Hume eventually makes an argument for free will—and becomes the fundamental problem in the history of psychology. While empiricism serves, followed in one direction, as the base of an observational (usually called "empirical") science recording the information that comes from the external world stimulating our senses, it also serves, followed in another direction, as the base of skepticism, since we can know nothing but ideas in the mind. In our daily lives we can set philosophy aside, as if it raised puzzles, not truths, and act as if we are who we think we are, by whatever inspiration, intuition, or even biological determinism. We can see ourselves as free selves, an outlook perfectly suited to the temperament of the majority of Americans.

The Continental European tradition from which structuralism emerges is not quite as willing to compromise with determinism. The analyses of Karl Marx are the most influential modern example. There is the assumption, whether in Comte or Hegel, that historical forces have, so to speak, a life of their own; that humankind is immersed in these; that human thought is consequently constituted by the process in which it participates, whether or not any individual person knows this. In modern structuralism this process is language. Of course, even Marxism promotes human action, so the problem of the efficacy of will is not finally resolved, an enigma that can be traced back to the *Ethics* of Spinoza, who would, paradoxically, have us "choose" to act in the way that we *must*. But this approach is not congenial to most Americans.

When, for example, many American writers comment on the growth of technology, they reject "the zeitgeist theory of technology, which holds that man's inventions have a life of their own, beyond man's control" (Slade 31). American writers for the most part will, like Sidney Hook, opt for man creating history, not vice versa. Marx, of course, believed that technology was a positive accompaniment in the movement toward a just society and human well being and that the primary forces at work were economic, rather than technological. But while a Marxist historical materialism is the most important influence on those French thinkers from whom Americans have derived the recently imported ideas that have influenced literary criticism, Americans (aside from thinkers whose specialty it is to support Marx) are basically most uncomfortable with the Marxist, or any other, theory of historical and economic determinism. Some can feel at ease with the Marxist theory of "alienation" since this allows a link to a moderately optimistic psychology.

Ultimately, Americans choose a theory of unified self and free will. This makes clearer the choices of the New Critics described in the previous chapter. The New Criticism begins in Richards with an underpinning of a biological psychology not incompatible with determinism. (J. B. Watson's *Behaviorism* [1924] appeared the year before Richards's *Principles*.) The persistent interjection into the New Criticism of ideas inherited from Romanticism is, for literary criticism, equivalent to what we find elsewhere in American thought: the attempt to counteract the inevitable consequences not of science itself, but of the philosophical basis of science in empiricism which, as most of the Enlightenment thinkers recognized, leads quickly to determinism and refutes free will. Technology is then seen as an example of how free will is sacrificed. The real issue is the advocacy of a system of values that empiricism cannot justify. But the New Critics could not be other than empiricist. Americans are Lockeans at heart. They could only strive to incorporate—while citing poems from a literary period (the early seventeenth century) before empiricism, but not before science, developed—theory from a literary period (Romanticism) in which concepts of human freedom, creativity, and, in a mixed way, hope were prominent. This is the source of their theoretical incongruities. They had no other choice, for literary scholars will go to literary sources, which are mostly, sometimes only, what they know.

During a time first of economic depression and then of war, when technology seemed itself to be becoming the evil it was supposed to do away with, the New Critics were compelled to turn to Romanticism. It is quite revealing to read Jacques Barzun's comment on the rehabilitation of Romanticism following World War II: "Romanticism has become respectable again" (Barzun [1961] xiii).

In reviewing the reception of structuralism and post-structuralism in the United States, then, it will be necessary to emphasize how concepts of self and freedom underlie the acceptance, non-acceptance, or reformulation of literary critical theory. We must examine how a critical movement arising in France as a deterministic empiricism progresses toward the same skepticism as did empiricism two hundred years earlier, and we must discern how that very skepticism provides an entrance for American critics to move, as usual, from the consequences of a determinism whose logic empiricism can never refute to a reassertion of human freedom and creativity.

The values sacred to most Americans are self-determination, individuality, opportunity, and physical well-being, operative within a supportive rather than constraining community in which work and family life are chosen and hence satisfying. Technology both promises to increase and threatens to diminish these values, all of which can be related to the concept of the "free self." The concept that the self is a distinct, unified entity of subjectivity residing in the world is not unlike that envisioned by Descartes. Such a self seems most inharmonious with the findings of science, since, if a universal cause and effect becomes a premise, then the self and all its actions must, so it logically appears, be determined, as is everything else. That the self might be an immaterial entity somehow apart from strict material cause and effect has had most of its philosophical support undermined over the three hundred years since Descartes, though a strong religious inheritance has kept the idea vital.

The effort to maintain the belief in a "free" unified entity of self to the maximum extent feasible, given the aggregation of scientific knowledge, is a predominant motivation even for the "man in the street." No less is this true in literary criticism, for which that portion of the scientific and philosophic community which rejects such a "self" becomes the adversary. The search for a "truth" other than scientific truth is augmented in the New Criticism the further one leaves behind the early works of Richards. This development has been used to illustrate the process, the avoidance over time of purely scientific explanations by incorporating mitigating factors, even if incompatible. Not that the "dual" truth of the New Critics is overtly used as evidence for "freedom" of will; but the search for some truth other than science is motivated fundamentally by a need to maintain faith in the freedom of self that science on every front seems to belie. (In recent times, one notes the attempts by humanists to account for free will by turning science upon itself: by using Heisenberg's proof of "indeterminacy" in small particle physics or by pointing again and again, with alacrity, to Gödel's proof of the necessary "incompleteness" of mathematics.)

In assessing the reception of structuralism in the United States, concepts of "self," of what the human being basically is, how mind is constituted, will be placed in the foreground. The constitution of mind is the basic concern of the modern linguist, and of structuralism specifically, whether in Lévi-Strauss, Barthes, Lacan, Foucault, Lacan, Althusser, or Derrida. We will find, however, that in concerning themselves with the constitution of mind, the French structuralists do not, like the Americans, demonstrate the need to preserve, at whatever cost, the idea of the "free," unified, autonomous, Cartesian-like self. Quite the contrary: they are repudiating it.

Existentialism

The French structuralists follow in time, and come to replace, the French existentialists. Before scrutinizing structuralism, it is important to recognize what is philosophically being discarded.

The term "existentialism" has been applied to encompass the thought of many writers—philosophers, theologians, and even novelists—who themselves would not identify their work as representing a single school of thought. It is a variation of phenomenology (for a basic review, see Grossmann [1984]). It is obviously not possible here to comment at length on Sartre, Heidegger, Jaspers, Dostoyevsky, Nietzsche, Camus, Kierkegaard, Tillich, Niebuhr, and others who have been called existentialists; but a brief and perhaps unforgivably condensed review will clarify certain philosophical issues.

It must be said that the structuralists and post-structuralists do not spend much time analyzing existentialism. While they take quite seriously the precursory phenomenologists, Husserl and Heidegger, who do receive special consideration from Derrida, they largely put aside existentialism as an inadequate methodology that addresses prominent issues of human concern in what perhaps should best be seen as a literary vein, rather than a philosophical one. Admittedly, cultural considerations are substantial: one generation must reject its predecessor if its own work is to appear unique and important. The reaction against existentialism was, for thinkers in France during the 1950s and 1960s, equivalent to asserting their intellectual autonomy; the structuralists were to "take over" French intellectual life from those who had dominated it for thirty years (Thody [1983] 108).

In *The Order of Things* (1966), Michel Foucault points out that the most prevalent modern concept of "man" arises after the order of the world can no longer simply be attributed to God. Man seeks to understand himself through himself, though he soon recognizes the limitations of such an approach, since he becomes at once subject and object in the study. The very "finitude" of man that causes the limitations are at the same time then purported to be, in the nineteenth century and into the twentieth, the very conditions of knowledge. "Modernity," writes a commentator on Foucault, "begins with the incredible and ultimately unworkable idea of a being who is sovereign precisely by virtue of being enslaved" (Dreyfus and Rabinow [1982] 30).

While the critique is meant to apply to philosophy from Kant forward, it is most useful in discussing existentialism, which Foucault seems most immediately to have in mind.

The concept of freedom, and the responsibilty this entails, is what, principally, binds together the thought of those classified as existentialists. In the works of the writers listed above, we find a self-conscious, introspective "self" that is persistently aware of the compulsion to choose, to act. Burdened with the anxiety that this need causes, the self seeks to realize its own meaning and potential, which it cannot do except by its own exertions, through its own strengths. "The unconditional imperative," Karl Jaspers asserts in *Way to Wisdom*, "comes to me as the command of my authentic self. . . . I become aware of myself as of that which I myself am, because it is what I ought to be" ([1952] 55). Metaphysics, systematic theology, rational ethical systems, public opinion, all fall away, prove flimsy, as human beings face their choices situated in a world in which meaning can arise only from human thought and action. They must carry on with risk and uncertainty, yet with faith that meaning and even justification can be achieved, despite the knowledge of an unavoidable mortality and in the midst of a threatening despair and dread.

Even existentialist thinkers of a religious persuasion cannot diminish the anguished courage with which decisions must be made, although some are comforted, as is Paul Tillich, that despite the "lack of ultimate necessity, the irrationality, the impenetrable darkness of fate" ([1959] 45), we can participate in "something which transcends the self" (165). The human dilemma is inescapable: it is the paradox of choice, of freedom, where we ourselves are both the guides and the followers. In Kierkegaard, undaunted in his commitment to Christianity and in his belief that humankind has a relation to "the absolute," "the knight of faith is obliged to rely on himself alone" (*Fear and Trembling* 90) even though he acts "by virtue of the absurd" (67): "to exist as the individual is the most terrible thing of all" (85).

Though the human condition is no less easy for existentialists with theological values—Maritain in France, Buber in Austria and Israel, Berdyaev in Russia—the dreaded absurdity is intensified in those writers for whom God does not exist. What measure of humankind then remains? The world is a court where we are both judge and jury, a court of last appeal and no appeal. "All man's alibis are unacceptable: no gods are responsible. . . . Man is free" (Kaufmann 46). Of course, this freedom does not suggest the optimism of the Enlightenment; on its borders lurk anxiety, despair, perplexity, and death. We learn that "the solitude of the self is an irreducible dimension of human life" (Barrett 34).

The best-known representative of existentialism to those in the United States was Jean-Paul Sartre. In his *Being and Nothingness* (1943; English translation, 1966), Sartre proposes that while the objects of the world are each an *en soi*, an in-itself, the human being is a *pour soi*, a for-itself. "It is impossible to define in the pure terms of the In-itself what is revealed to a For-itself as exteriority to self. That exteriority can be discovered only by . . . a consciousness" (260). "Human freedom precedes essence in man and makes it possible; the essence of the human being is suspended in his freedom. What we call freedom is impossible to distinguish from the *being* of 'human reality.' . . . There is no difference between the being of man and his *being-free*" (30). "My freedom is anguished at being the foundation of values while itself without foundation" (46). In his popular essay, likely his best-known work in the United States, "Existentialism is a Humanism" (1946; in Kaufmann [1957]), Sartre writes, "Man is free, man is freedom" (296). Only through free choice do humans define themselves. Human "existence" precedes human "essence." We are not pre-defined; we define ourselves by choosing, acting. "Man first of all visits, encounters himself, surges up in the world—and defines himself afterwards" (290).

In *What Is Literature?* (1947) Sartre emphasizes the social commitment of the author and the reader. The most important function of literature is the appeal from the freedom of the author to the freedom of the reader, an engagement that will bring about a free society. "One does not write for slaves" (59). "In a classless society . . . the writer might be a mediator for all" (76). Interestingly, Sartre asserts that "the writer appeals to the reader's freedom to collaborate in the production of his work" (40), a view that can be linked to more recent reader-reception theory. The approach has little patience with a literature produced solely for esthetic effect. Sartre demands a straightforward prose, one that furthers the interests of a moral and political commitment to human freedom.

Although this meager exposition of existentialism is perhaps more of a caricature, omitting the technical philosophical issues, this brevity is not inappropriate. It is really the mood, tone, and generally popularized conclusions of existentialism—that there is freedom and no source of meaning or value beyond individual commitment—that has influenced literary thought and theory in the United States. Philosophy, in a strict sense, has not been an issue at all. Anglo-American philosophers, at least those philosophers who comprised what Marjorie Grene calls the "Major Establishment," immersed in positivism and analytics, could not have cared less about existentialism, which did not seem to them to qualify as "philosophy." Existentialism was to breathe upon America a cultural ambience.

Nevertheless, some additional matters must be raised in reviewing the transition to structuralism in France. Structuralism rejects the Cartesian self. In structuralism the self is constituted from without; the self is a dependent variable, which is consistent with Marxism. Most of the thinkers mentioned above have a view of subjectivity not inconsistent with that of Descartes, a view of the human self as unified, autonomous, self-determined, endowed with the capability of a truth-bearing (because truth-creating) introspection, free from the customary scientific definition of causality, since only through such beliefs can individual freedom become a first principle. Sartre, for example, states that "there cannot be any other truth than this, *I think, therefore I am*" ("Existentialism Is a Humanism" 302); and one of the Marxist criticisms of Sartre is that he was a blatant Cartesian. Since phenomenology assumes that incontrovertible ("apodictic") truths can be based on introspection, it is incompatible with orthodox Marxism, in which the contents of consciousness are historically determined. This Cartesianism will not, of course, impede Sartre's reception in the United States; it will, rather, be part of the attractiveness of existentialism. But in France it will mean that the structuralists will not pay Sartre much homage.

It must be mentioned that Martin Heidegger, whose ideas serve in many ways as the foundation of Sartre's work, differs in at least one important way. He rejects (or at least qualifies more clearly than Sartre) the Cartesian self. Although there will be more to say about Heidegger later, it can be noted here that Heidegger saw the human being not as a unified self, an entity in one's head, gazing out at the world from its internal chamber (as if it were "the ghost in the machine" condemned by Gilbert Ryle), but as somehow co-extensive with the environment. The truth of things "reveals" itself, looms forth "unhidden," to a person whose very existence is the field of interaction that defines both subjectivity and the world at once (*Being and Time* [1935]). This approach is in many ways not incompatible with structuralism, for which environmental interaction also defines and constitutes the self. While Sartre recognized that knowledge of ourselves must be mediated by the existence of others, that the existence of others is indispensable to an individual existence, he describes the process (ostensibly following Heidegger) as the confrontation of Cartesian selves, through "looking" at one another, for example (*Being and Nothingness*

310). In part because of this view, a sophisticated language theory is not found in Sartre—nor is it really needed, any more than it is in Locke.

But Heidegger's approach to self puts language in a most critical position, and he devotes substantial attention to it in *Poetry, Language, Thought* and *Way to Language*. If the self is inextricably interwoven with the environment, language becomes external and internal simultaneously, in a way that fits quite nicely with what the structuralist will do with Saussure's notions of *langue* and *parole*. A significant point of contention will, however, arise. For Heidegger, the emergence of truth, its presenting itself to us un-hidden, *precedes* the propositions that we make about it. There can be knowledge in the silence that precedes speech, as works of art exemplify. This approach will be unacceptable to the post-structuralists, for whom an immediacy of revealed truth, an immediacy of presence, cannot precede language.

We do, then, find attention paid to Heidegger and not to the other "existentialists," who are, whether they say so or not, Cartesian (recall Husserl's *Cartesian Meditations*) in respect to the starting point of personal subjectivity. Heidegger's phenomenology stands in a unique position as an attempt to advance past Husserl by denying the possibility of somehow standing back from objects, the external world, without any predispositions (the phenomenological "reduction" or "bracketing" in Husserl's *Ideas for a Pure Phenomenology*). Heidegger progresses toward, perhaps nearly reaches, an elimination of the subject/object duality congenial to the post-structuralists. John Llewelyn writes that Derrida's "programme" begins in the work of Heidegger and "could never have been envisioned without it" (*Derrida on the Threshold of Sense* [1986] 33). Steven Melville agrees (*Philosophy Beside Itself* [1986] 60). Nevertheless, Derrida will accuse Heidegger of not progressing far enough along these lines.

In empiricism, the mind is a structured capability, a potential to organize perception; it does not contain *content*, for content would then be "innate" knowledge. We have seen the problem this causes. Assuming that the capabilities of the mind are in some way structured, then would not this structure determine the *form* content will take (the elements of folklore, in Vladimir Propp, for example), and is this not in some sense equivalent to what we mean by "content"? A strict empiricist would answer in the negative, but it is not clear that this is a defensible answer, as Kant understood. Because existentialism, for the most part, requires a Cartesian self and Cartesian introspection as its method, it is not an empiricism. (The fundamental Cartesian truths are not *dependent* upon "experience.") This is why existentialism was never accepted within academic philosophy in the United States. But the linguistics of structuralism is certainly an empiricism. It can accordingly dismiss existentialism without any extensive analysis; if the basic suppositions are erroneous, it hardly matters what follows. (Similarly, Sartre will dismiss structuralism as a-historical, not in the interests of revolution.) The basic supposition of phenomenology, of which existentialism is a branch, is that knowledge, a foundational knowledge, can be obtained by the self looking inside itself, by personal attentiveness to mentality. Whether introspection can be a source of knowledge (an issue as well for a literary criticism attempting to account for the cognitive value of poetry) is a matter of contention in American psychology, too, as comments in the next section will illustrate. For the structuralist, the derivation of the knowledge of the mind from a perusal of one's own mind is a misguided proposal.

We shall see how this empiricism is expressed in Saussure and in Lévi-Strauss. One path leads to a proposed new science, the science of "semiotics" that Saussure called for; another leads to a new skepticism, to deconstruction theory.

In existentialism, as in most philosophy, language can be used to describe, as best possible, the way "reality" is, at least for the human perceiver. But in the study of language, language itself is both the instrument of study and the object of study, which raises special considerations, of the kind that some epistemologists raise by asking how the human brain can be the instrument that studies itself. Perhaps we are trapped in a language that determines reality for us, and perhaps we cannot get around the fact that language is a "prison-house." That language is used to circumvent the limitations of language was not always a problem, even if there were those, like Sapir and Whorf, who understood that language itself takes part in formulating reality (the Sapir-Whorf hypothesis). The possibility of "objectivity" has been the normal point of view in the West, supported ever since the Book of Genesis, in which Adam names the animals. Alternatives have customarily appeared, and to many still appear, a dead end. In the New Criticism, for example, it is assumed that one form of language (criticism) can be used to explain another form (poetry). This possibility (or impossibility) of using one form of language as a "metalanguage" to talk about another form (it is also the predication of psychoanalysis) will be an essential component of the challenge offered, and the controversy stimulated, by the importation of ideas from France.

Anguish, according to the existentialists, arises in the face of an experience that creates dilemmas, incongruities, and uncertainties that no accumulation of knowledge or fact can ultimately resolve yet that nevertheless require human action. It should be possible to understand the function of poetry as transmuting this insight about the human situation into poetic form. This approach would demonstrate a comparability between existentialism and the New Criticism. The psychological resolution, distinct from the revealing of truth, that I. A. Richards attributed to the poem, especially through a balanced reconciliation of opposing or conflicting elements, can be said to reflect a basic human need, the need for psychic equilibrium in the midst of a world of discrepancy.

"What we call existentialism in philosophy," writes Frank Lentricchia, "is merely a thinner, generalized version of the unresolvable experiential tensions that are 'dramatically entangled' in the linguistic complexities of the organic poem" (234). While the words "merely" and "thinner" are unfortunate choices, the point has a certain validity. If, as we have seen in Hulme, human experience is fundamentally a chaotic flux into which we attempt to introduce order, then the poem may function to organize the chaos, which is, however, also to admit to it. "Irony" in Brooks could specifically serve this function by balancing the contradictions that comprise the human condition. "The transition from Richards to Brooks," Lentricchia continues, "is the elevation of irony from its place in the private psyche of the poet to the key to the human experience at large" (235). He cites Krieger's *New Apologists*: "Brooks considers our actual experience in the world to be infinitely complex. . . . Only the poet is able to handle this complexity" (Krieger 119).

It can be contended, in keeping with Ransom and Winters, that the resolutions (not answers or solutions, but balance and reconciliation) in the poem are *conceptual* ones, that the poem embodies the conceptual dilemmas of life's purpose, human nature, the existence of a deity, and so on, to which literary form brings a satisfactory esthetic organization. Literary language would, then, provide a response to conceptual dilemmas, while esthetic satisfaction would not depend upon "truth" at all. Language would serve both to illuminate the irresolvable incongruities of experience, as does the philosophy of existentialism, and to bring to these an apparent order that makes them bearable.

As we have previously stated, the crucial matter for American intellectuals generally is freedom, not the intricacies of philosophy. Americans are usually impatient with philosophy. When the impact of existentialism in the United States is analyzed, the emphasis must be on the support it gave to a generation seeking freedom of action, self-fulfillment or "actualization," and personal knowledge of their inner

"selves." Consistency of theory would be of trivial consequence compared to what, perhaps cynically, might be called mental health. (Ayer
has recently written, not without sarcasm, "the popularity of existentialism . . . appears to have been mainly due to the mistaken belief that
it prescribed a concrete way of life" [*Philosophy in the Twentieth Century*
(1982) 232]). What follows summarizes and advocates an interpretation
of occurrences in the 1950s and 1960s that will contribute to an understanding of the environment into which structuralism was eventually received, and sometimes welcomed.

The indefatigable and relentless promotion of free will, choice,
and self-definition is exactly what made existentialism, or at least something that was called "existentialism" in the United States, acceptable
to certain Americans in the 1950s. The receptive audience consisted
not of American philosophers—analytic philosophy was sovereign—
but of those who, with meager philosophical sophistication (university
students, for example, and some of their younger instructors in the
humanities), were seeking to make "sense" of life in modern technological times, to locate values that science did not seem capable of
yielding. Some social critics looked to a native American humanism to
support their aspiration, turning to Jefferson and to a vision of America
"the way it was meant to be." But a liberalism of *leftist* politics was
also evolving. Interestingly, even when we look back at the "radicalism" that was an intellectual movement in America during the 1930s,
we often find "an outwardness and a receptiveness to European ideas"
(Gilbert 4). Though the 1930s radicalism disappeared by the 1950s,
because of World War II, Stalinism, and McCarthyism, the growing
liberalism of the left also borrowed from Europe. It borrowed existentialism, which not only was an admirable free-will manifesto but also
was allied, through the politics of Sartre and others, with the political
left in France. A sizable group of those in the humanities (many of
whom are today's academic establishment) were captivated by a popularized existentialism, by the accessible portions of the work of Sartre
and Camus, especially in such fiction as *Nausea, The Plague,* and *The
Stranger* or short essays, like those in *The Myth of Sisyphus,* that, once
translated, entered the university curriculum without causing even a
suspicion of the complexities of Husserl and Heidegger. As that generation matured, a segment of it would eventually bring existentialism
into psychology (the movement after many years culminates in Yalom's
Existential Psychotherapy [1980]), a philosophical back door. This helps
us to understand the genealogy of certain therapeutic alternatives in
psychology, the "self-actualization" movement and the accord of post-

war therapists (Fromm, Frankl, and so on), many of whom, like so many other intellectuals, came to the United States from Europe over the years. (The "migration" is documented by Fleming and Bailyn, and by Hughes.)

A point of view is distinct from philosophical argumentation. What was needed was an outlet for the selfhood of a generation filling the universities, seeking the education their parents had never acquired, ready to manage the professions and society, too, in an era of economic prosperity. The increased standard of living and the optimism would last through the early 1970s. Ignoring the pervasiveness in existentialism of dread, meaninglessness, and death (they had not known war), and finding that existential anxiety was not unlike their own yearning, this generation could accept the view that humankind might continue to adhere to a belief in the autonomy of self, beyond social constraint. (Those radicals of the 1930s who were still active in the 1960s would be caused much aggravation by this untempered, usually ahistorical, characteristic.) They also believed in their powers of free will in the face of the inexplicable given of an existence in a world they did not make, nor apparently did anyone else; a world in which no longer could be found the ultimate purposes and meanings of the type that might have once comforted them in the religion to which the parental generation lukewarmly gave allegiance. They would be forced to depart the world entirely in a certain number of decades, to their dismay; yet it was a world that, despite all this, allowed for purpose, striving, ambition, justice, social change, personal meaning, and even heroism.

The attractiveness of what was thought to be "existentialism" has been here attributed to the social needs of a portion of a particular generation in America. Existentialism arose in France in a situation unlike any known in America, the occupation of its territory by an enemy nation. By the time it came, as an attitude, to the United States, existentialism's position had already been modified in France. Furthermore, the importance of existentialism as an intellectual movement in France is much more notable that its reputation in the United States. Despite the influence of the existential outlook on some portion of a certain generation engaged in studying the humanities, existentialism had little influence on the professional intellectual class and its practices, whether in social, political, or physical science. Nevertheless, to literary critical theory existentialism contributes support for a proposed freedom and a selfhood thought to be threatened by the domination of science and technology.

Behaviorism and the Alternatives

An important issue remains if we are to understand the transition of ideas. Two decades ago, the major influence in the United States on how human beings were perceived and defined was psychology; and the most prosperous enterprise of psychology was behaviorism. From a discussion of behaviorism, which is at the antipodes from existentialism and which, more than any other branch of science, called forth responses from and provoked disdain in many persons whose primary interests were in literature and language, it will be possible to determine what needs and conflicts influenced American doctrines of the self and free will, and in this way to move back toward the theory of literary criticism as it is situated in the midst of the intellectual movements that encompass it.

Psychology is the one science in which many literary critics have an interest and claim some knowledge, and much criticism has relied on psychology for conceptions of human thought and action. A basic, perhaps *the* basic, dispute in psychological theory is rooted in the two alternatives for achieving knowledge derivable from seventeenth- and eighteenth-century empiricism, the alternatives that the New Critics attempted to amalgamate by combining a scientific criticism with a tendency toward Romantic notions of poetic truth and creativity. Empiricism allows the fortification of "empirical" inquiry, in which fundamental ideas, or "facts," are presumed to come from the imposition of the external world upon the mind through sensation. Alternatively, empiricism also allows an introspective or reflective inquiry in which (since all one can know are the ideas in the mind, the existence of material reality being insusceptible of proof) fundamental insight comes from personal inspection of the content and processes of mind, with the recognition that, unlike public phenomena, the content of a single mind is directly available only to one person.

The history of psychology has demonstrated that these two apparently incompatible approaches call for an exclusive methodological choice. Either persons will be studied in the same way that external reality is studied, by the scientist recording the results of observing the outward ("observable") behavior of others, or they will be studied by attempting to reach into the mind itself through the reports of subjects engaged in introspection. In the first case, language will be a form of behavior like others (like eating), without the assumption that language is a revelation of what the mind itself really *is*. In the second, language has a privileged status and can reveal the structure and fundamental operations of the mind.

Literary criticism has need, however, of a coherent theory of mind with a methodology that would somehow combine the two approaches that psychology has kept apart. We have seen the difficulties that emerge when the poem is treated as an external object whose subject matter originates in the operation of private mentality that is hardest to explain, creativity. The dual-truth theory of the later New Criticism tries to straddle the two realms by using a terminology—irony, paradox, union of opposites—that attributes to a linguistic object the characteristics of a subject. In effect, the New Critics use a structural (syntactical) vocabulary together with a semantic one without sufficiently distinguishing between the two. It is the merit of structuralism that it attempts to clarify the relation and the distinction between structure and meaning.

In accounting for the reception of structuralism and post-structuralism, the theoretical choices available in psychology from the 1940s to the 1960s in the United States are, then, significant, especially as these involve theories of language.

Whether psychology is to concern itself with "mind" or with "behavior" is a controversy pervading the science. The sundering of mind and body is evident in Descartes, for whom the material body is known as other external objects are known. The body is, accordingly, an object of scientific investigation, while the immaterial "substance" of the mind, not subject to the laws of physics, can be known only through a philosophy based on the "apodictic" truths obtainable through introspection. The form this duality takes in Locke has already been described. The philosophical issues have not changed over two centuries. First, Is the mind an immaterial entity? The modern scientific consensus, and that of modern philosophy, is that it is not. Second, Is the mind a material entity? The difficulty is in the wording of the question. There is certainly no physical organ that we can name "the mind"; although mentality seems to occur in the brain, it does not make sense to say that the brain is the mind instead of saying that what we call "mind" is a function or capability made possible by the structure of the brain. The consensus seems to be that it is unwarranted to call mind a "thing," which would be to retreat, perhaps unwittingly, to the Cartesian position, to the belief in a "ghost in the machine." Third, Can the mind cause behavior? If the mind is a function and not an entity, then it would appear that the contents of mind are generated within a physical causal chain; although there is mentality (thought), it cannot (so goes the modern argument) be an unconditioned cause of behavior. It is at best part of the causal chain. This determinism is, as we have said, a sticking point, for it denies the free will that most of us find essential to believe in. Numerous thinkers seek a route of escape, either by simply positing freedom at the outset (as in existentialism) or by placing the issue beyond the reach of science (as in such appealing, even when unconvincing, works as those of J. C. Eccles). A positive answer seems to be a matter of faith, though this is not, for many, to discredit such an answer. Even within a deterministic theory, whether psychoanalysis, Marxism, and much of recent psychology, room is made, somehow, for choice and responsibility based on insight and self-knowledge.

A fourth question is perhaps the most difficult of all: Can we know the mind, discovering what it really is and how it works? The perplexity is that if the mind is not an entity (so perhaps we should say "mind," not "*the* mind") but a process or a function, how can a process or function get to know *itself* as it really is? Surely we are acquainted with our thoughts, but this is not equivalent to knowing the mind itself. This last statement may be a misleading one: if the mind is not an entity, perhaps there are only thoughts to know, thoughts that appear either as part of a determined causal sequence (that is, will counts, but it is not free) or as a by-product of physical causality, which is the theory of epiphenomenalism.

Is it not impossible to know how thought is structured, how it functions, how the mind "works"? Some say yes, some no. (The debate is analyzed by Howard Kendler, to whom a portion of what follows is indebted.) The mind of a person is directly accessible only to that one person. Even if someone *tells* us what is on his mind, there is still, obviously, no direct way of knowing the content of another mind. Nothing can be observed. If someone says he is in pain and has a "pained" expression, nevertheless, we cannot inspect that pain, we cannot know it or feel it. If we could, it would be our pain (see the various essays edited by V. C. Chappell). Since we cannot observe thought directly, there are those who say that science, being "empirical," need not concern itself with thought. Behavior is observable and is, therefore, the proper subject matter of psychology. This is the theory of behaviorism. (The theory is reviewed in books by John McLeish and by Brian Mackenzie.) Language, too, should be seen as a behavior, the utterance of sound. The scientific psychologist need not take it as evidence for the unobservable contents of mind, which become a scientific irrelevancy—although, to be sure, those contents remain the most interesting of all concerns to most of us.

There is a contrary view: that the mind is open to our personal inspection; that such inspection yields respectable evidence for how the mind operates; that we can report upon this; and that these reports, when coordinated and correlated, are knowledge of the mind. This view is called "phenomenology" (sometimes "experientialism"). To the behaviorists, such phenomenology is useless, for they argue that what is not publicly and *directly* observable to a community of observers has no place in science, wherever else it may find a place. According to the behaviorists, whenever the phenomenologist looks inside at the mind, what is found is merely caused by the strategy of exploration. What is considered a piece of evidence is predetermined by the methodology, so that selection is always operative as a bias and there can be no "objective," scientific phenomenology. Kendler writes that "different experiential worlds are *created* by different methods of phenomenological exploration" (62; emphasis added), and that no phenomenological method will ever be agreed upon by all those who call themselves phenomenologists (45).

It is important to recall that we are here addressing the history of American psychology, where the controversy between phenomenology and behaviorism dates back to the beginning of the twentieth century. American psychologists have been largely unconcerned with the European "phenomenology" that has been discussed earlier, that of Hegel, Husserl, Heidegger, and the existentialists, although this, too, shares the value of introspection. We will return to this when we trace the influence of European thought on American literary criticism. In the United States, the debate takes place between those who follow in the tradition of Wilhelm Wundt and E. B. Titchener and those who follow in the tradition of J. B. Watson.

While we cannot give full attention to the theories of these psychologists (the history is given by Leahey [1980]), a few generalizations can be made. The methods of Wundt, who wrote in Germany at the end of the nineteenth century, included subjective elements as they are presented in consciousness. Similarly, Titchener, who wrote in the United States during the first quarter of the twentieth century, also used introspection. Titchener believed that the mind was composed of sensations and images of sensations (*Outline of Psychology* [1897]). The basic elements of mind are the simplest sensations of our experience; these elements are connected in the mind by a process he sought to elucidate, in an approach similar to, though much more sophisticated than, that of Hume. It is most intriguing to note that the name Titchener gave to his psychological theory was "structuralism."

The opposing school of thought, behaviorism, was founded by J. B. Watson, who also did his major work (*Behaviorism* [1924], for example) during the first quarter of the twentieth century. Watson investigated the relationship between changes in the environment (stimuli) and human behavior (response); there was no need to make reference to mind, the contents of consciousness. The two schools of psychology battled for preeminence, Titchener and Watson the champions on either side. Titchener lost, and behaviorism, customarily abhorrent to literary practitioners, became the predominant, and ultimately the exclusive, hypothesis in American psychology.

Conclusion

The distinctiveness of a literary critical theory, the separateness and independence from other disciplines frequently seen as desirable by critical theorists themselves, depends upon the development of a unique object of study, a specialized professional methodology and vocabulary, and a consensus about the aims of criticism, about what is to count as knowledge. But if literary criticism is to be a distinct discipline (and this is an open issue), we must ask what criticism is to be distinguished *from*. For criticism to claim a territory, it must first have a geography.

The New Critics attempted, with much success, to repeal the subordination of literary studies to positivist philology and history. It is not, of course, possible or desirable to sever completely literary criticism from neighboring disciplines. It is the *interaction* of these disciplines with criticism—whose purposes remain distinct from theirs and whose method, as a formalism, can be in principle isolated—that is important. The modern critic practices in an environment that includes critical theory but is hardly dominated by it. Some commentators lament what seems to be the minor role of literary criticism in modern society; at the same time, some recent critics write as if Western civilization itself depends upon their researches.

By reviewing aspects of science, technology, philosophy, and psychology, I have attempted to clarify what kinds of intellectual forces have been brought to bear on criticism, which at best will exist in a homeostasis with them, as well as to prepare the way for an analysis of the cultural influences upon the change in the perspective of literary critical theory.

CHAPTER FOUR

Transition in Critical Perspective

The New Criticism proliferates within an environment in which technology rapidly advances, substantiating for many the qualifications of science to provide an encompassing worldview, including knowledge of humanity. The investigation of human behavior, ethics, and culture becomes allied with a scientific, deterministic psychology and sociology, an evolutionist biology, and a quantitative economics. In psychology, the dominant force becomes the version of behaviorism promulgated by B. F. Skinner. Human action is determined by the environment, to which behavior is a conditioned response; a behavior is likely to be repeated if the organism is rewarded for it (*Science and Human Behavior* [1953]). No longer is it necessary to discuss—except to dismiss their scientific relevance—thought, mind, intent, will, planning, memory, or any other functions of mentality, like feelings and belief. All of these, whether they accompany behavior or not, are irrelevant to the understanding of it. A science can go no further in eliminating from consideration that which had been most central to the literary critic. Personal creativity, as customarily defined, and also free will are not even theoretically possible (*Beyond Freedom and Dignity* [1971]). Since the meaning of a poem in the New Criticism is inseparable from its organization, and organization is the result of will (craftsmanship) exercised upon insight (inspiration), a deterministic materialism is unsuitable for the New Critics, since it can validate only a positivist criticism. (The literary critics eventually come to recognize this: the references to behaviorism are favorable in Richards's *Principles* and condemnatory in Wellek and Warren.)

In this milieu, the interests of a traditional literary criticism would surely come to be seen as remote from the major forces shaping the intellectual world of ideas. It was part of the task of the New Critics to adapt to this estrangement. They did so by admitting to the legitimacy of scientific knowledge while at the same time arguing that it alone was inadequate for an understanding of ourselves and the world. This dualism of cognition had the effect of institutionalizing (Graff, *Literature Against Itself* [1979] 137) instead of mediating the separation between those in the sciences and those in the humanities (the controversy caused by C. P. Snow's *The Two Cultures* [1964] is exemplary), each with their own "truths."

Transition to the 1960s

The strategy for literary criticism through the early 1960s was to seek an adversarial truce with science: incorporating some of its methodology, by taking the literary work as an autonomous object of study, and turning to the past, following the example of Matthew Arnold, for values and outlooks that allow literature to retain importance as one looks toward the future. But turning to the past may be called a reaction on the "right," similar to the seeking of late eighteenth or early nineteenth century social values, which we find in the southern agrarianism of some of the New Critics (Tate, Warren) and in many of the writers cited earlier who discuss technology in America. The political and religious conservatism of T. S. Eliot is a notable example of the attempt to stabilize the future by calling on the past, and his emphasis on "tradition" typifies the approach, wherever it is found.

There were few other places to turn in a politically conservative society that had experienced economic depression and World War II, that had entered a "cold" war with Russia and supported the activities of Senator McCarthy. (All of these events contributed to the disappearance of "radicalism.") A turn to continental European culture for ideas was not generally acceptable. (Had not, as an aside, the parents or grandparents of a rising generation of soon-to-be-educated professionals based some of their own values on leaving Europe behind them?) It was thought that a retrieval of fundamental American values could be combined with the techniques of science to manage successfully a modern democratic society. Even behaviorism was thought to have the potential to increase social well-being, by providing a method for modifying the environment so that human behavior would be cooperative and productive (as in Skinner's utopia, *Walden Two* [1948]). Significant changes in the functioning of the political structure would not, could not, be widely advocated for a few years.

The gradual introduction of Romantic theory into the New Criticism can be seen more clearly in this light. It was part of the attempt to retrieve from a past era literary (and hence, on the surface, politically unobjectionable) values that could assist in counteracting what were seen by literary critics as the worst aspects of modern technological society, in which the literary critic was obliged to play a role. The New Criticism could assign to literature the highest cognitive as well as creative values, both elevating and defending its stature. The best available tactic was, accordingly, to retain the technique of empiricism for literary criticism by claiming that literary criticism could itself be a separate scientific-like enterprise—distinct from the reliance on "extrinsic" disciplines, such as late nineteenth century "positivism," particularly in philology or history—while at the same time incorporating values of freedom, creativity, and personal human endeavor found in a Romanticism that, as Barzun has clarified, became "respectable" following an unrespectable association, in some minds, with the totalitarian movements of the late 1930s. This was a most appropriate move in a conservative environment. As the environment changed and theories incorporating the views of those on the political "left" became more accessible, the same values, particularly freedom, would again be promoted and enhanced, from a new perspective. Existentialism would provide one link to Europe in this regard because it shared the value of freedom with Romanticism; indeed, existentialism has even been called a modern Romanticism (Krieger, "The Existential Basis" [1966]). The quick replacement of structuralism by post-structuralism and the uses of the latter in the United States will later serve as another example of how the value of freedom is preserved by critics, even when, in this case, the founding theory hardly supports it.

We have earlier commented that the New Critics were viewed as traditional and conservative, whether by writers who saw them as reacting against the modern capitalistic industrial technocracy or by those who saw them as ultimately collaborating with the technocratic establishment, evidenced by the integration of the method into the universities. That the New Critics could but operate in a conservative political climate has in recent times, especially with the influence of Marxist criticism, often been held against them. It can be well argued that the rise of the study of "English" in American universities was associated with the educational needs, and the cultural indoctrination, of an expanding professional middle class. In America, as Terence Hawkes asserts of the "institutional expansion of English" in England, the solidification of the discipline can be "linked with the notion of a cohesive national culture, identity, and purpose" (*Shakespeherian Rag* [1986] 121). Furthermore, the New Criticism's "disinterested reconciliation of opposing impulses" has been said to permit "committing yourself to nothing . . . political inertia" (Eagleton, *Literary Theory* 50). The sophistication, wit, poise, and balance admired in poetry by the New Critics have been identified as characteristics of a "decaying aristocracy" still "revered by a sycophantic middle class" that is interested in emulating status and dignity (Hawkes, *Structuralism and Semiotics* 155). Certain writers, like Stanley Edgar Hyman and Arnold Goldsmith, have pointed to what they see as a contrasting group of writers on the "left," citing, for example, F. O. Matthiessen's *The Responsibilities of the Critic* (1952). The focus of the New Criticism on literary form has often been accused of being a way of escaping considerations of social power, politics, and public action (by Lawrence Lipking, for example), an escape that some have seen as endemic to criticism in the United States, even now (Said, "Reflections" [1983]).

All of this may be unfair to the New Critics, whose writings in many places do seem to contain the belief that criticism will contribute to human self-knowledge and to knowledge of the world and in that way beneficially affect modern civilization. Their theory of a non-scientific "truth," whether we find it insightful, vague, or unwarranted, certainly endeavors to go beyond formalism. The New Critics—at their best, if we are allowed such a value judgment—were for the most part "liberal" in the sense that Edmund Burke and John Stuart Mill were liberal. They espoused the very stance that over time, by an inversion, has come to be called "conservative": a liberalism of the "right." However, in many places in their essays on non-literary topics, the New Critics were undoubtedly reactionary and perhaps bigoted. Aspects of some of them, including Eliot and Tate (and a number of writers like to introduce Pound at this point), do not deserve much admiration. One certainly could ask whether the major historical events of the time have much of an effect on the American New Critics, although they have been defended by Robert Heilman against the charge of ignoring history. Such considerations are often part of the reasons why some recent critics vehemently reject the New Critics, even as they exercise a critical method that, in most instances, the New Critics would not take issue with. In fact, it is a method that the New Critics have taught them, a method that was itself at one point "revolutionary," displacing both positivist historicism and empathetic impressionism.

Furthermore, the uses of Romanticism made by the New Critics, in the context of empiricist theories that really have no place for it, is most important, we have argued, because it illustrates the need of American thinkers (at least the "humanists" among them) to retrieve or fabricate a structure in which freedom has a central place. That need bursts forth most prominently in the culture of the 1960s. In the study of literature, a new generation of students, many of whom are today faculty, having fully digested the practices of the New Criticism, begin to establish their own intellectual identity, which, as is customary, must call forth a rejection of the elders.

That the New Criticism's increasing accommodation with Romanticism reflected the temper of the times is manifested by developments in the 1960s, when the theoretical discrepencies emerge as political ones. For a sizable group of young people studying in the humanities and social sciences on college campuses, the technological forces in society came to be identified with a harmful "establishment," with industrial control, military might, and an indifference toward social injustice. This identification was not, of course, newly invented by the younger population but was in part the outcome of the increasing influence of thinkers on the "left." The political environment was charged with ambivalence and conflict: there are protests and the arrest of protestors; a liberal president is assassinated, as is the leading civil rights leader; a war is fought and despised, seen as necessary and senseless, an ethical commitment and a moral shame; both evangelists and "rock" musicians prosper.

Despite an acute awareness of the dangers of simplification, we must summarize a number of developments here. The universities required large numbers of faculty during the 1960s and a large proportion of those given positions in the social sciences and the humanities (in English departments for example) advocated a point of view on the "left." Simply to call this political "left" a Romanticism would be an unforgivable ploy. (It was not, of course, a "Marxist" left, rather an exasperation to Marxists, except in a few isolated instances.) But if we ask what characterizes such movements as Romanticism *and* those in the 1960s, some similarities emerge. Two are of particular importance. First, they share the belief that human relations—political, social, economic—must change radically and change rapidly, that the world must become a better place to live. (We might compare the aftermath of the French Revolution to that of World War II.) Second, intense personal experience can be a validation of (a non-scientific) "truth," whether through poetry, love, sexuality, strong feelings, an induced mind-altering state, or a "religious experience" that is different from the experience of religion. Both of these characteristics are founded on the presupposition of human freedom, which we have argued is the fundamental issue in identifying the predominant influences on the American outlook. In brief, a "Romanticism," which in the New Criticism is a form of leverage or flexibility in the dominant empiricist outlook, comes to be of primary influence. By "Romanticism" we must now understand a generic term for propositions concerning free will, social change, heightened personal experience, and a truth (as the New Critics' amalgamation of opposites) available through this experience.

But since a turn to "Romanticism" is, in America, a strategy to preserve philosophical "freedom" within a basic empiricism that logically cannot lead to freedom, we cannot expect a Romanticism ever permanently to take hold of theory. It never does: it is usually a tactic of reaction *against* theory, a qualifying of theory, which remains empiricist, as the quick importation of structuralism and the rapid growth of linguistics in the late 1960s and throughout the 1970s illustrates.

The battlefield is always, in the Anglo-American tradition, *within* empiricism, not between empiricism and something else. "Something else" entirely, such as philosophical "idealism" or "rationalism" (we will soon need to discuss Noam Chomsky), is customarily dismissed as useless metaphysics. Coleridge attaches himself to the cart of German idealism only to pull it back toward psychology, which is why the New Critics rely on him. Ultimately, "freedom" becomes a somewhat subversive tactic inside the camp of empiricism, legitimated in part by what we have called a "loophole" in empiricism, the logical possibility of skepticism. The process will become clearer when we review the effect of a "skeptical" (Humean) post-structuralism on (a Lockean) structuralism. Skepticism is a consequence of the recognition that we cannot prove ourselves to know anything but our own ideas; yet these ideas we know from introspection, and it is only through introspection that freedom (of will, of choice) seems, intuitively, a human possibility. Likewise, the conflict between a psychology based on introspection (Titchener) and behaviorism (Watson) also occurs within empiricism. The two psychologies are both empiricisms, in different guises, in different phases.

The generation of future professional teachers of English (now in mid-career) were in their younger days in that very environment when a "Romanticism" (personal freedom, social change, the truth of intense personal experience, the rejection of a purely scientific worldview) most strongly influenced the peer group in which most of them participated. But such a "Romanticism" was more a "lifestyle" than a theory, for which in their professional work (for those whose professional work would involve theory) they would someday need a legitimate empiricist alternative.

In retrospect, it is apparent what the criteria for an alternative approach to the New Criticism would have to be. First, such an approach would have to deal with the unique though publicly unobservable properties and functions of the human mind, with mentality, which behaviorism in psychology had tried to purge, as a causative agent, from science. Second, it would need its own scientific legitimacy; criticism would need to stand as a justifiable autonomous discipline, would need to be a form of "knowledge," capable of validation. Third, it would have to account for language. Fourth, it would have to relate to the functioning of human society, giving insight into the relationship between literature and the context in which literature is produced.

Each of these four issues is dealt with in the following sections.

Concerning Mentality

During the history of psychology in America, as we have shown, the theory that introspective reporting might yield scientific knowledge of the mind was challenged on the grounds that the object of science must be publicly observable and that introspection only leads to a substantiation of the theory that has validated its use, which is to say that it is not truly induction but a self-fulfilling hypothesis. Whether this charge is justified, whether it amounts to any more than saying that science determines its object, is not here the issue, for such pendulums are always in motion. But the victory of behaviorism over Titchener's "structuralism" lies behind the New Critics' focus upon the poem and their elimination of the author's (or reader's) intent or biography from critical analysis. For this reason it would not be possible for "phenomenological" criticism, whether found in Croce's *Aesthetic* (1902) or in Sartre or Georges Poulet, to command the center of the critical stage.

Yet by the middle of the 1960s, a psychological theory like behaviorism becomes, whatever its scientific merits, incompatible with the increasing interest in individuality, selfhood, achievement, and personal self-knowledge that arises in the younger portion of the general population, who for demographic reasons (and the fact that they fill up the universities) command attention. Deterministic scientific theories become no less supportable or rigorous (although classic behaviorism becomes reworked by the artificial intelligence theorists), but they become, for many, not socially satisfying. There arises the dilemma that, while science might be a fine thing, the logical consequences of the scientific worldview can be offensive. But since the territory of the sciences (eminence in university faculties, government-funded research) was on its own ground unassailable, the reaction needed to be at first "extra-curricular." A generation that defined itself as non-conformist looked toward Eastern religions, "beat" poetry, occultism, drugs, popular music (the lyrics of "rock" music through about 1976 should be a primary source of information), and a peer consensus fortified by dress, hairstyle, and living arrangements. Much of this, we are contending, is a reintroduction of freedom and self-determination—the values of Emerson and of Whitman—that the logic of science cannot, for philosophical reasons, condone. Philosophy, however, is hardly the major issue; and we have stressed as a repeated pattern the deep-seated antipathy to the social and "spiritual" consequences of technology. Essential to the growth of the American society, technology brings the material benefit that, paradoxically, both confirms the strength of the society and attests to its weaknesses; it creates the very leisure in which its shortcomings can be contemplated. Empiricism fuels the optimism of the Enlightenment: science can bring health and happiness to all, with which even Marx would agree. Yet in recent times we find two world wars, a devastating economic depression, the impersonal human relations of urban life, and continuing tension on a global scale and anxiety on a personal one. Still, it is impossible for most of us not to remain empiricists; this is our heritage. We accept it, we lament it, and we turn continually to incompatible sources for relief, for freedom once again.

The use of Romanticism in the New Criticism is similarly motivated. A "Romantic" link to existentialism formed as political thought moved to the left. Krieger finds the link to existentialism already formed in the later New Criticism, although he admits that demonstrating so early a direct connection is perhaps not possible (Krieger, "The Existential Basis" 1230). Again, we see this as a surreptitious reintroduction of freedom into an empiricist population. (It is an interesting sign of those times that perhaps the most popular book on existentialism, by William Barrett, was titled *Irrational Man* [1958].) The most informative place to look in the 1960s is not in the criticism of poetry but in the criticism of fiction. The need for a belief in human freedom, supported by a popularized existentialism in the face of much contrary evidence, is illustrated by the innumerable analyses of the fiction of choice and search for self: the fiction of Sartre and Camus, of Melville, James, Conrad, and Joyce (not without pessimism; see, for example, Eugene Goodheart's *The Cult of the Ego*). Allied with this was the psychoanalysis of authors and fictional characters and, as a formalism, interest in "point of view," as in Wayne Booth's *Rhetoric of Fiction*. It might even be argued that the criticism of poetry in the United States lost its predominance because it did not (aside from approaches like that of Frank Kermode in *Romantic Image* and the various major biographies) address themes of personality.

At the same time, however, around the 1960s, existentialism was losing influence in France; and this is a most important point. While American critics were moving toward a reinvigoration of concepts of freedom and a consequent focus on self-knowledge derived from personal examination, the French were moving away from such concepts toward a more sophisticated form of determinism, based on Marx and linguistics. This was structuralism. *The two cultures were crossing,* and structuralism was the crossroads at which they met (Roland Barthes periodically directing the traffic), both for a time in the same place but heading in opposite directions.

Behaviorism, our most entrenched psychology, never had much influence in France, the country of Descartes. Perhaps behaviorism was uninteresting in a country that had Piaget.

The growth of a "popular" psychology, distinct from the experimental psychology of the university laboratory, illustrates the process through which European ideas are naturalized as citizens of the United States (as, literally, were the authors of them who came from Europe). For example, while orthodox Freudian theory offers little succor to those who maintain an anti-deterministic position, psychoanalysis in the United States evolved toward a therapeutic commitment to freedom of choice and self-expression. Unconscious conflict was interpreted as human struggle; overcoming repression became a form of conquest and self-mastery. What originated in a pessimistic deterministic outlook soon effloresced into ego psychology, "gestalt" therapy, transactional analysis, and other encouraging therapies, such as those based on the heartening developmental theories of Erikson and Maslow. The "stages" of development in both writers are an idealization of the progress of a contented, educated, hard-working, self-assured citizen of America in the 1960s. All these theories were sanctioned by a new generation of humanist psychologists who found behaviorism repugnant.

The appropriation of Freud is an outstanding example of how a doctrine can become of great importance both in France and in the United States, seeming to form a bridge between the two cultures while, in fact, being used for different purposes. In France, the focus is on a *philosophical epistemology* that assumes the centrality of subjectivity: the encompassing question is whether the "subject" is a Cartesian-like (or even Christian-like) entity or a "constructed" content of consciousness, as in Marx and the structuralists. In the United States, the focus is on a *scientific psychology* that does not necessarily assume the centrality of subjectivity: the question is whether the self-consciousness of the subject is at all relevant to understanding behavior. That is, the field of study is differently divided. In France, consequently, psychoanalysis will be subsumed within a linguistic structuralism to help account for the constitution of the self by forces external to it, in conformity with Marxism, of which to some extent structuralism is a variation that substitutes linguistics for economic history. In the United States, psychoanalysis will barely find room in the "science" of psychology at all, despite the arguments of those who assert to this day that psychoanalysis is a (testable) science: it will, in its optimistic derivations, relate to science almost as a counterbalance, serving the same function as the Romanticism of the New Critics.

This helps account for why structuralism can be "invented" in France. The partitioning of disciplines determines the possible choices. In the United States, because the boundaries are differently drawn, structuralism will not be a native product; indeed, it will flourish only momentarily in American soil, in part because of what will someday be seen as the *anomalous* work of Noam Chomsky. (In literary criticism the link is Northrop Frye, who, while a structural formalist, was hardly a structural linguist or epistemologist.) We can look at the reception of Jacques Lacan in a related way and find that his psychological theory—with its concept of desire as a movement through (linguistic) "signifiers" set loose from any determinate "signifieds"—is certainly incompatible with American psychology; yet his concept of the "mirror stage," since it resembles the notions of developmental psychology, will assist those who wish to Americanize him.

Modern French structuralism, like Titchener's earlier "structuralism," presupposes the possibility of access to the human mind. The advantage of the more recent theory is that the content of the mind *is* language, not that language is simply used to convey the contents of the mind. Furthermore, language is publicly observable yet private, too. In France, this responds to the epistemological question of the constitution of self; in America, it responds to the psychological question of language acquisition and use by "elevating" linguistics to a position where deterministic behaviorism cannot reach it.

Criticism, Modern Science, and Kuhn

The issues addressed immediately above should clarify why, given the cultural environment, a new literary theory would have to include subjectivity as a category of the discipline. "Writing" and "reading" would eventually come to the foreground in America. A new, acceptable, literary theory would also have to be a science, or enough like a science to make its practitioners feel a participation in scientific rigor—

a rigorousness for which, in fact, the "close reading" of the New Criticism had prepared them.

American literary criticism has always had to contend with a powerful science, since rapid technological achievement seems to verify that scientific inquiry can lead to knowledge of the world, while other forms of knowledge have no such imposing evidence of their practical accomplishments. The reputation of Einstein is a quite remarkable phenomenon. Furthermore, departments of English are located in colleges of liberal arts, side by side with psychology, sociology, anthropology, economics, and history, all of which have for some decades claimed scientific validity.

That the study of literature might also be a science or like a science was asserted by the New Critics. They began, in Richards, by subsuming criticism to psychology and eventually, in Wellek and Warren, declared that "literary scholarship has its own valid methods which are not always that of the natural sciences but are nevertheless intellectual methods" (16). The important term is "natural." A contrast is being drawn not with "unnatural" science but with the "human" sciences. The authors mean that "natural" science need not apply "values" to the object of study, neither to its structure nor to its function (the sun is neither good nor bad, nor is the shark) while "we cannot comprehend and analyze any work of art without reference to values" (156). From a certain recent perspective, however, it is just this elimination of value from inquiry—which would have made criticism meaningless to the New Critics and probably to most of the other critics who have ever lived—that the structuralists saw as a solution to the separation of science, philosophy, and criticism. A major step toward structuralism, paralleling developments in many disciplines, was the acceptability of the belief that value, "evaluation," need not be the primary task of criticism. ("Judgment" is given over to the cognitive sciences, and "pleasure" is no longer a term of assessment.) This step could be taken because there was a new "science" at hand, one that the New Critics had not had available to them: linguistics.

The rise of linguistics allows the emergence of a "scientific" criticism because linguistics places language at the very center of a scientific study. It is for the first time no longer necessary, if criticism is to be scientific, to rely on an theory external to language itself, neither on psychology, sociology, or history, nor on the philology of nineteenth-century positivism. The New Criticism may be said to be a failed science, a wrong turn toward rapprochement with science, for the very reason that it had no coherent scientific methodology unique to language. Its vocabulary remained anthropomorphic (seeking to "objectively" describe poems in mentalistic terms), and it had to promote alternative poetic "truths" that no science whatever could reach. Accordingly, it had to rely on a system of evaluation based, as we have seen, on a tendency toward a Romanticism that science does not allow for.

At the same time, however, the New Criticism does conform in one important way with modern scientific practice: the viewing of scientific description (especially in physics) as "models" of the way things are, rather than as the "truth" about them. This probably results from the philosophical pragmatism of Dewey and others and from such achievements as the demonstration by Russell and Whitehead, in their *Principia* (1910), that arithmetic need not be innate (a priori), as Kant believed, but is an "analytic" construction. No longer is the electron a little planetary unit circling about the nucleus of the atom: there evolves a mathematical model of the electron that allows no definite assumptions about what the electron "really" is. Similarly, the economists have their models (as in the recent debate over "supply"-side and "demand"-side economics), as do the sociologists (functionalism, for example). The biological concept of genetic transmission is especially interesting, since it is based on a model of DNA as a coded molecule. The code consists of the innumerable possible arrangements obtainable in long sequences of a very few amino acids, a model with a "grammar" much like a linguistic one. (Those codes are described by Umberto Eco in *A Theory of Semiotics* [1979].) In each of these models, the terms in the lexicon take their meaning from the total context of the theory in which they are used; they have no independent meaning. But this is quite compatible with the idea in Brooks, which we have earlier called his most important contribution, of irony as a principle of structure, the idea that any poetic statement "bears the pressure of the context," that there is a constructed contextual meaning in addition to the everyday meaning. Brooks's notion of "dramatic appropriateness" can quite easily be said to lead to the description of a poem as a "model," created by the poet, of some portion of experience; the "reality" of the poem is contextual. To say this, of course, is to deny that poetry can contain the "truth," if truth is to be a correspondence with the way things really are. The New Critics ultimately arrived at this dilemma, for they still assumed that science was a form of descriptive (propositional) truth, and they wanted poetry to be "true," too. The theory of "models," apparently unavailable to Brooks and the others, might have been a solution (albeit temporary): science and poetry organize experience, at least along this line of argument, in comparable ways.

That all language, all "texts" whatsoever are a construction of meaning from a lexicon whose terms have no meaning apart from the structure that contains them is, of course, the basic premise of structuralism. It is what Saussure means when he states that "there are no positive terms," only terms defined by their "differences" from others in the system. Theorists come to propose that poetry is not a special form of contextual language practiced against a background of referential language; instead, all language is contextual, and poetry calls special attention to this. The New Criticism concludes, therefore, with a theoretical position, applied to poetry, that can be said to resemble recent theory, which is why the American post-structuralists have sometimes been called the New New Critics.

Thomas Kuhn's *The Structure of Scientific Revolutions* (1962) is most helpful here. Each science is based, in "normal" (Kuhn's term) circumstances, upon a "paradigm." This fundamental consensus of the professionals in a given science (Copernican astronomy or that of Einstein, Darwinian evolution or Mendelian genetics, and so on) is an encompassing view, for a time seemingly unchallengeable, about the particular field of study consisting of beliefs, "rules and standards for scientific practice" (11). (A "model," a term not used by Kuhn, is not a paradigm but the result of a paradigm.) The acceptance of the paradigm causes scientists to perceive the world as they do at any one time in the history of a science. If the paradigm changes, which is what Kuhn means by a "revolution," we can say that "scientists are responding to a different world" (111).

Two points in Kuhn are especially significant here. First, Kuhn (not unlike the New Critics) is advocating a contextual theory within the empiricist tradition. While his theory might lead to a complete relativism, perhaps even skepticism, he must, however, retain the belief, somewhat qualified, that we can make contact with the world through basic sensation. "Is sensory experience fixed and neutral?" he asks. "I find it impossible to relinquish entirely that viewpoint," even though attempts at some "neutral language of observations now seem to me hopeless" (126). This position—obviously taken as a matter of preference, not proof—creates a problem in linguistics: Can there be a neutral language? Russell and the early Wittgenstein answer in one way; Whorf, Saussure, and the later Wittgenstein answer in another. This linguistic problem, specifically the problem of how statements come to have meaning, will come to serve, by the 1970s, as one of the bridges between literary theory and science.

Second, Kuhn raises the question of whether succeeding paradigms come closer to the truth about the world as it is. His answer is,

again, much in keeping with the researches of those whose preoccupation is with language and literature. There is "no independent way
to reconstruct phrases like 'really there'; the notion of a match between
the ontology of a theory and its 'real' counterpart in nature now seems
to me illusive in principle" (206). If, in addition, a change in paradigm
causes "a different world" to be perceived, the issue of whether language constitutes the "self" is raised. If the history of science shows
not a cumulative progression toward the real truth but successive shifts
of conflicting paradigms (of convention), then the history of science
might be analyzed solely as the product of pervasive social forces rather
than of individual innovation. (Kuhn does not proceed in this direction,
perhaps because the consequences of such an analysis would approach
an unsolicited Marxism.)

Again, one can recognize a ground upon which the scientific
(-like) legitimacy of one approach to the study of literary texts, and
not only them, can be based—as can various theories of "convention"
(of what, in the literary work, is "really there") in Gadamer, Todorov,
Iser, and Fish. It is a ground which, we might say, requires some seeding
from French linguistic structuralism, but whose soil has been well prepared.

Scientific Criticism: Frye

The *Anatomy of Criticism* (1957) must be given a place of distinction
when describing the transition in critical perspective that occurred between the New Criticism and the structuralism that came to America
in the 1960s. In the *Anatomy*, Frye organizes ("creates" would be too
strong a term) the principles upon which a "scientific" critical methodology can be based; moves forward the debate concerning the "truth"
of literature so that the dual-truth theory of the New Critics can be
subsumed in a poetics well beyond a reinvigorated Romanticism; and
thinks his way almost, but not quite, all the way through to a view of
language compatible with the linguistics of both the structuralists and
the post-structuralists.

The volume is an "anatomy," not a "taxonomy," for it takes
literature as a single entity, like an organism with diverse internal
structures, rather than a collection of individual works related externally by a classificatory system whose value would be more organizational than functionally explanatory. (It is not necessary to review
the "anatomy" itself, with its "modes," "symbols," "myths," and "gen-
res.") While the New Critics treated each work in isolation, Frye—while
not denying the unity of individual works—addresses the system within

which each work exemplifies the overall structure of the system. This system can then serve as the object of a science. It can be explored like other systems addressed by science (the cosmos, forms of life, physical matter) with a methodology unique to the system, so that criticism is not subsumed in other disciplines. "Criticism is a structure of thought and knowledge . . . existing in its own right." Knowledge comes, as in other sciences, through an "inductive survey"; the "evidence is examined scientifically" (5-8).

The New Critics, of course, also believed that criticism should be a separate "objective" discipline, but insofar as their theory accounted for individual works, rather than for the system in which they participate, the development of a scientific criticism was impeded. Furthermore, the New Criticism's emphasis on evaluation is discounted by Frye. He believes that evaluation is a matter of taste, conditioned by a variety of personal and social forces, so that "in the history of taste . . . there are no facts" (18). Criticism is not to be concerned with value judgments. The object of science must be publicly "observable" by the investigators, a rejection of phenomenology that can be related to the predominance of behaviorism in psychology. Authorial intent or the mental processes of the reader are, as for the New Critics, outside criticism. It has been noted that Brooks applied mentalistic terms to poetic structure, terms such as "paradox" and "irony." Frye uses terms that depend on human mentality as well: for example, he defines the "ironic" mode as that dealing with individuals "inferior in power or intelligence to ourselves," the reader (34). But there is a difference. In the New Criticism, the terms of analysis describe an *effect* upon the reader, and in that sense they are psychological. In Frye, though he is not always consistent (the definition of the ironic mode presupposes a comparison on the part of the reader), psychology is not at issue, for while the terms obviously require that humans with minds exist (e.g., Frye's numerous character types) they are meant—and in most places throughout the work are used—as the identification of structural elements of the kind we find in Propp and Greimas. Such elements exist as atomistic entities, transportable from one work to another, like the physical elements that enter into chemical compounds; they are elements of plot and character, rather than of psychic impact. Such is the requirement of a science of literature that is to resemble, as other disciplines were hoping to resemble, "natural" science.

As for the truth of poetry, Frye's position is similar to that of the New Critics. He draws the distinction between "descriptive" and "assertive" language and literary language. "Literary works do not pretend to describe or assert, and hence are not true, not false" (74). Some years later, in 1973, Frye will write in *The Critical Path* that "there are two contexts for verbal meaning: the imaginative context of literature, and the context of ordinary intentional discourse" (14). Literary works may best be "described as hypothetical" (*Anatomy* 74), a concept resembling Brooks's "dramatic propriety." Similarly, "sign values of symbols are subordinated to their importance as a structure of interconnected motifs" (74).

Frye, however, reminds us not only of the New Critics in this regard, but of what is to come as well, for he advises that we "admit the principle of polysemous meaning" (72), which is, as we shall see, a necessary result of his approach to language. That the meaning of a literary work is, in principle, not unitary means more than that there are distinct "levels" of interpretation (the literal versus the allegorical, for example). It means that interpretation is, in principle, inconclusive—that interpretation cannot be exhaustive, now a pillar of much modern criticism. It is, however, also important that while in structuralism the linguistic "code" is the *condition* of meaning, in Frye it is likely best to say that the structure he identifies does not *determine* meaning but organizes or systematizes works that in themselves have meaning, although, at the level of system itself, there are meanings not readily available through the single work, as when the various classifications of myths are said each to represent a season—e.g., Winter—in nature.

Frye writes that when poetry "is applied to external facts, it is not its truth but its applicability that is being verified" (93). He here allies himself with philosophical pragmatism, in which truth has an "operative" definition, as it has in logical positivism (in A. J. Ayer's *Language, Truth, and Logic*, for example), and consequently with the approach to scientific truth that Kuhn espouses. It should be recalled that I. A. Richards had a comparable approach: poetry has a psychic function, a "use."

In the *Anatomy* Frye does not have a formal linguistic theory, but his comments are easily integrated into a modern formal linguistics. For Frye, the "order of words" (by which he means a linguistic system itself, specifically the literary system) must have a "center," because the "order of nature as a whole" is "imitated by a corresponding order of words" (96). That is, a referential attachment to the world is maintained, somewhat like that of the structuralists, who do not, however, limit the notion to literary language alone. The "reference" is not, clearly, equivalent to mimesis; rather, the entire system of literary language imposes a linguistic order or structure upon the world, which is itself orderly—there is a correspondence that is not the same as a description of reality as it "really" is. Frye refers to "the possibility of a self-contained literary universe" (118).

By the end of the *Anatomy*, Frye goes much further in the direction of an assumption axiomatic to structuralism. He admits that in his argument we are "led to the principle that all structures in words are partly rhetorical and hence literary and that the notion of a scientific or philosophical verbal structure free of rhetorical elements is an illusion" (350). The qualifying word "partly" is of interest here; Frye seeks to maintain the "descriptive" and "assertive" components of language. Though a similar point is made in Kuhn and in Richards's *Philosophy of Rhetoric* (metaphor, says Richards, is "the omnipresent principle of language"), it leads Frye to a surprising speculation. Two pages later he asks, "Is it true that the verbal structures of psychology, anthropology, theology, history, law, and everything else built out of words have been informed or constructed by the same kind of myths or metaphors that we find in literature" (352)? Here, too, Frye is quite cautious, and he concludes that these various non-literary languages cannot be "nothing but myth and metaphor." He suggests that there is an objective world that unifies (somehow) the various distinct language systems.

It is clear why Frye must maintain his reservations. If all language whatsoever is like literary language, then the separate system of literary language that he has been at such pains to define as a separate field of scientific criticism no longer remains distinct. This is a conclusion with which the structuralists will be quite comfortable. Lentricchia, who discusses Frye at some length in *After the New Criticism*, argues that Frye has dismantled his own system by raising these issues (as if Frye, like most, deconstructs himself at the last minute); but Frye is in fact clear and fully aware about where he—like Kuhn in his speculation on a "neutral" language—wishes to draw the line.

Other passages in the remarkable *Anatomy* attract attention, given what has happened since. For example, when Frye writes that "the contract agreed upon by the reader before he can start reading is the same thing as a convention" (76) and later that whether or not something is a work of art "cannot be settled by appealing to something in the nature of the thing itself" (343), we cannot help but call up the work of Fish, of the German "School of Constance" (Jauss and Iser), and books like Ellis's *The Theory of Literary Criticism*. There is also the recognition of what will come to be called "intertextuality": "the new poem, like the new baby, is born into an existing order." "Any poem," Frye states, "may be examined . . . as an imitation of other poems" (96-97), a Bloomian proverb. Lastly, that the structure of the literary system centrally involves myth is another link to the structuralists, specifically to Lévi-Strauss.

More important for our immediate purposes is that Frye exemplifies precisely the strategy that we have designated as characteristic of the temperaments of most American critics (that Frye himself is Canadian is, for these purposes, irrelevant): beginning in a rigorous classical empiricism only eventually, once the logical consequences of that branch of empiricism which supports science and hence determinism are encountered, to interject and superimpose concepts of human freedom which they cannot forsake. It has already been suggested that this strategy will be found in the reception of structuralism and post-structuralism in America. Frye asserts that civilization is "the process of making a total human form out of nature, and it is impelled by the force . . . of desire" (105), a fine (and in this work gratuitous) insight. But positing "desire" as a primary motivation does not lead Frye to a determinism, as it does Freud (and Lacan). Quite the contrary: "the ethical purpose of a liberal education is to liberate, which can only mean to make one capable of conceiving society as free, classless, and urbane" (347).

"The imaginative word," Frye states in *The Critical Path*, "opens up for us a new dimension of freedom, in which the individual finds himself again, detached but not separated from his community" (131). Frye attempts to reconcile freedom with the deterministic consequences of the empiricism that underlies his critical method. Since freedom implies free will, there is an "irony" that "consists in the fact that such freedom eventually collapses into the fatality it tries to fight against"; he continues, "the only genuine freedom is a freedom of the will which is informed by a vision, and this vision can only come to us through the intellect and the imagination" (132). Moreover, "in this kind of freedom, the opposition to necessity disappears: for scientists and artists and scholars, as such, what they want to do and what they have to do become the same thing" (133). This bipartisan position, reminiscent of Spinoza, well reflects the tensions for the humanist and literary critic seeking at once a foundation for practice compatible with science and a substantiation that the concept of freedom has a validity and an applicability for which literature is essential.

Frye, like his colleagues in Anglo-American literary criticism, wishes to be a scientist of the highest order but not at the expense of humanism, particularly as this involves belief in free will. This is hardly a negative criticism; it may even be a saving grace, defending, in a technological society dominated by a scientific worldview, possibilities that such a view cannot include and at the same time cannot exile, even if the only evidence comes from the very introspection that science has disparaged.

In seeking to discover the encompassing literary structures determining the individual structures of specific literary works, which altogether form a comprehensive single system, Frye need not go outside what has traditionally been considered the literary canon. This procedure is itself compatible with the New Criticism, even though the thematic and dynamic characteristics discovered are different. Frye might be said to have done a New Critical close reading of literature itself conceived as a single text. His criticism might be called a Meta-New-Criticism. At the same time he is, in his unique way, a "structuralist," since no element in the system can be said to be fully understood without knowing its place in the system. This raises the controversy over the descriptive referentiality of language; for where is the opening toward reality in a system that itself seems closed within its own boundaries? It is the juxtaposition of both these elements that makes the *Anatomy* serve so well as a transitional bond between the two critical schools.

Like both the structuralists and the New Critics, Frye's approach is a-historical. The literary system exists, to use Saussure's term, as a "synchronic" system—all at once, with individual works, regardless of the time of their composition, placed in a framework that exists in some absolute timeless sense. It is not, therefore, an evolutionary approach. This is Frye's distinction from Eliot and others for whom "tradition" was a historical term, each new work modifying, changing the shape of, the tradition as a whole. The history of literature, then, is distinct from Frye's "science" of literature.

While Frye provides an anatomical science of literature, the *Anatomy* lacks certain features essential to the structuralist and post-structuralist movements. Aside from the comments on human "desire," there is no theory of the workings of human mentality or the nature of the self, although from our present perspective we might find an obvious one implied. Additionally, there is no sophisticated linguistic theory. Both of these features become desirable ones, for the reasons outlined throughout these last two chapters, and they will make structuralism attractive to American critics.

The Political Context

Although some analysts have asserted that the New Critics and the American structuralists and post-structuralists avoid or neglect the relevance of literary criticism to immediate social concerns or its political implications, changes in critical theory can be related to the political environment of the mid-1960s through the mid-1970s. Of particular importance is the linking (whether warranted or not) of recent criticism with the politics of the "left."

We have proposed that the thinking during that decade of a sizable group of predominantly, though not exclusively, younger people can be called "Romanticism" insofar as it combined an advocacy of rapid social and personal change—a future-oriented pervasive belief in a liberating rapid progress in the "quality" of human life and relations—with an emphasis on the individual personality, particularly on the truth-bearing qualities of intense human experience. Such an intensity was often defined by the strength of accompanying feelings and emotions, a surer guide to truth, it was said, than logical reasoning alone. These beliefs were manifested in a group that can be characterized as young, middle class, and economically advantaged. (The civil rights movement would require broader definitions and the connection between that movement and the "counter-culture" would demand a separate analysis.) That group most directly interacts with the universities and with the professions, which they join. Social change was to involve modifying governmental structures and procedures; transferring political power, especially at the federal level, to those in agreement with the need for creating social justice and personal opportunity (employment, education) through major social legislation; modifying human awareness and promoting personal "growth" so that human social relations would improve and be based on a universal equality (the elimination of racism and sexism) and so that individual action would be undertaken with full consciousness, awareness, and responsibility; and changing the relations among nations so that they would be based on a harmony of interests, not conflict. War, particularly the war in Vietnam, would cease.

This social program was politically on the "left"—although the meaning of "left" was, to use Frye's term, polysemous—for the following reasons. (What follows is preposterously oversimplified, but we must advance our argument.) The left in the United States meant, for the most part, the liberal wing of the Democratic party, with which the proponents of the movement usually associated themselves. Equally important were certain connotations of the term "left," which often caused the advocates of change, in more conservative minds, to be associated with values and actions perhaps disruptive, certainly challenging, to traditional American society; to be associated with the "left" that in Europe often means Marxism. First, encompassing social change was linked, often not for good reasons, with the Marxist analysis of capitalism, particularly because of the indiscriminate use of the word "revolution." Second, the opposition to the war in Vietnam was sometimes interpreted as (and sometimes was) support for the opponents, who were Marxists ("communists"). Third, beliefs about "truth" in America customarily rely upon public consensus. The emphasis on the priority of personal values over community consensus, *if* the personal values are radically non-conformist, can be (somewhat illogically, given American history) interpreted as an undermining of American values. While personal insight based on experience is, to be sure, very much the American way, non-conformity is (paradoxically) not encouraged, for such insight is usually condoned only when it is interpreted as in some way advantageous to society. Fourth, we have pointed to the importation of a popularized existentialism: Sartre, like other French existentialists, was a Marxist. Similarly, the application of Freudian psychoanalysis to cultural change was often promoted from a Marxist background, in the *Eros and Civilization* (1962) of Herbert Marcuse, for example, who came from the Frankfurt school. Fifth, the movement on the "right" sought political rejuvenation through a reliance on an America of the past, on the Constitution, on Jeffersonianism, and on the rights of individual states. A movement called (by whomever) the "counter-culture" could be interpreted as non-American. Since the political system set in opposition to the American system was Marxism, what might appear to be a rejection of one could be seen as an acceptance of the other. Sixth, the use of the term "left" could (mistakenly) be identified with the radicalism of the 1930s, which was Marxist. Seventh, some people on the left called themselves Marxists, and among these some few in fact were.

This enmeshing with the left by so substantial a portion of the population, notably within the universities (where many faculty as well, especially in the humanities and social sciences, had adopted positions on the left), brought about the circumstance that both theories and theorists for a time needed, among those whose reception most counts, a *legitimation on the left*. The "right" was chastised as anti-intellectual, reactionary, a mixture of racism and warmongering; its proponents were not growing in personal self-awareness, emotional freedom, and behavioral expansion, but were conservative, unimaginative, and "uptight." Now the New Criticism, as we have shown, is on the "right." ("In general," Frye asserts of the New Criticism, "the movement, at least in America, was anti-Marxist" [*The Critical Path* 21].) Some of its most notable practitioners were from the South, "agrarians," with a critical method that seemed politically noncommittal or (worse) had embedded in it an orthodox ideology supportive of the status quo. Eliot's conversion is frequently mentioned. The belief in an autonomous poetic object might, in fact, be attributed to the conservative role in American history of two texts, the Constitution and the Bible. When the New Critics turned to Romanticism, it was to derive a psychological poetics; for models of poetic practice they looked elsewhere, to more conservative times. There was no receptivity to discovering in the nineteenth-century Romantics the "existential" "Romanticism" that characterized the 1960s, and there was no identification with the stance of the Romantics toward the French Revolution, toward the rejuvenation of all human relations (which Abrams traces in *Natural Supernaturalism*). For these reasons alone the New Criticism became unappealing, even while the methodology of close reading remained permanently sanctified.

This need, beginning in the mid-1960s, for a legitimation of theoretical (academic, scholarly) thought by the left was manifested in the rise of a socially oriented criticism tha was significantly influenced by Marxist criticism (by Gyorgy Lukacs, for example) and by such works as Sartre's *What Is Literature?* The failure of this approach in the United States was that it did not, and cannot, create the type of scientific criticism that makes such criticism a distinct discipline. Criticism becomes subordinated to sociology; even the production of writing eventually becomes understood in sociological terms (on the model, for example, of Pierre Macherey's *Literary Production* [1978], which argues that "the work is not *created* by an intention . . . it is *produced* under determinate conditions" [78]). At best, the critic can extract "themes" from literature (the rise of the middle class, the subjection of women, economic relations) and show how these reflect the times, encourage change or reaction to change, and so on. An important part of the innovation of structuralism—which itself is founded in Marxism, with language theory accounting for the contents of self—will be that it will not classify thematic content by its meaning and import but will break up narrative into *functional* elements that themselves serve as *structural* elements. This method is much more in keeping with a scientific poetics than is the practice of a sociologically oriented criticism that extracts thematic elements which are not in themselves structural but are given structure in the form of genre. In any case, a sociological criticism, while it did have a validation on the political left, could not be the scientific theory sought for over forty years; and the impact of such criticism on critical theory in the United States is small.

The theory that will come to be legitimated on the left and at the same time be a critical science incorporating a coherent view of self, language and literature—fortunately compatible with the methods both of the New Criticism and of Frye—will be a linguistic structuralism.

Linguistics and Chomsky

The increased interest in language from the mid-1950s onward is evidenced by the growth of scholarship, and graduate education, in linguistics (Lehmann [1981]). The annual bibliographies of the Modern Language Association over the past twenty-five years provide ample documentation. For literary critical theory, linguistics has the necessary scientific legitimacy that, by association (even by the administrative structure of university departments), increases the alliance between literary studies and those disciplines that might look upon literary studies as subjective and scientifically inconclusive. The absence of a comprehensive theory of language impeded the New Criticism from advancing as far as it might have liked to go in establishing a scientific criticism; such a theory is missing, although at the time it was not much missed, in Frye as well. There had, of course, been a tradition of linguistic scholarship in America for a long time, influenced by such landmarks as Leonard Bloomfield's *Language* (1914). Yet because linguistics was for the most part affiliated with the same scientific outlook as behaviorism, particularly the exclusion of introspection—reports or opinions of the user of language, in contradistinction to the objective analysis of publicly observable (audible) speech—the discipline was, like behaviorism, of minimal value to literary studies.

A change occurs with the work of Noam Chomsky. Not that his own research has much to do directly with literary criticism; but it fits so well into the cultural environment of literary critical theory, and it has so many of the characteristics sought by literary critics for their own discipline, that Chomsky's work became a most important factor in creating a setting in the United States for the reception of structuralism. Some writers, like Jonathan Culler and Philip Pettit, have even identified Chomsky's publications as a key to structuralism itself, even though, in fact, they are hardly compatible. A review of Chomsky's linguistics will demonstrate how it came to serve as a gathering point for theorists in America, how it came to represent what was *needed*, while his theory itself, we shall see, is most unlike typical American research.

The first advantage of Chomskian linguistics is that it confirms that the science of language is a distinct discipline—the very tactic that literary critics were seeking to successfully exercise. It is true that, for Chomsky, linguistics is subsumed as a branch of psychology (Smith and Wilson 22), since language is but one of a number of cognitive processes. In an essay reviewing his work of more than twenty years, Chomsky writes that "linguistics is simply that part of psychology that is concerned with one specific class of . . . cognitive structures" (*Reflections on Language* [1975] 160). At the same time, and more importantly, language has "its own principles and rules, which are different in kind from those governing other cognitive systems" (Smith and Wilson 32). That is, language cannot be understood by examining some cognitive function other than language; it cannot, for example, be understood through a learning theory confined to addressing the other "classes" of human or animal cognition. The way we recognize faces, or the way we learn to ride a bicycle, does not account for the learning of language. The major implication of this is that the dominant psychology, behaviorism, cannot found a linguistics on its own theoretical principles: "such methods when applied to language produce nothing but falsehoods or trivialities" (Searle, "Chomsky's Revolution" 4).

It is interesting to realize that the New Criticism had been created in a similar way: by I. A. Richards subsuming criticism within psychology, which provides scientific respectability, after which criticism can more and more leave psychology and set up shop on its own, also with its "own principles and rules." We might even say that the way linguistics was to relate to psychology is the way some modern critics would like criticism now to relate to linguistics, as a relatively autonomous sub-discipline. Linguistics would be subsumed under "semiology" and, perhaps, semiology under psychology (or, more intriguingly, vice versa), and in this way a broad synthesis might occur.

For Chomsky, humans are specifically adapted to learn language, just as they are specifically adapted to walk or eat. The human "mind" (a term we shall return to) is *innately* endowed with the capacity for language acquisition. This point is not controversial; obviously anything a person can do must come from what *can* be done, and what *can* be done must have an underlying basis in the capacities with which the human is born. But language raises special problems. Language is extraordinarily complex; an analysis of its structure reveals such an intricacy of rules, such a diversity of acceptable patterns, that it would be most unlikely for a child, who learns language relatively quickly, to learn the system simply by emulating others, by copying what they say, especially since many sentences that are spoken have not ever been spoken or heard before by the child. Furthermore, the speaker, if not a grammarian, is unaware of the governing rules that he invariably uses, once he learns the language. We know what is correct usage and what is not.

Now it might be proposed that although an analysis of language reveals rules, the rules do not have to be in the possession of the speaker. (We can walk without knowing the principles of physiology.) This is not Chomsky's view. Admittedly, the child learns the language that is spoken to him, and not some other, but this cannot be like learning the rules of etiquette or of a sport. Not only are the rules of language not consciously known to the speaker, but the speaker has the capacity to generate what is, in principle, an infinite number of sentences. To account for the ability to acquire language requires, for Chomsky, the assumption not merely of the innate *capacity* to do so but also of an innate *structure* to which each individual language conforms, although languages differ one from another. This innate structure is, or contains (the possible differences are too complicated to pursue here), the fundamental rules of grammar, a "universal" grammar underlying all languages, a grammar that has "psychological reality." The rules are actually in our possession, located in our minds; if they were not, it would hardly be possible to learn so complex a structure as language simply by listening for a couple of years to those who speak it. (If this were possible, adults should be able to learn new languages easily, which they cannot.) These rules of universal grammar are part of the mind. They are *in* the mind at birth, and an immersion in the environment of a specific language causes these rules to be brought to bear, at a biologically determined age, on the acquisition of language. To the vocabulary of a specific language the speaker applies the rules of a grammar—an interaction between innate structure and the particular language learned—that permits the creation of acceptable sentences, a "generative grammar" that is "a set of rules operating upon a finite vocabulary of units, which generates a set (finite or infinite) of syntagms . . . and thereby defines each syntagm . . . that is characterized by the grammar" as "well formed" (Lyons 125).

It is not possible here to provide the substantiation for Chomsky's theory or to enumerate the various rules of grammar that the mind is said to contain for speakers of all languages. (The theory is initially described at length in *Syntactic Structures* [1957]; for a summary see William Chisolm, *Elements of English Linguistics*.) Whether grammar has an innate psychological reality, whether there are universal rules underlying all language, and so on, is not a settled issue and perhaps cannot in principle be settled (which would make Chomsky's theory a metaphysics). Even if similar rules underlie all language, that is not itself evidence for the innateness of rules; it is evidence only for the similarity of languages, which might be occasioned by human society, brain physiology, and so on, imposing upon a human "capacity" rather than an innate "structure," especially a structure that seems to hold innate "content." But what is at issue for literary critical theory is not the details of the theory (any more than the details of Frye's theory) but the suppositions upon which it is based. These suppositions, it can be argued, are attractive not so much because of the explanatory value of a Chomskian linguistics but because of the intellectual milieu, because they support that kind of theory that appeals to those in the humanities and at the same time is considered scientific (or at least not entirely unscientific) by those in the social sciences.

If one looks at Chomsky's theory bearing in mind what has been said throughout these chapters about the need of American thinkers to work in an empiricist tradition and at the same time to escape from its ultimate logical consequences—a determinism and a strict scientific worldview in the midst of a technologically dominated society—we can see just how befitting is Chomsky's theory.

While behaviorism, to the chagrin of literary critics and their intellectual allies, banishes "mind" from science, Chomsky embraces it. Smith and Wilson write (erroneously, but still worthy of quotation) that Chomsky was "probably the first to provide detailed arguments from the nature of language to the nature of mind" (9). For Chomsky, the distinction between mind and body is a valid one. Even if by "mind" he does not mean an immaterial entity, nevertheless, mind is not the same as "brain," even if brain is the necessary precondition of mind. "When one hears a sentence one analyzes it, and that is an act of *mind*" (Lyons 361). It should be quite clear by now that, since Chomsky accepts the notion of an *innate* structure/content in a "mind" that can be defined in some way other than by biology and physics (at least as we currently know them), he is defending the very supposition that Locke had attempted to refute. By doing so he again raises the issues that have been addressed in our first chapter. Chomsky is a Cartesian, and (without embarrassment) admits to being one (e.g., his *Cartesian Linguistics* of 1966): he is a "rationalist" in the sense in which this term is philosophically distinguished from "empiricist." "His results vindicate the claims of the seventeenth-century rationalist philosophers, Descartes, Leibnitz and others, that there are innate ideas in the mind" (Searle, "Chomsky's Revolution" 19). The mind is not a blank screen at birth; knowledge does not come only from experience; the mind has innate "ideas," although, as has been said, it is not ever fully clear in Chomsky where the boundary is between structure and content, which is clarified more in Kant than in Descartes. Chomsky places philosophical empiricism in the opposing camp of the behaviorists; and he is correct that behaviorism is a consequence of one branch (Locke's, not Berkeley's or Hume's) of empiricism. The approach to language of this form of empiricism—language learned like everything else from experience *only*, language as nothing more than a conditioned behavior, like driving a car—is an approach "which assigns a fundamental role to segmentation, classification, analogy and generalization" (learning the language by imitating other speakers and simultaneously deducing or learning the rules). Such an approach is "mistaken in principle," writes Chomsky, in the same essay in which he classifies theory as either E (empiricism) or R (rationalism) and declares himself an R (Chomsky, *Reflections* 217). Chomsky is, of course, also responding to the linguistics of Bloomfield, whose writings are strictly empiricist. The mind, for Chomsky, does not merely have "potentialities," what might be called the passive kind of capabilities that even Locke would have had to admit to. Rather, it has "powers," it is an *active* faculty (216; Chomsky is alluding to Leibnitz here).

That the reference to powers of the mind will perhaps be a reminder of Coleridge, whose Romantic poetics is used by the New Critics (as Chomsky's theory can be used) as a defense against an unqualified empiricism, should not be surprising. The effectiveness of Chomsky's theory to a significant extent depends upon the rebuttal of the empiricism of those sciences and philosophies that exclude mind from the scientifically knowable and that simultaneously have determinism as a logical consequence, a rebuttal needed by a certain portion of the "humanistic" intellectual establishment for reasons we have repeatedly stated.

Chomsky's theory aside, his pushing or taking a major part in the pushing of B. F. Skinner (or let us say Skinnerianism) from what seemed to many an unvanquishable fortress may have been, in the long run, an achievement second only to confirming linguistics as undeniably and perhaps even irreversibly a distinct and separate discipline of research. (Chomsky was, again, continuing his adversarial relationship with the linguistics of Bloomfield, who accepted behaviorism and accordingly attacked any form of "mentalism.") Skinner's *Verbal Behavior*, an attempt to demonstrate how the acquisition of language can be accounted for on the principles of behaviorism (operant conditioning, reinforcement of behavior, stimulus-response theory, language as a *behavior* explainable without reference to mind, even thought being no more than inner speech, a conditioned behavior) appeared in 1957, the same year as Chomsky's *Syntactic Structures*, for which, by the way, Chomsky could not find an American publisher. Two years later, in 1959, Chomsky published an extensive and now famous attack on Skinner's book. Basically, the article focused on the inability of behavioristic learning theory to explain the rapid acquisition of language, given its stupendous complexity, or to demonstrate how rule-dependent sentences are generated by speakers for whom the rules cannot be consciously stated, or to account for the creativity of language, the fact that speakers both can utter sentences they have neither said nor heard before and can in principle create numberless sentences.

Chomsky, as the history of the debate is now interpreted (see the essays in Harman, ed. [1974]), had the advantage; and linguistics soon became a field, at least in the United States, indebted to him for its premises. Another issue, however, must be raised by again recalling the conflict between Titchener's introspective "structuralism" and Watson's behaviorism. Chomsky's theory relies on the reports of speakers, on the ability of speakers to recognize, by saying that they do, when a sentence is well formed or not. This is in part a confirmation of the innateness of grammatical structure. Including in his methodology what Chomsky calls "intuitions" is, in the words of Smith and Wilson, "an extremely suspect part of Chomsky's theory . . . not scientific, not amenable to direct observation" (40)—the very criticism that Bloomfield, or Watson, would have directed at Chomsky. Again, it is my contention that those who provided the warmest reception to Chomsky, literary scholars included, did so for the same reasons that no literary criticism could be acceptable unless it took mind into consideration—the reasons, by the way, that bring William James, the most adroit of introspectionists, into prominence in literary criticism (the "stream of consciousness," for example).

It must be repeated that in America, the controversies are customarily *within* empiricism; and this is no less true here. An introspective science and one that excludes introspection can, as we have shown, both be empiricisms, since empiricism admits that knowledge may come from sensation (perception) as well as from reflection. Chomsky's turn to what he calls a Cartesian theory is a strategy similar to the New Critics' turn to Romanticism. Both outlooks are attempts to reinvigorate the notion of a distinct, autonomous, primary entity of self, a self that can acquire one form of knowledge through introspection. The truth of that form of knowledge is validated by experience, though not logically *dependent* upon it. Such, too, was the Cartesian-like self of the American "counter-culture" (which is why it was not Marxism, in which the self is a construction). The technique only apparently escapes empiricism, by trying to expand its boundaries rather than by leaving it—a strategy that ultimately, in an empiricist context, does not work for long. Even today the bonds between Chomskian theory and mainstream psychology have weakened. It is cognitive psychology that has come to the fore, information and artificial intelligence theory, not incompatible with behaviorism at all, the psychology that began in such works as Miller, Galantner, and Pribram's *Plans and the Structure of Behavior* of 1960 (Leahey [1980] reviews some of the history). "New lawlike generalizations about cognition are being discovered every day by scientists who worry not one iota about the metaphysical nature of the underlying processes" (Flanagan 214). John Lyons refers to cognitive psychology's "brief fling" with Chomsky (392). It might be predicted that in a society where empiricism is the norm, no theory (Chomsky's included) that is affiliated with "rationalism" will endure.

Nevertheless, the popularity of Chomsky's theory can be explained in terms of the cultural milieu, in terms of what the intellectual ranks that include literary critics are looking for. It purports to be a science; it includes room for the human mind; it places language at the center of concern. We found in Frye's *Anatomy* ideas that seem compatible with what we know is to follow in subsequent critical debate; so, too, with Chomsky. His distinction, for example, between "competence" (the capability to apply the system of rules, the grammar, of a language) and "performance" (what is actually said by any individual) has been related to Saussure's distinction between "langue" and "parole." The relationship is spurious since "langue" itself exists nowhere, it has no "psychological reality" in any one mind, like Chomsky's grammar. Yet "competence" and "langue" do have in common that neither is *observable* and thus can be challenged as a valid scientific concept.

Quite importantly, Chomsky's theory had the legitimation of the political left that, at least in America, had come to be essential. He had a prominent place in the pages of the *New York Review of Books*, side by side with Freud. This legitimacy on the left was the result of Chomsky's political activities. A member of the "left" of the 1960s and 1970s, he published a number of writings on American foreign policy (e.g., *American Power and the New Mandarins* [1969]). "There may not be a perfect integration of Chomsky's linguistics and political activities, but the connection needs to be explored" (Hymes 330). This political allegiance helped create an acceptance for his linguistic theory; such can be surmised by noting how incompatible any Cartesian (or Leibnitzian, or Kantian) "science" is with customary American predilections. When the politics cooled, the theory became less plausible. Furthermore, the theory is actually *in*compatible with Marxism, since Marxism in any form, including structuralism (to which Chomsky is hardly the "key"), takes the self to be a consciousness constructed, fabricated, by the social environment. Marxism is an empiricism, not allowing innate knowledge or content of any sort.

Our purpose is not to question support for Chomsky's theory (it may be true) or to say that it should have been more like structuralism or Marxism. It is to argue that the theory was appealing, as structuralism would be, for cultural reasons, just as the dual truth theory of the New Criticism, embedded in a basically empiricist poetics of purportedly objective analysis, was also appealing to those Americans who sooner or later must rebel against the empiricism that is in fact essential to them.

This appeal can be demonstrated in Chomsky just as it has been in Frye. When Chomsky speaks of his opinions on non-linguistic matters, he takes what should by now be seen as a characteristic approach. He states that, when we try to explain human behavior, perhaps we are forced to admit the possibility that "the human mind is inherently incapable of developing scientific understanding of the processes by which it itself functions in certain domains" (Chomsky, *Reflections* 156). He is referring to free will. He cautions that he is not "urging this conclusion" but that it cannot be ruled out (157). Does this not, carried a little farther, resemble, even lead toward, a dual theory of truth, scientific truth and truths not available to science, found in the New Critics? "It is an interesting question," Chomsky writes in *Language and Mind*, "whether the functioning and evolution of human mentality can be accommodated within the framework of physical explanation, as presently conceived" (83).

It is the creativity with which language can be used that underpins these various assertions of Chomsky. "The central problems relating to the creative aspects of language use remain as inaccesible as they have always been" (*Language and Mind* 84); " 'the creative aspect of language use' remains as much a mystery to us as it was to the Cartesians" (*Reflections* 138). Descartes was able to confirm belief in free will by placing the truth about the mind in a realm inaccesible to science, which was to deal with the body. We are on quite familiar ground again. And as Descartes believed that human mentality was qualitatively different from anything possessed by animals, so Chomsky writes, "there seems to be no substance to the view that human language is simply a more complex instance of anything to be found elsewhere . . . in the animal world" (*Language and Mind* 63).

That the speaker has, in principle, the capability to produce an unlimited variety of sentences is, then, not simply a matter of mathematical permutation and combination. "Human language . . . is free from the control of independently identifiable external stimuli or internal states. . . . It is thus free to serve as an instrument of free thought and self expression" (*Cartesian Linguistics* 29). It is the desire, once again, to introduce freedom into a scientific environment that cannot philosophically support it that is, for Chomsky and many others, so powerful a motivating force. "In investigating some of the most familiar achievements of human intelligence," Chomsky states in *Problems of Knowledge and Freedom*, "we are struck at once by . . . the character of free creation within a system of rule" (88).

The work of Chomsky is important because it combines all of the elements necessary for a theory to have been acceptable in the 1960s and 1970s among the group of thinkers that includes those responsible for tending to literary criticism. It claims scientific validity, yet it admits into science human mentality; it allows for the "empirical" as well as the introspective, the self-reports of subjects; it employs a scientific methodology while conceding that such a methodology is limited and cannot encompass all important truths. It permits notions of "creativity," even of the mysterious Romantic kind that Coleridge inherits from German idealism, although, as in Coleridge, the notions are transmuted into psychological rather than philosophical (in the strict sense of the term) speculation. It places language at the center of attention; it is legitimated by the political left. Finally, it offers, even if only as a possibility, a way out of determinism, a purpose also served by the turn, of others, to Romanticism, existentialism, or the "humanistic" psychology of Erikson, Fromm, Maslow, or Perls, depending on their temperament, their education, and their theoretical sophistication.

On the other hand, Chomsky's theory, because of the admittance of innate content, is not an empiricism. In the United States a theory needs, in the long run, to be this too, as structuralism is, at first. In the next repetition of the cycle, the escape from *that* empiricism, necessary once again, will be post-structuralism.

CHAPTER FIVE

Structuralism I:
Theory and Method

Structuralism in its earliest formulation has a genealogy that includes Ferdinand de Saussure, Russian Formalism, Prague structuralism, the anthropology of Lévi-Strauss, and the analyses of literature by French writers such as Roland Barthes, Tzvetan Todorov, A. J. Greimas, and Gérard Genette. By the time the fundamental structuralist approach becomes widely known in the United States during the early 1970s, through publications summarizing the movement, it has already undergone radical revision, even a rejection of certain basic assumptions, a response that is named "post"-structuralism.

This circumstance confounds a simple history of structuralism in the United States, for it arrived as a theory already being dismantled, a theory at once new and remodeled, both instructive and flawed. The situation is complicated by the fact that the revisionists can also be considered part of the very structuralist movement they were refashioning. In addition, the sequence of the publication of structuralist-related works in the United States does not reflect the evolution of the approach in France, further confusing matters. Culler's *Structuralist Poetics* was published in the United States in 1975, by which time the publication in France of Derrida's *De la grammatologie*, which inaugurates post-structuralism, is an event seven years old. *Of Grammatology* was published in the United States in 1976; yet de Man's *Blindness and Insight*, which relies upon Derrida, was published in 1971, the year *before* Jameson's *The House of Language* (1972), an analysis of basic structuralist assumptions preceding post-structuralism. Some of the authors referred to by Culler, and also by Scholes (*Structuralism in Literature* [1974]), were at the time not available (or minimally available) in English. Certain essays of Todorov are translated in 1977 (*The Poetics of Prose*) and his important essay of 1968, *Introduction to Poetics*, is published in translation in 1981, by which time it is a historical document. Similarly, Genette's essays of 1966-72 are published as *Figures of Literary Discourse* in 1982, while Foucault's *The Order of Things*, published in France in 1966, is available in English as early as 1970, the same year that the papers from the influential 1966 Johns Hopkins symposium were published (edited by Macksey and Donato), papers that bring together the ideas of Todorov, Barthes, Lacan, and Derrida. Of course, in France, too, the works of structuralist writers of very different dispositions intermingle and overlap as the authors contend with one another and deny commonality, each claiming to have exited from the beaten path. But the circumstances are further complicated in the United States by the sequencing of translations.

In addition, even when critical approaches to textual material share, or appear to share, a common methodology, the underlying attitudes may be different depending upon whether the author speaks as a linguist, a literary critic, a philosopher, a reading theorist, a social critic, a Marxist, or some combination of these.

Nevertheless, there is a level of analysis that draws together the diversity of individual commentary, a level at which the most important issues are the conditions through which human mentality comes to have content and to function. Whether the practitioner knows it or not, the application of any critical method presumes an epistemological choice. Whether literature is seen as a coherent structure, as a communication, as an organization of experience, as a historically evolving system, as a coded hidden meaning, or as a personally creative act or a situationally determined one, each view presupposes some belief concerning the constitution and capability of the human mind.

Saussure

Structuralist theory is founded, in part, on a model of language proposed by Ferdinand de Saussure. "In itself, thought is like a swirling cloud, where no shape is intrinsically determinate. No ideas are established in advance, and nothing is distinct before the introduction of linguistic structure" (*Course in General Linguistics* 110). Words do not, then, as for Locke, serve as markers that convey notions of a world whose structure and order are received into the mind through perception and afterward objectively described through, represented by, language. Language itself structures the world; the world known is determined by the language used. Language is, of course, used to express thought: "speech sounds are only the instrument of thought and have no independent existence" (9), and "facts of consciousness which we call *concepts* are associated with representations of linguistic signs or sound patterns by means of which they may be expressed" (12). But organized thought and language are contemporaneous; thought does not preexist language. The *sign* (a word) unites *signifier*, the acoustical entity, and *signified*, the "concept." These "two elements involved in the linguistic sign are both psychological and are connected in the brain by an associative link" (66). The acoustical entity and what it signifies are bound together in a single unique unit, the sign, in the way, says Saussure, that hydrogen and oxygen bind together to form water, which has properties possessed by neither of its constituents. What is signified is not a demonstrably existent object in the world outside us, but a concept in the mind.

There are evident logical problems in these assertions. In particular, it is not clear what "concepts" might be. They seem not to be pictures of things in the world derived from sensation, else they would have a mental existence even without language, and the fact that they can be signified seems to give them some independence (how else have an "associative link"?), which is then, however, denied. The declaration that two elements form a single linguistic unit creates rather than solves a problem. Once the sign, particularly the "signified," is reconsidered so that the analogy of hydrogen and oxygen, both demonstrably separate substances, no longer pertains, that problem will come to undo an orthodox structuralism.

Saussure's concept of the sign is formulated in the empiricist tradition. His "concepts" clearly have a family resemblance to Locke's "ideas"; and Locke, too, believed that any "articulate sound" could serve so that "a word is made *arbitrarily* the mark" of an idea (*Essay*, III,ii,1; emphasis added). Geoffrey Thurley has acknowledged that Saussure's theories are "borrowed" (with, for Thurley, "disastrous consequences") from Locke and that they "introduced empiricist language critique into the French tradition" (170-71). It is, in fact, Saussure's empiricism that provides the ground for his "scientific" method and provokes the "associative link." In the early years of this century Saussure can step away, but not run away, from Locke and Hume, especially in what was a conservative academic environment.

The real innovation, however, is not in the notion of the sign but in Saussure's proposal for how signs *relate* to each other. Any given linguistic sign (a sound, as distinct from, say, direct visual or pictorial representations such as the "icons" or "indexes" of Peirce) is "arbitrary" insofar as there seems to be no external connection between the sound of the word and the concept it signifies. The meaning of a word does not derive from its self-sufficient reference (or from any natural attachment) to a concept; the word has meaning only within a system of interrelated units distinguished from one another by their acoustical variations. "The system as a united whole is the starting point, from which it becomes possible . . . to identify its constituent elements" (112). In a linguistic system "there are only differences"; there are no "positive terms" (118). No term (word) has any meaning standing alone: language is a system of numerous units of sound, each differing one from the other. These differences compose the language, which means that these differences in sound partition and distinguish concepts. "The content of a word is determined in the final analysis not by what it contains but by what exists outside it" (114)—the rest of the system. In literary criticism, for example (to look ahead momentarily), writes Terry Eagleton in *Literary Theory*, "you become a card-carrying structuralist only when you claim that the meaning of each image is wholly a matter of its relation to the other. The images do not have a 'substantial' meaning, only a 'relational' one" (94).

The modern French structuralists reasoned that if what we know of the world is formed, shaped, by language, then language may be said to constitute our knowledge of the world. What is known, therefore, is not any world-as-it-really-is but only language itself, the total collection of sounds, a system of acoustical differences structuring thought. Language is not "referential." Saussure does not go quite this far (although that has apparently long been forgotten) because of his retention of an empiricist definition of the single sign. Throughout the work of the early structuralists there is an effort to accept both Saussure's definition of the sign and his definition of the system of signs, which have no necesssary connection. His concept of system, in the right hands, eventually escapes the Lockean empiricism, on which the definition of sign is established, by the abolition of the idea of the "concept" as that which is signified. Although linguistics usually declares itself an empiricism, a "science," the concept of a linguistic system that is itself responsible for partitioning the world must eventually undermine empiricism (as in Sapir and Whorf, too). Empiricism can only assert its basic premise that all ideas come from experience *if* language "refers" to those ideas, if language is a tool of exploration and not that which turns out to be itself the object of exploration. How else to maintain the bond between language and the real world?— unless, of course, one turns, like Chomsky, to rationalism (innateness), which we have seen is likely not to be an enduring choice for empiricists. If language is not referential, or at least cannot be proven to be referential, empiricism is pushed over its limits. But at the limits of empiricism is not, in an empiricist setting, a turn to idealism or rationalism but a turn to a Humean skepticism. This is what will happen in literary criticism in the United States.

Perhaps Saussure himself recognized the limitation of, the incongruities in, the approach. He himself never published the theory. The Saussurian theory of system, furthermore, is one of those tautological scientific hypotheses—like evolutionary theory that the fittest survive, in which the fittest are then defined as the survivors—a theory incapable of refutation. For even supposing that a deity gave all humankind one language in which every word did, in fact, exactly correspond in some non-arbitrary way to a segment of the one true reality, it would still be possible to make Saussure's assertions and baffle any opposition, since the circumstance that the acoustic elements of language differ one from the other is undeniable. An "arbitrary" language could not be distinguished from an un-arbitrary one. But no statement about reality or mentality is demanded by this assertion. That there is not one language but many does not, logically, change the situation, a recognition that brings about Chomsky's assumption of a universal grammar.

Nevertheless, what is unresolvable in Saussure has been used (perhaps through various "distortions," see Angenot [1984]) in literary criticism to maintain simultaneously that the literary work is explicable by "immanent" criteria alone (by citing Frye's Anatomy, Russian Formalism, portions of the New Criticism, Todorov, etc.) and that literature refers to the process of mentality through which the "chaotic" world is organized. Although that process cannot, at least not after Kant, lead to direct knowledge of the world, it can lead either (the following classification of authors is admittedly somewhat artificial) to an understanding of the conditions of meaning (Jakobson, early Barthes, Genette), of the function of meaning in human life (Foucault, Lacan, de Man), of the creation of meaning (Derrida, Hartman, Iser, Fish), or of the relationship between meaning and "reality" (Althusser, Jameson, Miller)—all of which have been seen as the goal of structuralist and post-structuralist literary criticism.

In France, the structuralists for some years investigate language and literature under what they methodologically handle as an empiricism, primarily because of the influence of orthodox Marxism, which is an empiricism. But as Marxist theory moves beyond a theory of economics (likely because the economic predictions of the collapse of capitalism no longer seem convincing [see Lefevre]), moves toward a general theory of society and mentality, studies of language and literature also change. Once the orthodoxy that the economic "base" strictly determines all other structures, the "superstructure," is modified into the concept of a mutual interaction between structures (as in Louis Althusser's *Lenin and Philosophy*, Raymond Williams's *Marxism and Literature*, and Fredric Jameson's *The Political Unconscious*), language can itself assume a creative role: "the signifier . . . [can] be seen to have an active function in creating and determining the signified" (Coward and Ellis [1977] 3). Theory can then incorporate the Marxist position, in opposition to Cartesianism and existentialism, that the contents of consciousness and, therefore, the "self" are constructs determined by the environment, including language. Interpretations of Saussure, accordingly, parallel Marxist thought.

In the United States, Marxism has not been the major issue (important new work is, however, currently being done; see Nelson and Grossberg). Certainly Marxism has not been the major issue in literary criticism. Rather, the undermining of strict empiricism that results in France from a prolonged logical analysis of the implications of Saussure's theory is used to escape the logical consequences of empiricism (materialist determinism) through the same process by which the New Critics had adopted elements of Romanticism. This is why the acceptance of post-structuralism (Derrida) is so immediate, why the early structuralists never really establish a foothold except, perhaps, when they confirm the New Critical insight that the meaning of a literary work is determined by its own internal structure. Saussurian theory becomes fuel not for Marxist revisionism—although it satisfies the requirement for a theory on the "left"—but for critical theories of writing and reading, for a new form of textual analysis, of close reading, without a necessary challenge to customary non-Marxist concepts of self. (Miller, for example, seems to hold quite traditional religious beliefs [Atkins 64]. And the affiliations of Hartman and Bloom with their own religious tradition are basically traditional ones.) Even according to Derrida, "deconstruction" is a specifically American strategy (Davis and Schleifer [1985] 87). American critics, we shall show, while pointing to structuralist linguistics for what we have seen to be the necessary scientific legitimation of theory, move quickly, with skepticism as a vehicle, to assertions of human freedom and creativity again (just as Hume did), hardly a possible conclusion to be drawn from Saussure or his successors.

Structure and the Subject

The assumption that an understanding of the elements, processes, and rules of language serve as a foundation for critical theory and method places structuralist literary criticism, more specifically theoretical "poetics," either as a sub-discipline within linguistics or at the side of linguistics as a neighboring discipline with a method, a "rhetoric," comparable to, but not identical with, linguistics. Structuralist linguistics proposes to identify the primary elements that comprise language, elements that themselves may have no meaning (e.g., phonemes). These are united in meaningful units (words), combinable into higher orders of meaning (sentences) that are, in a regulated way, associated in more complex structures (as, for example, narrative). The meaning of any unit in the system is dependent upon its relationship to all other units. To analyze how language is used by the speaker and received by the listener as well becomes an attempt of structuralism, although this is not equivalent to the prior identification of elements and their rules of combination. (The word "structure" comes from the Latin *struere*, to build.) This distinction—often left indistinct because structuralist writers address both issues—has consequences for literary critics, who will, like the linguist, first seek to identify the elements, themselves nonliterary, that combine to form a literary object and afterward to explain the writing of literature (as a process) and the reading, the reception, of it.

It is assumed by structuralists that the system of language, its construction, is explicable without reference to the intentions of the user: the structure of mentality is derived from the observable structure of language, rather than presumed to be knowable as itself a cause of language. Structure can be analyzed as if it existed autonomously. "It would seem a generally valid thesis that for every *process* there is a corresponding *system*," wrote Louis Hjelmslev, "by which the process can be analyzed and described by means of a limited number of premises" (*Prolegomena*, qtd. in Culler, *Structuralist Poetics* [1975] 7). In literary criticism, structuralism "seeks to establish a model of the system of literature itself as the external reference for the individual works it considers" while being "as scientific as possible," according to Robert Scholes (*Structuralism in Literature* [1974] 10), who cites Eichenbaum's statement that "literature, like any other specific order of things, is not generated by facts belonging to other orders" (i.e., other disciplines, like psychology or sociology) "and therefore cannot be reduced to such facts" (77). There is, consequently, as in Russian Formalism, "an insistence on the autonomy of literary scholarship" (Erlich, *Russian Formalism* 171), although in structuralism the reliance on linguistic theory remains.

While the disciplinary autonomy of literary criticism and the concept of a structural determination of meaning have been identified in the New Critics and in Frye, there is a fundamental difference between them and the structuralists. The former adhere, as has been shown, to a "humanist" concept of "self," not incompatible with Cartesianism, Romanticism, and a psychology oriented toward the individual psyche, while the latter see the contents of consciousness, in keeping with the ideas of Marx, as constructed by cultural systems, including language, which create the contents of individual mentality. "It is not the consciousness of men that determines their being," declared Marx in his 1859 Preface to *A Contribution to the Critique of Political Economy*, "but, on the contrary, their social being that determines their consciousness." The multitudinous interpretations of Marx do include humanistic ones, incorporating human freedom and individual self-fulfillment, often based on Marx's 1844 manuscripts (*Economic and Philosophical Manuscripts*), the *German Ideology* (written with Engels in 1846), *The Eighteenth Brumaire* of 1852, and other early writings (see the anthology edited by Feuer). The structuralists, however, while by no means ignoring these writings, are in temperament more allied with the outlook of the *Capital* of the 1860s, which is quite different in expression from the early writings. Marx himself, it can be argued, was more and more forced over the years to yield to the deterministic consequences of his own empiricism. Structuralism cannot be understood without recognizing that it is largely an attempt to transpose Marxism into a new linguistic and epistemological context that replaces both the early Marxist Hegelianism (to avoid philosophic idealism) and the later vocabulary of economic determinism, with the intent to retain a scientific empiricism in a form more compatible with the linguistic interests of the structuralists than is the positivistic "historical" social-scientism of the late nineteenth century.

That consciousness is constituted, that its contents are explicable through an analysis of the social structures into which the individual is born, is of great importance. "What is at stake in the encounter with the structural 'turn' is the Western mind itself" (Fekete [1984] xiii). The influence of Lévi-Strauss is predominant: he argues in the Overture to *Le Cru et le cuit* (1964) that if myth, which appears to be "an apparently free outsurge, and a seemingly unbridled inventiveness," can be demonstrated to "presuppose laws which operate at a deeper level"—if, that is, "the human mind appears as determined even in its myths"— then "it must be determined in all its manifestations" ("Overture," in Ehrmann 44). Lévi-Strauss refers to the "unconscious elaborations which are the actualities of minds" (47); we can address structure "unconcerned with the identity of its occasional bearers" (49). He agrees with Paul Ricoeur's assertion (citing Ricoeur's 1963 article) that his, Lévi-Strauss's, approach is "Kantianism without a transcendental subject," that is, epistemological structure without subjectivity as its cause. In a related way, the impact of Russian Formalism is in large measure attributable to the belief that the system of literature evolves through its own laws, regardless of the initiative of any one writer. Such a "genre" theory can, with some manipulation, be integrated into the structuralist creed.

Meaning and Narrative

The difficulty in structuralist literary criticism, a difficulty that post-structuralism uses to unravel it and upon which American commentators seize, is the relationship of structure and meaning. Although a meaningful entity, whether a language or a novel, presupposes structure, it cannot, in fact, be shown that structure *accounts for* the existence of meaning.

The early structuralists, for example, place emphasis on "binary opposition," which is found in the linguistics of Saussure, the phonology of Jakobson, the anthropology of Lévi-Strauss (in *Structuralist Anthropology* [1958]; and see Scheffler), and in the discussion of narrative by Greimas and drama by Barthes (*On Racine* [1964]). Binary opposition is assumed to be a fundamental process of the human mind, reflected by the structures of meaning. Yet binary opposition of elements that themselves have no meaning is not the same as an opposition of elements that already have meaning, and the transition from an analysis of phonetics to that of a literary work may have more of a methodological resemblance than a theoretical unity. For Jakobson to show that language can be studied, using binary opposition, "just as a phonic system, putting aside its conceptual aspect" (Pettit [1977] 12), that is, setting aside Saussure's "concept," is fundamentally different from identifying two primary devices basic to all language, metaphor and metonymy. Even if studies of phonetics and of aphasia (by Jakobson and Halle [1956]) reveal dualities in both cases, the "dualities" are incompatible, one being quite comprehensible without a semantics and the other incomprehensible without one. Similarly, that Lévi-Strauss can find that the Oedipus myths address a duality, the "chthonous" origin of man versus the "autochthonous," is still another matter altogether—as would be many other analytical dualities; the common distinction between reason and passion, for example, or the logically analytic definition that everything can be divided into *a* and *not-a*. Again, asserting that duality is inherent in the non-meaningful elements of language is different from asserting the duality of meaningful elements, for the former need not suppose any subjectivity (note the duality in the genetic code, computer language, the mating of animals, and small particle physics) while the latter can assume its duality only to a conscious subject who must *use* the system. It is, then, hardly apparent that the structure, in this case "duality," itself accounts for or explains meaning.

An interesting discrimination is made by Emile Benveniste, who notes that while phonemes, morphemes, and words are, in a given language, finite in number, the number of possible sentences is infinite. There are "different levels in linguistics," that of sign formation and "that of language as an instrument of communication . . . language as a living communication" (qtd. by Strickland [1981] 18).

In structuralism, the link is made between the two levels—the elements that combine to make a meaningful unit and the combination of meaningful units—in order to apply a model of the mechanics of language to the mechanics of a meaningful structure composed of language. Such a model is needed to advance still further, eventually, to a theory of the uses of language, to communication theory. The link is a tactical bridge between structure and semantics, in no way inherent in Saussurian linguistics but a consequence of the elimination of the Cartesian subject; that bridge is buttressed as it becomes recognized that semantics has been left out of the original system.

The development of the structuralist theory of narrative manifests how the analysis of a system of *meaning* poses certain problems, the solutions to which ultimately come up against a barrier, that of accounting for the *presence* of meaning, of justifying the presumption that meaning is derivable from the system, rather than vice versa.

In the 1920s, Vladimir Propp had already drawn the distinction between the performers of action in a folktale (people, animals) and the function in the tale of an action, concluding that the basic structure of the folktale is the sequencing of functions, "stable, constant, elements in a tale, independent of how and by whom they are fulfilled." The function of an action is determined by its context in the tale. Propp, in his *Morphology* of 1928, finds thirty-one functions; all need not occur in any one tale, but they occur, in whatever subset, always in the same order. The structuralist principle applicable here is that a structure is composed of isolatable classifiable elements and that these elements have significance only when positioned in the structure. This mutual interdependency of the elements and the structure resembles Saussure's linguistics, which Propp did not know. It is the juxtaposition of the two writers that yields the original suppositions of structuralist narrative theory.

Subsequent writers, whether they agree with Propp in specifics or not, use a similar approach. Claude Bremond, agreeing that there are functions but that Propp has not explained how, at any point in the narrative, a diversity of possible outcomes seem to present themselves, devises "a system of schematic representation that would clarify the relationship of all the logical subsets in an entire narrative," based on triadic sequences (qtd. by Scholes 96). Lévi-Strauss pares down Propp's functions to a few by amalgamating logically related functions (cited in Culler, *Structuralist Poetics* 213). Greimas—for whom the elementary concepts of thought are binary (*Sémantique structurale* [1966]), such as up/down, left/right, dark/light—posits, according to Scholes's review, "a level of thought prior to language, in which these rudimentary oppositions are given anthropomorphic shape" (103). They are transformed into "actants" in a narrative, actants that reflect the binary terms disjunction/conjunction, which in narrative become separation/union and struggle/reconciliation and take the triadic form of subject/object, sender/receiver, and helper/opponent. A triadic model like Bremond's is found in Todorov's analysis of the *Decameron* (1969): actors, actions, and objects are interrelated in the same way that grammatical units are in individual sentences. The tales are said to be structured, based upon, three verbs—to modify, to sin, to punish. Larger thematic motifs can also be considered structural elements, as in Rene Girard's study, *Deceit and Desire* (1965), of "triangulated" desire in the novel.

An inspection of some of the writing of Tzvetan Todorov will reveal not only the basic assumptions of structuralist narrative criticism and its methods, but as well—since Todorov in the 1960s is attempting to integrate the basic structuralist sources with the innovations as they appear—the weaknesses of the approach that will lead to the revisions of most influence in the United States.

"Structural analysis . . . was created within a science," the science of linguistics. In literary analysis "we are 'doing science' " (Todorov, *Poetics of Prose* [1977] 30). It has been noted that this scientific legitimation will be welcomed by American critics. In this science, "the goal of investigation is the description of the functioning of the literary system, the analysis of its constituent elements, and the discovery of its laws . . . the scientific description of a literary text" (249). There are discoverable "general laws of which the particular text is the product" (Todorov, *Introduction to Poetics* [1968; English translation, 1981] 6); and each work is "the manifestation of an abstract and general structure" (an idea already familiar to American critics through Frye) "of which it is but one of the possible realizations" (*Introduction* 7). Consequently, "the individual work is not an ultimate goal for poetics" (*Poetics of Prose* 32), since "particular works are instances exemplifying" the system as a whole (235).

The application of these principles proves them to be not quite so congenial as they first appear to the critical methods of Todorov (and other structuralists), who assumes that the "analysis of narrative permits us to isolate formal units" that comprise the individual works (*Poetics of Prose* 113), that "every text can be decomposed into minimal units" (*Introduction* 41). First, as structuralism proceeds, agreement is never reached on what these minimal units are, or even on how the definition of a minimal unit can be agreed upon. In various places the minimal unit in narrative may be handled at the level of a grammatical construct, a figure, a character, the action of a character, the function of the action of a character, the meaning of the function of the action of a character; or at the levels (all found in Todorov's *Introduction*) of logical, temporal and spatial order or of narrative syntax (e.g., the "narrative proposition" that "Y is a king"). Although the narrative sequence is composed of elements, the relationship between elements and sequence is not clear. Still, it is difficult to see how it could be a *causal* relation. The fundamental problem is that nothing that exists is the "product" of laws. Rather, the reverse is true: laws are the product, the result of rationality applied to phenomena, to what is found to exist. Order is discovered in what occurs; statements that describe the order—descriptions whose validity is customarily ascertained in science through the confirmation of prediction—are called laws. But it is gravity as a property of objects that causes objects to attract one another—or, preferably, this attraction *is* gravity. The *law* of gravity causes nothing. It might be said that this is splitting hairs, that all that is meant is that the order of narrative, narrative in general, can be described. But the order of narrative can *necessarily* be described because classifying a work as narrative has already been done. If consistencies are found in the Russian folktale, it is because one already knows what to count as a Russian folktale. We will not count *Middlemarch*, and if someone sits down today intentionally to write a story structured like a Russian folktale, we will not count that either. What is a folktale is presumed in advance of the analysis. That planets go around the sun is not a law of planets; it is now part of the definition of a planet. That planets obey the law of gravity tells us nothing about planets specifically. Now we can say that the law of gravity causes planets to travel in ellipses, and that this had to be discovered, since it is not part of the definition of planet. The laws of planetary motion, however, have nothing to do with the generation, the production, of planets, yet the "laws" of narrative are presumed, somehow, to relate to the production of narratives. Todorov reasons "as if there existed what one might call a *generative narrative grammar*, which would *govern* the formal construction of any narrative literary work" (Donato, "Of Structuralism" [1967] 567; emphasis added). But that Todorov finds similarities among literary works is not really a matter of causal laws but of "transformational" schema. Such schema are spatial, not temporal, demonstrating that certain literary works have the same topology.

One might note, hoping for a preferable analogy, that the production of new humans (or the evolution of new species) can be understood through the laws of biochemistry. Nevertheless, the laws of molecular biochemistry certainly do not account for the higher-order properties of the entire system (teleological behavior; consciousness; or even evolutionary adaption, since "random" mutation theory is a ploy). Some scientists assure us that, someday, physiochemical laws will account for macrobiology and even for psychology. Even this assurance is an admission that no one yet knows how to bridge this gap, any more than that between the "objectively" describable elements of a narrative and its overall structure of meaning or its function as meaning. Todorov himself states that "the phenomena of signification [meaning] which constitute the object of interpretation, do not lend themselves to 'description.' . . . Hence, in literary studies: what can be objectively 'described'—the number of words, or of syllables, or of sounds—does not permit us to deduce the meaning" (*Introduction* 5). Todorov is attempting to distinguish between linguistics, poetics, and interpretation in a way that has led reviewers of structuralism to assert (perhaps as a compromise) that structuralism deals with the "conditions" of meaning and not with meaning itself. However, structuralism generally assumes some connection between the conditions of meaning and meaning, a supposition that can be questioned; for the conditions of a phenomenon do not explain it unless the phenomenon itself is *defined* as the sum of the conditions. If, for example, the "conditions" of life at the most fundamental level are lifeless (oxygen, carbon), the aggregation does not account for the level of organization called life (any more than knowledge of sodium and chlorine will account for the taste of sodium chloride, salt). If, on the other hand, we begin with basic living elements (e.g., cellular metabolism), then life is presupposed and the unity of the entire organism, its being "alive," is not thereby explained. Similarly, the non-meaningful elements of language can be a condition of meaning without accounting for meaning, and the combination of meaningful elements in narrative, which presuppose meaning but not literature, myth, and so on, can be a condition of narrative without accounting for it.

The assumption of the connection between meaning and the conditions of meaning is, then, assumed but never demonstrated. It is assumed because Saussure assumed it, with the connection being the "concept." But to assume a "signified" is not to account for meaning, but to presuppose it. Despite the wish to base literary analysis on Saussurian principles, there is nothing in poetics that can correspond to the Saussurian "concept," which is proposed in order to maintain an empiricist link to reality (and was therefore quickly found to be the weakest part of the theory), in avoidance of solipsism. No other kind of connection has been discovered. If Todorov admits the distinction between description and interpretation, he also admits that "one could object that . . . we have not managed to 'explicate' narrative, to draw general conclusions from it. But the state of studies of narrative implies that our first task is the elaboration of a descriptive apparatus." At this point we "do not seek to name the meaning of a text, but to describe its constituent elements" (*Poetics of Prose* 119). By referring to our *first* task, Todorov is employing the same tactic as the neurophysiologist who assures us that his discipline will someday explain mentality: perhaps so, but nothing today substantiates the aspiration.

Literature would have no interest—or existence—were it not for the communication of and/or reception of meaning. The structuralist approach is called a science because it is believed by structuralists that linguistics is an empiricism (in distinction from Chomsky; recall Chomsky's *Reflections*) and that literary scholarship can be founded upon it. Empiricism, it has been noted, posits that all complex ideas are built up from simple ones, that, as in structuralism, a structure is an aggregation of elements. But the empiricist assumption, before Hume's skepticism, is that an *orderly* knowable world is impressed upon the mind by sensation, which gives us "ideas," and that language expresses or combines these ideas. Meaning exists in empiricism because reference exists. Saussure bonds reference to mentality alone, to the "concept" (so reference becomes, in fact, non-reference), rather than to the world, which is for us (as for Bergson) an incoherent amassment of sensation until it is organized, by language. Man himself "does not exist prior to language," writes Barthes ("To Write" 134).

But this Saussurian bond undermines, instead of supporting, empiricism because it makes meaning a *characteristic*, a property of a system of language rather than the *function* of a system of language, which in a strict empiricism would be nothing but a collection of arbitrary sounds conventionally used to make public mental content caused by perception. The structuralists pursue this pseudo-empiricism until it falls apart because, once the primacy of individual mentality as a factor in explanation is abolished, there is no accounting for meaning, only the recognition that, to be sure, there *is* meaning. The structural narratologists, writers like Bremond, Greimas, and Todorov, recognizing the impossibility of directly linking non-meaningful elements (e.g., phonemes) to narrative meaning, begin with elements that themselves have meaning, as if these, once assembled, could offer insight into meaning at higher levels because they are the "conditions" of meaning. But the encompassing meaning of a literary work, or its formal unity, may result from a combination of elements that are not its cause (as two plots might be the same while sharing not one sentence in common), unless the aggregation of elements is considered to be the work itself (the sequence of plot elements is the plot). Such a definition might describe literary form without ever providing the link to literary meaning (interpretation), even if Todorov tells us, without much evidence beyond an apparent reliance on Jakobson, that "the relation between poetics and interpretation is one of complementarity par excellence" (*Introduction* 7). No analysis of the non-meaningful elements that form a cathedral—materials of construction, certain geometric forms—will lead to an understanding of the meaning of a cathedral. (A more American example is the difference between the "objective" description of a football game and understanding football used by Searle in *Speech Acts* [1969].) And if we identify as elements the meaningful constituents—an altar, a cross—we will find that the elements are really determined by our overall understanding of the meaning of the cathedral, not the reverse.

Of narrative the same is true, and the structuralists come themselves to recognize this as the basic structuralist approach wanes. In 1968, Todorov is writing that literature probably cannot be a totally autonomous discipline because its simplest "atomic" elements (e.g., single words or sentences) are not themselves literary. Nevertheless, "it is very possible that we can reconstitute a specificity of literature . . . but at a molecular level and no longer an 'atomic' one. Literature will be a crossing of levels" (*Introduction* 70). This crossing of levels is here asserted in the midst of its own denial in order to hold together the structuralist enterprise. By 1980 Todorov, in his new preface to the 1968 essay, writes, "the same empirical object has an infinite number of properties, and each theoretician can—in theory—select those that suit him, leaving the rest aside" (*Introduction* xxii), which is to concede the failure of the early structuralist approach. Culler, quoting Greimas, states that "as Greimas notes, one can choose at random a series of elements in a text, treat them as a set, and construct some general category encompassing them all: 'it is always possible to reduce an inventory taken on its own to a constructed sememe' " (*Structuralist Poetics* 87).

The essays of Genette have a similarly mixed perspective. He asserts that the "message in the code" of a literary work is "uncovered by an analysis of the immanent structures and not imposed from the outside by ideological prejudices" (*Figures* 7). Nevertheless, although Genette as a structuralist maintains the immanence of structure, "structures are not directly encountered objects. . . . They are systems of latent relations, conceived rather than perceived, which analysis constructs as it uncovers them" (11).

Signs of the vulnerable spots in structuralism appear from the beginning, as theorists qualify the applicability of the "linguistic model." Lévi-Strauss in *Structural Anthropology* recognizes that "to derive from language a logical model" applicable to "other forms of communication is in no sense equivalent to treating the former as the *origin* of the latter" (83; emphasis added). He is referring to non-linguistic components of behavior, "attitudes" rather than "nomenclature." Kinship phenomena, for example, "though they belong to another order of reality . . . are of the same type as linguistic phenomena" (34). Barthes, in *Système de la mode*, handles fashion (dress codes) on the same premise. If, however, a form of communication is not structurally related to language in a causal way, then all we have is an argument for an effective comparative methodology, an analogy, not an argument for the discovery of any truth about anything, for in what way *are* they related? Relation assumes causal connection *at some level*: humans and primates are related not because one causes the other, but because some causal factor exists that is common to both. Todorov, trying to address this issue, states at one point that the structure of language *is* causally related to the structure of narrative and other forms of discourse, that the relation between them "is not only functional but also genetic." However, he promises to provide the evidence for this assertion in the future ("Structuralism" 162).

It can, of course, be argued—and Lévi-Strauss seems at times to do this, in speaking of basic binary oppositions, for example—that the internal structure of the human mind is such that it causes similar structure to be found in diverse systems (language, kinship, myth). But this use of "causes" is well on the way to philosophic *idealism*, which is exactly the philosophy that structuralism wishes to reject. Even Todorov at one point in the *Poetics of Prose* speaks of the existence of a "universal grammar" not limited to language alone, which "will have, evidently, a psychological reality" (109). For Lévi-Strauss to admit that structuralism is Kantianism without the transcendental subject (Ricoeur's statement is made not without irony) leads sooner or later back to Kant. And to avoid "cause" by positing that perhaps the structure of mind and of "reality" are similar, as Scheffler attributes to Lévi-Strauss (65), is also no more than the abhorrent metaphysics that structuralism purports to avoid. Structuralism, then, finds itself in a dilemma. It attempts, in support of Marxism, to demonstrate that social structure causes the content of mentality, and at the same time that these structures are like language, which clearly has no existence—as social structures might (in bees, for example)—beyond mentality, whether or not a natural language precedes any given user of it. Structuralism as a theory must open a path first into skepticism and then, if taken far enough, unwittingly or not, into idealism. A Saussurian-like non-reference theory of language does this as it paradoxically founds structure on mental organization while it denies any causal power to mentality. (Positing unconscious mental causes is, obviously, logically of no help.) This dilemma is behind the move in post-structuralism to eliminate "origins," for to have admitted origins into structuralism is to court idealism costumed as an empiricism.

Because literary works are composed of language, the assumption that the science of linguistics will encompass poetics, including a necessarily semantic component, is not an unnatural hypothesis, although the structuralists, at the stage discussed here, do not substantiate it in discussing narrative unless they limit poetics to linguistic analysis or proclaim, as an avowal, the theoretical union. When Todorov says he agrees with Benveniste that "it is the capacity of a linguistic unit to integrate itself into a unit on a higher level" ("Structuralism" 129), one can easily understand that the word "capacity" is being used ingeniously. His next sentence is that "the meaning of a word is defined by the combinations . . ." and so on; but the difference between "defined by" and "capacity" is the very crux of the matter.

It is, of course, possible to declare a position contrary to structuralism, admittedly with equal dogmatism, as American critics will tend to do. "A language is a very different sort and order of thing from plot structures," writes Barbara Smith, "and there is no good reason to assume a priori [!] that the specific criteria for a grammar of one would be at all relevant to a theory of the other" (*On the Margins of Discourse* [1978] 180). Throughout this study we have been arguing that, critical methodology be what it will, the fundamental issue for Americans is the adherence to the concepts of freedom and the autonomous, Cartesian-like self. The denial of these concepts is the essence of structuralism and serves as the only real bond between the various structuralists, who otherwise themselves assert their differences with colleagues so strenuously that certain critics have been led to "question the very existence of structuralism as a meaningful concept" (Macksey [1970] ix).

The real significance of structuralism is not, however, at the level of critical technique, which is an attempt to employ the methods of empiricism in a field not entirely congenial to it (as we have demonstrated in the New Criticism). Rather, structuralism's significance lies at the level of the concept of human subjectivity, of self. In a well-known passage in *Le Cru et le cuit*, Lévi-Strauss says that "we are not, therefore, claiming to show how men think the myths, but rather how the myths think themselves out in men and without men's knowledge" ("Overture," in Ehrmann 46). Individual subjectivity as commonly understood—a conscious, personally motivated, self-knowledgeable individual, a self as entity, in contact with a reality that can be uncovered, revealed, in the process of mentally discovering it—is rejected. Replacing it is a concept of the self, or more exactly of subjectivity, as constituted by systems, structures, in which each newborn human is immersed. It may be that the approach to myth in Lévi-Strauss is much like the approach to disease, for which medical textbooks give symptoms, causes, and prognoses without any attention to any individual person who happens to be the carrier of the disease (although there is no disease apart from the carriers). Such an approach has its weaknesses, as we have discussed, and may be untenable when applied to systems of meaning. Nevertheless, when Eugene Donato ("Of Structuralism" [1967] 94) writes that Lévi-Strauss, by maintaining "the discontinuity between the order of the signifier and the order of the signified" (whether Lévi-Strauss does do this is another issue), is permitted "to avoid dealing with the problem of an individual subject," he (Donato) is reflecting the American predisposition, the need for this "individual subject." Because it is not found, in this case (and for good reason) in Lévi-Strauss, it is said to be "avoided." But Lévi-Strauss hardly can be accused of "avoiding" this matter.

The need in structuralism to preserve the notion of the constructed or constituted self dictates the application of the method. When a nonreferential theory of language tends to skepticism, the post-structuralists, as we have said, will abolish "origins" and, further, will abolish the "immediate presence" of phenomena, even of primary chaos, to consciousness. (This presence we find in Husserl and Heidegger; and it should be recalled that phenomenology itself is, or can be, based on the empiricism of Berkeley.) The post-structuralists refuse to be coerced into re-creating Kant's transcendental subject, which in fact they would re-create if they did not rely on empiricist skepticism instead. And meaning, the existence of which cannot be denied, will be generated, as in Nietzsche, Freud, Lacan, Deleuze, Goldmann, or Derrida, from the rediscovery of "desire."

The problems and dilemmas that have been identified in the early structuralist theory of narrative call forth a number of options in American literary criticism, of which, at this point, two main branches can be identified: the theory of writing and the theory of reading. Both of these will reintroduce the subject as an active agency and attempt to integrate such theorists as Peirce and Chomsky, and also employ speech-act theory (on speech-act theory see Austin, *How To Do Things* [1975]; Searle, *Speech Acts* [1969]; Ohmann, "Literature as Act" [1973]).

The rise of theories of reading will be especially significant in the United States because of the many books of Barthes that are translated and the widespread recognition given to Culler's *Structuralist Poetics* and De Man's *Blindness and Insight*. By 1980, the year of the publication of Fish's *Is There a Text in This Class?*, even Todorov is declaring that "every work is rewritten by its reader" (*Introduction* xxx). At the same time, a provocative approach to writing, including the writing of criticism itself, is taken by Miller, Bloom, and Hartman, in some measure based, not without contortions, upon the influence of Derrida.

But before these occurrences are discussed, it is necessary first to turn again to the basic structuralist theory, this time as it addresses not narrative but poetry.

Structure and Poetry

Early structuralist writings analyze poetry according to the arrangement and distribution of the elements of language used in a poem. The arrangement of grammatical and syntactical elements is such that a special form of meaning is generated—special in the sense that poetic meaning is not to be taken merely as reference or thematic statement, which the devices of poetry ornament, but to include the recognition of how language itself functions. Poetry makes evident the workings of language, the conditions of creating meaning, by calling attention to these workings through an emphasis upon its own devices. Whatever else a poem may be about, which interpretation will attempt to discover, it is also about itself as a linguistic construction. Structuralism will ask, primarily, not what the poem means but how it works. Structuralists do eventually come to offer interpretations of poems; and this will raise again our earlier issue of what connection there might be, in structuralist theory, between meaning and the conditions of meaning.

Leaning upon Jakobson, Culler tells us in *Structuralist Poetics* that the poem is a "structure of signifiers which absorbs and reconstitutes the signified" (163). In ordinary language, that is, the signifier and signified are bonded together in a way that has become customary, conventional, and unquestioned. By loosening or opening up a distance between signifier and signified, the signifier can be used in creating a new context for it, the poem. That the bond between signifier and signified can be infiltrated in poetry will be of much consequence to the post-structuralists, for it raises the issue of whether the bond has, all along, meant anything at all in relation to a knowledge of reality in *any* use of language. Perhaps there is only context, only interrelated signifiers. In "early" structuralism, it is assumed that the manipulation of language in poetry does not call into question the existence of signifieds, although the implication is that, in poetry, organization of the signifier determines, or one might say redetermines anew, the signified. Of course, Saussure, Lévi-Strauss and others recognize that the world, reality, might be partitioned in alternative ways, for which myth, poetry, and narrative all give evidence, although the stability of a language at any one point in time makes the average user unaware of alternative structures or realities.

The basic structuralist theory of poetry evolved from the gradual transformation of the Russian Formalism that Roman Jakobson brought with him to Prague. It is the eventual juxtaposition of what Jakobson and his colleagues meant by structuralism (Prague structuralism) and what Lévi-Strauss meant by it that appropriates the discussion of poetry into the structuralist mainstream. In truth, for reasons to be addressed later, poetry lends itself far less than narrative to the version of structuralism developed in France, where, consequently, little attention was given to poetry by structuralists.

Victor Erlich's work on Russian Formalism points out that the Formalists rejected the idea that poetry can be defined by differences between propositional statements and emotive ones (as we have seen in Richards), or between statements that carry truth values and those that do not (as in Warren, Ransom, Brooks). Both ideas the Formalists would see—as to some extent we have done this in tracing the influence of Coleridge on the New Critics—as psychologizing (*Russian Formalism* [1955; rpt. 1965]; also on Russian Formalism are books by Peter Steiner [1984] and by Ewa Thompson [1971]). Nor is poetry simply image making. Furthermore, no theme or motif is excluded from poetry; in this there is an agreement with the New Critics from Hulme onward.

"The material of poetry," Erlich is quoting Zirmunsky, "is words. . . . Poetry is verbal art" (175).

For Shlovsky, the verbal art of poetry consists of a "making strange," *ostranenie*, a process of defamiliarization. The habitual is put in a new light, a "sphere of new perception" (cited in Erlich 176; also see the anthology edited by Lemon and Reis). The perception of that which is made strange is thereby intensified; perception is reinvigorated. For our purposes, a discrimination needs to be made between making the *language* strange, having language accordingly call attention to itself, its workings, and making a *subject* strange, like the wheelbarrow in Williams's poem. The former use makes Formalism not only distinct from other theories—since it has likely never not been recognized that poetry, even poetry that confirms the reader's worldview, calls a focused and renewed attention to its subject—but makes it also of use to structuralism, because linguistic mechanisms, not meaning, become the basic structural elements.

It is the latter use that is of interest to Brecht, who wished to defamiliarize the commonplace because the familiar comes to seem permanent and timeless, which retards social change (Brecht, *On Theatre*). In the mid-1960s, Geoffrey Hartman too saw this "defamiliarization" as important: "society is always based on some form of social lie or vital myth," which over time loses vitality. "The dead convention can be restructured and revived, as it is in all authentic art" ("Anglo-American Adventure" [1966] 143). Even through the 1980s the concept retains its vitality, and Roger Fowler founds his "linguistic criticism" on literature's "deliberate devices for defamiliarization" ([1986] 37).

Shlovsky, moreover, accepts the presupposition of a history by asserting that what is made strange is that which has become, over time, familiar. But we must understand that the theory does not require history; for at any one moment in time (the synchronic) the language is complete as it is. A seeming-strange is a present occurrence, no matter, in truth, what the past has been (in the way that nothing in the world would be different if we, granted the contents of memory, and everything else were created five minutes ago). Historicism is not essential to formalism, and over time "formalism came to represent the a-historical attitude of the early twentieth century" (Kristeva, "The Ruin" [1973] 103). While Jameson, as a Marxist, is attracted to the historical, diachronic aspect of Shlovsky's work, which suggests "a new concept of literary history . . . abrupt discontinuities, of ruptures with the past" (Jameson, *Prison-House* [1972] 52), and while most of us, Saussure included, believe there has been a past history of language and literature, the belief is not essential to the *analysis* of literature, or language, at any single moment. This is Saussure's essential point. "Historicity as evaluative reaction . . . plays no role in the narratological variant of French structuralism" (Fokkema and Kunne-Ibsch, [1977] 71).

In fact, the historical aspect of Shlovsky's theory and Russian Formalism has been welcomed not for historical reasons at all but because, by assuming such a literary history, *generative* "laws" immanent to the literary system itself can be posited. Literature is in these terms a law-governed system, independent of authorial intent—a most agreeable notion for the structuralists, even though, as we have shown, the "laws" of narrative discovered by the French structuralists are not *temporal* laws of cause and effect (neither Propp, also a Russian Formalist, nor Lévi-Strauss need history in method) but "transformational" rules showing topological relationship, which is different from succession. Difference in time does not introduce the efficacy of time; and the structuralist use of a linguistic model is "spatial," as if the whole system and all its transformations existed as a single event, in the manner of Hegel. Such a view is perhaps ultimately derived from notions of a deity who comprehends all of time simultaneously. It is at the level of combining law-like systematics with the centrality of linguistic mechanisms, devices—where history, although useful, is logically unnecessary—that structuralism integrates formalism.

The writings of Jakobson are not merely representative of the structuralist approach to poetry; they are definitional. Stressing that while the acoustical sign, the sounded word, is (through what Saussure would call "convention") allied with a referent, the alliance is not an identity or an inseparability, as a naive user of language (although Locke is hardly naive) might suppose. The word itself has a value detached from reference, and poetry, oriented to the "sign" in its own right, is constituted by these values. At first Jakobson focuses upon the phonic aspects of words, refining the theory of binary opposition, with some indebtedness to Trubetzkoy; but over the years the emphasis shifts "from phonetics towards semantics or more exactly, toward the interrelations between sound and meaning" (Erlich, *Russian Formalism* 184). Because poetry intentionally manipulates the bond between word and referent, signifier and signified, the way is opened to concepts of the ambiguity of poetic meaning and the creation of new signification through linguistic structure, distinct from language reflecting reality as it in fact is (mimesis).

It is important to note—in momentarily looking ahead—that the underlying theoretical consequence that will eventually emerge is not that, as in the New Criticism, poetic language creates its own reality while scientific language is propositional and hence truth-bearing, testable, (the dual-truth theory of a time when scientific achievement seemed unchallengeable). Rather, the consequence is that poetry demonstrates that language wherever used is composed of structured signifiers, systematized among themselves by differences or oppositions and linked to signifieds in a way more tenuous than even Saussure realized, so that ultimately "the whole notion of reality itself becomes suddenly problematical" (Jameson, *Prison-House* 33).

In his important essay entitled "Linguistics and Poetics" (rpt. in DeGeorge and DeGeorge and in Sebeok), which was the "concluding statement" at a conference at Indiana University in 1958, Jakobson begins by reasserting the scientific credentials of poetics, which "may be regarded as an integral part of linguistics" (76), an "objective scholarly analysis" (87). By 1958, nearly forty years after he left Moscow for Prague, Jakobson sees the necessity of including in his presentation some rudimentary communication theory, an eventual turn in early structuralism which American critics will make central, although it really has little to do with basic structuralism. "Any verbal behavior is goal directed," Jakobson says; he offers one of those models with an "addresser" at one end and an "addressee" at the other, with theoretical terms and arrows placed between the two. The theory takes advantage of Hjelmslev's five "functions" of language—the "cognitive," "expressive," "conative" (influencing), "phatic" (contact-making, like "hello"), and "metalinguistic" (a reference to the code use itself, like "Am I clear?")—to which Jakobson adds a sixth, the "poetic" function, based on the ideas, mentioned above, originating as a part of Russian Formalism. The poetic function is a bridge to bring Jakobson back, in this notable essay, to structural analysis, which had always been his main concern in poetry.

The poetic function focuses "on the message for its own sake." Poetry is, regardless of thematic content, about what it is for a message to be made, about the very functioning of language. (That it makes no difference whether the poem is called a "message" or not might be noted: some of the popularity of the essay, which is mostly metrical analysis, might be attributed to its susceptibility to recent communication theory.) Poetry, "by promoting the palpability of signs, deepens the fundamental dichotomy of signs and objects" (93). All of the grammatical and morphological components of language are used in poetry to yield meaning, which is dependent upon the components. Through poetry, one can view how the formal constituents of language—whether sound, parts of speech, tense, sentence structure, and so on—*determine*, for Jakobson, meaning. There are "poetic resources concealed in the morphological and stylistic structure of language, briefly, the poetry of grammar and its literary product, the grammar of poetry" (discussed by Erlich, "Roman Jakobson" [1973]). That is, the poem is organized so that similarity of linguistic structure at a non-semantic level is used to determine, to cause in the reader, similarity at the semantic level: connections of meaning are caused by connections between sound, grammar, and syntax, and the formation of these relationships is essential to the poetic generation of meaning. For example, "it would be an unsound oversimplification to treat rhyme merely from the standpoint of sound" because "equivalence in sound . . . inevitably involves semantic equivalences" (107 and 109). In this way, rhyme brings about meaning within the poem, aside from considerations of whether the two terms have semantic relation in other contexts or in the "objective" world.

The same can be said of other devices of language. In his most direct statement of his poetics, Jakobson asserts that "the poetic function projects the principle of equivalence from the axis of selection into the axis of combination" ("Linguistics and Poetics" 95). He is referring to Saussure's distinction between "associative" relations between words that might substitute for one another at a given point in a sentence (e.g., the numerous nouns that might be used in the place where a given sentence names the subject) and the "syntagmatic" or rule-governed sequential relations between parts of a sentence. In poetry, where an "equivalence" of grammatical or sound structure is found in the syntactical (combinatorial) sequence, there too can be ascertained a semantic equivalence.

Jakobson's methodology is well demonstrated by his approach to Baudelaire's "Les Chats" (in an article written with Lévi-Strauss in 1962). A sentence or two is sufficient illustration: "All the personal forms of the verbs and of the pronouns, and all the subjects of the verbal clauses, are in the plural . . . except in the seventh verse . . . which contains the only proper noun in the poem and the only instance where the finite verb and its subject are both singular" (130). Lines end in nouns or adjectives; all feminine rhymes are plural. The poem is broken into various blocks whose constituents are compared and contrasted: "an intricate web of binary oppositions" (Erlich, "Roman Jakobson" 18). Significantly, the step is taken from this level of analysis to the meaning of the poem; the former is said to yield the latter. The cats are linked to the human condition; there is discovered the union of the themes of lovers and scholars; and "the poet of 'Les Chats,' liberated from love . . . meets face to face and perhaps even blends with the universe delivered from the scholar's austerity" (" 'Les Chats' " 146).

That the linkage between the two levels can be confirmed in the manner of Jakobson is questionable. To repeat, the constituents of meaning do not logically account for meaning; it may be, to the contrary, that meaning accounts for what shall be considered significant in the internal structure. Structural analysis is, then, to some critics, more a defense of a reading than a cause of it. (Such a critique is applicable to Lévi-Strauss's reading of myth as well.) Michael Riffaterre, for example, attacks Jakobson's analysis of "Les Chats," challenges the significance of the "discoveries" (perhaps nearly all the subjects are in the plural because the poem is, after all, about cats) and presents an entirely different reading of the poem. Culler discusses Jakobson's analysis of one of Baudelaire's "Spleen" poems, in which Jakobson finds that first-person pronouns are only in the odd-numbered stanzas, that "adjectival participles . . . are symmetrically distributed in the odd stanzas," and so on (Culler, *Structuralist Poetics* 60). Culler believes that "only by starting from the effects of a poem" (73) can we then identify the structures that contribute to the effect: Jakobson is producing, not discovering, relevant structure. Numerical summary "leads to the indiscriminate postulation of structures" (66).

For Riffaterre and Culler, of course, the belief that a reader-oriented theory is preferable to fundamental structuralism motivates their evaluation of Jakobson's approach. And it is quite true that reader theory is an alternative to structuralism and not, as Culler seems to believe, a needed refinement of it. In attacking what he sees as the pretensions of "stylistics" (particularly focusing on Milic's *Unconscious Ordering*, [1966]), Fish states that the stylistician assumes that to read is to aggregate discrete units of meaning so that they add up to a completeness, as if the text were already ordered and filled with its meaning before the reader arrives. In his view, the activities of the reader constitute a "structure of concern" (apparently, for Fish, the encompassing expectation brought to the poem) "which is necessarily prior to any examination of meaningful patterns because it is itself the occasion of their coming into being" ("What Is Stylistics" [1973] 148). Without much generosity, Fish refers to the "monumental aridity of Jakobson's analyses" (149). Similarly, Barbara Smith writes, "No analytic method can produce an interpretation and none can validate one."

For our purposes, a most interesting aspect of these critical responses is that there is, at base, actually a turning away from empiricist concepts—a familiar tactic of American critics—specifically, a turn away from the notion that large meanings are dervived from the atomistic assemblage of little ones and toward the notion of an embracing irreducible meaning or unified context, just as we found in the New Critics, although they would not much agree with Culler's or Fish's reading theory, since they would hope to find an immanent meaning in the poem. More will be said about reader theory later on.

The problems in crossing the line from the analysis of the non-meaningful elements inherent in the structure of language to that of the meaningful elements that comprise larger meaningful entities have already been reviewed in the discussion of narrative. "The ambition of structuralism," writes Genette, "is not confined to counting feet and to observing the repetition of phonemes: it must also attack semantic phenomena" (10). In poetry as well, the connection between the conditions of meaning and meaning itself remains a puzzle. It cannot be resolved by asserting that language has structure (which is tautological), that structure has elements, and that therefore the elements are the "conditions" of meaning. In his introduction to the article on "Les Chats," Lévi-Strauss states that, while poetry can be analyzed at various levels—the phonetic, the syntactic, and the semantic—myth, "at least in the extreme, can be interpreted at the semantic level only" (Jakobson and Lévi-Strauss 124). In myth, that is, Lévi-Strauss is unconcerned with the specific verbal expression; he is seeking conceptual relationships, for the myth might be "said" in innumerable ways. Structuralism applied to myth, then, does not need to ask how the line is crossed between meaning and the conditions of it. When it comes right down to it, meanings at the deepest level in Lévi-Strauss are *interpretations* of the meaning at the "surface" level of storytelling, which is why Freud and Marx, also seekers after subterranean meaning, can be claimed as allies. (Interpretation is, in fact, also at the heart of Piaget's "structuralism" and Goldmann's "genetic structuralism.") That the interpretations turn out for Lévi-Strauss to have a *diagrammable* structure of oppositional elements is more critical for the underlying epistemology than for the interpretation itself.

Formalism is not equivalent to structuralism, and Jakobson's Prague "structuralism" is, in fact, a formalism. The epistemological issue is central because much structuralist theory, including that of Lévi-Strauss, presupposes the obsolescence of the Cartesian self in favor of a self whose content is fully determined by exteriority. But the analysis of poetry by Jakobson need not contain such a supposition at all, which is why some critics see no more in it then a New Critical close reading pushed as far as it can go. There is much truth to this: we have said that structuralism "appropriates" the analysis of poetry (the friendship of Jakobson and Lévi-Strauss may have something to do with this), which is not derived in structuralism from the same presuppositions as the analysis of narrative. The analysis of poetry remains a "formalism," a variety that attempts to remain an empiricism and fails at the point where the line is crossed into poetic meaning. This process is not unlike that of the New Critics as they seek help in Romanticism. The early French structuralists claim the support of Russian Formalism because it can be used; but usefulness does not make formalism a structuralism. In formalism, the object *as we know it* is explicated on the basis of the structures that compose it. No special epistemology is presupposed. The New Critics and the Russian Formalists need no philosophy. In structuralism, on the other hand, objects of study (language, myths, social systems) have a structure of relational elements whose import is not that of the object as known to the users; those users have no idea of the underlying structure or its "real" meaning, which structure mediates and, in fact, hides. (No one would say that Freud was doing a New Critical reading of dreams.) Structure is the cause of the subject, not its knowledge.

Even Lévi-Strauss distinguished formalism from structuralism. The former, to him, maintains the form/content duality; "but structure has no content: it is itself the content, apprehended in a logical organization conceived as a property of mind" (qtd. in Caws 83). Furthermore, formalist poetics does not exclude a direct "reference" theory of language in general, which structuralism has claimed to disqualify. That poetry casts in a new light the signifier/signified relationship or that the statements of poetry cannot be adjudicated true or false does not indicate that language does not refer to reality as it is. It indicates only that *meaning* has no existence independent of language, likely because neither one can any longer be assigned a ground (e.g., the deity) external to humanity, as Sartre recognized. Formalism does not "deny that there exists a real world external to the signifying mantle that language casts upon it." "Oxen exist . . . but the *concept* of an ox . . . exists solely as part of a system of meaning," of language (Bennett [1979] 5; emphasis added).

Poetry is quite different from myth, and the poem cannot, like a myth, exist in numerous analogous forms. The poem is just the one thing it is, not an assemblage of variants of an idealized poem. The analysis of poetry, then, becomes unlike myth analysis, and this difference calls forth in many American critics the belief that the idea that literature *is* a language (as Lévi-Strauss, focusing on myth, believed all cultural systems to be) and can be analyzed as such is not quite so appealing as the idea that literature is *in some ways* like a language.

The structuralist's linguistic model can be used, accordingly, as a metaphor or an analogy only; it can provide suggestive technique, not an encompassing poetics.

Narrative seems midway between myth and poetry. (Interestingly, drama in structuralism is treated like narrative *or* poetry and has no independent status.) Since narrative encompasses everything from multiform folktales to James's painstaking novels, the structuralist project gets entangled here, for reasons commented upon earlier, when shifting from meaning to its "conditions." This entanglement, in literary criticism, is the primary cause of the perplexity, not to mention the incredulousness or animosity, of some American commentators on the movement.

Conclusion

American writers have been interested in the interrelation between the New Criticism and the poetics of structuralism, especially since it can be justly concluded that American literary critics have, to a large extent, appropriated structuralism as an advanced technique for the close reading of literary texts. "Even for those who scorn the New Critics . . . the close reading of texts remains the normative procedure" (Cain [1984] 107).

The New Critics most often treated the individual poem as an autonomous object, the "verbal icon" that has in recent years been much disparaged. In structuralism the emphasis has been on the system of literature as a whole, a law- or rule-governed system, an approach that Frye legitimated in America. Structuralists do analyze single literary works; when they do, some American critics feel comfortable saying that the structuralists are doing nothing new, since both approaches treat the poem primarily as an object rather than as the product of authorial mentality (which covers up, of course, the discrepancy of what "mentality" itself might mean). "W. K. Wimsatt said that the poem is an act, but that it must be hypostatized as 'a thing between the poet and the audience' before it becomes available for criticism. . . . Linguistics has generally adopted the same methodology" (Ohmann [1973] 90).

Early structuralism, like the New Criticism, presupposes an "ideal" reader. When structuralism was presumed to be a science, knowing the truth was still a possibility. The reader is the bridge of "formalism" between the New Criticism and structuralism. Shlovsky's notion of making-strange must assume a reader for whom this strangeness exists: like the New Critical vocabulary, "defamiliarization" is a quasi-psychological term used as if it were objectively descriptive. Formalism makes assumptions about the subjectivity of the reader that structuralism, at the level of epistemology, must in its classic form deny; this state yields an incompatibility (formalism seems untenable), which soon generates a reading theory to escape from the problem it believes it is resolving.

The New Critical methodology is designed to yield interpretation, an interpretation of a meaning that is *in* the text, not an imposition upon it. If multiple interpretations are possible, it is because the text itself contains them, in the ambiguities that are characteristic of poetic language (as those elaborated by Empson). The structuralists seek the mechanisms through which meaning is generated, the ground of interpretation. The permissibility of multiple interpretation illustrates the inherent and unavoidable arbitrariness in the bond between language and that which language signifies.

Structuralists handle linguistic elements that do not themselves have meaning (phonemes, grammatical structure), creating the problem of the link between the conditions of meaning and meaning. The New Critics avoid this dilemma by identifying the elements of poetry at the level of meaning (metaphor, irony, paradox, reconciliation of opposites) with a vocabulary that ultimately lacks "scientific" justification for a linguist, since it presupposes not only a psychology but a semantics which it does not consciously avow. (The exception is Brooks's later writing, where "irony" becomes a structural term, for contextualization, rather than a rhetorical one.) While the New Critics and the structuralists believe that meaning in poetry is created contextually, the New Critics maintain a belief in alternative forms of language. The science/ poetry distinction and the dual truth theory are unnecessary in structuralism, since the specialness of poetry is that it manifests in a unique way the characteristics of language wherever used.

Whether structuralism and the New Criticism are seen by any critic as more like than unlike one another can be attributed to beliefs about matters other than critical methodology. Structuralist literary methodology cannot by itself legitimate structuralist philosophy, nor can New Critical methodology legitimate its humanism. Both a fundamentalist and an atheist, to take a simple example, can use the methods of biology to reinforce their prejudices. That a method may be founded upon a philosophy is not the same as that method necessarily presupposing the philosophy: empiricism, for example, yields both introspective psychological theory as well as its behavioral opponent.

An intriguing suggestion is made by Todorov in the 1980 preface to his 1968 essay. Apparently referring to the Kantian notion of the ep-

istemological autonomy of art, applicable in structuralism and formalism to the autonomy of the literary system or the individual work
and including such concepts as organic structure and untranslatability,
he states that "the ideological bases of structuralism are the very ones
that romantic esthetics had elaborated" (*Introduction* xviii). Todorov
barely suggests what he might mean by this. It is tempting to say that,
in 1980, Todorov is reflecting the same process that we have argued
is central to American criticism. As the New Criticism begins allied
with an empiricism and over the years, because of its inadequacy in
explaining the creative process, drifts into Romanticism, so the process
is repeated—again through the inherent propensity of empiricism to
give birth to skepticism—as structuralist literary criticism, which is also
purported to be based on an empiricism (linguistics), begins to show
similar incapacities, motivating once again a movement toward theories
that allow for an explanation of creativity, and toward revised theories
of reading, writing, personality formation, ideology, and human desire.

CHAPTER SIX

Structuralism II:
Reception and Critique

In its original form, before the revision brought to it by Foucault, Derrida, Lacan, and others, structuralism has had little lasting impact on American literary criticism. It was, in fact, a momentary attraction, a newsworthy European event reported in a few widely read critical books and anthologies whose purpose was to translate the ideas of French authors. Structuralism was presented by its originators and its reviewers as an empiricist science (since its skeptical and idealist ramifications were not recognized by its proponents). As I have asserted, such a science is not, in the long run—because of the implications of determinism—in keeping with the prevailing outlook of American literary critics and most of their colleagues in the humanities. In addition to encouraging a reappraisal of the utility of Marxist thought for literary criticism, the main function of early structuralism in America was to confirm the scientific legitimacy of criticism and to demonstrate the alliance between criticism and both linguistics and theories of the mind. As we have seen in an earlier chapter, these had become the criteria—following the work of Frye and Chomsky and a decade of leftist politics—for a critical theory to receive close attention in the United States.

But scientific determinism could not replace the New Criticism; for while such a determinism in France might overthrow the freedom-based phenomenology of an existentialism in which the autonomous subject was presumed, Americans were, on the contrary, seeking to reestablish notions of freedom and human autonomy in reaction to behaviorism and the implications of technological dominance. For this reason we have said that the two cultures were *crossing* and that structuralism was a meeting place, an exchange of information at a crossroads before the travelers went their own way. The French then proceeded further into a post-structuralist determinism in which change is causally generated by subjectivity but not by a Cartesian subject; the Americans moved toward a theory of literary deconstruction quite compatible with the freedom of the subject, even if not with the "apodictic" assured truths of Descartes or Husserl. In each case, however, there has been a related change, with different results, from the structuralist focus on the human as fundamentally structurable *intellect* to an emphasis on the human as fundamentally structurable *will* or desire, another movement within that age-old duality, the great-grandfather of all philosophical debates.

Before we consider the revisions to basic structuralism, it will be informative to consider some critical responses to structuralism—English-language responses from the perspectives of reading theory, language theory, history and politics, and empiricist epistemology (addressed sequentially in the following sections)—which will illustrate how structuralism was, almost simultaneously, received and reformulated.

The Process of Reading: Barthes, Culler

The topic of "self," which we have proposed is the underlying major issue, will be discussed below in Section IV. Critics writing in English will generally assume a critical stance that does not incorporate the structuralist epistemology, unpalatable to Americans, except for the Marxists, who attack structuralism, as we shall see, for other reasons.

A primary strategy to circumvent or (perhaps more accurately) to ignore the structuralist epistemology is to understand the relationship among signifiers and signifieds as a matter of "convention," resting, uneasily, upon Saussure's attentiveness to the "arbitrary" association of a sound and a concept. This leads to a theory of reading based on established conventions. The major premise of such a theory is that both meaning and structure in a literary work result from the interaction with the text of the reader, who brings to the work expectations, derived from having *learned* the functions, purposes, and operations of literature, together with a range of predispositions and beliefs shared with other members of the society. Meaning and structure are not exclusively properties of the text, which are then objectively discovered by the reader; the reader is, to an extent, the co-creator not of the text itself but of its meaning, import, and value. He *subsequently* supports that meaning with a formal (structural) analysis that, if successful, verifies his overall view of the text.

The theory of the reader became available as a critical methodology to critics of structuralism though a lineage distinct from structuralism. (The history is traced in Robert Holub's *Reception Theory* [1984] and, from an American perspective, Steven Mailloux's *Interpretive Conventions* [1982].) In the 1930s, Roman Ingarden developed a theory of reading in which the structured levels of the literary work, which offer a schematic framework to the reader, contain points of indeterminacy that the act of reading completes, fills in, which Ingarden calls "concretization" (*Literary Work of Art* [1931]; an English translation appeared, significantly, in 1973). There is a distinction between the structure of the work itself and the various individual concretizations; this structure is knowable in the literary work, which as an object stands distinct from both author and reader, an idea not incompatible with the New Criticism, for which Ingarden can be seen as a precursor (Wellek, *Four Critics* [1981] 57). In 1960, Hans-Georg Gadamer's *Truth and Method* was published in Germany; an English translation appeared in 1975, the same year as Culler's *Structuralist Poetics*. Gadamer proposes that any critical method, whether of texts or natural objects, is applied to achieve results, the value of which has been predetermined by social context. While the results constitute meaning, this meaning is distinct from truth, if truth is assumed to be the permanent impersonal facts of the matter that the scientific method, emerging dominant over three centuries, is said to reveal. For Gadamer, as for Heidegger, understanding, meaning, is always historically grounded, like humanity itself. Interpretation of a literary text, accordingly, depends upon the specific situation of the observer, who has a "horizon," a specific historical context from which he can interact with the past, with a history that itself encompasses, as a coherent transformative process, movement and change. Interestingly, Gadamer's analysis of texts has also, like Ingarden's, been compared to the New Criticism (Holub 45). It is a pertinent speculation that reader theory comes, by the 1980s, to occupy, in part through Culler, what seems to be (although on the level of philosophical theory it is not) a mediating, even mollifying, position between structuralism and the New Criticism in the United States.

Most recently, the reader-reception theory of Hans Robert Jauss and Wolfgang Iser, work still in progress at the University of Constance, has received increased attention in the United States. Since this work is, for the most part, published in English translation following the initial Anglo-American reception of structuralism (Culler does list an article of Iser in the bibliography of *Structuralist Poetics*, although there is no citation in the text), we will reserve a discussion of it, and of Stanley Fish, until the last chapter.

An apparent legitimation for transforming structuralist theory into reading theory is taken, as well, from the work of Barthes. This accounts (not fully, of course) for Barthes's great popularity in the United States; for what he does is to use structuralism as a medium to unite structuralist and customarily non-structuralist ideas. Barthes's linking of an early existentialism with a later reading and writing theory, while passing through the structuralist environment, makes him appealing to Anglo-American writers.

The earliest influence on Barthes was existentialism. In his first books, notions of freedom quite alien to structuralism are evident. His attack on ideology in *Mythologies* (1957; English translation, 1973) and his review of fashion codes in *Système de la mode* (1967) seem to propose that the purpose of demystification is to increase the potential for human choice. In *Writing Degree Zero* (1953; English translation, 1968), Barthes says that "the choice of, and afterwards the responsibility for, a mode of writing point to the presence of freedom" (17), an idea taken from Sartre's *What Is Literature?* In another place ("Structuralist Activity") he writes that structural analysis involves man's "history, his situation, his freedom."

Barthes's *On Racine* (1964) and *Sade/Fourier/Loyola* (1971) both begin with the view that interpretation comes through a conflict, a confrontation, of different modes of discourse, that of the writer and those of diverse readers, a reading theory founded only tangentially in structuralism. In speaking of *S/Z* (1970), Culler and Philip Thody both interpret the approach as if it were a conventional reading theory. Thody finds "the codes and structures already existing in the reader's mind" (Thody [1977] 94); Culler finds an "attempt to explain how readers make sense of novels" (Culler, *Barthes* [1983] 88).

Over time, Barthes's view of the critical activity comes to seem allied with post-structuralism: he describes a literary work as "a galaxy of signifiers" (*S/Z*) and, in *New Critical Essays*, speaks of analysis entering "into the play of the signifier" (79), "advancing not into the text . . . but into its own labor" (89). This leads Barthes to a theory that the text is an object of pleasure and, eventually, in *The Pleasure of the Text* (1973), to bliss (Barthes's notorious *jouissance*) itself: "the subject gains access to bliss by the cohabitation of languages working side by side" (4).

Most of Barthes's works, then, can be easily appropriated (or misappropriated) by interpreters of structuralism, such as Culler, who use Barthes more for the purposes of a reading theory than as structuralism itself. His writings emphasize the creative role of the reader and critic, not incompatible with existential selfhood. Yves Velan asserts that, at the level of the literary *interpretation* that structuralism is used to validate, "the subject re-enters the world; . . . the work of Barthes gathers together its [the subject's] movements"; and he continues that for Barthes "structure, language, and desire are all the same thing" (Velan 328). It is this unique intermixture of the subject with a theory that purports to refute it that allows Barthes to occupy so central a place in the reception of structuralism in America.

The initial response of a number of Anglo-American critics to structuralism relies, then (whether such a reliance is fully acknowledged, fully recognized, or not), on the premises of a theory of reading, premises quite distinct from the propositions of structuralism. Jonathan Culler is representative. In *Structuralist Poetics* (1975; hereafter cited as *SP*: Barthes has the longest listing of citations in the index), after demonstrating at some length the inadequacies of Greimas and Jakobson, whose approaches are, in fact, central to basic structuralist literary analysis, Culler proposes a "structuralist poetics" founded on a theory of "convention and naturalization," a theory of reading (*SP*, Chap. 7; also *The Pursuit of Signs* [1981], Chap. 3). "The meaning of a sentence" (Culler cites Derrida in support) "is not a form or an essence, present at the moment of its production and lying behind it as a truth to be recovered, but the series of developments to which it gives rise" (*SP* 132). Furthermore, for literary works, "what we speak of as conventions of a genre . . . are essentially possibilities of meaning, ways of naturalizing the text and giving it a place in the world which our culture defines" (137). The reader naturalizes, seeks and, sure enough, finds meaning. "Whatever one calls the process, it is one of the basic activities of the mind. We can, it seems, make anything signify" (138). This naturalization consists of bringing a new text into an alignment with models of discourse already familiar to us, which gives to the work, for the reader, *vraisemblable*, a term Culler takes from Todorov. Culler outlines the various "levels" (cultural conventions, literary ones) at which naturalization produces coherence.

It is clear that this is not structuralism at all, despite the title of Culler's book, despite his citations of Derrida and Todorov. That Julia Kristeva (in *Semiotikè*) has stated that "intertextuality comes to take the place of the notion of intersubjectivity" (qtd. favorably in *SP* 139) is hardly supportive of a reading theory based on convention. Structuralism makes presuppositions about the mind and the self that reading theory need not make because reading theory is basically a psychological or a sociological description. Reading theory attempts to describe *what* happens during reading, which is different from describing *how* or *why* it happens; but these latter concerns define the structuralist project. Structuralist "conditions" of meaning are not "conventions" of meaning. The plot elements of Propp or Greimas, or the myth elements of Lévi-Strauss, are not explicable by convention. Nor is it accurate to say that Saussure and Peirce agree that "the task of semiotics is to describe . . . *conventions*" (*Pursuit of Signs* 24; emphasis added). And certainly the structure of mind cannot be "convention," although the structure of mind permits convention-making. Reading theory is compatible with any number of epistemologies since it deals not with the properties of mind but with an evident function of mind (making sense of things), which to describe is not to explain. Structuralism, contrariwise, is itself an epistemology. The tactic is one we have already identified in the process by which the German idealism of the late eighteenth century is transformed into a psychology by Coleridge, which makes it usable to the New Critics, who then, as Americans are wont to do, can ignore philosophy altogether. Even Culler recognizes that "in structuralist parlance naturalization tends to be thought of as a bad thing" although "it is an inevitable function of reading" (*SP* 159). That it is an inevitable function of reading may be the case; but since it would be so for an empiricist, a rationalist, an idealist, a phenomenologist, or even for a cognitive psychologist with behaviorist tendencies, it is irrelevant to structuralism in particular. For example, *vraisemblance* "need not depend on the claim that reality is a convention produced by language" (141). This statement is true; nor need *vraisemblance* depend on the structuralist concept of self or mentality, nor need it not.

The turn to the reader allows an escape from the ramifications of structuralism by diverting the discussion from the consideration of the constitution of the mind to the consideration of how the mind, whatever its constitution, seems to function in a social context. The term "convention" is used to signify socially produced expectations, a matter different from that important to Lévi-Strauss and the other structuralists, the fundamental structures of mentality. It should be noted, in addition, that convention (like men wearing ties) usually presupposes the possibility of identifying an origin, which we cannot say, as Derrida will show, about linguistic meaning and structuration. The issues are complex, as the earlier discussion of Chomsky has mentioned: there is a need to distinguish between *capacities of* the mind, which everyone would admit need to exist if there is to be mentality at all; *structures in* the mind that predetermine the structure of the world, whether at the level of classification (e.g., the theories of binary opposition) or of perception (Kant on space and time); and structured *content of* the mind, whether innate knowledge (as Descartes) or innate rules (as Chomsky).

But reader theory demands no choices among these. In America, an avoidance of such choices allows a falling back to the already familiar assumptions about who we are. Reader theory is, in fact, quite compatible with notions of free will, of a free subject engaged in reading. But it is equally compatible with a determinism that defines the subject-reader as *created* by the narrative, as do Coward and Ellis, who write: "the subject is constructed in such a way that it is not questioned by the flux of the text. . . . Narration rather sets the subject in place as the point of intelligibility of its activity," so the subject becomes (seems) "homogeneous," "fixed in a relation of watching" (Coward and Ellis [1977] 50). Reader theory is also compatible with an ideology based on coherence of meaning as a necessary attribute of mind or, as for a Marxist, an ideology based on coherence as a socially determined process that functions to obscure underlying conflict, an approach in which the critic "fills in the gaps" of the literary work "and smooths over its contradictions, domesticating its disparate aspects and defusing its contradictions" (Eagleton, *Literary Theory* [1983] 181).

Equally important, since reader theory in America does not imply that familiar notions of self are inapplicable, it will participate in the generation of a writing theory based on creativity as a "free" process. The question of "intent," a "hermeneutics," which the structuralists have no use for, will again become important (to Paul de Man, for example). E. D. Hirsch has already been mentioned. Geoffrey Strickland, to give one example, writes (in England, as did Culler) that whatever we say of a piece of writing "presupposes an assumption on our part . . . concerning the intention" of the writer ([1981] 35). A psychology of writing, amalgamating psychoanalysis and gnosticism, emerges in Harold Bloom (e.g., *Anxiety of Influence* [1973]). This question of intent is then intermingled with speech-act theory, and the structuralist epistemology is forgotten, as revisionists transmute poststructuralism into deconstruction.

The transformation of structuralism into theories of writing and reading happens quite rapidly. Structuralism is a momentary occurrence, a flurry of activity, a boisterous challenge quickly made safe, in part by Culler (see Norris, *Deconstruction* [1982], Chap. 1), and folded into reading theory by those trained to read within the New Criticism, folded into a branch of social psychology on the one hand and into advanced close reading techniques on the other. It might even be said that the Anglo-American concept of "structuralism" is itself a text created by the rejection of it.

Language and Meaning

Whether the "linguistic model" is suitable for systems other than language—whether, that is, myth, literature, or other meaning-bearing systems, like fashionable dress (Barthes, *Système* and *Elements of Semiology*) can be thought of as themselves "languages"—is questioned by many critics writing in English.

The general consensus is that meaning for humans does not exist apart from language, that language is not simply—as it is for the classic empiricists—a tool or medium through which preexistent ideas in the mind, produced by perception and a subsequent process of association that unites primary ideas into more complex ones, are shared with others. (That language is itself the sharing it seems to make possible is an approach that has been widely accepted because of the influence of Wittgenstein's *Philosophical Investigations*.) On the other hand, the consensus argues, since other meaning-bearing systems themselves presuppose the existence of language in society, their meaning is contingent upon a prior order of meaning. Consequently, these systems are not themselves languages; and at best the linguistic model offers helpful insights into a potential critical methodology.

Early on, it was recognized that while a methodology resembling linguistic analysis may be applicable to literature, nevertheless, literature or literary works are likely not, as systems, the same as languages (Donato, "Of Structuralism" [1967]). To Pettit, the structuralist's linguistic model, for the literary critic, is an "approach," a "metaphor" (100). Also, following his presentation of structuralist interpretations of literary works, Culler concludes that the value of developing interpretive "schema" (his examples are Barthes on Racine, Gennette on Proust, Heath on Joyce, and Foucault on Roussel) is "totally independent of the linguistic model" (*SP* 109). The title of the John Fekete collection, *The Structuralist Allegory* (1984), is suggestive of the manner in which structuralism is considered in various of the essays, as a (faulty) model derived (with some deformation) from linguistics but not demonstrably applicable to other human systems. "The autonimization of language and the objective world must itself be accounted for," writes Fekete, "and the language paradigm cannot do that on its own because that is the premise it takes for granted" (234).

One major issue has already been treated at length above: Can meaning in literature be *accounted for* by elements that, at the primary level of analysis, have themselves no meaning? Or can the structure of meaningful but non-literary elements (sentences, actions, functions) found in literature account for the overall meaning, function, or existence of literature? Structuralist formalism may not sufficiently consider literary meaning, Scholes believes, "because even in linguistics the role of semantics in unclear" (Scholes 12). (Semantics has, of course, rapidly become sophisticated in the last decade.) "Linguistic description," Scholes continues, "will not solve the problem of literary response" (39). For Pettit, "the general structuralist argument about narrative is that, just as in a sentence, it is more or less *mechanical* articulation of the text which produces its meaning" (43; emphasis added); Fekete, in stronger terms, states that structuralism "overstates the colonization of the event by the structure, and so fully enslaves meaning to the rule of an automatic system" (237). Finally, from Culler: "Linguistic analysis does not provide a method by which the meaning of a text can be deduced from the meaning of its components" (*SP* 95).

Of particular importance to American theorists is the work of Chomsky. As we have discussed in a previous chapter, in Chomskian theory the learning of any particular language is dependent upon grammatical rules innately preexisting in the mind of the individual, a universal grammar (*Syntactic Structures*). Since any acceptable utterance generated by the speaker of a language is governed by grammatical rule, even if unknown to the speaker, it may seem logical to relate this theory to the structuralist theory of narrative (or to Frye's theory) in which each narrative is but an example of, and a product of, a rule-governed narrative system (miscalled narrative "laws"). Might not, then, the underlying grammar of narrative account for narrative utterances, with the elements of narrative corresponding to the elements of speech, which would be combined in a regulated way whether or not any individual author recognized the regulatory substratum? The Chomskian model might then be seen as similar to the structuralist model.

Interestingly, the Anglo-American writers raise this possibility with some frequency, whether they accept it wholeheartedly or not, while the European structuralists find no need to address Chomsky as if he is somehow a linguistic compatriot. (Of equal interest is the fact that no need was found for an English translation of Saussure until 1959.) In truth, the differences between the structuralists and Chomsky are much more significant than the similarities, which are superficial and can only be proffered by American writers because (as with other issues) the fundamental philosophical premises are kept at a distance.

It must be remembered that, for Chomsky, sentences are generated (his is a "generative grammar") by the application, usually unconscious, of innate grammatical structure, equivalent to rules, to the specific lexicon learned by the individual. The universal grammar has a "psychological reality"; it has real existence in the human mind. Such a position, we have shown, is Cartesian and reinforces the concept of the unity of self as an entity: but it is exactly the Cartesian self that every structuralist finds preposterous. Lévi-Strauss, we recall, stated that the myths think themselves in men, not that men think in myths; the contents of consciousness, including the "self," subjectivity, are constituted by the systems into which the biological (human) organism is born. For a Cartesian, the subject *uses* myth; for the structuralist, what we call the subject *is*, in part, the myth. The distinction, to reiterate, must be kept firm between a *capacity* of the mind, its functional potential—which needs to be a supposition of any empiricism, Locke's, Marx's, or the structuralists', if we are to account for why there should be human thought or language at all—and innate *content* of some sort, whether Descartes' apodictic knowledge or Chomsky's grammar. At this level, Chomsky and the structuralists are philosophically most incompatible.

Suppose it is argued that, since the system of narrative in its entirety, as for the Russian Formalists, follows laws independent of authorial intent, this system may be compared to language which also develops according to laws not determined by the speakers. First, the development of a language over time is irrelevant both to Chomskian theory and to structuralism. As Saussure points out in the chapters of the *Course* that deal with language "diachronically," such change is often explicable by historical forces external to language (migration, conquest); and even if some change happens to be the result of lawlike regularity inherent in language (vowel shifting, etc.), this is irrelevant to analyzing a language as it exists for the speaker(s) at any moment in time, which is the only way one comes to learn language. Similarly, structuralist narratology is not literary history (Shlovsky is a formalist but not a structuralist) since, as has been mentioned, the laws proposed for narrative are really transformational topological relationships, which do not presuppose the causal efficacy of time. Second, for Chomsky, sentences are generated by the underlying grammar, while, as has been argued above, the "laws" of narrative cannot be said to generate narrative, and the use of "law" in such a sense is a confusion in Todorov and others. Furthermore, that all folktales have a similar structure can only be attributed to the same kind of "lawful" causality to which one attributes (to shift to a simple example of biological causality) the fact that human hands are generated with five fingers only if one excludes from causality human intellect, the mentality of the subject, in both cases. Although a structuralist might readily wish to exclude intellect in this way, a Chomskian cannot, since, to a Chomskian, mind has innate content. Admittedly, since Chomskian theory does not have a developed semantics, there is an area of possible overlap, but this area is so blurred that no conclusions are warranted, at least not by American literary critics of structuralism.

Further, the underlying rules of grammar can be determined by describing what the user of language does or does not take to be an acceptable sentence. This is not applicable to literary works: there is certainly no innate grammar of narrative that generates works classifiable as acceptable or unacceptable. Pettit, whose book attempts to substitute a Chomskian model for a structuralist one as if it were a preferable version of structuralism, recognizes that it is not possible to say what is an "impermissable" text (15-18). We cannot identify, Terence Hawkes maintains, the "non-novel" ([1977] 65). Culler, who believes Chomskian theory is a key to understanding structuralism, attempts to circumvent this difficulty by inferring that, since Chomsky's view of language involves rules and norms of utterances, and since literature as well seems to follow rules and norms, a connection can be made. But Culler's reading theory depends upon a *learned* system of "conventions," while Chomsky's language theory is meant to combat what he sees as the naive learning theory of the behaviorists. That "literary competence" might be called "a set of conventions" (and that they may be learned is hardly a controversial point) "for reading literary texts" (*SP* 118) has no relation to Chomsky's theory of language "competence," the ability of a speaker to generate a theoretically infinite number of sentences because the basic grammar—which has *not* been "learned"—is in the mind ready to be applied to the learned lexicon of the speaker's language. Culler and Pettit both propose that they are Chomskians; but, without innateness, this is an inconsequential Chomskianism. Again, there is some failure in these critics to achieve any philosophical depth. They concentrate instead on critical practice and methodology because the philosophical issues are usually not of basic importance to Anglo-American critics, to whom philosophy may appear on the one hand like a sterile positivism and on the other like a baffling metaphysics.

Fredric Jameson early understood that Chomsky's theory is quite the reverse of Saussure's. He interprets structuralism, in *The Prison-House of Language*, to some extent as the "afterlife" of a discredited Saussurian linguistic theory in non-linguistic disciplines, such as literary criticism. (It is notable that in a recent work Jameson takes the view that narrative may be a fundamental way of organizing the world, as if narrative were like a Kantian category of the mind. See Jameson, *The Political Unconscious* [1981], and the synopsis in Dowling [1984].)

In a non-scholarly, basically sarcastic article, George Watson also asserts that Saussurian linguistics, by the time of structuralism, had long been "overturned" ([1975] 50). Catherine Belsey agrees that Chomsky's "transformational generative grammar . . . is not post-Saussurian" ([1980] 38), that is, not allied with Saussure through theoretical influence, descent, or comparability.

It should be mentioned that Jean-Marie Benoist argues that Chomskian generative grammar should not be placed in opposition to structuralism, that Chomskian theory does not reintroduce free ego but is quite consistent with Saussure's langue/parole model, for which it "opens up new frontiers" ("The End of Structuralism" [1970] 38). Our analysis here and in Chapter Four does not, obviously, support this view.

The analysis of the relation of Chomsky to structuralism is further complicated by the fact that, in linguistic research in America, the term "structuralism" was long reserved for the linguistic theories of Bloomfield and those with similar approaches, whom Chomsky attacks. That this American linguistic "structuralism" can be shown to be incompatible with European structuralism does not make Chomsky an ally of the latter because he rejects the former, although the topic cannot be treated at length here (see Hymes and Fought [1981]).

Chomsky's theory of language, then, cannot be used to support structuralism. Where this support is attempted in literary criticism, the most significant philosophical issues, which place Chomsky and the structuralists in opposite camps, are inactivated.

History and Politics

In any area of inquiry, incorporating the historical process is essential for critics with a Marxist outlook, for whom all social phenomena are time bound and have meaning, at the highest level of understanding, inseparable from historical interpretation. Furthermore, in orthodox Marxism the economic system of production and exchange, the "infrastructure," determines the boundaries of the structure and function of the other social systems, the "superstructure" of law, education, politics, family life, and religion. These assumptions have had implications for literary criticism, especially as the evaluation of structuralism is concerned.

The proposal of the Russian Formalists that the literary system has its own internal laws that govern its evolution was met with rejection by orthodox Marxist theorists early in the twentieth century (see Erlich, *Russian Formalism*, Chap. VI), for whom the notion that "literary change can be seen not as a response to, or a by-product of, social change but as . . . self-generating and self-enclosed" (Hawkes 71) was unacceptable. While Trotsky (in *Literature and Revolution*) could admit that artistic creation transforms the content of reality through artistic laws and that historical materialism cannot provide *evaluative* criteria for works of art, nevertheless, ultimate causal explanation for why art is as it is in any historical period must be accounted for by Marxist historical theory. When Eichenbaum attempted to distinguish between the "evolution" of the literary system—which could evolve according to its own internal dynamics—and the "genesis" of literature (the difference, that is, between transformation and cause), his position was taken as anti-Marxist (Erlich 109).

Although some of the formalists, including Jakobson, eventually attempted to diminish the theoretical gap between formalism and Marxism (an attempt recently renewed by Tony Bennett), the use of formalism made by structuralism has emphasized, for Marxist critics, the ahistorical nature of both approaches. (Formalism is not itself structuralism.) Saussure distinguishes between "diachronic" historical linguistics—typified by the nineteenth-century philologists—and "synchronic" linguistics, the latter an analysis of language at one point in time. This is not to say that Saussure denied history (most of the *Course* is on language history), but that the method for which he is best known, the method attractive to the structuralists, is not the historical one. Lévi-Strauss, for example, in *The Savage Mind* (1962) attacked Sartre's emphasis upon history in the *Critique of Dialectical Reason*. There has been, consequently, an effort on the part of Marxist critics to correct what they identify as a one-sided view. "Structuralism," Eagleton laments, is "hair-raisingly unhistorical" (*Literary Theory* 109). Lentricchia persistently finds structuralism ahistorical, severing subjectivity from historical reality. The major task of Jameson's *Prison-House of Language* is to reintroduce the diachronic into synchronic structuralism: "My guiding thread and permanent preoccupation . . . has been to clarify the relationships possible between the synchronic methods of Saussurian linguistics and the realities of time and history itself" (Preface, x). Jameson finds that the early structuralist theory cannot be accepted because it ignores the reality of history, because the structuralist concept of sign "forbids any research into the reality beyond it" (106). He asserts that the work of Derrida "comes to split open the husk of the older system" and does incorporate time; yet since "time" is, for Derrida, "latent within the sign itself" rather than an independent reality, Jameson sees this as the limits, and the limitations, of structuralism, which as a theory remains unsatisfactory (187-88).

That structuralism is fundamentally an idealism becomes an accusation of the Marxists. Insofar as the earlier formalist and subsequent
structuralist approaches grant an evolutionary autonomy to mental
constructs, to literature and language, they are judged to lead to a
philosophic idealism. The formalists were neo-Kantians, Trotsky declared, whether they knew it or not. And Tony Bennett notes that
"apart from a period of brief flirtation in the early 1960s, Marxists have
come to regard structuralism as a new idealism" ([1979] 20). Ricoeur's
comment on Lévi-Strauss's Kantianism has already been quoted; and
Jameson accepts the pertinence of the view that it is "to the dilemmas
of Kantian critical philosophy that, consciously or unconsciously, structuralism remains a prisoner" (*Prison-House* 214). "Structuralism," for
Coward and Ellis, "ultimately rest[s] on idealist presuppositions" (2).

To charge a philosophy with idealism is, for a Marxist, to hurl
an insult. It is important to recall, however, that the structuralists themselves believed that their theory was quite compatible with Marxism;
it assumed that the self is a determined construction and that, as Marx
proposed, the contents of consciousness are created by the social system. We have said that within this view of the constructed self, structuralism might be seen as a Marxism in which language as a determining factor replaces economics. This replacement may not succeed,
because it substitutes a mental structure for "reality." (The structuralists, of course, would say that language is an objective non-personal
reality.) But this is not to refute the structuralist motivation, which is
actually to avoid idealism. To redefine the common ground between
Marxism and structuralism becomes the work of Louis Althusser.

An early criticism of Russian Formalism by orthodox Marxists
was that its methodology was "a product of the decadent and spiritually
sterile ruling class," that it was "simply a cultural survival, one of the
relics of old Russia amidst the revolutionary upheaval" (Erlich, *Russian
Formalism* 106-7). When Sartre wished to express his disdain for the
structuralists, he said that the method was a "trick of the bourgeoisie,
an attempt to substitute for the Marxist vision of evolution a closed
inert system where order is privileged at the expense of change" (qtd.
in Scholes 195). It is quite true that the structuralists, like other French
intellectuals, have little love for the bourgeoisie. In Barthes's long essay
in *Mythologies*, "Myth Today," he uses the word "myth" in a derog-
atory sense to denote that mental process of the bourgeoisie which
solidifies their shared ideology by turning their historically contingent
beliefs into apparent universal and everlasting truths. Much of this is
merely name calling; the same invectives have been hurled at the New
Critics. In recent work on literature and ideology, the vituperation often

remains prominent. For example, while the ultimate "scientific" legitimacy of structuralism might have been "more a strategic moment in an open-ended process than an attainable goal" (Macksey and Donato ix), it is quite another thing to declare that "structuralism was the dupe of an alienated theory of scientific practice, one powerfully dominant in late capitalist society" (Eagleton, *Literary Theory* 122). What is and is not bourgeois cannot be settled here.

Still another concern is the relationship of structuralist and poststructuralist theory and literary criticism to political action. Those who believe that criticism should, as a social activity, contribute to beneficial change often point to what seems to be the disaffiliation between politics and literary criticism, which those who lived through the active 1960s might not have expected to occur. The conservative political views of the New Critics have been mentioned; their literary criticism gives little indication of the important political events of the 1940s and 1950s. Because of structuralism's legitimation on the left, and its having issued from the usually politically heated French intellectual environment, it might have been anticipated that politics and criticism would become allied.

In 1974 Scholes wrote that structuralism "worked against nationalism and against egotism in general" (190), that it was "a move away from adversary relationships in political processes" (193), that it would "help us to live in the future" (200). Some years earlier Peter Caws had written, "structuralism, in effect, advocates an engagement with the world" ([1968] 817). Still, the political role of structuralism has been minimal, certainly with no effect in the United States. Even in France, the response of structuralist theorists to the political events of the 1960s, in particular the Paris student uprisings of 1968, was meager compared to what activists might have anticipated (see the essays in Kurzweil [1980]). (Also, the left did not gain political power in France until Mitterrand took office in 1981.) When he first published the volume of essays that comprise *Beginnings* (1975), Edward Said believed that structuralism would, in America, reopen the issues of political commitment and the questioning of the status quo. In his Preface to the 1985 edition (by which time deconstruction had become prominent), he states that recent literary criticism "has come to resemble the old New Criticism in its formalism, in its isolation of literature and 'literariness' from the world." William Cain agrees: "the spirit of reversion, withdrawal and isolation remains deeply rooted in literary studies, and the New Critics are in large measure responsible for it" (111). Said accuses himself with "having failed totally to have predicted this surprising turn," which he attributes to circumstances "largely

American and academic" (xii). In another volume he condemns the "relative absence of the historical dimension in criticism" (*World, Text, Critic* [1983] 168). Since criticism occurs within a structure of power and authority, the lack of historicity in the long run legitimizes the existing power structure: "the culture validates the humanist, the humanist the critic, and the whole enterprise the State" (*Beginnings* 175).

The assessment of the historical and political dimensions of structuralism has customarily, then, been an unfavorable one, whether because of a presumed incompatibility with Marxism (a position we do not support) or a failure to incorporate history, to repel idealism, to escape ideology, or to contribute to social improvement. Much, though not all, of this falls outside purely theoretical considerations; yet the issues are not for that reason less germane.

The Concept of "Self"

The underlying major issue in the reception of structuralism in the United States—whatever critical method might be avowed—is, to repeat, the concept of the "self." As early as the well-known conference held at Johns Hopkins University in 1966, the controversy begins on American territory. (The papers are collected in Macksey and Donato [1970].) In his introductory presentation, Macksey cautions that "semiotic formalism" raises the "risk of divorcing understanding from the contingency of the *individual* experience in its depth" (12; emphasis added), and in one of his later responses he calls literature a "free, unmediated act" (37). In neither of these statements, obviously, would certain members of the audience, which included Lacan and Derrida, take delight. The papers preceding and likely anticipating those given by Lacan and Derrida, and the audience responses, frequently address, even in a combative way, the matter of self. Georges Poulet, for example, states, "I need absolutely for my own kind of criticism what I would call with Descartes, the *Cogito*" (88). Later Lucien Goldmann asserts, "when it becomes a question of transforming society . . . there are no longer any individual subjects" (101). To the opening paper of the conference, a quite conventional talk by Charles Moraze on "invention," with examples from the self-reports of scientists about what invention feels like, Lacan responds from the audience, "Who invents? There would be no question of invention if *that* were not the question. You [Moraze] consider this question resolved." Lacan raises "the term *subject* as something distinct from the function of individuality you introduced" (42-43).

To reinforce the contention that the concept of the subject fundamental to structuralism is found unappealing by American (or, more precisely, Anglo-American) critics of the movement, we will again cite the authors mentioned earlier in this chapter, who seek a way back toward traditional concepts of self that allow for a more congenial explanation of freedom, will, and creativity in order to preserve the customary American predilections.

" 'Man' disappears under structural analysis," Culler says, and he quotes Lévi-Strauss's *Savage Mind*: "the goal of the human sciences is not to constitute man but to dissolve him" (*SP* 28). This aspect of structuralism first became well known in English because of the relatively early popularity of the writings of Foucault. In *The Order of Things*, translated in 1970, Foucault argues that the concept of "man" is an invention about two centuries old. In "Abecedarium Culture," Said recognizes that in Foucault, whom he reviews at some length, man is "no longer a coherent *cogito*"; "man is dissolved . . . turning finally into little more than a constituted subject, a speaking pronoun, fixed indecisively in the eternal ongoing rush of discourse" (*Beginnings* [1985] 286-87). Gilles Deleuze has called Foucault's work "a cold and concentrated destruction of the subject . . . a dismantling of unifying pseudo-syntheses of consciousness" (qtd. in Macksey and Donato x). Robert D'Amico calls attention to structuralism's "exclusive emphasis on objective ordering at the expense of subjectivity," with which he takes issue ([1984] 164). And we have previously quoted Fekete: "what is at stake in the encounter with the structuralist 'turn' is the Western mind itself" ([1984] xii). Seyla Habib, whose approach is derived from the Frankfurt School, calls for philosophy to regain its "commitment to the dignity and autonomy of the rational subject" ([1986] 15).

In earlier chapters we have traced certain American responses at the level of culture, psychology, philosophy, science, linguistics, and literary criticism to demonstrate that the segment of the intellectual population that contains literary critics repeatedly rebels against what is a logical consequence of classic empiricism, namely determinism, in order to incorporate what are for them more satisfying views of selfhood and creativity. It has also been shown that empiricism can lead to skepticism, which often legitimates the escape from the empiricist determinism. Analysts of structuralism manifest the same propensity.

Lentricchia, for example, who is critical of the movement, states that "Saussure's notions . . . are profound determinisms" (115); consequently, the goal of structuralism is "to demonstrate a monolithic determinism" (127). Whether Saussure would think of himself as a determinist is doubtful; what he did say was that "the sign always *to some extent* eludes control by the will" (16; emphasis added). But the point here is Lentricchia's rejection of determinism.

Culler defends individualism with some fervor. Even if language is structured as the structuralists assert it is, "individuals" do exist and *"choose* to speak and what to say." We can't dispense with the individual subject," for "meaning moves through him." "He assimilates its rules"; one must consider "his judgments and intuitions" (*SP* 29-30). Needless to say, this is not philosophy but credo. Scholes's attraction to structuralism is in part based on the mistaken assumption that it is compatible with traditional humanist, and politically liberal, values; and the conclusion of his book is almost a paean to human potential. To Fekete, writing with more philosophical rigor, structuralism "excludes evolutionary, axiological, and praxical dimensions of human *agency*" (234; emphasis added). "We must reconceptualize the process that leads to the formation of efficacious agency on the individual and social levels . . . to rediscover the place for substantive rationality" (xviii). Gyorgy Markus, in the same volume, makes the point that structuralists need, in fact, to account for their own subjectivity since they meet with "insuperable difficulties as soon as they are confronted with the task of self-reflection, of justifying their own claims to truth" (123). (This is the argument that writers against free will would have to admit that their own writing is not done freely, etc.)

We will assert, again, that these strategies are motivated by the same needs that motivated the New Critics to move toward Romanticism at a time when deterministic behaviorism was the dominant psychology.

Scholes professes, in the name of structuralism, a typical non-structuralist outlook when he maintains that "the simple forms of literature come into being as a response to ethical and interpretive needs" (49). When he presents his own theory, it involves the relationship between fiction and human experience: literature "offers a perspective on our own situation. . . . We are engaged in seeking our own position in the world" (133). This is recognizably derived from an existentialist position and is a position affiliated with that of certain earlier writers who see literature as part of the process by which man supports the "fictions" by which he lives, the "social lie or vital myth" referred to by Hartman ("Structuralism" [1966] 143). Some of the literature addressing the human need for creating sustaining fictions is reviewed by Lentricchia, who cites Wallace Stevens ("the vogue of Wallace Stevens in the 1960s"), Kermode, and the work of Vaihinger. There are two approaches to the fictionalization of reality: in one, addressed by Lentricchia, the objective reality revealed by science is so inhospitable

to humankind's needs, aspirations, and self-image that fictions are created to make the world bearable; in the other, all descriptions of reality
are "fictions" insofar as reality itself is, in principle, unknowable. The
former position is an esthetic social psychology. The latter is somewhat
loosely affiliated with the structuralist position that, because language
is a self-enclosed non-referential system, it does not describe reality
itself. This view is indebted to both Kant and the empiricists—which
is the paradox that unravels structuralism. Perhaps these "fictions" are,
in modern guise, the "grand narratives" whose incapacitation and loss
defines for Jean-Francois Lyotard the basic condition of postmodernism
(*The Postmodern Condition* [1984]). Now that we know the writings of
Derrida, the signifier "reality" seems to some extent to have been privileged here by the writers of the 1960s, since it is difficult to determine
how one can know what a fiction is without at the same time knowing
what reality might be, or how one can know what non-referentiality
is without knowing what referentiality is, too. (The same dilemma led,
in the nineteenth century, to the post-Kantian rejection of the unknowable thing-in-itself.) In any case, the intermingling of these various schools of thought is more a diversion from structuralism than a
method of understanding it.

In Said's *Beginnings*, the criticism of structuralism supports a theory of human "intention." "A major thesis of this book is that beginning is a consciously intentional, productive activity" (372). He refers
to "beginning intention—which in history is human will" (361). Since,
obviously, structuralists also know that there are people in the world
who (seem to) have intentions, Said's approach is not really, as he
intends it, a "criticism" or "modification" of structuralism, in which,
to Said, "the origin and the beginnings are both hopelessly alien to,
and absent from the stream of discourse" (316). The terminology indicates that Said is referring to both structuralism and the revisions of
the 1970s. The central matter here is that Said, like other critics, has
a basic antipathy for the structuralist doctrine: at one point he states
that "there is a comic side to their industry. The intensity of their
dedication often reminds one of Molière's characters" (321). Behind
this is a by now familiar theme: "A major criticism of the structuralists
is, I think, that the moving force of life and behavior, the *forma infor-
mans*, intention, has been, in their work, totally domesticated by system" (319).

The temperament of Anglo-American writers is illustrated, perhaps anecdotally, by Edmund Leach's candid response to Lévi-Strauss's
idea of *esprit*, which refers to a human mentality distinct from the
autonomous individuality of the subject (what Said refers to in Foucault

as "transpersonal mind" [*Beginnings* 293]). Leach admits, "I have to confess that, when it comes to the crunch, I have no clear idea of what it is that Lévi-Strauss is really taking about" (Leach [1966] 248).

An intriguing aspect of the controversy over the nature of self is the assertion of certain Marxists that notions of an independent, unified, and free-willed self is a creation of capitalism. Hawkes, for example, quotes with favor Barthes's *On Racine*: "literature is that ensemble of objects and rules, techniques and works, whose function in the general economy of our society is precisely to institutionalize subjectivity" (qtd. in *Structuralism and Semiotics* 153). The view of Coward and Ellis that narrative can participate in the constitution of the self has previously been mentioned. Coward and Ellis attempt to reconcile the determinism of Marxism with a theory of the "productive" possibilities of self (the major dilemma for all determinisms which, despite their premises, exhort human action, praxis) by basing the constitution of the self, via Lacan, in "contradiction." Eagleton refers to the "classic bourgeois ideology" concerning self and "man" (*Literary Theory* 58). In his explication of Jameson, William Dowling speaks of the "master code" permitting the New Critics to "allegorize" literature, a code that remains invisible to the readers who share its ideological supposition: "the idea of an integrated identity, a whole self, a stable and balanced individual psyche" (106). Dowling suggests that this idea of self is an "ideological reverse image of the estranged and alienated and fragmented reality that is modern life under capitalism" (106). "The ideology of liberal humanism," writes Belsey, "assumes a world of non-contradictory . . . individuals whose unfettered consciousness is the origin of meaning . . . a free, unified, autonomous subjectivity" (67). The writing of Althusser is of prominent importance on these matters. While such conclusions are of use to American critics as part of the legitimation of theory on the political left, they are usually intermixed into a sociology of alienation based on the early "humanism" of Marx and do not—as, in France, does Joseph Gabel's *False Consciousness*— address the philosophical underpinnings.

Issues of Marxism aside, more than one section above has emphasized that literary critics, often using the methodology of structuralism as an advancement of close reading and meticulous analysis in their striving to go beyond the New Criticism, frequently bypass the philosophical issues altogether. This tactic is made possible because there is no *necessary* connection between a philosophical system and a specific methodology. In bypassing these issues, however, the most significant implications of structuralism are absent from the analysis; structuralism in that way can be appropriated but not accepted.

It is, finally, most important to understand that the most recent writers (since, say, 1977) on structuralism cited throughout this chapter are including the structuralist revisionists (Foucault, Derrida, Lacan) in their scope of review. This substantiates the view that structuralism in *all* its forms possesses an underlying determinism that is incompatible with the dominant Anglo-American critical temperament. Structuralism, then, was itself but a momentary meeting place for two cultures that were *crossing*, one heading away from the determinism of behaviorism and the scientific method toward renewed concepts of freedom, the other heading away from the freedom of phenomenology and existentialism into determinism.

Empiricism, Once Again

Empiricism explores and defines the limitations, boundaries, constraints, and conditions of human knowledge, relying on the proposition that what is external to mind is introduced as "idea" into mind through the mediation of the senses. Sensation and perception, while serving as conditions for knowing the world, also call into question the status of knowledge: we can know nothing directly but these ideas. Furthermore, since various ideas cannot be shown simply to be aggregated from sensation —ideas of consciousness, free will, self, immortality, and God, for example—the empiricist needs recourse to introspection, the "reflexion" of Locke, to complete the empiricist system, although the union of these two dimensions of empiricism yield philosophical problems not resolvable within the system.

The success of the scientific method, however, has served to legitimate empiricism despite its contradictions; and empiricism has, in general use, often come to mean no more than gathering data through the senses, which is called "empirical." I have kept that adjective distinct from "empiricist," using the latter to refer to a philosophy, not to the scientific technique that it undergirds. Empiricism, it has been argued, is the fundamental influence on the Anglo-American outlook; but at the same time, that a logical consequence of empiricism seems to be a materialistic determinism calls forth numerous strategies to reinvigorate alternatives, a persistent current of countermeasures.

The linguistics of Saussure and the "linguistic model" of the structuralists is founded on the supposition that linguistics is, or should be, an empiricism. The nineteenth-century positivists, philologists, and historians certainly believed in empiricist doctrine, which they applied to *historical* processes. The novelty of Saussure's theory was the assumption not only that the study of linguistic change over time is an empiricist enterprise, but also that a language at one point in time is an existent "object" of study and can be investigated by the methods of empiricism. Yet empiricism is a theory of perception in which "meaning" tends to stand for a consensus concerning the truth of the matter, a referential consensus. Language "means" insofar as those who exchange it share the experience to which linguistic sounds refer. Language is a tool to convey one's mental ideas, which, of course, in a way sets language outside the explanatory powers of empiricism: in classic empiricism, once the system of perception, cognition, and "association" is set in place, language is introduced as a medium of exchange.

But if the workings of language—much different from changes in language over time, which show nothing about its workings as *communication*—are themselves to be explained through an empiricism, difficulties arise. First, language can only be itself discussed in language. To discuss language is to remain inside it, and the possibility of isolating language as an object becomes a puzzle. Pettit, for example, attests that structuralism tries to "put language among the things of the material world" (10), which he attributes to the "vice of Anglo-Saxon empiricism" (23). That language needs to be understood by the application of itself to itself is a dilemma that brings some critics to view structuralism as trapped (in a prison-house) inside the phenomenon it has attempted to scientifically isolate.

Second, if language is scrutinized with an empiricist method as an object in the world, it can only be viewed as an assembly of "sounds," since "meaning" certainly cannot be an object in the world. How one is to get from language as a system of meaniningless elements to language as meaning is left unsettled by structuralism. And as we have said earlier, that language as a system of sounds is found to have a structure of differences simply reveals the ramifications of a tautology, for it is not conceivable for language not to have such properties. For language to have meaning it must have reference, which is why Saussure needs to retain the notion of a "concept" (really the Lockean "idea"). But, again, reference cannot be explained in a strict empiricist way. For the word "reference" itself to have a meaning, it would have to refer to a "concept" derived from "experience": yet the only experience that supports the concept of "reference" is our "reflection" on what we seem to be doing when we use language. This introspection, however, has no explanatory power if what we wish to explain is the apparent relation between the ideas, the concepts, and an external real world. (This is the door to skepticism, and Chomsky's turn to "rationalism" cannot help us here.) The two aspects of Saussure's theory—the system as "difference" and the sign as signifier/signified—are meant to generate, in two different ways, an empiricist linguistics. But the theory rests from the beginning not on linguistic "facts" but on contradictions inherent in the way the problem is configured; for facts about the "conditions" of meaning are facts about the conditions of language, not about language itself, which is inextricable from meaning. Similarly, at a higher level of organization, Lévi-Strauss determines the conditions of myth, which are facts about those conditions and not about myth itself, except where Lévi-Strauss crosses the line into interpretation. Hawkes quotes Barthes's statement, from *Critique et vérité*, that criticism "cannot be a science of content . . . but a science of the conditions of content" (57). In our analysis of structuralist literary theory, this problem of interrelating elements of meaning, conditions of meaning, meaning, and interpretation of meaning has been considered a central problem. Structuralism raises the problem—similar to the problem philosophers have of the impossibility of getting from *is* statements to *ought* statements—but cannot solve it.

In contrasting Titchener's introspectionist psychology with Watson's behaviorism, attention was given to Kendler's criticism of the "phenomenological" (introspectional) theory. Kendler maintains that the results of any process of introspection that tries to determine the basic irreducible elements of sensation, and hence consciousness, are predetermined by theoretical suppositions. There can be no "neutral" ground on which to stand so that sensation itself, unbiased by language, can be detected in its pure state (the state that Husserl's "bracketing" would create). Kuhn assents, though reluctantly, to this view.

Structuralism is positioned, or would like to be positioned, around the tenet that *knowing* whatever is known, sensation included, is mediated by language. Certainly there can be sensation without consciousness (film, for example) and perhaps (who can say?) conscious sensation but without self-consciousness (in animals, for example). Structuralism says or implies either that sensation itself is mediated by language or that knowledge (making sense of) sensation is mediated by language. Language, socially existent preceding individual consciousness, constitutes individual consciousness. There is a "primacy of language over subjectivity" (Belsey 60). The basic "elements" that an introspectionist is searching for are, consequently, linguistic; for without language, sensation (or perception) is not itself elemental (atomistic) but rather an amorphous, unorganized, inseparable, chaotic mass. Despite the arguments of certain positivists (e.g., Russell, the early Wittgenstein), there are no pure unmediated atomistic elements of sensation to discover. Language, for human consciousness, becomes more basic than our own sensations, since these are unknowable as such without linguistic mediation. (A newborn can have sensation but no subjectivity to know its sensations.) Yet it is the "knowableness" of consciousness that defines human consciousness.

If knowableness is mediated by language, and if language is a mental construct, then structuralism is open to the charge of idealism; language becomes, as if it has been substituted for the Kantian categories, an inescapable matrix that determines reality, that both determines and *is* consciousness. But it is extremely important to understand what the structuralists believed they were doing, for although idealism can logically be drawn forth as a consequence of structuralism, the structuralists certainly were themselves not so naive as to deny in ignorance that they were idealists while they, in some obvious sense, were.

Idealism is, of course, dependent on innateness, on a priori knowledge (causality, spatiality, temporality), subsumed in Kant's categories. Innateness presupposes self-hood. The self is not a construct but is itself the constructor. Is not Kant "a founding spirit of the German Romantic movement" (Scruton 138)? Consequently, Ricoeur's assertion that structuralism is Kantianism without the transcendental subject is an oxymoron. Idealism substantiates the transcendent subject.

The structuralists, with their linguistic model, did not belief they were invoking idealism; quite the contrary (note Eco's denial of idealism at the conclusion of his *Theory of Semiotics* [1979] 317). Rather, they took language not as a mental construct but, unlike idealism, as the constructor of mentality. They could then assert that the elements of mind are the elements of language. But if language preexists individual consciousness, which it fashions, then language can be treated as an object in the world (like behavior to the behaviorist, like the poem to the New Critic), as a system existent outside the mind. *The elements of mind*—traditionally locked inside the head and available only through reflection—*are externalized*. This is essentially the most important structuralist step.

Admittedly, this strategy, driven by empiricism, may not work, probably because the "language" that is made an object in the world is its systematic properties and not its semantic ones, since meaning cannot be so object-ified. Idealism, which is a theory of intelligible meaning, then reemerges. It reemerges as a philosophical system which has posed better (even where unacceptable) solutions to certain problems of the structuralists than the structuralists themselves can; but this is not to say that structuralism *is* an idealism, even if one is led back to idealism, which for an empiricist (not to mention the Marxists) is to throw suspicion, with good reason, on structuralism itself.

There is, however, a preferable, perhaps complementary, analysis. Kant's idealism developed as a response to Hume's skepticism, which, as everyone knows, roused Kant from his "dogmatic slumbers"; and Kant attempted to demonstrate the illogicality of skepticism by showing that the human "understanding" that Hume employs to philosophize, itself, by its very structure, yields the knowledge that Hume denies can ever be known for sure.

In between empiricism and idealism, then, came skepticism, a logical consequence of empiricism. This is, assuredly, the same movement to be found in structuralism. Structuralism, as an empiricism, yields skepticism, not idealism. And idealism only may seem, afterward, a consequence because we already know Kant's response to Hume, already know how well idealism begins to work where empiricism falters.

Conclusion

Structuralism, as it originally appears, possesses the various attributes that literary critics would like to find in a critical theory: scientific methodology, a theory of mind, a theory of language, and a leftist political alliance. Nevertheless, the strict empiricism that it purports to exemplify (whether well or ill founded) and the evident determinism of a Marxist-based theory of the self as a construction quickly provokes dissatisfactions, criticisms, and rejections. Regardless of the ground from which they are argued, these criticisms represent the persistent attempt by (Anglo-)American "humanists" to circumvent the very empiricism that they frequently claim legitimates their own critical activity.

We have followed this process in the development of the New Criticism as it begins in Richards's empiricist psychology and gradually strives to integrate components of Romanticism. It is significant that structuralism has been linked to Romanticism, in a passage cited earlier, by Todorov (*Introduction* xxviii). Similarly, Scholes devotes some space to finding "the roots of structuralist thinking in romanticism" (168). Scholes's argument is quite weak, a piecing together of Shelley's Platonism (shall we believe, with Scholes, that "Shelley has the spirit of a social scientist"?), some unrelated statements by Wordsworth, and passages from Coleridge's *Biographia Literaria* (e.g., "the best part of human language . . . is derived from reflection of the acts of the mind itself," from Chapter XVII), which Scholes views as a work of linguistic science. Passages in Coleridge can, of course, be found that will prove him an empiricist or an idealist, a psychologist or a religionist (many of the important issues are raised in Owen Barfield's *What Coleridge Thought*), because his purpose is to use as leverage within the English amalgam of the Enlightenment and neo-classicism a foreign metaphysics that can, in an empiricist environment, never take hold. The frequent focus of the deconstructionist critics upon Romantic poetry, like the New Critics' attentiveness to Romantic theory, is telling. That there are those who wish to associate early structuralism and Romanticism (a most ungainly fellowship) helps to reemphasize the tactical strategies we have been tracing in criticism, the finessing of empiricism.

The "classic" structuralist movement—from Saussure through Lévi-Strauss through literary analysts like Jakobson, Greimas, and Todorov—undergoes major revisions as the works of Foucault, Lacan, and Derrida appear, revisions that have uniquely affected American critical practice.

Basically, the inseverable bond posited by Saussure between the signifier and the signified, the two constituents of the sign, begins to weaken. A gap appears, a gap that widens into the abyss of skepticism, into which tumble many traditional notions of truth, logic, language, and literature. For example, a critical stance toward any object of study customarily presupposes a language suitable for the analysis; the languages of literary criticism or of philosophy or of psychology appear as "meta-languages," an order of language in which another order can be analyzed. But if all language is of a single, a common, order, then the concept of meta-language vanishes. We are left no longer with the possibility of discovering truths, but only with the prospect of discovering the mechanisms of texts and the relationships between texts (intertextuality), which cannot be prioritized on any truth-bearing scale.

Post-structuralism, the revisions to purportedly empiricist structuralism, is this skepticism, as will be shown in the next two chapters, a skepticism initiated by the recognition that once the "signified" as a Saussurian "concept" can no longer be supported, we are left with the "signified" as itself another "signifier." The system of linguistic signs becomes a self-contained, endless, internally self-referential system of signifiers whose meanings are generated by their own network. This is, first, like Berkeley's recognition that nothing, after all, can be known but ideas, the content of mind, and, second, like Hume's recognition (once Berkeley's deity is set aside) that if only ideas can be known then skepticism immediately follows. That idealism can subsequently ensue is, at least at this stage, not the point.

The history of philosophy from Hobbes to Hume finds a parallel in the movement from Saussure to Derrida. The structuralists are Lockean empiricists; Derrida is their Hume.

There are two structuralist approaches to the literary work. The first, not unlike Frye's, investigates the work as a part of a larger system, possessing no meaning independent from the system as a whole. The second views the literary work itself as a system (without, to be sure, discounting its membership in the larger literary system), so that each work in its own right comes to illustrate a theory of language and literary functioning. While the former view will gain adherents (Bloom, for example), the latter, because it offers a continuity with the New Criticism, will become the American practice, the deconstructionist practice. The lessons of the New Criticism will not be forgotten; they will be reformulated in a new theoretical context. Like a word or sentence in a poem, the technique of critical practice, too, is understandable only in its context, the theory it comes to serve.

As American critics seek to open up space for self, freedom, and creativity, they will transform (even before they really understand it) the theory imported from France, a theory of a constructed self, of determinism. As this occurs, the emphasis will move from a consideration of the human being as structured intellect to the human being as will and desire, reflecting on the one hand the migration in philosophy from Kant to Schopenhauer in the nineteenth century and on the other from Husserl to Heidegger and Sartre in the twentieth. Early in this study we noted that even Hobbes, Locke, and Hume had need of a rudimentary theory of will or desire underlying human nature in order to account for how the whole system of humanity and society is "energized" in the first place. Desire theory, then, is at all times available, when called upon, in empiricism. (Even behaviorists may lean upon drive-reduction hypotheses.) A bond between the two cultures is Sigmund Freud—half empiricist, half metaphysician—who plays a Coleridgian role, as the links are tightened between Freud and Marx on the left and American humanist psychology on the right.

The transition occurs quickly for American literary critics. They receive and reject the orthodox structuralist doctrine in short order yet are nonetheless stimulated and intrigued by it; they are made alert to the intricacies of literary critical theory, which begins to grow in university departments of literature as a sub-discipline of much interest, while the work of the revisionists, Derrida in particular, comes to the fore.

CHAPTER SEVEN

Post-Structuralism I:
Foucault, Lacan, Althusser

In its application to literary criticism, structuralism appeared, at first, to meet the criteria demanded of a critical theory in the United States in the late 1960s: it was, presumably, an empiricist science; it incorporated linguistics; it addressed the problem of human mentality; and it issued from the political left. Nevertheless, shortcomings were quickly identified in each of these domains, as we have seen, inadequacies that challenged the usefulness of structuralism for literary criticism, particularly from the point of view of American theorists.

The linguistic model, based on Saussure, while illuminating the "conditions" of meaning, is insufficient to account for the presence of meaning or for the encompassing systematic unity of literary works. And the model cannot—as if this might save it by explaining the "production" of meaningful utterance—be reconciled with Chomskian theory, which in any case, as a "rationalism," is itself vulnerable. The epistemology undergirding structuralism, quite clear in Lévi-Strauss, is not compatible with the prevailing Anglo-American predisposition and was ignored or discarded, which is to vitiate the structuralist project. Theorists on the left, whether Marxist or not, deplored the apparent elimination of history, the absence of time as causative, and the residue of a politically detrimental ideology. The assumption that an empiricist science can adequately handle literature was, as always, questioned, customarily because a science encompassing mentality (excluding, as Americans do, a phenomenological "science") usually ends by dispossessing mentality, through behaviorism and physiological or sociological reductionism.

Post-structuralism, in its application to language and literature, begins with the recognition that the epistemological consequences of structuralism unravel the empiricist presuppositions of the Saussurian-based linguistic model, particularly because the original notion of the "signified" reflects a commitment to a form of empiricist "knowledge" that evaporates under scrutiny. After a general introduction, the analyses of Foucault, Lacan, Althusser, and Derrida need to be reviewed, especially with regard to their relevance for literary criticism.

Post-Structuralist Suppositions

The point of view to be outlined is not, to be sure, the consensus of a group of thinkers who call themselves "post-structuralists" or who believe that the foremost importance of their work consists of a critique of structuralism. It is best to think of post-structuralism as a set of related approaches to a similar problem—the relation of self and language—which together, when set beside (or inside) structuralism, disclose its underlying inconsistencies and force it to its theoretical limits. These approaches form no unified theory; nevertheless, on certain issues a harmony (which always consists of different notes) does emerge, and this will be the emphasis here.

Science requires an investigator, a methodology, and an object of study, and it assumes a distinction between the three. The investigator obtains results; the results are knowledge of the object. But while empiricism justifies the scientific method, empiricism cannot, in the long run, provide a justification for itself: empiricism legitimates scientific practice but at the same time raises, often despite itself, the question of the philosophical status of science. Locke's philosophy yields Hume's skepticism; empiricism deconstructs itself. Although fundamental to the customary Anglo-American outlook, empiricism becomes from another point of view—one that is usually found confusing, metaphysical, or indefensible by English-speaking philosophers—the statement of a problem, not the solution to it. That problem has been addressed by German philosophers from Kant to Heidegger, as well as by certain French thinkers from Sartre and Merleau-Ponty to Derrida.

Two issues emerge in approaching post-structuralism. First, if the "subject" (human consciousness) is itself to be the "object" of analysis, how can this subject be situated in regard to itself as an investigator? The problem became prominent in Kant. In his "transcendental deduction of the categories" and in his analysis of the "ideas" of pure reason (e.g., freedom), Kant proposed somehow to discover a philosophical knowledge encompassing human mentality by working from within the very confines of intellect that would seem to place on knowledge the unavoidable limitations (Foucault's "finitude") that Kant would surpass. Second, and similarly, if the structuralist hypothesis that knowledge of the world and self, regardless of the organizing discipline (physics, psychology, literature), is ultimately language, whether natural or invented (like mathematics), then in what way can language be the implement of understanding itself? If knowledge is contained within language, the container itself cannot be viewed from an external vantage point.

The post-structuralist view is that these dilemmas are implicated in Saussure's definition of the sign as composed of "signifier" and "signified." We have argued that this definition is an attempt to retain empiricism, since the signifieds, called "concepts," resemble the "ideas" of Locke. What any signifier signifies, however, cannot be divulged except by using more words, more signifiers. The neat formula for the sign gives way in post-structuralism to Saussure's further speculation that the linguistic system is composed of terms that have meaning only insofar as they have a collective systematic integrity; and it is concluded that the chain of signifiers cannot yield irreducible signifieds. What language is pointing to is itself: what exists are "texts." The idea of a knowable reality independent of language is rejected. The early structuralists recognize that language cannot be called "referential" in the customary sense; nevertheless, like Saussure, they do not advance to the point where objective knowledge is discarded. Since structuralism is promoted as a "science," truth is available at some level, even if it is only truth about language and the mental structures that it both engages and establishes. "There is not a single book or study by Lévi-Strauss which does not offer itself as an empirical essay which can always be completed or invalidated by new information" (Derrida, "Structure, Sign, and Play" 259). In post-structuralism, the descriptions of the linguistic structures and codes discovered by structuralism are themselves also viewed as linguistic constructions, fabricated in analysis. They are not viewed as "reality," which is itself always an interpretation ultimately embedded in linguistic structures. The premises of an innovative theory of literary interpretation can already be detected here.

In post-structuralism, knowledge of the world derives from the interaction between a primary, originally contentless, subjectivity and a language that pre-exists the user of it, which generates the "self" ("ego"). Since language determines what is (thought to be) known, rather than serving as the medium through which knowledge independent of language is publicly expressed, traditional philosophical "solutions" lose their ground. That an ordered, objectively knowable reality imposes itself on the mind, as Locke believed, through a mechanistic sensation or perception cannot be verified, in this view: "I don't believe there is any perception," Derrida has said ("Structure, Sign, and Play" 272). That the order of language might somehow correspond to the order of reality, even if it does not objectively "describe" reality, likewise cannot be substantiated. Even the belief that basic sensation yields a chaos or disorder that language orders cannot be said to be a fundamental truth, since words like "chaos" and "disorder" are themselves but members of a linguistic system. Lastly, even the understanding that philosophical systems are ultimately ungrounded in truth is not itself an encompassing truth; that very understanding is but another configuration of language. To call the structuralists or the post-structuralists "idealists" is therefore not accurate, since idealism presupposes a use of language that yields truth, the meta-language of philosophy. We have argued that the early structuralists are empiricists, which might also be said, with reservations, of Lacan and Foucault; and we will call post-structuralism, as an integration, a skepticism since—and it is Derrida we have specifically in mind—all truth is eventually undermined. No longer does philosophy, Paul Ricoeur's "vigilant watchman" of philosophical discourse, have privileged access to truth.

The strongest and most evident bond between the post-structuralists and the structuralists is their agreement that the self (the subject, mind, ego, cogito) is not a Cartesian-like entity but is constituted, and that this constitution is by and in language. Structuralism, however, is a theory of human *intellect* (reason, understanding, cognition, thought), which causes it to be a "synchronic," ahistorical theory whose structures are related transformationally, topologically, rather than causatively. Time is factored out, as in an algebra or taxonomy; what are identified are structural and functional resemblances (as in the structure of all narrative or the function of all poetry), rather than sequential determination. At the same time, the content of intellect, which is equated with the self, is in structuralism determined by language or language-like social structures, which makes structuralism a philosophic determinism. That is, it presupposes a behind-the-scenes mechanical causality, which it cannot demonstrate because it assumes the validity of the scientific method rather than demonstrating it, which of course science itself is not obliged to do. As a "synchronic" mathematics can be applied to a "diachronic" astronomy, so do the structuralists attempt to apply the synchronic system of language to humans, who, like the heavens, exist in time.

The post-structuralists reinstall time into the theory of language and self by identifying as primary not intellect, but *desire*. Subjectivity, being desire, then becomes generative, not merely receptive. The subject, or ego, that which is generated, can be constituted over time; it becomes a process (as it was to Freud), not simply a product. Derrida recognizes that structuralism does not "permit the conceptualization of intensity or force" (*Writing and Difference* 27). This important shift of theory accounts for the role given to generativity in post-structuralism. It has earlier been mentioned that even the classic empiricists needed to assume a basic human desire in order for behavior to be activated, to provide the human system with causative energy. In structuralism, the synchronic properties of structure can be allied with (but not, as we have seen, equated with) formalism, including an atemporal formalist literary criticism. Foucault, Lacan, and Althusser, however, all require the reality of history. The interactions of discourse are time-bound. The static binary opposition of Saussure or Jakobson is replaced by a productive binary dialectic. (Derrida will attempt to account for time by having it produced within the system of signification, a complexity that will be addressed later on.) If the interactions of discourse are time-bound, a formalist literary criticism, a "new" New Criticism, can be linked to literary history (a generative intertextuality), and desire as a productive force can be used to readmit "creativity" into critical theory.

The promotion of desire and creativity does not, of course, solve the philosophical issue of "freedom." Freud was a determinist, as was, eventually, Marx. In European post-structuralism, the term "free" is not incompatible with determinism, for it refers to a certain bounded psychic and social space—a "space" that is the primary metaphor of post-structuralism—in which desire has limited free (unconstricted) room to operate. This is not the same as "free will," if the term is used to denote a procedure of making personal decisions, free choice, whose causality is free intellect. We have been maintaining that in America the latter concept is confused with the former, and that while post-structuralism has been employed in America as a reaction against determinism, particularly against behaviorism, in Europe it is determinism that becomes reinforced by post-structuralism.

The transition into post-structuralism is marked by the movement from a *linguistic* model to a *literary* model. In the structuralist and post-structuralist critics, language and literature are analyzed as systems of elements that derive their meaning from the overall system whose unity they constitute. For the structuralists, however, although the systemic relations determine the significance of any element, the methodological approach is to demonstrate how the system is built up of elements (phonemes, words, narrative functions, etc.), which is the basic presumption of an empiricist science: that the whole can be explicated as a unified assemblage of its parts. We have already discussed the difficulties this engenders in moving from the primary elements of literary works to the embracing meaning of literary works, since at some point a line is surreptitiously crossed between non-meaning and meaning. In a "literary" model, the whole is greater than its parts; and the methodology begins with a *presumed* systemic unity and proceeds to a disentangling of elements, rather than vice versa. The analysis can never be exhaustive: some meaning is always left over, left unfathomed, unaccounted for. The analysis always has some unfilled "space"; vacancies are found in the predicated unity of any text.

As a consequence, the emphasis in literary criticism changes from "sign" to "text," from "language" to "discourse." And not only in literary criticism, for all forms of discourse come to be seen as textual, as literature, analyzable in terms of a "rhetoric," not infrequently based upon a "classic" rhetoric, such as that of Quintilian. Literary criticism becomes a model for all criticism. If, for example, speech, to Derrida, is subsumed in "writing," then its reception becomes "reading" (interpretation) rather than "listening." In post-structuralism, the bottom of analysis, however, is never reached because the "subject" performing the analysis is himself, in fact, constituted by the very object under observation, language. As the critic proceeds, the light sooner or later dims. Ultimate origins, first causes, experiential "immediacy," the couplings between signifiers and signifieds, retreat even as we begin to sense their nearness.

We have already seen how Culler attempts to transform structuralism into reading theory based on "convention." We have said that the most significant role of Barthes for American literary criticism is as a mediator between structuralism and a reading theory more palatable to American critics, as when he writes, in *Critique et vérité*, that literary language is "enigmatic . . . and the critic composes rather than recovers the sense of it" (qtd. in Davidson 33). Deconstruction in America is as well a reading theory, one that goes well beyond Culler and Barthes and claims a post-structuralist alliance that we need to explore further.

While the New Critics, to generalize, believed that the immanent meaning of a poem was obtainable with a degree of surety equivalent to the rigor of the critical method, the new reading theorists will demonstrate that meaning is not contained in the text itself but created by the confrontation of text and reader: meaning is not discovered *in* the text, but is effectuated by the reading of it.

In post-structuralism the metaphor of "space" assumes substantial importance. At significant points in the various theories, there is a reliance on a "space" to provide the room for subjectivity to *generate* meaning. This space becomes the site for the operations of "time"; as a consequence, time can be reintegrated into formal notions of structure, which in early structuralism have a spatial but not a temporal dimension. Derrida's *différance* has both a spatial ("differing") and temporal ("deferring") aspect. This metaphorical space originally opens up between Saussure's signifier and signified as the bond between the two weakens. (And one might recall Henri Bergson's theory, in *Time and Free Will*, that time is conceptually spatialized in Western thought as points along an infinite line.) Into this originally linguistic space is set, depending on the author, the concept of "man" (Foucault), the human ego (Lacan and Althusser), "being" and knowledge (Derrida), as well as, in literary criticism, the indeterminacy of texts, interpretation, the psyche of the reader, social conventions, and the gaps inside language itself between words and meaning, between reference and rhetoric, between texts themselves, and between tropes, devices, logic, and intention.

Foucault: The Order of Things

In "classical" thought, before the end of the eighteenth century—according to Michel Foucault in *The Order of Things* (*Les Mots et les choses*, 1966; English translation, 1970; cited hereafter as *OT*)—the representational quality of language was not questioned, and the knowledge of man's mind, his situation in nature, and his limitations assumed its place in an encompassing systematic, tabular, ordering of knowledge. (Of relevance here is "the great chain of being" examined by Arthur Lovejoy [1936].) Knowledge was the totality of observation classified and categorized through the medium of a language, taken as a system of referential signs connected by logical operations, suitable to represent external reality. Classical thought was, accordingly, not "ever able to know man as he is posited in modern knowledge," as "a being such that knowledge will be attained in him of what renders all knowledge possible" (*OT* 318).

Knowledge, following a "fundamental event" in the late eighteenth century, becomes a function of humanity, which generates knowledge rather than merely uncovers it: "there is a nature of human knowledge that determines its forms" (*OT* 319). Accordingly, knowledge becomes formally dependent upon the human constitution. "The rightful limitations of acquired knowledge . . . are at the same time the concrete forms of existence" (248), which themselves can only be known within those same limitations. In the earlier "table" of knowledge, the "*activity* of human beings in constituting the table could not itself be represented," and once the need to account for this activity is recognized, "man, who was once himself a being among others, now is a subject among objects" (Dreyfus and Rabinow 20 and 28). Man becomes "he who ties together all the interlacing threads" of knowledge (*OT* 248), and this activity is itself the form and boundary of knowing.

The "fundamental event" is the "withdrawal of knowledge and thought outside the space" in which language had previously been granted full representational status; and it is contained in the "Kantian critique," which "marks the threshold of our modernity" (*OT* 242). As an "archaeologist," Foucault is unearthing a replacement of one *episteme* by another. In the *Archaeology of Knowledge* (1969; English translation, 1972), Foucault defines an episteme as "the total set of relations that unite, at a given period, the discursive practices that give rise to epistemological figures, sciences, and possibly formalized systems of knowledge." The change in episteme—a notion which might be compared, although it has much broader scope, to Kuhn's "paradigm"—is "paralleled by an accompanying genesis of consciousness" (*OT* 71).

The reason for such a shift is not readily explicable: Foucault leaves "the problem of causes to one side" (*OT* xiii). Consequently, it is not quite accurate for Jean-Marie Benoist to say that Foucault elucidates "the systems of rules and systematic distinctions which *account for* the transition from one episteme to another" (*The Structural Revolution* [1978]; emphasis added). Demonstrating sequence is not to show cause.

The modern episteme arises when "*non-representable realities*" are discovered, when it is asked "what lies in the depth behind" the appearance and apparent organization of the world (Cooper [1981] 46; emphasis added). Addressing economics, biology, and language, Foucault finds that "labor, life, and language" in the new episteme "appear as so many 'transcendentals' which *make possible* the objective knowledge of living beings. . . . In their being they are outside knowledge, but by that very fact they are conditions of knowledge" (*OT* 244; emphasis added).

Foucault demonstrates that in the theory of language (and all other signs) used in the episteme of the sixteenth century, which preceded the "classical" episteme, signification consisted of three components: the "marked" object (in modern terms, the signified), the "marker" (the signifier), and a presumed resemblance between the two. "Resemblance" was essential in all disciplines of study; knowledge seemed unverifiable without some "real" link between marked and marker. Following the exchange of epistemes, the appearance of the classical, which lasts through the seventeenth and eighteenth centuries, this concept of resemblance disappears; it is replaced by a theory of representational language. In the next change of episteme, at the end of the eighteenth century—by which time human activity becomes the condition not only for the existence of knowledge but also for its form— there is a disappearance of the possibility of considering language solely as a representational (denoting) structure, as an assemblage of conventional symbols operated upon by the mechanisms of a (basically Aristotelian) logic functioning to represent directly the reality presented through the senses. Language acquires its own internal systematic structural integrity, which is distinct from the "use" of language. "The dimension of the purely grammatical" emerges: "Language consists no longer only of representations and sounds that in turn represent the representations" (OT xxx). Language becomes "no longer linked to the knowing of unequivocal things," through direct representation, and gains "an historical depth" (Cooper 53). A language "consists also of formal elements, grouped into a system, which impose upon the sounds, syllables, and roots an organization that is not representation" (OT 235). That is, the internal structure of language becomes prominent as the properties and functions of "finite" humankind (the invented "man") become the formal architecture of knowledge.

From the perspective taken in this study, Foucault attempts to create a coherent "modern" episteme where none exists. The modern outlook, at least in philosophy, as we have stressed throughout this study, has evolved from the disparities between empiricism, which both supports the scientific method and leads to skepticism, and Kantian and post-Kantian idealism (including its influence on Romanticism). The reconciliation of the two, or their replacement by a more encompassing system that accounts for them both, is the project of Hegel and, later, the phenomenologists; it has proven unsuccessful. Foucault writes from the viewpoint of French culture, in which none of the major philosophical events (nor those in economics or science) took place. His modern episteme seems, at root, an attempted integration, a harmonizing, on French territory of disparate importations. From the Anglo-American perspective the model is inapplicable. The British empiricism of the beginning of the eighteenth century remains the fundamental philosophical disposition in England and America. The Kantian revolution in philosophy, central to Foucault and Continental philosophy, has consistently met with rejection, not integration, although we have tried to illustrate how it emerged indirectly, using the impact of Romanticism on American literary criticism as the example, as a "check" upon the deterministic consequences of empiricism.

Despite the extensiveness with which Foucault treats language as "representation," an order of logically organized signifiers, he does not deal with the British empiricists at all. The approach, however, clearly takes its most influential form in Western culture from them. Consequently, only by showing how the modern episteme differs somewhat from orthodox Kantianism (by slightly adjusting his episteme) can Foucault show how the episteme "explains the appearance of a positivism" (*OT* 245), the very positivism that characterizes, in his description, nineteenth-century language theory, which is in fact more readily explicable by the evolution of empiricism.* The nineteenth-century philologists and the twentieth-century linguists cannot, by Foucault's means, be made colleagues of Kant. We have already remarked on the concept of the "arbitrary" association of signified and signifier in Saussure, whose concept of the sign is an empiricist compromise, and on the space that eventually opens between signifier and signified, a space pried open by what we see as a form of skepticism (the waning of the signified). Admittedly, it is a skepticism that must take into consideration (though never yielding to) the work of Kant, which, obviously, Hume did not have to do. When Foucault addresses the severance of language and reality, skepticism is ignored. Foucault's modern episteme is at bottom the influence of Kant on the history of philosophy; more specifically, the influence of Kant on phenomenology in France. That episteme is a local fabrication of unity and coherence, crafted to hold conflicting forces that contend throughout European and Anglo-American thought in an unresolved tension by the citation of sources that must frequently appear to a non-French reader as esoteric and provincial.

Whether there is epistemic change or whether Foucault's version of it is correct is a separate matter from his influence on post-structuralism.

---

*Timothy Reiss, who acknowledges Foucault as the source of his method, has done just such a study in *The Discourse of Modernism* (1982). He demonstrates how "a discursive order is achieved on the premise that the 'syntactic' order of semiotic systems (particularly language) is coincident both with the logical ordering of 'reason' and with the structural organization of a world given as exterior to both these orders. This relation is not taken to be simply one of analogy, but one of identity" (31). This description refers to the modern "analytico-referential" discourse. Persons central to the very wide-ranging discussion are Francis Bacon, Kepler, and Galileo; Hobbes and Locke are also cited numbers of times. The impressive application of method by Reiss, while reliant on Foucault for an initial inspiration, is distinctly embedded in the very empiricist tradition that Foucault circumvents.

J. G. Merquior, for example, argues that Foucault's theory is not "a proper story" (71), since the "monolithic" nature of the purportedly successive but hardly interactive epistemes yields a "watertight view of epistemological breaks" (62). What is important, however, is to understand, first, that in describing a displacement of frameworks, in each of which humankind is differently defined, Foucault is not accounting for the processes by which the content of human consciousness is constructed; this was the project of Lévi-Strauss and other structuralists, and of Lacan, Althusser, and Derrida. While Foucault can, he believes, show that "man" (as a generic term, "humankind") as we now conceive of it was "invented" at the end of the eighteenth century, this archaeology is not to advocate, at least not as a logical necessity, the structuralist epistemology. Foucault calls those who classify him as a structuralist "half-witted," with "tiny minds" (*OT* xiv). A structuralist, as we have seen, must account for the formation of the content of *individual* consciousness. In addition, for the structuralists the "conditions" of meaning are the properties (the elements) of language (or literature, myth, social institutions). These are discoverable through an empiricist methodology and are not, as for Foucault, subsumed within the influence of a Kantian transcendental metaphysics.

Foucault's conclusions are, however, "*post*-structuralist" because they lend, by their own route, support to the critique of early structuralism, calling into question the possibility of objective knowledge and of an independent subject for whom knowledge is an acquisition. If knowledge can "take up residence in a new space" (*OT* 217), then— whether Foucault is *methodologically* a structuralist or not—knowing as a human function is made relational. To demonstrate that the belief in representational language is an impermanent one is also, as Foucault admits, to forsake the idea that we can objectively come to know a reality that precedes the discourse that purportedly reveals it. And in Foucault, as in Derrida, even his own discourse cannot find some privileged center, some meta-linguistic ground that privileges its own analysis. Hayden White goes as far as to say that Foucault follows Nietzsche "in the perception of the 'madness' of all 'wisdom' and the 'folly' of all 'knowledge,' " ("Foucault" 81). This forsaking of wisdom will, as a primary consequence, in John Rajchman's analysis, force us to dissociate our hopes from "realizing our essences," an impossible realization whose possibility was constructed by the nineteenth-century "utopian" imagination. Foucault, to be sure, frequently displays an impatience or exasperation with "humanist" views.

If discourse functions "within the regulated exchange of the episteme" and if archaeology "does not refer to a 'subject,' 'mind,' or 'thought' that evidently gave rise to discourse," then "man is unable to account for the formations or transformations of his discourse" (Leitch [1983] 50-52). In *The Order of Things* we find the post-structuralist perspective but without the structuralist methodology. Foucault himself comes to recognize that this perspective is implicated in *The Order of Things*: by the time of the preface to the English edition, he reflects that if the history of science is "the whole spontaneous movement of an anonymous body of knowledge," then it might be asked "whether the subjects responsible for discourse are not determined," and he rejects any approach that would lead to a "transcendental consciousness" (*OT* xiii-xiv).

The use of the spatial metaphor, the rhetorical center of post-structuralism, is a quite powerful one, perhaps related to an early tradition that God created the world by withdrawing from the plenum of Himself and leaving an empty space, in which creation could occur.

Foucault's most ingenious tactic in *The Order of Things* is to propose that "man" in the modern sense was created in the "space" created by the severance between language and representation. At the same time, this metaphorical "space" between word and object, signified and signifier, will be exactly the same place where others will insert the creativity, indeterminacy, and infinite possibility of language, as well as the creation of self. The creation of "man"—by which Foucault at first says he does *not* mean the growth and constitution of the *individual* psyche—and the creativity of language are intermixed together in post-structuralism into theories of the evolution of personal subjectivity as a linguistic phenomenon. What is, for Foucault, a theoretical space in which "man" can be *placed* becomes the same space, in Lacan and Derrida, in which individual subjectivity can be *generated*. When Said accuses Foucault of "reducing the originality of any writer he reads to a deliberate accident occurring within the latent, ordered possibilities of all language" (*Beginnings* 294), he is straddling the line between determinism as it might apply to a transfer of epistemes and a psychological determinism. The two are related but not identical. Similarly, when White quotes Foucault to the effect that "man composed his own figure in the interstices of that fragmented language" ("Foucault" 101), there is no clear distinction between "man" in general as a philosophical concept and the subjectivity of one specific person as a psychological concept. Foucault likely believes in determinism in both domains; but our point here is that the union between them is only a shared metaphor, that of "space." That very metaphor is the foundation for almost all of what is called "post-structuralism." Reading theory will situate interpretation in this very same space.

The confusion between "man" (humankind) and "a man" (a person) is not Said's or White's alone; it is what makes Foucault's work, which is basically a history of ideas as artifacts (as archaeological objects), appear to be so much more. At critical points we detect a shift from history to epistemology, not accompanied by an announcement of intentions. To Foucault, in *The Order of Things*, linguistics is not merely one science among others viewing the same set of facts, as human behavior can be examined within psychology or biology. Linguistics offers "the principle of a *primary* decipherment"; for linguistic analysis is "constitutive of its very object" (397; emphasis added). That the function of language may itself constitute the object of discourse is at the least a skeptical and at the most a Kantian-like critique of knowing; and Foucault begins to use such a critique as if it were a way of talking *about* epistemes (a critical meta-language), rather than simply a component of one (historical) episteme. He does ultimately give his archaeology a privileged epistemological vantage point, which allows him to make such statements as "men believe that their speech is their servant and do not realize that they are submitting themselves to its demands" (297). To say that men believe one thing while another is the case is, however, to put forth the possibility of the very kind of "truth" that is simultaneously being subverted. And where Foucault himself seems to admit that truth is not ultimately knowable, the admission is based on a "truth" revealed by insights into language.

Foucault is, of course, not alone in this dilemma, which is fundamental also to the theory of ideology in Althusser. It is the dilemma inherent in Marxism, in which a consciousness constituted by social institutions—by language (not economics) to the structuralists—is exhorted to gain an overview of itself. Derrida will acknowledge that there is no choice but to continue to write, accepting the dilemma, within the very "logocentric" schema that one must disassemble. The language of human knowledge becomes only the knowledge of human language. In an interview recorded in *Tel Quel* at about the time when he was writing *The Order of Things*, Foucault stated, "A number of us, I think, including myself, consider that reality does not exist, that only language exists" (qtd. in Cooper 28).

In *The Order of Things*, the opening of a linguistic "space" that is presented as an event in the *history* of philosophy and language theory is rhetorically transformed into an *epistemological* "emptiness" or "vacancy," which once was filled by the ground of knowledge (God, perhaps) and the soul, essence, or self of the individual. Within that space is now "Desire, Law, and Death, which outline, at the extremity of analytic language and practice, the concrete figures of finitude" (*OT*

378). Critics who focus upon the historical (archaeological) aspect can assert that Foucault is reinstating time into structuralism: language "activates a complex historical archive" (Leitch 149), and Foucault's work "may well lead to the recovery of a regard for historical scholarship" (Butler [1984] 136). On the other hand, critics who emphasize Foucault's apparent reevaluation of the possibility of truth can assert that he undermines or evades historical knowledge: if history is but one form of knowledge, then one cannot "expect to understand the links between those forms of thought historically" (Jameson, *Prison-House* 194). Either view is supportable by the text, by the multiple configurations of Foucault's "space."

Foucault's comments on literature in *The Order of Things* are deployed to illustrate a consequence of the dispossession of one episteme by another. In the sixteenth century, the words of a language are thought to stand in a relation of "resemblance" to things. "Language is not an arbitrary system; it has been set down in the world and forms a part of it" (*OT* 35); and the way in which words are "linked together and arranged in space . . . reconstitute the very order of the universe" (38). In the succeeding classical episteme, the function of language is "representational," and the bond between a sign and what it signifies needs to be questioned, explained. Consequently, "the profound kinship of language with the world was thus dissolved" (43).

When *Don Quixote* appeared, as the sixteenth-century episteme was drawing to a close, the integrative "resemblance" of language and the world had been eroded: "similitudes have become deceptive." Yet, according to Foucault, one can hear a "deeper discourse, which recalls the time when words glittered in the universal resemblance of things" (47). In the seventeenth and eighteenth centuries, during which "the art of language was a way of 'making a sign,' " signification (through representation) characterized literature: classical literature "really was composed of a signifying element and a signified content" (43-44).

In the nineteenth century, language, severed from any necessary representation of reality, becomes an autonomous system in its own right, with its own structural genealogy (a "history"). Then "literature as such" emerges. Literature becomes "a *particular* language . . . the untamed imperious being of word . . . a manifestation of a language which has no other law than that of affirming" its own "existence" (299-300; emphasis added). We can relate this notion to Kant's esthetics, which we will address during the discussion of Derrida. But this is also Foucault's link to early structuralist literary criticism—both to Russian Formalism and, especially, to Jakobson's "poetic function" that "focuses on the message for its own sake" ("Linguistics and Poetics" 93)—although Foucault's own literary comments in the mid-1960s are based, like his analysis of "man," on the "space" that opens up in language as early structuralism weakens.

It is not in *The Order of Things* but in Foucault's *Raymond Roussel*, written shortly before it, that some theoretical statements on writing can be located. Roussel's work demonstrates that literary style is not intended "to duplicate the reality of another world, but by means of the spontaneous redoublings of language, to *discover* an unsuspected space and to *recover* therein things never yet said." The space at the heart of language is evidence of "an absolute vacancy of being, which it is necessary to invest, master, and fill up by pure invention" (both quotations are addressed by White, "Foucault" 87.

We have already become familiar with this "space." It is through Derrida as well as Foucault that it will influence American literary critics. This approach to literary theory in Foucault does not last, although it is significant for our purposes because it is during these years that Foucault comes closest to centering himself within the transitional developments of structuralist thought. His later work on prisons (*Discipline and Punish*) and on sexuality (*The History of Sexuality*)—like his earlier work on the clinic (*Birth of the Clinic*) and on insanity (*Madness and Civilization*)—focuses upon the relationship between discourse and power, combining Nietzsche on power and Marx on ideology. This work is no longer affiliated with structuralism, which by the mid-1970s is, in any case, no longer a movement.

Because of the prompt availability of his work in translation, Foucault's influence on Anglo-American literary criticism has been to reinforce the early structuralist concepts of language as an autonomous system, of the individual as constituted by language, and of language as severed from any reality beyond that which it itself creates. His writings have also served as a transition to, rather than the source of, the most radical consequences of such beliefs.

Lacan: Language and the Unconscious

For Jacques Lacan, as for Foucault, the humanist concept of self has become inapplicable and outmoded (for synopses of Lacan, see Ragland-Sullivan [1986]; Lemaire [1977]; Bowie [1979]). Lacan will contend that the self, conscious and unconscious, is a linguistic construction, the imposition of language on desire.

"Subjectivity" (consciousness) before language, before the creation of a "subject," is, in Lacan's psychology, pure desire, a desire which, as in Freud's model, is thwarted in early childhood, rendered unable to express itself with absolute freedom. The mechanism of this constraint is initiated by "the name of the father," representing "law" (the coercion of power), a concept corresponding to the Oedipus complex. When about one year old, the pre-linguistic child, not yet subject or ego, having observed itself (literally) in a mirror, gains, intuits, an image of itself as a unified being, "an ideal unity" (*Ecrits* [1966; English translation, 1977] 19; cited hereafter as *E*). The child "imagines" itself as a unity, an entity. Since the child is, at that point, still weak and dependent, "toddling," there is a discrepancy between the intuition of "ideal" unity (self sufficiency) and the present dependency, and the mirror image is "invested with all the original distress resulting from the child's intra-organic and relational discordance" (*E* 19). This discrepancy is a gap, a lack, a rupture, between the imagined unification and the current absence of it. When the constraints and confinements of primary desire are imposed by the "name of the father" (the significance of the father or the phallus, rather than the physical person or organ), there is an external demand that the child configure desire to conform to these constraints. This configuration, occurring in the space of the gap or lack, is the subject, an ego, *created by* a language that pre-exists the child and that accordingly determines not only how the world shall in the future be known but also what the knower, the subject, *is*. The child must enter the Symbolic Order, the order of language, which then constitutes both the subject and the knowledge of the subject. "The law of man has been the law of language" (*E* 61). Since this formative imposition of language is repressive, a domination of pre-linguistic desire by the social institution of language, an "unconscious" is formed simultaneously with consciousness, with ego. This unconscious, coeval with consciousness, is as well a linguistic form. "The appearance of language is simultaneous with the primal repression which constitutes the 'unconscious'" (Lemaire 53). Furthermore, and most significantly, since the language that constitutes the subject is imposed upon the child by others, the subject itself is a construction fashioned only in relation to otherness, to the Other. "The subject is spoken rather than speaking" (*E* 71). To misunderstand this, to hold to the belief in an objective, autonomous, free entity of Cartesian-like self, a self permanently separated from not-self (the other), is "the most profound alienation . . . in our scientific civilization" (70). The subject, for Lacan, has existence only insofar as it continually addresses itself to an other. "What I seek in speech is the response of the other. What constitutes me as a subject is my question" (86).

Notably, "the semiotization of Freud" has been called "the signal accomplishment of the sixties" (MacCannell and MacCannell [1982]

37). Whether Lacan's theory is correct cannot be debated here. What is germane, for our purposes, is that the creation of self, of the subject, occurs in a "space," which corresponds to that space in which Foucault places the creation of "man"—a space not only, in Lacan, between subjectivity as desire and its image of unity, or between desire and its object that has been rendered unobtainable (the mother), but also between language and the world (any proposed "objective" reality), the space that Foucault describes opening in the nineteenth century when the notion of language as "representation" dissolves. "When the subject takes the place of the lack," Lacan has said, "a loss is introduced in the word, and this is the definition of the subject" ("Structure as an Inmixing" 193).

This much-utilized "space" in post-structuralism can be traced back, to reiterate, to the untenability in Saussure's definition of the sign as a bonded signifier and signified. Lacan represents the Saussurian sign as numerator and denominator in an algebraic fraction, as S/s, the signifier "over" the signified. He then asks what the "bar" in the fraction represents, only to find that it is "a barrier resisting signification" (E 149). Since the signified cannot be described, discussed, or explained without resorting to more language, "no signification can be sustained other than by reference to another signification" (150). What language refers to is itself. Once again, any knowledge about what reality might be outside of language is unobtainable—as post-structuralist literary critics will declare. Even to posit such a "knowledge," a knowledge existing but beyond our reach, is to fail to understand that the inquiring subject as well as the object of inquiry are both constituted within the very language of inquiry. There is an "incessant sliding of the signified under the signifier" (154); the signified is forever evasive.

In Lacan, then, the self, subject, is formed in what is for post-structuralism a multipurpose space: a linguistic gap; a psychic incompleteness in the quest for unity; and a separation between desire and its object. Lacan cannot, as he admits, say what the "bar" is between signified and signifier. It turns out to be, in fact, no-thing, nothing at all, the empty place where, as in Foucault and Derrida, generation and creativity can occur. This space is a figure of speech, a word that denotes what cannot be denoted, cannot be named; it serves the same function as Derrida's différance. "The lack of the lack makes the real," says Lacan, "which emerges only there, as a cork" (Four Fundamental Concepts of Psycho-Analysis ix). Such space cannot be a scientific concept; it is the gap, consequently, where we find that skepticism must be situated.

Although a Kantian-like metaphysics might also be placed here, such a move is obviously unappealing to Anglo-Americans, who in literary criticism will use Lacan as if he is either a supporter of deconstruction, for whom this metaphysical space has become the limitations of figural speech, or a psychoanalyst, for whom this space has become simply absence.

For Lacan, however, the theory of desire is clearly a larger philosophical issue. He recognizes that Spinoza sought to escape from the domination of desire by permeating everything that exists with the "universality of the signifier," with the one substance that Spinoza names God. Desire in Spinoza becomes manageable, conquerable, incapacitated, by looking at it from the vantage point of a fundamental truth, a "center" (what Derrida will call both a "center" and a "transcendental signified") that grounds all other truth. Lacan, obviously, cannot follow Spinoza. "Kant is truer"; his theory is one of "desire in its pure state," by which, we gather, Lacan means that for Kant human knowledge is created by and through human activity, from which it is inseparable. Nevertheless, even Kant would have us control desire by a more firmly grounded understanding (his transcendental signified is Reason), an impossible procedure, in Lacan's theory, since the control of desire through external imposition has created the subject in the first place (the discussion is in *Four Fundamental Concepts* 275). Interestingly, Lacan nowhere mentions Schopenhauer, whose primary "Will"—clearly a source of Freud's "drive" theory—is Lacan's "desire" reified as a universal force.

Lacan states in *Ecrits* that the ego cannot be found in a "false recurrence to infinity of reflexion," that the ego "is a topological phenomenon whose distribution in nature is as sporadic as the dispositions of pure exteriority that condition it" (*E* 134). We take this to be equivalent to Hume's confession that, when he reflected upon consciousness, he found only the mobile, ever-changing contents of consciousness and no permanent substratum of self. John Llewelyn observes that, according to Husserl, Hume's inability to "get a firm hold on the difference between psychology and phenomenology" caused him to turn to skepticism rather than to what might have been a phenomenology (Llewelyn, 16). From our point of view, Lacan's qualification of Kant is, then, a resurgence, admittedly in a phenomenological environment, of Humean philosophy, of skepticism.

The psychoanalytic theory of Lacan can be variously utilized in literary criticism, and Lacan appears in the literature of critical theory in diverse contexts. Lacan himself is not a literary critic. There is, however, a well-known article ("Seminar") in which he analyzes Edgar Allan Poe's

"The Purloined Letter." Poe's story is based upon a letter whose contents are never revealed. Twice stolen in similar circumstances, it is both times placed in an unconcealed location: the first time because the attempt to hide it in full view of those in the room would arouse suspicion, and the second time because hiding it in a secret place would be, for the detectives who are looking for it, more obvious than leaving it in open view on a desk. Although the article is at critical points written in Lacan's most perplexing style, the best interpretation seems to be that for him the letter represents a "signifier" whose "signified" (the content) is, like language itself, hidden, elusive, and presumed rather than known (cf. Belsey 140-43; Barbara Johnson's *The Critical Difference* contains an article on Lacan, Derrida, and Poe). The letter, then, is used as a "floating" signifier; it moves from one person to another, corresponding in function to language, which is fundamentally the exchange of signifiers between speakers and listeners who are bonded by the signifiers of language that have created their selves, egos, in the matrix of Others. "The Purloined Letter" becomes an allegory of Lacanian linguistic theory.

Lacan's speculations, however, can be given a wider application to literary criticism. First, they may serve as a foundation for a theory of both the writer and the narrator. "No discourse . . . is ever addressed to anyone but the good listener." (In the therapeutic environment, it is the psychoanalyst who serves this function as listener.) "The Other is, therefore, the locus in which is constituted the I who speaks to him who hears" (*E* 141). This "I," which a person uses to refer to himself, is an objectification of the subject; it is not itself equivalent to the subject, who, being constituted by language, cannot unequivocally be signified by it. "Discourse of self, then, is a perpetually distanced speech, emptied of the real, elusive subject" (Said, *Beginnings* 299). The subject is "in effect represented in symbolism which may be the personal pronoun 'I' " (Lemaire 88). This suggests two approaches: analyses of the "I" of the poet in lyric poetry and of the narrator in fiction. In both cases the critic might demonstrate how the authorial "I" is derived from authorial subjectivity, or how the creation of the "author" as well as of the narrator rests upon the expected reception of the reader. Such an approach is related to Iser's "implied reader" and to Barthes's description of the "death" of the author in *Image/Music/Text*, but with the added dimension that the existence of the reader, as listener, can participate in causing the actual coming into existence of the self of the writer and his narrative surrogates.

Second, as a corollary, Lacan's thesis might be used to account for the existence of the reader, by viewing the process of reading as analogous to the primary construction of self. Esthetic effect might be explained as the undergoing of a re-creative transformation.

Third, having come into the order of language through an initial force of repression and an alienation of the object of desire, the subject, the self, trapped in the language that composes it, may be said to move along a theoretically unending linguistic chain of signifiers. While from one point of view (Eagleton's Marxism, or Jameson's) this entrapment is an unhappy idea, it can also lend support to a literary criticism that takes joy in the infinite progression, the never-ending possibility, the "pleasure of the text" that is Barthes's ultimate position and that we find, too, in Hartman.

Fourth: since in Lacan *all* language resembles "literary" language and is based upon metaphor and metonymy (recall Jakobson and Halle, *Fundamentals of Language*), his work fits well (as the preceding two paragraphs have perhaps indicated) with deconstruction. There is, for Lacan, no meta-language; there is only "the birth of truth in speech . . . the reality of what is neither true nor false" (*E* 47). We will discuss deconstruction following a review of Derrida.

Fifth: in Lacan the unconscious is a language. This language functions primarily through metaphor and metonymy, which Lacan allies with Freud's "displacement" and "condensation" in dreams. In post-structuralism *all* language, we have said, is like literary language—figures and tropes, rather than direct representation. If "the unconscious is 'like poetry' " (Bowie, "Lacan" 144), then literature can be seen to be structured as, and to some extent generated by, the unconscious. That literature is about the workings of the unconscious is, of course, the premise of decades of psychoanalytic criticism. The approach has traditionally been interpretive, a revelation of the true meaning of a text—not unusually a psychoanalytic autobiography of the author—based on thematic and narrative content, which is a much different matter than either structuralism or post-structuralism.

Some recent Lacanian-based criticism, collected in *The Fictional Father*, edited by Robert Con Davis (1981), continues this interpretive psychoanalytic tradition. In his introduction Davis writes that "since the operations of the psychoanalytic subject and the text are synonymous . . . many of the same laws govern both" (3). In narrative fiction we will therefore find seduction, primal scenes, and castration. The unifying theme in the various essays, Davis continues, is the "absent father"; this absence is correlated with the "lack" or "space" that we have traced in Lacan and others. "The development of narrative . . . is fully dependent on the structural absence that initiates it," the absence of the father (8). The father also appears as the "name of the father" (Lacan's "law"; Davis's example is Zeus in the *Odyssey*). "In short, the father is a 'no,' "—that is, both absence and injunction—"that initiates narrative development" (13). While this type of criticism yields some fine results (as in the earlier work on Faulkner by John Irwin), it remains a search for the underlying meanings of texts, although its emphasis on the text itself as a structure marks a change from the earlier focus on the unconscious of the author. It combines, in an important way (like Lacan's lecture on *Hamlet*, in Felman [1982]), a New Critical methodology with a renewed psychoanalytic perspective.

A sixth application of Lacanian theory concerns feminist literary criticism. Insofar as Lacan accounts for the formation of self, the approach is of particular use in demonstrating how gender identification is created and maintained. Since Lacan understands femininity, like all other aspects of self, "in terms of its construction," a discussion can center explicitly around "the issue of women's relationship to language. In so far as it is the order of language which structures sexuality around the male term [the "phallic term"], . . . or the privileging of that term which shows sexuality to be constructed within language, so this raises the issue of women's relationship to that language and that sexuality simultaneously" (Jacqueline Rose, Introduction to *Feminine Sexuality* [1982] 54; also see Ragland-Sullivan, Chap. 5). The analysis, accordingly, can be applied from a feminist perspective to a disclosure of the ideological and psychological assumptions incorporated into literary structure and character development, as well as to the social reception and function of literary works.

The underlying incompatibility between the concept of self in structuralism and post-structuralism and that concept of self most attractive, generally, to American theorists can be exemplified by Lacan's response to Anglo-American psychoanalytic practice, which he deplores.

The work of Freud, according to Lacan, revealed that "the very center of the human being was no longer to be found at the place assigned to it by a whole humanist tradition" (*E* 114), a tradition that at one point Lacan attributes to "religious hypocrisy" and "philosophical bravado" (175). This humanistic, Cartesian self was retained, as has been discussed, in existentialism, the predominant philosophy in France when Lacan began to lecture; in the 1950s the works of Freud were not readily available in France (Wilden xiii). Lacan's work is meant to contribute to "the final demise of the *cogito* that Husserl, Merleau-Ponty, and Sartre once struggled with" (Wilden 310). In *Four Fundamental Concepts of Psycho-Analysis*, Lacan rejects "the soul, either mortal or immortal, which has been with us for so long" and all other "such simplified notions" (47). He disavows "the philosophical *cogito* ... at the center of the mirage that renders modern man so sure of himself" (*E* 165).

The recent growth of French interest in Freud's work followed after a long French resistance to psychoanalytic thought, an interest that proliferated, as Sherry Turkle documents in *Psychoanalytic Politics*, when theorists in England and in America thought there might be little new to say on the subject. Lacan's "return to Freud" is intended, in some measure, to rectify what he sees as the wayward and erroneous misappropriation of the Freudian texts in England and America. In particular, he condemns "ego psychology," an approach that stresses the inherent (immanent) strengths of the individual ego (the structure of "personality") attempting to adapt to its social surroundings, rather than the function of an ego that has been created merely to mediate between libido and the external environment. Ego-based theory is found in the work of Karen Horney, whom Lacan especially disparages, and Alfred Adler, who in places writes of the "unity" of the individual. Such theories are obviously irreconcilable with Lacan's. Lacan sees the Anglo-Americans as having transformed psychoanalysis into the medicalized "science" that has become the modern Freudian therapeutic establishment—a politically conservative establishment, since "adaption" to the social order is also submission to it.

It is of interest that in the standard English edition of Freud, edited by James Strachey, Freud's *Wunsch* is translated as "wish," which seems to promote the idea of the "individual," while French translators have used the word "*désir*." The German and English words are "limited to individual isolated acts of wishing, while the French has the much stronger implication of a continuous force" (*E*, translator's introduction, viii), the desire so central to Lacan's thought.

In analyzing the American reception of post-structuralism in literary criticism, this issue of self and desire will arise once again.

Lacan's influence has erupted into the Marxist debate concerning self, language, and ideology. Forging a union between Marx and Freud has been a paramount concern for certain writers. Both attribute the contents of conscious to mechanisms of repression—for Freud, the Oedipal repression of sexual libido; for Marx, the repression caused by a capitalistic economics that engenders a "false consciousness," an ideological substitute for an accurate, historically based comprehension of human purpose and function in the economic environment.

In an important study, *Language and Materialism* (1977), Rosalind Coward and John Ellis refer to Marx's concept of the "contradiction" that develops over time within the "relations" of production—the relations, that is, between persons, the classes in which they have membership, and the system of production, the economic system. Contradiction is masked by ideology, whose function is to create in the exploited producer, the worker, a consciousness that conceals this servitude and, in fact, makes the economic structure seem both beneficial and necessary. The psychic consequence of such a false and contradictory belief is alienation, experienced but not understood. The intensifying of contradiction eventually leads (theoretically) to economic upheaval, a replacement of one economic system by another.

For Marx, the contents of consciousness are caused by social institutions, a position we have related to the structuralist epistemology. "Morality, religion, metaphysics, and all the rest of ideology as well as the forms of consciousness corresponding to these," Marx and Engels write in *The German Ideology*, "thus no longer retain the semblance of independence." The "superstructure" of society, the legal and political systems, ultimately depends upon the underlying economic "base" (infrastructure). Consciousness is formed by and operates within this superstructure.

Coward and Ellis point out that the "Marxist account does not show how the contradictory processes of the individual subject are themselves constituted" (78), which is to say that Marx had no theory of psychology. For Coward and Ellis, it is necessary for a theory to account for the "imaginary relations" that construct the subject (his own psychic processes and fabricated self-image), as well as for the "real relations," reflecting the Marxist belief that history and social systems are objectively knowable, for the juxtaposition of these two separate relations yields the "contradiction." Both relations are necessary "if the subject is to produce itself at all"; and "only the articulation of psychoanalysis and Marxism can hope to give an account of such practices" (20). Lacan is of obvious relevance here, and Coward and Ellis, whose theory we cannot pursue further at this point, ground their "materialistic" conception of language on Lacan and the "formative role of the signifier" (100).

The Lacanian hypotheses can consequently augment the Marxist view. They seem allied with the thought of recent Marxists—even if they are not Lacanians—like Chantal Mouffe, for whom "every social agent is . . . the locus of many subject positions" and for whom, accordingly, "a given social agent is always precariously and [only] provisionally fixed" (172). In orthodox Marxism language is customarily identified as part of the superstructure, basically ideological. The work of Lacan demonstrates, on the contrary, that the constitution of the subject is itself language. This finding goes beyond a simple theory of ideology, of language as perpetuating distortion, since the conflictual forces impelling change (including change for the better) emerge in linguistic form, in the space, for Lacan, between desire and the social milieu. "Freed from the orthodox economist insistence on its secondary superstructural role," states Andrew Ross, "ideological practices have increasingly assumed the full significance of the[ir] 'specific effectivity' " (679).

We have earlier argued that structuralism is in part a transmuted Marxism, with the linguistic system given priority over the economic system, and that post-structuralism reinserts time, through desire, as a causal element, which a synchronic structuralism omits: a criticism directed at structuralism by most Marxist critics, a few of whom find a more fertile ground for amalgamation in post-structuralism.

Althusser

Any conciliation with structuralism is, in Marxism, controversial. This is illustrated by the response to Louis Althusser, a portion of whose work can be discussed in a Lacanian context. It has often been recognized that Freud's conceptual terminology is derived from the physics, biology, and economics of the late nineteenth century; the Freudian model is fundamentally "thermodynamic," incorporating the principle of the conservation of energy, and "hydraulic," relying upon a self-contained system of physical forces under pressure. Lacan's chief contribution has been to recast Freud in terms of a theory of language. To Althusser, Lacan has demonstrated that the "transition from (ultimately purely) biological existence to human existence (the human child) is achieved within the law of Order," Lacan's Symbolic Order, which Althusser names the "Law of Culture." "This law of Order is confounded in its *formal* essence with the order of language" (Althusser, *Lenin and Philosophy* [1971] 209; "confounded" here does not mean "confused"). Since the system of language precedes the subject, who is constituted by it, this Order "has been lying in wait for each infant born since before his birth and seizes him . . . assigning to him his place and role, and hence his fixed destination" (211).

The influence of Lacan can be detected in Althusser's essay "Ideology and Ideological State Apparatuses," contained in *Lenin and Philosophy*. Althusser here distinguishes between social apparatuses that are overtly coercive—the police, the courts, the army—and those that have ideologically covert formative influence on the individual—religion, the family, and most significantly, the educational system. These latter, the "ideological state apparatuses," assure that the individuals produced within the economic system, the "labor power," accept the system and work for it willingly, even docilely, unaware of their subjugation. The relation of the individual to the economic and social system, as the individual himself comes to perceive it, is, then, an artificial construction, language in the shape of ideology. Ideology is a "representation of the *imaginary* relationship of individuals to their real conditions of existence" (162; emphasis added), to the "real relations in which they they live" (165).

Since ideology "has the function . . . of constituting concrete individuals as subjects" (171), it plays the same role as language throughout structuralism and post-structuralism, but with a particularly Lacanian aspect. Eagleton remarks that Althusser's ideology serves the function of Lacan's mirror image: it reflects the "imaginary unified image of selfhood" (Eagleton, *Literary Theory* 173). For Althusser, the subject is "called to" or "hailed" by ideology; his response to this solicitation is what defines him, just as addressing and responding to the "other" defines the subject for Lacan. In a religion-based capitalism, for example, subjects are "hailed" as *"free* subjects," which causes them to avow their freedom in the midst of their subjugation and, as a consequence, to "work all by themselves" (*Lenin and Philosophy* 182).

In his "Letter on Art" (also in *Lenin and Philosophy*), which can be incorporated into a Marxist literary criticism and therefore receives praise from Eagleton in *Marxism and Literary Criticism*, Althusser declares that while art is itself produced within an ideological context, nevertheless, it allows us to perceive the nature of its own ideology. (This idea recalls the structuralist concept of literary language calling attention to the message, the code, the devices of language themselves.) With that perception we can move toward a fuller understanding of ideology that, for Althusser, comes through what he calls "scientific" knowledge. By promoting, here and elsewhere, the notion of an ideologically free scientific knowledge, Althusser—who as a Marxist cannot discard the idea of an empirical truth—is, of course, proposing a "meta-language," which post-structuralism in Foucault, Lacan, and Derrida ultimately subverts.

Althusser's approach is customarily praised or attacked by Marxists depending on the critic's attitude towards structuralism, of which Althusser is correctly seen as a representative insofar as he accepts a "linguistic model." It is important to realize that if ideology is given Althusser's definition, then even Marxism itself cannot be said to be free of it, since the self is everywhere a linguistic ideological construct. Benoist praises Althusser because he "has not flinched from denouncing all that long remained ideological in Marx" (*The Structural Revo-*

lution [1978] 32); at the same time, he criticizes Althusser for using psychoanalysis in a manner that leads away from structuralism, which Benoist defends. John Frow also states that Marxism has "the ability to make visible the frame from which its own categories and positions are derived" (*Marxism and Literary History* [1986] 24). On the other hand, Jameson, in his critique of structuralism, disparages Althusser for the philosophically "idealist" character of his thinking: "for Althusser, in a sense, we never really get outside our own minds"; accordingly, "action for him would seem to be a kind of blindfolded operation" (Jameson, *Prison-House* 106 and 108). Adam Schaff, whose book is an extended deprecation, from the viewpoint of an inviolable orthodox Marxism, of Althusser and structuralism, sees Althusser's attribution of ideology to Marxism itself as simply a result of Althusser's unfortunate disillusionment with party politics: Althusser's definition of ideology "makes both that term and the whole discussion based on it to be completely vacuous" (38).

Althusser's integration of a theory of language into his version of Marxism has ultimately had the effect of transforming the perhaps simplified notion of language as (merely) a component of the economically caused superstructure into the idea that language is one of the various components of the social structure that interact in a *mutual* (not a one-way) cause and effect relationship. (The economic component is but one aspect of the interrelationship, not, as it was to Marx, the fundamental causal one.) Such an approach has been particularly welcomed in Britain, where Marxism has been experiencing a revitalization into what Jonathan Arac sees as a newly influential "western Marxism" (*Postmodernism and Politics* [1986] ix). The approach has also gained some strength in the United States (see the essays in Nelson and Grossberg, eds., *Marxism and the Interpretation of Culture* [1988]). Raymond Williams declares that language is itself "a specific structure of social relations" (*Marxism and Literature* [1977] 140); accordingly, "cultural work and activity are not now, in any ordinary sense, a superstructure. . . . On the contrary, they are among the basic processes of the formation itself" (111; also see his "Base and Superstructure"). Chantal Mouffe opposes "the economic view of social evolution as governed by a single economic logic" (173). John Frow similarly reassesses the orthodox base/superstructure categorization: if Marxism is to accept the "challenge" of post-structuralism, it will need to "rethink the status of the dialectic and to build a semiotic politics on the ruins of a [what has been until now] metaphysics" (50).

We have earlier asserted that the Anglo-American effort to preserve the free self, threatened by the ramifications of empiricism, issues in a "humanistic" interpretation of Marx, in which the possibility for humankind to attain its freedom is defended. Fromm and McMurtry have been cited earlier as examples. The writings of those in and influenced by the Frankfurt school, some of whom eventually came to teach in America, would warrant much discussion, space permitting. (For a review of the Frankfort school from Horkheimer to Habermas, see David Held, *Introduction to Critical Theory* [1980].) In lectures given in the United States, Perry Anderson, from England, laments the undermining of the subject's action and role in history by structuralism, which he calls a "corruption of Marxism." Including Althusser in his attack, he finds the emphasis on language in structuralism an "exorbitation of language," which has attenuated the possibility of knowing the truth: "language," he declares, "is no fitting model for any other human practice" ([1984] 37 and 43). A flattering introduction to the volume is, by the way, contributed by Lentricchia.

In discussing both Jameson and Althusser, William Dowling finds that "the endless dismantling of such false structures"—by which he means ideology—"a repeated and hopeful gesture in the direction of that *freedom* that may ultimately be won from Necessity, [has come to] be the distinguishing mark of Jameson's criticism" ([1984] 55; emphasis added). Jameson believes, writes Cornel West, in a "notion of freedom" even if it cannot be "conceptually grasped": in this way meaning is preseved in history ("Ethics and Action" 127). Jameson, himself an American, looks forward to a social order which has "put behind it . . . the implacable *determinism* of an historic logic beyond the control of humanity," to a time when, in addition, bourgeois notions of "autonomous individualism" will also be discarded (*The Political Unconscious* [1981] 393; emphasis added), although Jameson's outlook often seems able to absorb, rather than discard, such notions.

Such speculations in Anglo-American scholarship (whether used in discussions of Althusser or elsewhere) are based, again, on the longstanding confrontation between empiricism and its alternatives, which are found at first appealing but ultimately discouraging. While Dowling may believe that an "infatuation" with nineteenth-century science drew Marxism into a "vulgar empiricism" (99), it is more accurately the case that Marx himself, during his residency in England, moved intentionally further and further away from Germanic metaphysics toward the empiricism that characterizes his later and most influential thought. Marxism is an empiricism, with the unavoidable implications of materialistic determinism, no matter how offensive this may seem to those in the humanist tradition. Structuralism maintains this empiricism; Continental post-structuralism is—from an Anglo-American perspective—the transformation of that empiricism into skepticism, similar to the transition in the eighteenth century. For a Marxist, however, skepticism is not a valid stance. Consequently, figures like Althusser stand *between* structuralism and a thoroughgoing post-structuralism, trying to maintain an uneasy balance between the search for historically based truth and a theory of self—whether in Foucault, Lacan, or, as we shall see, in Derrida—that renders the search futile.

In Foucault, Lacan, and Althusser, then, the essential themes of post-structuralism emerge. In addition to premising language as an autonomous system and the self as a linguistic construct, and as a result challenging the referentiality of language—issues which all were raised in early structuralism—the post-structuralists contribute a theory in which language has become a chain of signifiers rather than a system of Saussurian signs in which each signifier is bound to a specific signified. An empty space opens up within language, and this space becomes of paramount concern. In this space is nothing, no-thing, which nevertheless must be identified, discussed, and described. A generative desire replaces a passively structured mentality, intellect. What had formerly been considered the characteristics of literary or poetic language have come to be the characteristics of all language.

The reception of Foucault, Lacan, and Althusser (though the latter receives significantly less attention) by literary critics hardly does justice to the wide-ranging speculations of these writers. This reception is most often, psychoanalytic criticism aside, a reading of their work in a context in which Derrida is predominant; and the post-structuralist themes will come to be applied to literary criticism in a Derridian format.

CHAPTER EIGHT

Post-Structuralism II: Derrida

In his presentation at the 1966 Johns Hopkins conference, Jacques Derrida remarked that "structuralism justly claims to be the critique of empiricism," while at the same time he pointed to the empiricist assumptions of Lévi-Strauss: the belief in discoverable objective fact (about language and myth), validation, and scientific method ("Structure, Sign, and Play" 259; cited hereafter as "SSP"). During his discussion of Rousseau in *Of Grammatology*, Derrida admits that he himself is striving toward "a certain exteriority in relation to the totality of the age of logocentrism" (in which speech is presumed to correspond to the immediate presence of reality to consciousness). But since he has himself "defined the form and vulnerability of this empiricism," his own method—embedded in the very language he would critique by what might be called a "radical empiricism"—cannot give "methodological or logical . . . assurances": "empiricism destroys itself." Philosophy attempts to produce "truth at the moment when the value of truth is shattered," a process that, accordingly, cannot circumvent "the internal contradictions of skepticism" (*Of Grammatology* [1967; English translation, 1976] 162; cited hereafter as *OG*). Empiricism deconstructs itself.

We have already proposed that structuralism in its original formulation *is* an empiricism—based on the Marxist format in which, although consciousness is constituted, truth can nevertheless be empirically derived (somehow) from analysis. Post-structuralism demonstrates such a belief to be self-contradictory. Foucault, Lacan, and Althusser all retain an empiricist foundation, which their own work then intentionally subverts; each of them presents certain "scientific facts" of the matter (archaeological history in Foucault, psychology in Lacan, the acquisition of belief in Althusser), while offering a model of language and self that is incompatible with a belief in the availability of objective knowledge. This subversion of empiricism is, I have claimed, similar to the philosophical movement from Hobbes and Locke to Berkeley and Hume, from classic empiricism to skepticism. Furthermore, post-structuralism, culminating in Derrida, is this skepticism, which attempts to avoid, despite the accusation in certain critiques of the movement, the lapse into idealism. "The dismantling of logocentrism is simultaneously . . . a deconstruction of idealism" as well as of empiricism (Derrida, *Positions* [1972; English translation, 1981] 51; cited hereafter as *P*).

While many twentieth-century French writers apparently see the history of modern philosophy as consisting of Descartes, then a sizable intermission, then German philosophy from Kant to Heidegger, and finally recent French thought (i.e., themselves), the reception of structuralism and post-structuralism in America must be understood from within the Anglo-American perspective, in which eighteenth-century British empiricism remains fundamental, even into the twentieth century in the work of the positivists and the "ordinary language" philosophers. From this perspective, one wonders why, at a certain moment, philosophical thought in one tradition suddenly becomes pertinent to another. Why have the speculations of Derrida become attractive to American literary critics within *their own* tradition? This is a tradition in which philosophical idealism, Hegel, European phenomenology (with the exception of existentialism), and Marxism have certainly not been the primary issues for literary critics. Rather, the underlying avoidance of the deterministic and materialistic consequences of empiricism and scientific methodology will be emphasized, together with the maintenance of the creative human subject. Those same issues, in fact, account for the appeal of Romanticism for the New Critics.

Language and Truth

For Derrida, the "structures" of reality purportedly discovered by philosophy are meant to account both for the generativity, change, and transmutation that characterize life and the world as it is known to humankind and, as well, for the stable, unchanging ground of the structure itself. In philosophy generally, including recent "structuralism," ontological structure has "always been neutralized or reduced . . . by a process of giving it a center . . . a fixed origin"; the "freeplay" of structure, its generative potential, is "constituted upon a fundamental immobility and a reassuring certitude which is itself beyond the reach of the freeplay" ("SSP" 247-48). The names given to this steadfast center—including essence, existence, being, truth, consciousness, God, and man—designate what Derrida calls "transcendental signifieds," proposed groundings of the reality on which rests existence as we encounter it. Derrida rejects this stable foundation of structure, its "center," for it is substantiated only by the false belief that there is a level at which reality appears to humans directly, with an immediacy of presence.

For Derrida there is a "rupture," following which "the center could not be thought of in terms of a being-present." That rupture can be identified with the "space" Foucault shows opening between language and reality in the modern episteme, as well as with the space, as important to Derrida as to Lacan, between Saussure's "signifier" and "signified." The center has no "natural locus" but is itself a "function" of the structured system, which, since it is always expressed in language, turns out to be language itself ("SSP" 249). The ultimate truth-of-being is, then, unobtainable; and attempts such as Husserl's to reconcile the self-enclosed "totality" of structure with the grounding "origin" and "foundation" of structure are doomed to failure (*Writing and Difference* [1967; English translation 1978] 157; cited hereafter as *WD*). Modern structuralism is a "totalization"; therefore its implications subvert any notions of center. The structuralists themselves did not sufficiently develop the consequences of their theory, having neglected the rudimentary inconsistencies in Saussurian linguistics, inconsistencies that Derrida explicates in *Of Grammatology*.

It is Nietzsche who comprehended that the quest for truth emanates from motives of power impelled by desire, and that metaphysical systems yield not truth but structures of language substituting for truth in the name of truth. Throughout the post-structuralist literature, one encounters Nietzsche's well-known statement from "On Truth and Falsity in Their Extramoral Sense": "What, then, is truth? A mobile array of metaphors, metonyms, and anthropomorphisms—in short, a sum of human relations, which have been enhanced, transposed and embellished poetically and rhetorically, and which after long use seem firm, canonical, and obligatory to a people: truths are illusions about which one has forgotten that this is what they are; metaphors which are worn out." Founded upon language, a systematic philosophy is susceptible to being disassembled—in Derrida's term, "deconstructed"—to expose the rhetoric that supports it, a position Derrida amplifies in "White Mythology" (in *Margins of Philosophy* [1972; English translation, 1982]; cited hereafter as *MP*; the methodology is reviewed and applied in Norris, *The Deconstructive Turn* [1983]). Heidegger, who has substantially influenced Derrida, had insisted "on noting that being is produced as history only through the logos and is nothing outside of it," which indicates that "the difference between signifier and signified is *nothing*" (*OG* 23). Since, for Heidegger, Being emerges as knowable only in language, it is at once made present by words and hidden in the midst of them, a simultaneous revelation and concealment. Nevertheless, as mentioned in an earlier chapter, Heidegger does not, according to Derrida, go far enough. While it is true that for Heidegger, at the utmost extension of phenomenology, "the sense of being is never rigorously and simply a 'signified' " (*OG* 22), he does in places seem to privilege "Being" by locating it in an inaccessible silence beyond the processes of signification. In Heidegger, though certainly not as egregiously as in Husserl (whom Derrida discusses at length in *Speech and Phenomena* [1967; English translation, 1973]), the erroneous assumption of "logocentrism" emerges: Being (reality, existence) and humankind can interface with an existential immediacy and directness, which speech, presumed to be expression in its own immediacy, captures and transmits. Derrida finds such a belief unsupportable: there could never have been "a purity of sensory language" (*MP* 210).

Derrida recognizes, however, that the logocentric tradition, since it encompasses all philosophy from the beginning of history through the present day, cannot simply be dismissed: "we have no language . . . which is alien to this history" ("SSP" 250). We cannot get outside it; we can only wander about in it, exposing inconsistencies, patched up rips, and hidden false assumptions concerning the existence of real signifieds designated by signifiers that point to them. (Derrida's favorable reference to Charles Peirce, for whom "the so-called 'thing itself' is always already a *representamen* shielded from the simplicity of intuitive evidence," is notable [*OG* 49]; Peirce, who rejected the Cartesian self, is customarily the only American philosopher that the European structuralists and post-structuralists hold in high esteem.) Language is an infinitely interwoven fabric (textile, text) of signifiers, of language itself, with no demonstrable power of direct representation or reflection (mimesis) of a reality external to it. "*There is nothing outside of the text*" (*OG* 158). Yet "the difference between signified and signifier belongs . . . to the totality of the great epoch covered by the history of metaphysics." Nothing is conceivable for us" except in the language that we have inherited (*OG* 13), since this very language composes our consciousness itself.

As a consequence, there is no dominating "this stratum of 'tutelary' tropes . . . by what it has itself engendered"; language cannot transcend itself to explain itself, cannot "include under its own laws the totality of the field to which the product belongs" (*MP* 219). This includes, as he admits, Derrida's philosophy as well: even to say that all philosophical language is "metaphorical, resisting every meta-metaphorics" (*MP* 224) is to court the danger of forgetting that even the concept of "metaphor" is not somehow transcendent, that the very idea of metaphor "remains a philosophical product" (*MP* 228). Yet, looking back, one finds that as early as Aristotle it has been assumed that nouns indicate real, objective, autonomous "things" and that metaphorical language might be avoided by philosophers for the sake of clarity, or at least be recognized as only a rhetorical gesture. Derrida, however, unmasks even Aristotle's definition of metaphor in the *Poetics*, revealing the underlying complicity of unacknowledged, secreted rhetorical figures composing the Aristotelian poetics.

Hiding behind logocentric metaphysics is the assumption that the utterance of speech occurs together with and in the immediate presence of existence, the belief that there can be, or at the very least once was, perhaps when speech began, "a full speech that was fully *present . . .* an originary speech" (*OG* 8). The voice, speech, has always been privileged above writing, as if writing were merely the transcription of speech and so removed one step from the immediacy of experience: as if of speech one might declare, "I am conscious of being present for what I think" and that therefore "speech depends upon my pure and free spontaneity" (*P* 22). "The history of truth, of the truth of the truth, has always been the debasement of writing" (*OG* 3). Derrida contends, to the contrary, that speech relies upon "writing." Derrida is not proclaiming that graphic notation preceded speaking. He means that, since language is a system of differences—a system of differences, as Saussure recognized, without any "positive terms" (freestanding meaningful words)—and since the system exists prior to any user of it and in fact constitutes the reality of the user, then this system of differences is "always already" inscribed, formally constituted and structured *external* to the speaker. Even though it may seem, naively, that language exists somehow within the speaker, available to communicate thoughts that arise through the immediacy of an interaction with external reality (Locke's view), nevertheless, "the *exteriority* of the signifier is the exteriority of writing in general" (*OG* 14). While it has been thought, by Plato for example, that writing is but the (graphic) sign of a sign, it is more accurate to say that *all* language is but a structure of signs of signs, since the Saussurian "signified" has been eroded. Everything within the "play" of difference that comprises language, the "retention and protension of differences . . . a play of traces—all this must be a kind of writing before the letter" (*MP* 15).

We will note at this point, before turning to other aspects of Derrida, that the elevation of what he names "writing" to an honorific status will be used in American criticism to aggrandize the "act" of writing (authoring) and the reading of writing (criticism), although it is largely the aberrational, frequently perplexing use of the term "writing" by Derrida that underwrites this critical strategy.

In language, according to Derrida's reinterpretation of the Saussurian model, no signified "concept" can be "present in and of itself." Rather, every concept is "inscribed in a chain," within a "play of differences" (*MP* 11). These differences "produce the sense of the very thing they defer," Derrida writes in *Of Grammatology*: "the mirage of the thing itself, of immediate presence, of originary perception." "Immediacy" itself is a derived notion, a product of the signifying chain. To this "systematic play of differences, of the traces of differences, of the *spacing* by means of which elements are related to each other" (*P* 23), Derrida gives the name "différance," a neologism (the French *différence* with the penultimate "e" changed to an "a").

Différance is not to be taken as the name of a thing, event, or process. *Différance* is "literally neither a word nor a concept"; it has "neither existence nor essence. It derives from no category of being" (*MP* 3-4). The term functions to designate what cannot be designated because it is not any*thing* at all: *différance* is what is not. Every linguistic element exists only because of what it is not; each contains a "trace" of what is absent. The possibility of any sign, what allows it to be, "is anterior to all that one calls sign" (*OG* 62). The sign beckons forth what has already been and what may be: "this trace being related no less to what is called future than to what is called the past" (*MP* 18). What we call the present is, accordingly, not an immediacy of presence but is constituted within the sign by its use. The present is a construction appearing between the past and the future, which are themselves not directly known but constituted by the "trace"—the bond to an absence, a no-thing, that functions as what-has-been and what-may-be. This absence is both temporal and spatial. As space, it is the "differing" between signs, the gap that both separates and constitutes them; as time, it is the "deferring" of meaning, since meaning is never present but always being generated by the play of what is not present. The sign "is conceivable only on the basis of the presence that it defers and *moving towards* the deferred presence," which never arrives. *Différance*, then, is the "becoming-time of space and the becoming-space of time" (*MP* 9). (The English word "spacing," used in the translation, has both a temporal and spatial aspect.) Since the objects of our world are known only through language, "the field of the entity, before being determined as the field of presence, is structured according to the diverse possibilities . . . of the trace" (*OG* 47). Again, the trace—and *différance*, for which it stands as an alternative term—is not even itself present in a real present. Since it is "the similacrum of a presence that dislocates itself, displaces itself, it properly has no site" (*MP* 24).

Derrida has, of course, asserted that he must write within the logocentric tradition because no other language is available. His key words, his own technical terms, undermine the word. They speak from within the linguistic system, though that system is shown to have no place for them. Derrida will at times put his terms "under erasure," will use them and cross them out simultaneously, to indicate that they are saying what language lacks the capacity to say; they are referring to what cannot be signified, to what makes language possible. This is not to say that *différance* precedes language. The possibility of language is at once "anterior" to itself—which is why language is "writing" (the potential of language is pre-inscribed, since the system of differences always already precedes its use by any speaker)—yet there is no language anterior to language through which language itself can be understood. The anteriority must be addressed from within. But to be within language is to roam around in a system constituted by that which is not: *différance*, trace, absence, space. Though words must be used if anything is to be said, *différance* cannot itself be made into a philosophical entity but is "irreducible to any ontological or theological reappropriation": it is "the very opening of the space in which onto-theology—philosophy—produces its system and its history" (*MP* 6). "The trace is nothing. . . . It exceeds the question *What is*? and contingently makes it possible" (*OG* 75). We are told that "*différance*, in a certain and very strange way . . . is older than the ontological difference or than the truth of Being." *Différance* is "the play of a trace . . . whose play transports and encloses the meaning of Being" (*MP* 22), a play that is itself "the unnamable movement of difference-itself" (*OG* 93).

Derrida attempts to remove support for any notions of the self with which humanists (including American literary critics) have long been comfortable. Not unlike Foucault, Derrida wishes "to pass beyond man and humanism" ("SSP" 265). He emphasizes "the illusory autonomy of a discourse or a consciousness whose hypostasis is to be deconstructed"; certainly there is "no subject who is agent, author, and master of *différance*" (*P* 28). There is no autonomous, Cartesian-like subject who is situated in the world and looks out to perceive it directly. The major effort of Derrida is to take what he calls the "metaphysical principle" of the "*original self-evidence* and *presence* of the thing itself in person" and to put this "radically" into question (*WD* 164). Consciousness, as for Lacan, is a construction, "a *determination* of an effect within a system which is no longer that of presence but of *différance*" (*MP* 16). Lacan's ideas concerning the constitution of the self through the imposition of otherness, the forceable impression into the Symbolic Order, should be recalled.

Language is not, as it was for Locke, merely *used* by the subject. What constitutes language does not find its "cause in a subject or a substance . . . a being that is somewhere present" (*MP* 11). On the contrary, all one finds is a "desire" for such presence. "Man is that being . . . who has dreamed of full presence, the reassuring foundation, the origin" ("SSP" 265). Here is the impelling force of desire, which Derrida, like many others, needs in order to energize the human system. That force of desire, by the way, can be Americanized—just as we have seen Freud, clearly a determinist, Americanized—and turned into a support for self-knowledge and self-determination. But for Derrida, the self is constituted. "The emancipation of the sign constitutes . . . the desire of presence." This "becoming" does not happen *to* the subject; rather, "as the subject's relationship with its own death, the becoming is the constitution of subjectivity" (*OG* 69). Subjectivity is constituted by a relationship to its own not-being, as the sign is constituted by its difference from that which it is not. The outside world would not appear at all, there would be no consciousness, "without *différance* as temporalization, without the non-presence of the other . . . without the relationship with death as the concrete structure of the living present" (*OG* 71).

Here we may again recognize how, at the level of an analysis of self and consciousness, the link can be formed between French thought and American thought—which, it has been argued, are not heading in the same direction. The link is made through the passageways of a psychology of desire and a literary critical practice, rather than through Continental philosophy, with which Americans are impatient. American literary critics (and historians of criticism: Vincent Leitch, for example, and Culler in *On Deconstruction* and "Derrida") will attempt at once to use the linguistic-based critical methodology of Derrida (deconstruction); at the same time, however, they leave aside (or even turn on its head), for the most part, the epistemological consequences, which are, as a determinism, unappealing. Early structuralism was used in the same way—briefly, to be sure—as an analytic technique (e.g., a reading paradigm), rather than as a philosophy.

In Derrida's giving names, tentative or not, under erasure or not, to the unnamable, especially to that which *is not*, we hear echoes of a number of traditions that take us beyond the evident relationship

between structuralism, post-structuralism, and empiricism. Such naming of what cannot be named, such identifying of what is beyond
identification, such speaking of the nothing in terms of the something,
is also the intent, in (to use Derrida's words) a "very strange way," of
the poetic theory of most importance to the Romantic poets. It characterizes as well certain religious speculations associated both with
Western religion and with the Eastern thought that contributed to the
American intellectual milieu (and had an effect on some overviews of
modern science) of the 1960s and 1970s, as some alternative was sought
to a predominant scientific and technological outlook.

We will reserve a fuller discussion of these points until later, but
we can here, to anticipate, note the occurrence of the words "play"
and "freeplay" in Derrida. Through them he is referring to the generative and productive interaction among the terms of language that
comprise an unlimitable chain of signification at the heart of which is
difference, an absence, a what-is-not-there, even though we may, erroneously, take language to be signifying that which is immediately
present. "Freeplay is the disruption of presence": there are only "differences and the movement of a chain" ("SSP" 263). The terms are
important because in America "play" will, to some, be interpreted
much like "playfulness," and "free-play" much like "free-dom." Such
an interpretation is compatible with customary American predilections
pertaining to the "self."

That Derrida lends himself to an American transformation can
be illustrated by the Marxist response to him. Derrida's critique leaves
Marxism in no more possession of truth than any other system. (This
is his link to Althusser.) In *Positions*, an interviewer, Houdebine, states
that Derrida only refers to Marx "in a marginal fashion." Derrida replies, "It is probable that I have had nothing very original . . . to propose
on this subject" (*P* 51). When he is continually pressed on this issue,
he says, "Don't you see, once again, I do not believe that one can
speak . . . of a homogeneous Marxist text" that can itself be fully liberated "from the dominance of metaphysics" (*P* 74). We have said on
a number of occasions that structuralism is a Marxism in which the
linguistic system has been substituted for the economic system, relying
on the belief that consciousness is a product of social circumstances.
Derrida is not immune to such an approach (for applications of Derrida
to Marxism, see Ryan, *Marxism and Deconstruction* [1982]; Ryan, "Deconstruction and Social Theory" [1983]; Butler, *Interpretation, Deconstruction and Ideology* [1984]). On the other hand, for our purposes
here, Derrida's avoidance of specifically Marxist concerns characterizes
what makes him attractive to American critics, who, unlike the French,

have no difficulty separating criticism and politics. In addition, Derrida's "deconstruction" of metaphysics from Kant to Heidegger offers Americans a welcome excuse to place all these difficult philosophers at a distance while they focus on methodology and critical technique, often ignoring the most important philosophical issues in favor of a critical practice that elevates reading and the writing of criticism as personal, and personalized, activities.

Literary Critical Theory

"Deconstruction" is the name Derrida gives to the critical methodology that issues from his analysis of what a text is and how it might be read. The method (an interesting overview is given in Norris, *Deconstruction* [1982]) is imported into the United States under that title.

Derrida's dominant idea concerning the literary text is that, since language is a chain of signifiers that does not point to independently existing signifieds, texts do not portray a real world that exists independent of language. Consequently, criticism is to focus upon the text as a construct of language, a rhetorical fabrication that can be understood by being dismantled, deconstructed, in order to reveal its often covert rhetorical machinery. This procedure leads not to truth but rather—the benchmark of skepticism—to the understanding that where truth was thought to be there is only an absence of truth, its perpetual evasiveness, a vacancy, an empty place, which language has masked to create the effect of completeness and unity.

Derrida's best-known aphorism, "there is nothing outside of the text" (*il n'y a pas de hors-texte*), is preceded in *Of Grammatology* by the statement that, in the process of reading, one "cannot legitimately transgress the text toward something other than it, toward a referent . . . or toward a signified outside the text whose content . . . could have taken place outside of language" (*OG* 158). The basis for this is, to repeat, the prying apart of Saussure's signifier and signified, the ultimate outcome of the original structuralist venture. Language is all that humankind knows; and that is not equivalent to knowing any-*thing*. It is "impossible to separate, through interpretation or commentary, the signified from the signifier" (*OG* 159), to declare what the text is indicating beyond the language that composes it and other texts with which it interacts. There is only "the chain of differential references." What is customarily thought of as the "real" (existence thought of in its own right, independent of language) is found to be, in effect, a by-product of the text, "being added only while taking on meaning from a trace and from an invocation of the supplement." (This latter word

Derrida uses to mean both addition and completion, what is both extra and absolutely essential.) "And thus to infinity" (*OG* 159). All we possess is "the being-chain of a textual chain, the structure of substitution, the articulation of desire and language" (*OG* 163), the desire, in Derrida, for an unobtainable immediacy of presence, the non-existent origin of language in primary perception.

From these statements one could advance in a number of directions. First, in referring to the "real" as an addition, Derrida might be seen as commenting on Kant's well-known scrutiny, in the *Critique of Pure Reason*, of Anselm's "ontological argument" for the existence of God. Kant concludes that "existence is not a predicate," cannot be through definition an attribute or property of a thing. Along this path Derrida can be said to enter into the midst of idealism in order to "deconstruct" it at the point of reference to Being in and of itself, the same point at which he infiltrates Husserl and Heidegger. This would lead us again to conclude that Derrida is not an idealist and hopes not to be a phenomenologist. (Derrida's relation to Kant's esthetics is discussed below.)

Second, one might move in the direction of defining a "deconstructive" literary criticism, which we shall soon do. But third—and it is necessary to address this before proceeding— one might emphasize the relation of desire and language, the meeting ground of Derrida, Lacan, and Freud, which would lead us to reassert that Derrida is a determinist, that he helps "insure the growing prominence of linguistic determinism" (Leitch 15). Derrida's position on "freedom" requires some clarification here, for his statements in various essays that treat the literary text might be misinterpreted to legitimate "freedom" as a free and conscious decision-making process of an autonomous subject, the self as entity. Such a concept may be attractive to the existentialists and to humanist literary critics, and central to many theories of literary creativity, but Derrida certainly does not support it.

Most conspicuously, in "Force and Signification," a 1963 essay that appears in America in 1978 as part of the collection in *Writing and Difference*, Derrida states that "the will to write reawakens the willful sense of the will: freedom" (*WD* 13). He also remarks that "to grasp the operation of creative imagination at the greatest possible proximity to it, one must turn oneself toward the invisible interior of poetic freedom" (8); and he adds that writing demonstrates "a certain absolute freedom of speech" (12). Moreover, in what we shall call this "early" essay, Derrida claims that poetic freedom allows one to be "united with the blind origin of the work in its darkness" (8). The freedom is "the freedom to bring forth the already-there as a sign of the freedom to auger. . . . To create is to reveal." Further, "this revelatory power of true literary language as poetry is indeed the access to free speech, speech unburdened of its signalizing functions by the word 'Being' "; and literary language is "referring only to itself . . . a game or pure functioning" (12).

This 1963 essay represents the early influence of Heidegger on Derrida (with an infusion of Barthes and likely the existentialism of Sartre, which we will also detect in the American deconstructors) and is not compatible with what Derrida says later. The essay should be viewed as Derrida not yet matured. Since it appears in English in 1978, following the translation of *Of Grammatology*, together with later essays, the language of "freedom" can be interpreted out of context. Our discussion of Derrida's view of "self" should have made clear that Derrida is not Coleridge. In the 1971 interview contained in *Positions*, Derrida criticizes those who would try "isolating . . . a formal specificity of the literary work which would have its own special essence and truth" (*P* 70): all writing, literature included, works in the same way. In *Of Grammatology* we are cautioned that even that form of criticism which is a "doubling commentary," which attempts to repeat in other words what the text is saying, is not reproducing "the conscious, voluntary, intentional relationship" of an author to the real world. We have mentioned Derrida's statements that there is no "subject who is agent, author, and master of *différance*" (*P* 28) and that consciousness is "a determination or an effect" (*MP* 16). In the final essay of *Writing and Difference*, written to conclude the 1967 volume, Derrida's language is quite different from the earlier essay. "*To write is to have the passion of the origin*," although there is neither origin nor the opposite of origin to be found. There is only "a trace which replaces a presence which has never been present, an origin by means of which nothing has begun" (*WD* 295).

It is important to understand that, while Derrida might in the 1963 essay sound like an existentialist and even a Romantic, it is certainly not his *intention* to contribute to Romanticism. Nevertheless, that Derrida's approach to language has "Romantic" underpinnings—though these are developed along different lines than in the 1963 essay—is our contention. The intermixture of Derrida and Romanticism explains Derrida's reception in America. In fact, Derrida can quite readily be made to play a role in recent American criticism similar to the role that Coleridge played for the New Critics, who also separated the author from the work and who also made poetic language "contextual"—but without, it should be recalled, thereby challenging the autonomous self of the writer or the reader, referential language, or traditional humanist values, which we have found from Eliot through Brooks to Frye and Chomsky. A literary critical methodology that might be based on Derrida cannot, however, be a French "post-structuralism" without the accompanying epistemology. This point is similar to the one raised during the discussion of the Anglo-American reception of early structuralism. What is of importance is not the American *acceptance* of Derrida, but the special *use* that is made of him within a basically alien environment.

Deconstruction, as literary critical practice, disassembles a text to reveal that what perhaps has appeared to be a consistent and unified work is a structure of rhetorical strategies and maneuvers. The uncovering of that structure subverts the presumption of a coherent, non-contradictory, comprehensible (clearly interpretable) meaning. It is not, of course, that the writer is a charlatan: language itself, having no origin in the immediacy of the perception of an external reality, is by its very nature an ungrounded chain of signifiers. What Gayatri Spivak refers to as "the sleight of hand at the limit of a text" (xlix) is not simply a ploy, an error, or an unfortunate contradiction but is the boundary of language. Deconstruction exposes this limit, exposes the inconsistency and ultimate indeterminacy at the heart of the text.

For example, Derrida finds that philosophical writing is customarily based upon the assumption of an opposition—being/non-being, nature/culture, speech/writing, literal/metaphorical, science/art, and so on—in which one term comes to be privileged over the other. The recognition of the duality does not lead, in deconstruction, to the possibility of a reconciliation, a Hegelian synthesis at a higher level. Rather, the space opened up between the terms (like the post-structuralist "space" between language and reality, between signifier and signified) cannot be remedied by closing the gap through, for example, the insertion of other philosophical terms. The critic can invert the oppositional terms, showing that what seemed to be subsidiary is in fact paramount (as Derrida does for speech and writing) and in that way can turn on its head the philosophic text in order to expose its contrivances. But even in doing this the critic remains within the same language that he is attempting to deconstruct—since there is no other language available. Therefore he locates not truth, but only the place where it was thought to be but cannot be. Even the deconstructive critical text cannot claim the privilege of a critical meta-language. It is itself subject to deconstruction, and the critic can be said, in Culler's terms, to be "sawing off the branch on which one is sitting" (*On Deconstruction* 149). All language is deconstructible.

The customary "values of meaning or of content, of form or signifier, of metaphor/metonymy, of truth, of representation, etc., at least in their classical form, can no longer account for certain very determined effects of these texts" (*P* 69-70). Since language is not referential and its surface cohesion depends on differences rather than on positive presence or direct reference, the "effects" rest upon logical inconsistency and indeterminacy. "The system of a writing and of a reading . . . is ordered around its own blind spot" (*OG* 164). This "blind spot"— what will popularly come to be known as the *aporia* (Greek: "blocked path")—in its simplest definition is the point at which the underlying logical inconsistency of the text is discovered, unmasked. In its somewhat more profound definition, it is the place where the space residing in the midst of the text opens up. The empty space of difference and deferring is itself no-thing, cannot be named, can only be suggested by words that are not words (*différance, trace*); it is a space in which can be generated limitless, though not totally unconstrained, interpretation.

Since there is nothing outside (beyond, other than) the text and the text is constructed by a rhetorical chain of signifiers floating upon and within a space and time that it both constitutes and depends upon, in any work the critic finally confronts "an indefinitely multiplied structure—*en abyme.*" The critic comes to the edge of an abyss, into which he cannot avoid falling, an abyss that is not "a happy or unhappy accident" but a "structural necessity." Derrida continues: "Representation *in the abyss* of presence is not an accident of presence," for we have leaned that there is never an immediate presence of being (*OG* 163). The desire of presence—the yearning for "the reassuring foundation" that characterizes man ("SSP" 265)—is itself "born from the abyss (the indefinite multiplication) of representation, from the representation of representation," and so on indefinitely (*OG* 163).

This discovery in the text of the inconsistency, the rhetorical strategy, the indeterminacy, the "space," the "abyss," is not made because the critic is more perceptive than the writer of the text or because the text fails to include measures to avoid these pitfalls. Since there is never a "pure signified," the text can do nothing else than present signifiers. Consequently, the deconstruction of the text is not the disclosing of some remediable error; the deconstruction of the text is necessarily contained as a possibility within it. "Writing structurally carries within itself . . . the process of its own erasure and annulation" (*P* 68). A philosophical text may presume to undertake "the project of effacing itself in the face of the signified content which it transports and in general teaches" (*OG* 160)—which is to say that the text proposes to "serve as an obedient vehicle of thought" (Norris, *Deconstruction* 30) that *brings* that which it purportedly signifies *to* the reader. Nevertheless, an adequate reading of the text, "in the last analysis," will "expose the project's failure." "The entire history of texts, and within it the history of literary forms in the West, should be studied from this point of view" (*OG* 160).

What form such studying takes in the United States will be among the topics of the next chapter.

Language as Art

From the perspective of American literary criticism, what Derrida has done is to conceptually transform all language into the Romantic art-object, the work of art as it is given definition in Kant's *Critique of Judgment*. Because Derrida "poeticizes" language, his work can serve, in American literary criticism, to continue the gradual drift from empiricism toward Romanticism that has been traced in the thought of the New Critics.

In his *Critique of Judgment*, Kant asserts that esthetic judgments are a necessary part of esthetic enjoyment; yet such judgments, evaluative propositions, can never be supported by any objective or universal principles (for analyses of Kant's esthetics, see Donald Crawford [1974]; S. Korner [1955]; Karl Jaspers, *Kant* [1962]). It is hopeless to believe in the objectivity of esthetic judgment; nevertheless, there are universally valid judgments. Kant "denies the possibility of deductive arguments, rules, principles, and hence any conclusive reasons in esthetics," yet he asserts that esthetic judgments do have validity (Crawford 164). The validity, oddly, cannot be validated.

To Kant, the esthetic object is "purposive" although it does not have a "purpose." What Kant means by this has been much debated and often disparaged. While we cannot settle the issue here, it seems that Kant is proposing that, although the esthetic object has a structural coherence and harmony, an "organic" unity, these traits are not, in the esthetic experience, identified with any purpose. An animal, for example, appears to us as a coherent organic entity, but unlike a work of art, the purposes of its biological structures can be ascertained. We contemplate the esthetic object for its own sake, "as it is in itself." In modern philosophy this creates the discipline of esthetics by isolating the esthetic object as an autonomous (purposive, unified, organic) object, the basis of almost all literary theory that follows Kant, especially all "formalisms."

Furthermore, the esthetic object is enjoyed in a "disinterested" way. We are not concerned with the pertinence of the object to the demands of practical reason (ethics, action, acquiring knowledge). Consequently, the work is enjoyed free from the intellectual "concepts" of the "understanding" (Kant's technical terms earlier defined in *The Critique of Pure Reason*) on which the acquisition of knowledge, most significantly in the sciences, is based. To be disinterested means to take pleasure not in the "existence" of the object, its reality (for this would be allied with purpose), but in its "presentation." The esthetic experience causes pleasure because our cognition is free from the application of concepts or concern for purpose and can, as a result, achieve a pleasurable, "disinterested," equilibrium. The esthetic experience is "the consciousness of the merely formal purposiveness in the interplay of the cognitive faculties of the subject on the occasion of a presentation" (Kant qtd. in Korner 185).

The "play" in "interplay" is most significant here. In contemplating the esthetic object, "our cognitive power, the imagination and the understanding, are in harmony and free play" (Crawford 89). In Karl Jaspers's words, "the freedom of esthetic play is the most perfect, because it is unconfined by interest and reality" (*Kant* 79). The idea of free play becomes part of a Romantic esthetics through the work of Kant and through Friedrich Schiller's *On the Aesthetic Education of Man* (1795), in which Schiller declares that art is play. In the writings of Derrida, "freeplay"—which can now, accordingly, be viewed as linked to Romanticism—is a primary characteristic of language, although for Derrida "freeplay" does *not* refer to a subject freely playing, which for critics influenced by Romanticism will cause a misreading.

Derrida, then, is at once a "Romantic-ist" (by way of Kant) and a "determinist" (by way of his "radical empiricism"). This is his uniqueness. His position is a modern (post-modern?) version of Romantic irony, in which the irony has turned to empiricist skepticism. Furthermore, in Derrida the possibility of discovering objective and universal principles is *everywhere* rejected. While Kant establishes a similar limitation on esthetic judgment, in other areas he supports scientific knowledge. Derrida imposes this limitation on *all* language, which encourages our claim that Derrida has turned all language into poetry.

That the approach of the Kantian esthetics leads to a deconstructive literary criticism had already been understood by Jaspers, who published his study on Kant less than ten years before the publication of *Of Grammatology*, when Derrida would have been in his twenties. Jaspers argues that the numerous logical contradictions in Kant result from his attempts to achieve an encompassing vision by various routes of argumentation. Kant's philosophy is the gradual convergence of these routes, rather than the discovery of an absolute certainty, which, for Jaspers, is beyond attainment. "The aspiration to absolute totality does not mean that such a totality is given or attainable, or even that it is thinkable" (Jaspers, *Kant* 46). (Is not this "aspiration" the same as Derrida's "passion" of man for the "origin," striven for, but never reached, by searching from within the logocentrism where it can never be found?) Kant, says Jaspers, begins with a "skeptical method" that "lets a large part of the traditional metaphysics destroy itself" (45). A philosophical impulse "can elucidate itself in the form of a fundamental knowledge only if the particular argumentation logically negates itself and so permits the content of the philosophical act to shine forth" (42). Knowledge, "in striving to attain clarity concerning itself," requires concepts; yet knowledge "can only employ them by making at every step a logical mistake" (41). Whether Derrida be borrowing from Jaspers, we cannot say.

Heidegger's concept of "destruction" may be a more obvious influence on Derrida. Heidegger, notes Spivak, called for " 'a destructive retrospect of the history of ontology,' which 'lays bare the internal character or development' of a text"; and in the first French version of *De la grammatologie*, Derrida "uses the word 'destruction' in place of 'deconstruction' " (Spivak xliv).

Our point here, however, is the affiliation of Kant and Derrida. Not that Derrida, in his own opinion, is a Kantian. Derrida clearly takes pains to avoid Kantian idealism, and his view of the constituted self is incompatible with that of Kant, who believed that the skepticism of Hume might be refuted, that knowledge is available. Furthermore, Kant finds it necessary to appeal to "Reason" in order to arrive at certain forms of knowledge, to resolve what he calls "antinomies" (for example, that the world must have begun yet it cannot have begun in time; that causality seems ubiquitous yet man has freedom). For Derrida, there can be no transcendence of language by Reason, no superior position from which antinomies are satisfactorily comprehensible. But if the attempt to make Derrida a full-fledged Kantian is discarded and the comparison is confined within the Kantian esthetics, we then discover, in Kant and in Derrida, a congruence, an area where objective validity is forever elusive.

We could, of course, continue to find similarities and differences between Kant and Derrida, but that is far beyond our purposes. We might compare Kant's belief that time and space are not properties of things-in-themselves but are necessarily imposed upon them by human perception with Derrida's assertion that time and space are generated by language (*différance* as differing and deferring), which we might contend is Derrida's substitution of language for consciousness in order to maintain a notion of time and space as no-things. Derrida has substituted language for the Kantian categories.

To continue along these lines would take some time.* More important for our purpose here—which is to emphasize issues pertinent to literary criticism—is the recognition of how the esthetic object described by Kant is quite like language described by Derrida. One of the most persuasive approaches to analyzing Derrida—that taken, for example, by Christopher Butler—is to declare that Derrida ignores language as it is in fact *used* by human beings. Language is a communicative behavior; when language is used, both the user and the recipient have no difficulty in achieving clear meaning. The dispute between Derrida and the speech-act theorists hinges on this issue (see Searle, "Reply to Derrida" [1977]). It is argued that only by disregarding the fact that language is something humans *do*, purposefully, with an "intention," does Derrida find himself caught in an endless chain of

---

*Derrida's philosophical position is still being defined for readers in the United States. A variety of analyses by philosophers (as distinct from literary critics) of his position and its antecedents (some precursory texts have been collected by Mark Taylor [1986]) are currently being published. The translation of Vincent Descombes's *Modern French Philosophy* (1980) made available the notion that Derrida's work is the "radicalization of phenomenology," while Derrida simultaneously commits "the fault of empiricism" (141). John Llewelyn finds Derrida's "point of departure" in Heidegger. Steven Melville, noting that "Derrida's relation to Kant is of increasing centrality," locates Derrida's philosophical roots in Hegel, particularly in Hegel's *Phenomenology*. Mark Taylor, similarly, refers to Derrida's "preoccupation with Hegel." Irene Harvey, in *Derrida and the Economy of Différance*, distinguishes between Derrida's project and Kant's: while for Kant experience itself, albeit mediated by signs (language), is sufficient evidence that experience has an "origin" (a cause, the thing in itself), Derrida reaches a different conclusion— that even the "origin" is "itself a sign and a result." Harvey's analysis is, in our view, consistent with the approach that Derrida is rejecting Kant's *first* critique (*Critique of Pure Reason*), which does not at all necessitate rejecting the *third* critique, the esthetics. Finally, the attempt to relate Derrida to Wittgenstein is also of importance, in, for example, Henry Staten's *Wittgenstein and Derrida* (1984) and Marjorie Grene's "Life, Death, and Language."

Derrida does have an essay on Kant's esthetics, "Economimesis." Derrida interprets Kant's assertion that art is "free" (freely created) to (also) mean that art, for Kant, is free of the economic system (i.e., "for free") since it is believed to be produced outside the customary marketplace forces. Price, monetary worth, and gain are purportedly not of importance to the artist, "who does not work for a salary." Art is a sort of "immaculate commerce." This leads Derrida to argue that since art is unassimilated to the economic system, it is "undigested." But what cannot be digested is "vomit." Hence, Derrida considers "vomit" as a "general synthesis of transcendental idealism." This unpalatable essay concerns matters other than those addressed in our analysis.

ungrounded signifiers, in the abyss of skepticism and endless freeplay. Derrida does separate language as a system from language as a function, a consequence of his denial of the very subject that most Anglo-Americans will not forsake. What legitimates this strategy is the treatment of all language as if it were the Kantian esthetic object, detached from "purpose," experienced with "disinterest" (irrelevant to action or ethics), and inexplicable by means of any principles that can be objectively validated. This esthetic detachment in Kant and Derrida permits "free play." It may be precisely the extraction of purpose from language that leaves behind the metaphorical "space" on which post-structuralism is founded. Derrida places certain of his terms "under erasure" not only because he is a skeptic and must rescind his own assertions but also because poetic language, or language as poetry, holds itself free of "concepts."

Derrida is, in this sense, writing poetry. Philosophy, the search for truth, has become poetry (and from an Anglo-American perspective we recall Matthew Arnold). For Derrida, language in its entirety much resembles what we found the poem to be for the New Critics; and his denial of his own terms functions as New Critical "irony," a balancing of opposites, of what at once is and is not.

Language, Empiricism, Romanticism

The original structuralist linguistics was intended to be an empiricism. This intent made it (briefly, to be sure) appealing to Anglo-American literary critics, whose thought is embedded in an empiricism the logical consequences of which they consistently try to avoid. The scientific method legitimated by empiricism needs an "external" object of study. The structuralist attempt to turn language, which from an empiricist view is a construct of the mind, into an *externally* existent object of study (the system of language as it exists irrespective of the user) raises the dilemma of skepticism. If all we can ultimately know are the ideas in our heads (perceptual imagery, their combinations, and the words that stand for them, to the eighteenth-century empiricists; language, to the structuralists), then truth is unobtainable. We become, on logical grounds, trapped in the "prison-house" of language. To be sure, one can reach this conclusion without challenging the existence of the traditional "self" (although Hume raises the challenge). But post-structuralism in Derrida is not only the isolation of language as a Kantian art object: the post-structuralists have done more than make language in its entirety like the poem to the New Critics because, in addition, throughout structuralism the self becomes a linguistic construct.

By accepting that the subject, the self, is constituted by language, Derrida, like his structuralist predecessors, isolates language as his object of study. He accepts, however, the epistemological implications of structuralism in order to deconstruct idealism, phenomenology, and (most significantly for our purposes) empiricist structuralism itself, which he transforms, as far as it can go, into skepticism, in the same way that Hume undermined Locke's empiricism and at the same time completed the project of empiricism. "It may be said," Derrida writes of his own work, "that this style is empiricist and in a certain way that would be correct. The *departure* is radically empiricist" (*OG* 162). By creating terms such as *différance, trace, supplement,* and so on, Derrida stipulates the conditions of language, as well as its structure, outside of subjectivity, as if this can place language exterior (because logically prior) to self, which it has the power to constitute. His concept of "writing," that which is always already inscribed preexisting the individual, is meant to serve this purpose. Yet his terms, which from an empiricist perspective "reify" mental constructs, are then said not to be the names of any-thing; they are no-thing. But to name what cannot be named is to raise and recognize the difficulty that Derrida's object of study is not really an *object*. Nor can *différance* refer to a "faculty" of mind, for this would be to ascribe a property, an attribute, to the mind (the subject) as object, as thing. Derrida denies that possibility, since this would be to reify the subject, which is, in the European philosophical tradition he addresses, to court either rationalism or idealism.

Language cannot be seen by Derrida either as behavior or as communication (again, his debate with speech-act theorists illustrates this), for this would be to make language the "tool" of a subject. Nevertheless, his terms are certainly names (nouns), and his placing them "under erasure"—which we see as a poetic device, related to irony—cannot counteract their function as nouns. Without these names there can be no *object* of study. (Lacan, we recall, finds no name for the space represented by the bar in the formula S/s.) Since Derrida invents these names, they are surely, at the least, mental constructs (his). But for him to say that he is naming merely mental constructs would be to admit only to inventiveness, which is not a philosophical discovery (a move toward knowledge), not an escape from the consequence of structuralism that if the self is constituted by language there is no place to stand outside of language in order to discuss it. And Derrida—without a Cartesian or Berkelian deity to set things right, and without a Kantian subject—cannot avoid stopping, as he knows and accepts, at a skepticism, which logically is and historically has been situated between empiricism and idealism. He willingly forsakes truth yet, like Nietzsche, claims to know something; he claims to advance philosophy by, paradoxically, dismantling it.

Derrida recognizes that to deny a reality to what is defined as an *irreducible* reality is also to affirm it (the logocentric tradition cannot be escaped) since whatever is denied has a name. But if irreducible ideas—Derrida's "transcendental signifiers," the stable "center" of mobile structure—such as time, space, being, and substance are denied, what do we know about them that can be denied? If we say something can be known about them, then they have properties and are not irreducible terms, but a portion of the chain of signifiers. If they are irreducible, where do the "transcendental signifiers" come from in the first place? They must, it would at first seem, either reflect perception (empiricism) or, on the other hand, be spontaneous or necessary products of the mind (Kantianism and idealism). To refute the existence of unicorns, for example, is not to deny some essential irreducible "unicornness" but simply to reject the possibility of a certain aggregation of properties (like a horse, with one horn, etc.) each of which does have an existence (there are horses, there are horns). To assert that a collection of attributes cannot exist all in one entity is not problematic. Similarly, the ontological argument states that the existence of God cannot be denied because the concept of God is already in thought; but because Anselm provides the properties of God, defines God, Kant can then deny the proof, because there is no need to grant existence to what can be defined by the sum of its attributes. But to deny irreducible terms, "transcendental signifiers," is another matter. Kant cannot relinquish "intuition" (perception), God, and freedom, because these, for him, cannot be reduced to the sum of attributes.

Derrida first establishes and then denies what might at first seem his own transcendental signifiers: by first asserting that these names are a product of language itself and then denying that language is caused by subjects. But he also, perhaps with some circularity (which he recognizes), makes these terms (e.g., *différance*) signify the conditions of language in order that "language" does not become itself a transcendental signified. Since one can never escape language, never know it either for what it is in itself or as a faculty of a subject (even the "one" to whom we have just referred is a linguistic construct), the referential value of *any* term is ungrounded; the "signified" disappears, and the use of words as if they referred to things becomes indefensible, even though language cannot do anything else. Derrida's irreducible terms are, consequently, said to refer to nothing. To deny the existence of one's own fundamental terms is the extremity (and the fascination) of skepticism.

These philosophical issues cannot be pursued at length here, but their relevance to our discussion of American literary criticism, and particularly of the influence of Romanticism, is manifold. First, the naming of that which cannot be named much resembles the task of poetry in Romanticism, particularly as this involves the concept of the symbol. In addition, the structuralist and post-structuralist attempt to make language an object of study external to the user of language (to avoid intent and communication theory in favor of systems theory) resembles the isolation by the New Critics of the poem as object (self-enclosed system), in part based on Romantic notions of organic unity. Furthermore, if nothing can be known outside of language, then meaning is contextual—which is the position taken, concerning poetry, by the New Critics, whose opposition of referential language (science) and poetic language is derived from Romanticism and leads to a dual truth theory that may also be applied to early structuralism. To posit the possibility of knowledge *about* language itself (the science of linguistics) in the midst of the understanding that meaning is a product of language (contextuality) is itself a dual-truth theory, which Derrida recognizes as structuralism's flaw. If, furthermore, language is considered fundamentally rhetorical, "metaphorical," we are reminded that Nietzsche, and consequently Derrida afterward, is indebted to the German Romantics for this notion, since the theory that language was originally poetry is found there.

Derrida overcomes the dual-truth theory by presenting *all* language (not exempting science or the early structuralist's language about language) in the same way that the Romantics defined poetry. Derrida's theory is the poeticization of all language. This can be traced back to Kant's esthetics, which establishes the autonomous esthetic object. Derrida's theory is a poetics; and he himself frequently operates as a poet, creating in language meanings that cannot be separated from his own language, his own text.

But at the same time, Derrida can indefinitely postpone any "transcendental signifier" because he of course denies (as do the other structuralists and post-structuralists) the autonomous subject, which is essential to Romanticism. Derrida's "language" is poetry without any poets as cause. We recall Ricoeur's critique of Lévi-Strauss: that Lévi-Strauss was a Kantian without a transcendental subject, which we called an oxymoron. Derrida might be said to be a Romantic without the Romantic epistemology, for which his "radical" empiricism (skepticism) substitutes. If his epistemology can be ignored, as it will be in

America, he can be given an hospitable reception by literary critics in an environment where a "Romanticism" has already been put forth as a remedy to empiricism.

At the conclusion of Chapter Five, we quoted Todorov's comment that "the ideological bases of structuralism are the very ones that romantic esthetics had elaborated" (*Introduction* xviii), and it was assumed that Todorov, who does not explain himself, was referring to the Kantian notion of the epistemological autonomy of art. Since Todorov's statement was made in 1981, by which time post-structuralism was well advanced, we can now interpret it in light of our own analysis: in American literary criticism, empiricist structuralism and the post-structuralist revision contributes to the Romantic reaction to empiricism.

As the New Criticism began in a scientific empiricism and moved toward a Romanticism, justified, as we have earlier asserted, by the "loophole" (skepticism) in empiricism, so will empiricist structuralism in America shift (much more rapidly) for some critics into a Derridian mode (also through a skepticism) because of its "Romantic" qualities. In America, Derrida completes the movement of the New Critics, while, in France, he completes the structuralist venture—providing, perhaps to our surprise, legitimation both for an intensification of non-deterministic Romanticism in one culture and the intensification of a linguistic determinism in another culture, the two cultures heading, as we have often repeated, in opposite directions.

It must be added here that although American criticism came to require a justification on the political left, orthodox European Marxism has never become the major issue to American critics. The fact that Derrida refuses to privilege Marxism encourages for Americans a Marxless criticism purportedly on the "left," with political implications that we will review in Chapter Ten. Through its concept of the constituted self, Marxism generated structuralism from Lévi-Strauss onward in the first place, and it is at this epistemological level that the work of Foucault and Lacan can be best understood. But in the American environment, it is not the epistemology itself but the consequence of it that will become appealing. That consequence—that the truths derived within empiricism are unfounded if a non-referential (non-mimetic) language is made primary and irreducible—will be used in support of what will serve not as a rejuvenated Marxism but as a new skepticism.

The skeptical ramifications of French post-structuralism evolve in France from a critique of the metaphysical philosophy extending from Kant through Hegel to Husserl and Heidegger, the employment of that critique by the French existentialists, and the critique of that critique by Derrida. In this progression the British empiricists receive, in France, negligible attention. Within the Anglo-American tradition, however, empiricism remains the fundamental problematic, and the reception of the structuralists and post-structuralists in America must be understood within *that* tradition. That Locke posited two sources of knowledge, sensation (perception) and "reflexion" (introspection), creates—shall we say by the "space" created between these two—the basic conundrum, whether in philosophy, psychology, or esthetics.

While, from a viewpoint internal to Continental philosophy, the constant revisions of modern German philosophy appear to be major innovations and upheavals, from the Anglo-American perspective the entire movement can be seen as turbulence on the surface of a single relatively homogeneous continuity: the opposition to empiricism. A point of view is, of course, as important as what is viewed. An American reading of Derrida, for example, may be quite different from his own reading of himself or from the reading given Derrida by empiricist Marxists who detect a lapse into idealism. The Continental European tradition comes to seem pertinent in American literary theory because the movement from an empiricist linguistic structuralism to post-structuralism in Derrida parallels not only the movement from Locke to Hume but also the movement from a psychologically based empiricist criticism, in Richards, to the Romanticism of the later New Critics, like Brooks, in the 1950s.

The work of Frye and of Chomsky, both structuralists in their formalism and humanists in their ethics, is situated between the New Critics and structuralism. So is the importation of existentialism (and, for a time, the phenomenological criticism of the Geneva school) and of Freud in the 1960s, which served to provide support for the American humanist, who looked toward Europe for new ideas from within a milieu in which the strongest cultural (called counter-cultural) movements, those reviewed in Chapter Four, were those confronting the influences of science and technology, the consequences of empiricism.

The response to early structuralism, a phenomenon limited in America to a few years in the 1970s, has already been discussed. The response to post-structuralism is still in progress.

CHAPTER NINE

Deconstruction in America

The four critics at Yale University* who have been customarily classified as deconstructive critics—J. Hillis Miller, Paul de Man, Geoffrey
Hartman, and, to a lesser extent, Harold Bloom—do not themselves
acknowledge the theoretical unity of their work as a single body of
criticism; there are as many differences among them as among the
various New Critics or among the writers classified as structuralists or
post-structuralists. Nevertheless, common themes, beliefs, and approaches emerge in their recent work. Their collegial alliance has been
emphasized by their collection of essays called *Deconstruction and Criticism* (1979), their frequent references to one another in their essays,
and the similarities discussed by Miller in "Stevens' Rock" (1976), an
article that did much to encourage the notion of a coherent deconstructive outlook at Yale, which other writers, in praise and condem-
nation, assumed to be a "school" of criticism.

Each of these four critics produced a substantial amount of literary
criticism before integrating (or, in Bloom's case, counteracting) the influence of Derrida, whose celebrity grew rapidly following his appearance at the 1966 Johns Hopkins conference. Deconstruction in
America is, in fact, not French post-structuralism; it is a use of post-
structuralism that continues a movement in American criticism begun
by the New Critics, with, admittedly, significant modifications, many
of which have been responses to issues much wider than literary criticism. Furthermore, it is erroneous to perceive these four critics as
having undergone a Derridian conversion, after which they rejected

---

*These four critics are no longer all at Yale. However, since the deconstruction movement
arose, and achieved notoriety, when they were colleagues at the same university, I have
left the text as it was originally written, with the recognition that time, too, deconstructs.

their previous positions in order to preach as disciples a French post-structuralism. In each there is a continuity, and Derrida serves to advance their previous criticism into a new, but not foreign, critical territory, in the way that settlers push against a frontier on the margin of their own national geography.

Deconstruction and Post-Structuralism

If, from the Anglo-American perspective, Derrida transforms language into the Kantian art object, poeticizing *all* language, the student of language becomes much like the reader of poetry, without having to posit, as an alternative to poetry, a purely propositional scientific language, specifically a scientifically critical meta-language. At the same time, such "reading" appropriates both what had seemed to be the originally scientific legitimations of early European structuralist linguistics and also the undermining of that science in post-structuralist philosophy. A literary critical science, which the New Critics hoped for, becomes a critique of any critical science, which is expected to grant criticism a disciplinary autonomy as well as a prestigious place among rival, purportedly more scientific (in America, more authoritative) disciplines. American deconstruction does not, however, integrate the fundamental suppositions of structuralism or post-structuralism. These involve the radical redefinition of the self, which in Europe has Marxist underpinnings, that Americans, who seek to liberate the self, find unappealing. Claiming a post-structuralist foundation, "a handy source of philosophical grounding" (Norris, *Deconstructive Turn* 166), the American deconstructors customarily ignore the post-structuralist epistemology and focus, like their New Critical predecessors, on the analysis and interpretation of literary works. Structuralism, we recall, was originally to have replaced "interpretation." Deconstruction reopens the New Critical project: the description of the content of a poetry not subordinated to propositional truth.

The New Critics, however, located a stability and balance in the poem, a reconciliation of opposites, a reconciliation through unified "organic" form. The deconstructive critics also find a tension of "opposites," although these can no longer be reconciled. The social and cultural movements of the 1960s and 1970s—the importation of French existentialism, the disaffection with science and technology, the reaction against the determinism of a psychological behaviorism, the search for personal freedom and political harmony—and the eventual subsiding of the force of these movements (accompanied for some by disillusionment) weakened the socio/cultural base that had supported notions of stability, balance, harmony, and transcendent truth in art, human relations, and spiritual growth. Using a post-structuralist leverage that in Europe is directed at undoing any possibility of a Hegelian or Marxist ultimate synthesis of truth in historical time, the deconstructive critics, unconcerned with Hegel or Marx, find, on esthetic grounds, unresolved conflict, perpetual indeterminacy, and limitless irresolvable interpretation—Derrida's abyss and Eco's "unlimited semiotic."

This transmutation, the turning of the same poetic elements from a harmonious balance into an irreconcilable tension, is accomplished by an appropriation of the (metaphorical) "space" that grounds post-structuralism. Any reconciliatory bond that joins and harmonizes "opposites" dissolves, in effect, under a scrutiny analogous to that applied by Lacan to the bar in the fraction S/s. The history of that space begins with Saussure's phonetic theory, in which the linguistic system is composed not of positive terms but of difference, and the difference is a phonetic binarism, exemplified by such sequences as *cat, mat, met,* etc. Over time, the *phonetic* binarism becomes, in Jakobson, Lévi-Strauss, Greimas and others (see Chapter Five), and ultimately in Derrida's deconstruction, a *thematic* one; a schema formerly applied to paired differences of sound becomes applied to paired oppositions of concepts (in Derrida: presence/absence, being/non-being, nature/culture, speech/writing, etc.). The system of sounds is applied to systems of ideas. This generates deconstruction, in which "unity" is not an achievement but an illusion. The lexical model of the linguistic system is transferred to philosophical discourse ("logocentric" discourse) on the level of ideas—a most complex, and not easily recapitulated, turn of events. The space that Foucault, Lacan, and Derrida open up between the Saussurian signified and signifier then becomes the space between language and reality as well as between desire and its object; finally that space, as Derrida's *différance*, becomes the primary ontological category, preceding even ontology itself and not describable within it.

Significantly, this space is also made the location where self is generated, a space that remains a constituent of self (since self is language and language is difference), a space characterizing finitude and death. When this space comes to involve finitude and death, it can be seen as the post-structuralist's reevaluation of the existentialism they reject; it represents existentialist "absurdity," but without an autonomous subject for whom things are absurd. The self is now the absurdity, the absence that is the language of which the self is constituted, the groundlessness. At this level, the post-structuralist "space" is a "misreading" (a use and a conversion) of Sartre's "nothingness," converting his freedom into determinism. And at this point it can be suitably imported into America, to be received in an "existentialized" (and Romanticized) context, not as a determinism but, paradoxically, as a continuation of the quest for liberated self. In America, the post-structuralist space becomes situated in the already familiar area between wish and reality, religious longing and secular resignation, God and man, reason and passion, scientific truth and poetic truth, injustice and political equality. It becomes situated in the midst of a native Romanticism—not uncommonly incorporating aspects of a religious orientation—infused with a popularized existentialism, the space of Romantic "irony," which forms much of the character of the deconstructive critics, who seek in their work (quite unlike the French post-structuralists, with the exception of Barthes; and this accounts for his popularity in America) a role and a fulfillment that Romantic poetry has long enveloped. To accomplish this end, the deconstructivists elevate criticism to an (almost) equal rank with poetry, justified by Derrida's transformation (intentional or not) of language in its entirety into the Kantian, or (from an American view) New Critical, art object. The critic as reader becomes the critic as writer, the critic as poet-like. Reading becomes the central creative act, even for poets, whose poems are readings of other poems or self-deconstructive readings of themselves or of language itself.

Language as itself an artwork can be treated as if it were detached from the world (authorial purpose or intention, mimetic referentiality). Insofar as language can be treated as a formal structure provoking esthetic response, it yields its ground of meaning and retains only the formal properties of meaning (as it did in structuralism), for it becomes severed from purpose. Meaning becomes a property of language, rather than of its employment. This detachment from intentional use in post-structuralism calls forth the analyses of a number of English writers (Christopher Butler, Jonathan Culler, Geoffrey Strickland, Catherine Belsey) who, like E. D. Hirsch in America, cannot—and there is no reason why they should be compelled to—separate reading or writing from communication, from convention, the socially determined interchange of information (what Raymond Williams, in *Marxism and Literature*, calls "active practice" [169] and Joseph Ditta "the executive features of language" [5]). A number of American critics, both for and against deconstruction, will attempt to employ speech-act theory in literary criticism, as if this might remedy the post-structuralism with which, in fact, speech-act theory is incompatible.

The turn from "life" to "art," or from the world of action to the world of thought (or, in our present example, from speech as act to language as formal structure), has been said to characterize the Romantics, whose selves often seem in principle infinitely free and in practice constrained and shackled, like Shelley's Prometheus. This may also characterize the way many intellectuals in America view their situation. The acceptance of language as art, in the view of Marxists (who demand social change and praxis and for whom the turn to esthetics, if this suggests Kant, is a noxious idealism) and of others too, effects a political conservatism, perhaps a political irrelevance. This accusation is leveled against deconstruction, with justification. (For a contrary view see Peter Brooker [1982]; Michael Ryan, *Marxism and Deconstruction* [1982]; Christopher Butler [1984].) American deconstructive critics emulate the Romantic poets, whom they so admire, and they go even further by forsaking the possibility of truth altogether, which in an empiricist environment is their skepticism. Graff, in *Literature against Itself*, calls the Yale critics "radical skeptics" (145); Norris, in *The Deconstructive Turn*, refers to post-structuralism as "linguistic skepticism" (161); Denis Donoghue, in "Deconstructing Deconstruction," calls deconstruction "an extreme form of skepticism: an old story after all" (46). As the deconstruction of empiricism yields its skepticism, so does Romanticism deconstruct itself, which is the furthest extension of its irony.

In post-structuralism, which is a determinism, the self is constituted by the imposition of preexistent language on originally subjectless biological desire. In a Cartesian, existentialist, or Christian view (none of them determinisms) the self (or soul) has a primary ontological status, and this self experiences desire. The psychoanalytic theory of Freud can be interpreted in both ways. While the former interpretation characterizes French post-structuralism, the latter characterizes American psychoanalysis, which places it, at least during the 1960s and early 1970s, in opposition to deterministic behaviorism and, later, to cognitive psychology. Similarly, "phenomenology" can be defined either along scientific psychological lines (Wundt, Titchener), as in America, or along philosophical, non-deterministic ones (Husserl, Heidegger), as in Europe.

The American intellectual milieu has always displayed a basic empiricism persistently in debate with religious, spiritual, and esthetic countercurrents. Attempts at a truce have taken the form of deism, humanism, "classicism," dual-truth theory, and political agreements, such as the separation of church and state or the policy of freedom of expression, designed to acknowledge a philosophically ungrounded human self-determination. While, from one empiricist and scientific position, desire is treated like an organic fuel, energizing the biological system, from another position, also empiricist but at the present somewhat less scientific, desire provides the self's motivation. There is, accordingly, a difference between desire generating or fueling the constitution of the self and the self generating or activating desire. Americans usually recognize a "desire" that precedes self-consciousness and attribute this to "need" (for oxygen, food, love, etc.). But another form of desire (seeking, wanting, yearning) is posited, following self-consciousness, as an attribute of the healthy self, as if the self existed from the very beginning, at birth, but took some time to get to know itself. In the post-structuralism of Derrida and Lacan—which, from the Anglo-American point of view, looks like an empiricist skepticism responding to the non-skeptical empiricism of structuralism and orthodox Marxism (repeating, as we have argued, the transition from Locke to Hume)— desire precedes self and plays a part in constituting it. Adult desire, structured in language, is continuous with, of the same composition as, original biological "need." This is Freud's view, which in America has been tempered by ego-based psychologies of various sorts, a rejection of the notion that adult need is no more than infant "id" in a new guise, and a concession to a selfhood present from the beginning.

Literary critics in America are customarily allied with a view of the self as a unified, coherent, ontologically fundamental entity, engaging its desire in a quest for meaning or fulfillment (truth or salvation) while residing often in confusion and contradiction. This is also the Romantic disposition. The deconstructive critics in America are more strongly influenced by this tradition, even when they challenge it, than by the fundamental post-structuralist epistemology, which leads to determinism. This accounts for certain of their modifications of post-structuralism. For them, criticism is a personal quest. This is an underlying reason for the elevation of criticism to a status not unlike that of poetry itself. At the same time, however, they accept from post-structuralism the belief that, since language can never accord with reality, which therefore is never directly "present," truth is unobtainable. This quandary is intensified by an inability to relinquish the traditional "self," as do Lacan and Derrida (to reduce, perhaps, the anguish of existentialism). And since for a scholar, we suppose, a desire for truth is paramount, the deconstructive critics must admit to an irremediable desire for the unobtainable (still another version of the myth of Sisyphus), the most ancient of religious dilemmas and the most modern of personal ones.

Deconstruction can, then, be seen in the light of a personal quest. The post-structuralist philosophical speculations of Derrida are set off to the side by the American critics, called forth only insofar as they justify the critical *methodology*, which is not itself post-structuralism and not unlike the New Criticism. The absence of truth for Miller and de Man is used not to counterattack Husserl's "presence" and Heidegger's "Being" but to extract textual inconsistency and contradiction through close reading in a skeptical mode. The theoretically infinite openness of language, the "freeplay" which Derrida bases upon *différance* and the subversion of the signified, is used by Miller and de Man to support indeterminacy in critical interpretation and by Hartman to support a criticism based on freedom, on unconstrained creative pleasure and self-revelation. (Derridian freeplay is, however, *not* freedom; "freeplay" is a mechanical term, first used of machinery.) In the American critics, the structuralist constitution of the self by language becomes the self creating itself, self-creativity as a project of self, and, in Hartman and Bloom, a struggle for achievement and independence by the language-using critic or poet. Much of this deployment of post-structuralism retains religious or spiritual ties (except perhaps in de Man, who grew up in France): concepts of the sacred in Hartman, of Kabbalism in Bloom, of the absence of God in Miller.

The quests of Miller, de Man, Hartman, and Bloom appear throughout their critical work, quests in a world their readers know quite well, where truth is at the outset known to be an illusion: Miller seeking to know the presence of an-other, poet or deity (or perhaps only fellow critic); Hartman attempting to confirm the artistic/philosophic vision of the critic as seer; de Man striving for whatever mastery might be found, even if only of texts, in the face of mortality and time; Bloom wrestling with angels and devils (the great poets) to acquire the visions reserved for mystics.

J. Hillis Miller: Interpretation as Impasse

In *The Disappearance of God* (1963), Miller espouses a "phenomenological" critical practice with which he investigates a theme common to certain nineteenth-century authors. In the years that follow, this theme generates a critical technique of its own, Miller's version of deconstruction. The disappearance of God becomes the disappearance of unequivocal textual meaning; the absence of God is amalgamated with Derrida's *différance*, and space and absence become a critical methodology. Just as the content of Foucault's modern episteme turns from an historical phenomenon into his own critical position, so does the content of the authors Miller reviews historically and biographically become his own existential position, through the translation of spiritual alienation into textual indeterminacy.

In the criticism of the Geneva School, that of Miller's early mentor, Georges Poulet (most often called "phenomenological," although Poulet came to reject the term), the critic treats the entire work of a single author as "so many manifestations of the same personality" (Lawall [1967] 7). The critic attempts to interact with the personality of the author, a personality reconstructed through the texts themselves, "to reproduce his experience," to "duplicate" his "awakening," to provide "a comprehensive description of the 'author's' total experience" (267). To Miller in the mid-1960s, literary works "embody states of mind"; and the critic is to put himself "within the life of another person . . . to relive that life from the inside" (*Disappearance of God* vii; cited hereafter as *DG*).

For the authors whom Miller examines, God, though still believed in, is absent (a "terrible absence"); there is no longer evidence of "the divine power as immediately present" (*DG*, 2). (The Catholic eucharist is founded on the doctrine of "Real Presence.") The former "old harmony" in which language mirrored, corresponded to, all aspects of sacred and mundane reality—which Foucault will, at about the same time, also attribute to an earlier "episteme"—vanishes: modern literature "is part of the history of the splitting apart of this communion" (*DG* 3). God is hidden somewhere behind "the silence of infinite space" (6). The Romantics try to cross this space through poetry and symbol, "to create in the vacancy a new fabric of connections" (14). This circumstance is caused, in part, by the development of modern philosophy in Descartes and Locke, following whom (for reasons Miller does not provide but which should by now be clear from our analysis) "each man is locked in the prison of his own consciousness"; as a consequence there is, in modern literature, "a moving of once objective worlds of myth and romance into the subjective consciousness of man" (12). Furthermore, a growing sense of human history suggests "the arbitrariness of any belief or culture" (10). Facing all of this, a writer like DeQuincey, whom Miller treats at length, "trembles at the abyss" (DeQuincey's words, qtd. in *DG* 27).

Every theme raised here by Miller—the disappearance of immediacy, the opening up of a vast "space," language reaching for the inaccesible, man locked in a psychic prison, poetic symbol replacing directly referential language, belief as arbitrary—is clearly transportable into the post-structuralist setting. While Miller's analysis is of a dilemma of the very "self" (one-third Cartesian, one-third empiricist, one-third Romantic) that post-structuralism disassembles, nevertheless, most of the elements that can be reformulated into American deconstruction are already present here. Miller says of DeQuincey that "desiring immediacy, he is doomed to the mediate" (32); DeQuincey searched for an unobtainable harmony and unison (39); his essays lack logical progression, they have persistent discontinuities, and De-Quincey, through his style, tries "filling up all those chasms," tries to balance "polar opposites" (45).

Without requiring, as do the post-structuralists, the incorporation of Kant, Hegel, Marx, Husserl, or Heidegger—although one can sense the influence of an Americanized existentialism—Miller can eventually ground his critical deconstruction on the history of Romanticism and its aftermath in England. The influence of Derrida will not effect a total conversion for Miller but will confirm his understanding of the human predicament by validating a critical methodology. The absence of God becomes the impossibility of ascertaining certainty in textual analysis, the perpetual withdrawal of truth from language.

Miller's early "phenomenology" can easily be shed, since the method proves irrelevant to his interpretations: knowing an "author" through his works and knowing the works of an author cannot, in the long run, be considered distinct. The phenomenological critics of the Geneva School treated the entirety of a writer's work as a single evolving text in which emerges the "author"; the New Critics, however, treated each text as a distinct entity, like the Kantian art-object. In moving away from "author"-based criticism to individual texts, in part motivated by his reading of post-structuralism's dismantling of the self, Miller moves back toward the formal practice of the New Criticism, a practice that, in fact, serves him better to legitimate an *autonomous* discipline of literary criticism because it provides, as all the New Critics were well aware, literary criticism with a claim to its own special object of study by isolating poetic language and avoiding biographical or psychological temptations. Deconstruction, the new method in Miller's essays of the 1970s, utilizes the New Critical techniques of close reading while—and this is the major change—rejecting the possibility of "univocal" inter-pretation. Reading leads not to a unity of fundamentally coherent meaning but to what Miller calls an impasse or *mise en abyme* in "Ste-vens' Rock" (1976), a labyrinth in "Ariadne's Thread" (1976), a blank wall in "The Critic as Host" (1979), and blindness in "Theory and Prac-tice" (1980) (cited hereafter, respectively, as "SR," "AT," "CH," "TP").

In Wallace Stevens's "The Rock," Miller finds a wide assortment of words "uncanny with antithetical and irreconcilable meanings." A word can function as what appears to be a "fixed rock" and at the

same time be a "treacherous abyss of doubled and redoubled meanings" ("SR" 7). A poem "calls forth potentially endless commentaries"
(31). In Stevens's poem, "the meanings of all of the key words and
figures . . . are incompatible, irreconcilable" (10). What seems to be a
ground is itself not ground. "It is an abyss, the groundless," which the
poem both opens up and, simultaneously, "covers . . . over by naming
it" (12), the "impasse of language: *mise en abyme*" (11). The "redou-
bling" of meaning is elsewhere referred to as "repetition," which—if
threading a maze to solve it is used as a metaphor for critical interpretation—"might be defined as anything which happens to the line
to trouble or even to confound its straightforward linearity: returnings,
knottings, recrossings" ("AT" 68). We follow the thread as deeply into
the work as we can, until we reach "a discovery of the way it deconstructs itself." The mind can never reach the center of the labyrinth;
the blind alleys are never exhausted, but "they may only be veiled by
some credulity making a substance where there is in fact an abyss"
("AT" 74).

In "Stevens' Rock," Miller distinguishes between "canny" critics,
who are "Socratic, theoretical," and "uncanny" critics, who are "Apol-
lonian/Dionysian, tragic." The canny critic believes that literary study
can be rationally ordered "on the basis of solid advances in scientific
knowledge about language." Miller's examples are the structuralists—
Greimas, Todorov, Jakobson, and others—who profess "agreed upon
rules of procedure, given facts, and measurable results" (335). The
uncanny critics—among them Derrida and the Yale deconstructors—
recognize that literary analysis and the logic of criticism lead "into
regions which are alogical, absurd"; their criticism enters the labyrinth
and is itself labyrinthine, at once a "mapping of the abyss and an
attempt to escape from it," which never succeeds (336-37).

Although Miller bases his definitions of canny and uncanny on
references to Socrates and to Nietzsche's *Birth of Tragedy*, they can also
be understood as the empiricist implications of the two sources of
knowledge named by Locke, perception and reflection. Followed in
one direction, these legitimate scientific method; followed in another,
they yield skepticism. Miller's purpose is, after all, to reach the proposition that "there is no 'truth' of things" ("SR" 347), a skepticism. If
Miller turns to Continental philosophy for confirmation, it is not because he could not have found support in sources written in English.
French post-structuralism is imported to dissolve the bond that reconciles opposites for the New Critics, to replace it with an indeterminacy in literature that is then extended to cover all language (a
disciplinary imperialism). Miller accomplishes this by repeating, rather

than himself deriving, the conclusions of Derrida. That, for example, there is no strategy by which a critic can " 'reduce' the language of the work to clear and distinct ideas" ("SR" 324) readily follows from Brooks's critique of paraphrasing in *The Well Wrought Urn*. Part of the value of post-structuralism to Miller is that, since it occurs later than the New Criticism, it can therefore be used as a response to it; although the issues that lie deepest beneath Miller's criticism are those that he has addressed much earlier, in *The Disappearance of God*.

In a review of *Natural Supernaturalism*, Miller criticizes Abrams for treating language as mimetic, for proposing a "one-to-one relation" between works and their "sources," and for believing that texts have an "actual primary meaning." Abrams fails to find the ambiguities and contradictions that comprise all texts: "all of Abrams' readings can be put in question" (Miller, Review of Abrams [1972] 12). Basically, the review accuses Abrams of not treating his materials as Nietzsche, Derrida, and Deleuze would have treated them. If Abrams had asked why a similar "scheme" (attaining transcendence and salvation) is found in both the Romantic poets and their sources, he would have found that it is " 'programmed into' our Western family of languages . . . latently there in the lexicon, the grammar, and the syntax of our language" (10). There are three issues here: the availability of truth; the determination of patterns of individual thought by the patterns of the language in which that thought is expressed; and the possibility of singularly correct interpretations of literary works. On the first two, Abrams's position seems not incompatible with deconstruction. In Abrams's book we find a search not for truth (nor does Abrams say poetic language is mimetic) but for the transformation of ideas through "readings," a variation of intertextuality. And Abrams certainly would not deny that patterns of ideas become embedded in the language, even though he would probably not see them present at the origin of language—as does Miller, who writes: "as soon as there is man at all, man and his power of speaking, then the whole scheme is already latently there" (10). Yet Miller's position is not precisely Derridian, either, for the configuration of ideas that Abrams defines and Miller analyzes is not what Derrida means by the logocentric tradition, although, of course, it cannot (nor can any idea) be outside this tradition. Abrams can hardly be faulted for believing that poets think they are talking about something. Miller raises such issues primarily to attack the notion of a "univocal" meaning of a work. For him, there is an "inability of the critic to 'read' the work in any determinate or monological way" since, as he says elsewhere, it ultimately rests upon "incoherence and heterogeneity" ("CH" 610). Abrams argues for the validity of confirmable interpretation; Miller disputes this. Yet Miller himself will recognize that all of his theoretical statements must be based on the "concrete acts of interpreting particular works" ("CH" 614), which is Abrams's task. Miller has, in fact, an underlying purpose, the eradication of truth in language, which corresponds to the *historical* disappearance of the ground of truth, of God. Post-structuralism is used to place that issue within language rather than within history, as if this might *explain* the absence of truth that a historical relativism can only describe.

Miller's review of Joseph Riddel's *The Inverted Bell* has a similar format. Miller attacks Riddel for being too much like Heidegger and not enough like Derrida, for referring to the "mystery of the origin," the "presence of a presence," and so on, for redefining the "center" rather than rejecting it altogether (Miller, "Deconstructing the Deconstructers" [1975] 30). Here too, Miller's major issue is that truth cannot be located. Furthermore, great literary works are "ahead of their critics. . . . They have anticipated explicitly any deconstruction the critic can achieve" (31). That Riddel and Abrams are both accused of not conforming to Derrida places Miller in the position of Derrida's surrogate, as if all criticism must pass through the Derridian censor. Since Miller himself does not systematically develop any philosophy but accepts, and strongly suggests that others accept, the implications of someone else's philosophy, we are preempted from asking how Miller logically derives his principles. But Miller's aim is not simply to serve as Derrida's bulldog. It is apparent that Miller uses Derrida primarily to maintain the consistency of his own long-standing critical project, to "update" it, trying to account for the disappearance of the ground of truth, which motivates his insistence on indeterminacy in interpretation.

In various essays Miller asserts his concurrence with the post-structuralist view of the self. He determines that Stevens's "The Rock" is a "thorough deconstruction of Emersonian bedrock self." The self is "deprived of its status as ground by being shown to be a figure on that ground," a figure of language ("SR" 23). In "Ariachne's Broken Woof" (1977; cited hereafter as "ABW"), Miller shows that in Shakespeare's *Troilus and Cressida* the mind of Troilus is divided against itself, having to hold at once "two simultaneous contradictory sign systems centered on Cressida": Cressida as faithful and Cressida as unfaithful (48). Miller concludes that, if a mind can be divided against itself, this "puts into question the notion of the mind and of the self and sees them as linguistic functions" (51). This assertion certainly goes well beyond the evidence (that a mind sometimes cannot choose between interpretations), and Miller does not fill in the space between the text and his reading with much argument. Similarly, he finds that in Goethe's *Elective Affinities* there is a notion of "intersubjectivity as a relation between two independent selves," which says no more than that in the novel two people get to know one another. With this information he concludes that Goethe's work shows such a notion to be founded on the "philosophical and linguistic notions" of Western metaphysics, which the novel "unravels" ("A 'Buchstabliches' Reading" [1979]). What is demonstrated in these articles is that, if one wishes to accept a certain view of the self—in this case the post-structuralist one—then that is the way any self, including all fictional ones, can be interpreted. Yet no work of art can refute or confirm a psychology or a philosophy, because the psychology or philosophy of the critic precedes the analysis. Employing a critical method that yields in each work a fundamental level of interpretive indeterminacy, derived from Derrida's "deconstruction," Miller then takes the success of the method—which *must* succeed, because all that is meant by success is a logical consistency in application—as a reason to affirm, or seem to, the post-structuralist epistemology, a much different matter than the critical methodology.

But the "self" in Miller is, in fact, not quite the self that we have encountered in either structuralism or post-structuralism. In them there is a self that *is* language, while in Miller the self is bounded by, resides within, language. Miller states that "the most heroic effort to escape from the prisonhouse of language only builds the walls higher" ("CH" 230). This metaphor is of a self inside the walls, not a self that is itself the walls. It is helpful to note that Nietzsche, from whom the term "prison-house" is taken, was not professing a structuralist linguistics (Jameson's use of the term, remember, is a rebuttal of structuralism), although his attack on "truth" can be incorporated in such a linguistics. Nietzsche's sense of the self as entity was quite strong, even if the self is imprisoned. Miller continues: deconstruction "seems to give the widest glimpse into the other land ('beyond metaphysics'), though this land may not by any means be entered and does not in fact exist for Western man" ("CH" 231). Who, we may ask, is capable of performing this transcendent glimpsing if not one's transcendent self? (And does the land exist for "Eastern" man?) To subvert the notion of truth by showing that language can never be identical with univocal meaning is not to reduce the self to language. And to show that truth cannot be known is not the same as knowing that there is no truth. Miller speaks of "the place we inhabit . . . this in-between zone" ("CH" 231); the definition of this "we" (how else to use the term?) more resembles the Nietzschean self, or the Romantic self, or a "trapped" Lockean/

Cartesian self than the "constituted self" of Lévi-Strauss, Lacan, Derrida, or (the later) Marx.

Similar ambiguities in Miller's view of the self appear in his *Fiction and Repetition* (1982). In its first essay Miller states that "literature continually exceeds any formulas or any theory with which the critic is prepared to encompass it" (5). This leads him to identify "structures of language" in literary works that "contradict the [logical] law of non-contradiction" (17). He continues, "realms of man and nature are stranger than we had thought." Whether we study language, psychology, or physics, we find "unsuspected anomalies" that "defy or seem to defy elementary principles of logic and geometry." Literature, in its ability to defy logic, shares this "peculiarity" (19). This approach is clearly compatible with the empiricist scientific method and asks us to believe no more than that, despite theory and methodology, the world in some sense remains puzzling and often appears illogical. Undoubtedly, as Floyd Merrell remarks during his discussion of Miller in *Deconstruction Reframed* (1985), many scientists are themselves familiar with the predicament that science has its paradoxes and is not as clear-cut as it once seemed to be. But these scientists would surely discriminate, as Miller does not, between defying logic and *seeming* to defy logic (because of the incompleteness of knowledge), between the (possible) limitations on access to knowledge and the (likely impossible) violation of the "law" of non-contradiction, and between the illogical (which is error) and the alogical (which is irrelevant to logic; like music and, perhaps, poetry). That a literary critical method cannot fully encompass textual meaning and that a scientific methodology cannot fully describe the world are not equivalent. In the former indeterminacy, at least for Miller, is a property of the textual language, while in the latter the inexplicable is a failure of theory. Even if such failure in science is necessary, this makes indeterminacy not a property of nature but (as in Heisenberg) a limitation placed on measurement. In any case, the Lockean self is much at home here. Later, in the final essay, Miller declares that "the gaps between units of a text are not capable of being filled by some fluid medium, consciousness as a unifier. The mind is neither a space nor a substance but a function of its own sign-making, sign-made activity" (216). The gaps in a text can only be filled in by more words; but these generate their own indeterminacy, create additional gaps. Much could be asked about the meaning of the word "its" in the quotation. Miller's odd assertion here, that the mind is a "function" of what is in fact "its" own activity (sign-making), is generated by his reading of Derrida rather than logically deduced from his own notion of indeterminacy. While indeterminacy may follow from the post-structuralist concept of mind, the reverse proposition, that a conclusion about the mind follows from the indeterminacy of texts, is altogether different. Miller, then, in *Fiction and Repetition*, presents the human mind both as an inquisitive discoverer (apparently with some objectivity) of the perplexing and the inexplicable in the objects of the world *and* as a function of language as well, in words that indicate that something can logically be a derivative of itself. He retains the empiricist self—admittedly tempered by a skeptical doubting—even as he attempts to subvert it. He is motivated not by consistency in philosophical deduction (which is by no means to disparage the critical method or the interpretive insight), but by the necessity to come to terms with the discovery, which for him is a spiritual one, that meaning is ungrounded, that we need to "accept the silence and emptiness which is there" (224).

The biblical image in "The Critic as Host," Moses prevented from entering the promised land (the "glimpse into the other land"), is important. Miller's deepest concern appears to be a religious one. "Many people," Miller has written recently, "seem able to live on from day to day . . . without seeing religious or metaphysical questions as having any sort of force or substance" (Miller, "Search for Grounds" [1985] 22). During a recent symposium Miller said, "I see in Derrida a commitment to another kind of ultimate explanation which is not purely linguistic. . . . There is a genuine ontological dimension." He guesses that, if Derrida were to analyze *Daniel Deronda*, "he might say that the real explanation is a religious one" (Davis and Schleifer 89).

If the "uncanny" critics described in "Stevens' Rock" are not Socratic, it is likely because the transcendent in Socratic philosophy is knowable. "Uncanny" critics are not only Nietzschean but also like the existential theologians we have commented upon in an earlier chapter, for whom the ground of truth, God, is unknowable (the original meaning of "agnostic"). Such a recognition is then used to affirm the very freedom that we find supported in the deconstructive critics by indeterminacy, "free play," and origin-less language. The "deconstructive procedure," says Miller, may lead to "interpretation as joyful wisdom" ("CH" 230). Douglas Atkins calls Miller a "spokesman for religion in modern literature" and finds that "indeterminacy, patient and watchful waiting, the reading of signs" is a "biblical-like view of the world" (*Reading Deconstruction* [1983] 61 and 66). It is of related interest that Miller has asserted that deconstruction "views as naive" the "millennial" hopes of Marxism ("Theory and Practice" [1980] 612). The "self" in Miller is a self at the extremity of the process of severance from God, a circumstance well known to the Old Testament prophets.

That process of severance from what substantiates truth is described in its mid-course in *The Disappearance of God*. The severance yields a fearsome freedom. Like Foucault, Miller has defined a historical episteme from the outside and, via his critical practice, has joined it.

In his essay on Troilus, Miller argues that if the mind can be divided against itself "when two different coherent languages struggle for domination," then the possibility is raised that "language may be sourceless, baseless, not modeled on any mind divine or human" ("ABW" 49). That this is somewhat of a non sequitur in the essay is less significant than Miller's direction: if the mind is divided, this means it is not a unity; then the mind is not equal to itself, and the Aristotelian law of identity (A = A) does not hold. This logically undermines the "I am I" of God. Mind and self, then, become "without base in the logos of any substantial mind" ("ABW" 51). Knowledge, mind, self, and truth all seem to depend, for Miller, on mind as a unity ultimately resting on the concept of the mind, the self, of God—a position not unlike that of Descartes, Berkeley, or innumerable theologians. If knowledge of God becomes unobtainable, what else can we base action on? Indeterminacy is the consequence of the disappearance of God. A historically defined "space" has become an ontological emptiness.

Miller's conclusions about the self can also be placed in the context of his former alliance with the criticism of Poulet, a criticism which, for Miller, ultimately ends by having to recognize that "any stability or coherence in the self is an effect of language" ("SR" 346). Miller's deconstructivist position, then, can be seen as a logical outcome of his own evaluation of his earlier *critical* beliefs, which are, as we have said, distinct from thematic concerns (the difference between the method and the content of *The Disappearance of God*). Since the "author" whom one comes to know through the methodology of Poulet emerges in the texts, one can ask if the "author" is anything more than the texts themselves. Such an analysis does not need Derrida, and Miller welcomes Derrida through a door already opened. Miller's criticism can be seen as the result of the admixture of a phenomenological existentialism (Miller would have been in his twenties when existentialism came to America) and an empiricist skepticism, leading to an empiricist critical methodology, close reading, that reveals no fundamental meaning. By means of a critical method not unlike that of the New Critics, empiricism, through what we have called the loophole of skepticism, is again subverted. Only this time the result is not Romantic organic unity, but the irony of Romantic doubt (for the two-sidedness of Romanticism see Edward Bostetter, *Romantic Ventriloquists* [1963]). This doubt, in Miller and the other deconstructors, is cast abroad with all the Humean self-confidence of an achievement: an achievement attained in Miller's criticism by the unification of the space opened up in structuralist linguistics with the space opened up as transcendence retreated from us, or we retreated from it.

Paul de Man: Contradiction and Meaning

The most methodologically precise of deconstructors, de Man applies a technique for disclosing the self-contradiction inherent in both literary works and critical ones. This contradiction is not an authorial mistake or a correctable oversight but, because of the nature of language itself, ubiquitous and necessary. Language is used with semantic intention, but the fulfillment of intention cannot be either unambiguous meaning or an impeccable logic. Critical and poetical assertion, however insightful they may seem to the reader, float upon disunity, upon disparate meanings held together through rhetorical strategy rather than through logical continuity, a rhetorical strategy that is the essential mechanism of all literature and criticism, in which an apparent consistency of meaning is fabricated. Because intention is a cause of the use of language, while meaning is effected by and not simply transmitted by language, intention and meaning are not congruent.

In *Blindness and Insight* (1971) de Man treats the rhetoric of literary criticism; in *Allegories of Reading* (1979) he addresses literature and philosophy. In the former volume de Man displays the influence of Derrida on his critical technique; however, it is in the latter that there is a pronounced impact of the Derridian notions both of self and of language, particularly language as poetry, which we have traced in Derrida to Kant's esthetics. Consequently, the differences between the two collections require some attention.

In *Blindness and Insight* (hereafter cited as *BI*) de Man demonstrates that the apparently well-reasoned arguments of literary critics contain contradiction at their core; yet there is no alternative path to insight. Meaning is a cumulative effect, a summative quality of interrelating contradictions that can be organized but not overcome: "The contradictions . . . never cancel each other out, nor do they enter into the synthesizing dynamics of a dialectic." One meaning always lies "hidden within the other as the sun lies hidden within a shadow, or truth within error." This "negative, apparently destructive labor" of criticism leads to what can "legitimately be called insight" (*BI* 103).

The critic is himself unaware of his blindness, the self-contradiction that yields his insight, which he believes to be logically consistent and, as far as this can be achieved, error free. What de Man calls the "rhetoric of crisis" "states its own truth in the mode of error. It is radically blind to the light it emits" (*BI* 16). Critics announce their intentions, which they subsequently attempt to support, but the process is flawed and divided: the critics de Man analyzes all "seem curiously doomed to say something quite different from what they meant to say" (*BI* 106). The readers of criticism recognize the blindness of their predecessors, reorganize it, and thereby gain both the insight of the critics and a knowledge of the contradiction that brings forth insight. Each reader, of course, has his own blindness; and the criticism of criticism is not a matter of rectifying someone else's mistakes.

De Man's approach here is, significantly, person centered. It is author centered insofar as the deconstruction of a critical text reveals a discrepancy between an author's intent and his accomplishment, which one would think must be supported by a "psychology," a function that Derrida will come to serve. It is also reader centered insofar as "insight" cannot be a property of the text but only a state of mind of the reader. To achieve this state of mind the reader must, it would seem, be inevitably attuned to the intention of the author who proposes that insight has been achieved. The presence of a phenomenological criticism is detectable here, just as it is in Miller. "Insight" is used as a quasi-psychological term, as "irony" or "paradox" was used in the New Criticism.

The discovery of logical disparity necessarily requires the notion of a logic that can be violated. It would seem that, if we are in possession of such a logic, then we might achieve dominance over contradiction. What else could it mean to know logic? De Man's attention is, after all, given to propositional assertion, not to poetic statement. For this reason de Man's method, in *Blindness and Insight*, has often been seen (simply) as a mastering of other critics' texts, a critical one-upsmanship, despite his confession of his own blindness, which, of course, he does not (theoretically cannot) himself disclose.

There is some resemblance between de Man's proposals and Derrida's assertion that we cannot escape the logocentric tradition in our own reasoning. The resemblance is not, however, an identity, for in *Blindness and Insight* de Man reaches conclusions within logic, through logic, while Derrida, for whom logic itself is not a meta-language but a contrivance, must ultimately create terms to designate nothing, nothing (trace, supplement, *différance*) in order to legitimate the placing of his own reasonings under suspicion—to legitimate, that is, the impossibility of finding truth resident in language.

At this point de Man need not follow Derrida into this territory. De Man offers minimal speculation of the kind that characterizes European structuralism and post-structuralism. He develops neither a philosophical vocabulary nor an encompassing semiological theory. De Man's approach (the same can be said of Miller) is, in fact, somewhat the opposite of the post-structuralists'. The post-structuralists argue that if their epistemology ("archaeology" in Foucault, psychology in Lacan, philosophy in Derrida) is correct, then, as a consequence, we will find, since language is a chain of signifiers, that texts cannot be reduced to directly referential meaning: indeterminacy is the lack of referential ground, a ground that disappears when (after) the constitution of the self by language is recognized. De Man *begins* (as does Miller) by supposing that texts are created by authors to convey propositional meaning and then discovers that texts are self-contradictory. Such a supposition makes "indeterminacy" specifically a literary critical dilemma, an insight that might be supported by more than one epistemology. Because "deconstruction" is inherited from Derrida it might seem, at first, that the post-structuralist epistemology must logically be entailed by the critical technique. But it need not be, any more than an Anglo-American "structuralist" reading theory must contain the structuralist epistemology.

In his reading of Rousseau in *Allegories of Reading*, de Man tries to show that "the resulting predicament" of a deconstructive analysis is "linguistic rather than ontological" (300; cited hereafter as *AR*). In post-structuralism, however, the "predicament" is clearly, at the most profound level, an ontological one. To de Man, philosophy aside, deconstruction is itself methodologically sound, which has generated the apprehension among critics of deconstruction that deconstruction, while purporting to subvert all meaning, is itself (in de Man, at least, and likely in Miller) as much a formula for critical interpretation as was the New Criticism. De Man's technique does not, in fact, require a post-structuralist philosophy or any other philosophy. What the major philosophical influence on de Man might be is a topic to which we shall return.

In *Blindness and Insight* propositional prose is taken to be the model of all language. This occurs because de Man maintains a semantic theory of intention, of language as intentional communication, which makes his approach basically author centered. He means to attack "the notion that a literary or poetic consciousness is in any way a privileged consciousness, whose use of language can pretend to escape, to some degree, from the duplicity, the confusion, the untruth that we take for granted in the *everyday* use of language" (*BI* 9; emphasis added). But it must be noted that only by viewing all language, including poetry, as *propositional* (meaning as assertion in the ordinary sense) can the deconstructive technique applied to literary criticism in *Blindness and Insight* be said to apply to poetry as well.

In the foreword de Man states that, while he has not "extended the conclusions of the section on criticism to poetry or fiction," he believes that we can no longer "take for granted that a literary text can be reduced to a finite meaning or set of meanings, but see the act of reading as an endless process" (*BI* ix). It should be recognized that indeterminacy of meaning, whether in de Man or Miller, need not logically entail "endlessness" in interpretation; indeterminacy might, with equal logic, as *Blindness and Insight* illustrates, mean a finite set of (perhaps incompatible) meanings. If one comes to occasion the other in American deconstruction, there must be motivations beyond the critical technique.

There is an important shift of approach in *Allegories of Reading*, in which De Man discusses not literary critics but poets and philosophers. There de Man refers to both "literal" and "figurative" meaning, and he states that we find rhetoric "when it is impossible to decide . . . which of the two meanings . . . prevails." At this point, "rhetoric radically suspends logic" (*AR* 10). There is a surely a difference between a necessary internal contradiction in logical argument being masked by rhetoric and the "suspension" of logic by rhetoric. In the first case (in *Blindness and Insight*), all language is like propositional prose, without the privileging of poetic language; in the second, poetic (literary) language has a separate nature, with rhetoric more fundamental than logic, more than just a technique for masking inconsistency. Poetry, in *Allegories of Reading*, is that special form of language where "the deconstruction" "constituted the text in the first place"; it is not "something we have added to the text." De Man continues: "A literary text simultaneously asserts and denies the authority of its own rhetorical mode" (*AR* 17). Again, this is quite different from discovering internal contradiction in propositional prose. De Man shows that Rilke's poetry does not assert his inner feelings and emotions as they actually existed preceding the poem that expresses them: the poems put the "authority" of their "own affirmations in doubt" (*AR* 27). Furthermore, the poems "have no other referent than the formal attributes of the vehicle" (*AR* 32). But in *Blindness and Insight* de Man has, of course, shown that Rousseau's prose texts also deconstruct themselves, and he returns to Rousseau at length in *Allegories*, where he also attempts to demonstrate that Nietzsche, too, performed a self-deconstruction. In analyzing both poetry and prose de Man has moved, by the time of *Allegories*, from the notion of all language as prose toward a notion much closer to

Derrida's, of all language as poetry, with "literary" poetry being the form of language that recognizes this correspondence.

But de Man never follows this path to the end, as Derrida does. Instead, he retains the concepts of "literal" meaning and of poetry as "affirmation." If, however, one treats language as the making of, or as including the making of, supportable assertions, then it has long been known that logical is fallible: all argument must begin with first principles which themselves, as axioms, are presupposed. We recall Hegel's discussion of the impossibility of incontrovertible first principles in the *Phenomenology of Mind*. Philosophers have always shown errors of reasoning in one another's thought. That any propositional prose can be "deconstructed" is not a novel discovery. It is only by looking to poetry for prose-like affirmation or communication of propositional statement (even if about feelings and emotions) that de Man's version of deconstruction works as a technique. If poetry is non-propositional (as it was in the New Criticism, at least in that aspect based on Richards), such deconstruction is obviated. Derrida avoids this critique because his theory is not one of communicative intent, which always, even if surreptitiously, posits a self preceding the communication, a self using language rather than composed of it. That de Man finds assertions in poetry is, of course, not unusual, since that is the function of interpretation; but to subject these ideas to the standards of truth, logic, and consistency, and then to find that these do not hold (as in his analysis of the Romantic poets in "The Rhetoric of Temporality"), is perhaps to substantiate what has not, since the New Critics, been at issue. De Man seems at first to assume, as did Hobbes and Hume, that poetry makes logical, hopefully consistent, statements, and then, not surprisingly, refutes this.

De Man attacks the New Critics for being inconsistent because they posit the organic *unity* of a poem that they find to be composed of *contradictory* elements, an attack repeated in much recent criticism. The Coleridgian notion of the reconciliation of opposites is, however, not illogical (which is not to say that we ought therefore to accept it), although to de Man (and Miller) it is unattractive, not so much on logical grounds, but because it is more appealing to find that truth is ever absent, meaning ever illusory, and (which also does not need logically to follow) interpretation ever endless. The reasons for such an appeal are larger than literary criticism; they concern the state of humankind seeking truth in the modern world. Truth itself needs, now, to be undermined. The confidence (for want of a better word) that would allow a critic to adhere to a dual-truth theory (the optimistic aspect of Romanticism) has disappeared. This absence of truth is skep-

ticism, which in America does not require the post-structuralist epistemology (the whole point of the debate in France), although post-
structuralism is nevertheless imported as a modern verification of skepticism in a form particularly useful to literary criticism.

If what seem to be oppositions (contradictions) in poetry are not
reconciled, for de Man, but deconstruct the text, does this say something about the text or about the critic? (We are situated between Brooks
and Fish.) In Proust, de Man finds "the irrevocable occurrence of at
least two mutually exclusive readings" (*AR* 72). In what (whom), we
need to ask, does the reconciliation not take place? Similarly, if the
critic or poet cannot say exactly what he intends or must say what he
had not intended, understanding this seems to require as much a psychology as a critical methodology. Is there some unconscious Freudian-
like motivation that causes the "blindness"? Or are there things that,
though we may try, cannot be said? If so, why does the writer not
know this? These questions cannot be answered in terms of deconstruction—although they can be (whether well or not is beside the point
here) in French post-structuralism, which has both an epistemology
and a psychology. If truth has evaporated under the very same methodology (close reading, the discovery of opposition) by which it formerly was said to emerge (in the New Critics) and we therefore conclude
that "the allegory of reading narrates the impossibility of meaning"
(*AR* 77), then what must have changed, since the method has not, is
the environment in which the method is exercised. The search for truth,
if there is no truth, has come to be hopeless.

De Man was born in France (in 1919) and resided there through the
1940s, during which time the influence of German phenomenology
was shaping French existentialism. De Man's concept of the self is
modified but not radically changed (on de Man's persistent existentialism, see Lentricchia, Chap. 8) by the innovations of post-structuralism, which de Man uses to confirm both the self of phenomenology
and the critical reading practices of American New Criticism. The "self"
in *Blindness and Insight* is the self of phenomenology; and as the work
of Derrida is integrated by de Man into his essays of the late 1960s
and the 1970s, the outlook on the human predicament explored by
phenomenology is intensified. Post-structuralism does not (as it was
meant to do in France) replace an existentialized phenomenology in
de Man but is used to confirm it, creating a mixture of the self of
existentialism and the linguistically constituted self of post-structuralism—a mixture suitable in the American environment, where phenomenology has been read in the context of existentialism.

In his essay on Binswanger, for example, de Man distinguishes between the "ontological" self, with its "relationship to the constitutive categories of being" (as in Heidegger), and the "empirical" self, with its "concerns . . . as they exist in the empirical world" (*BI* 38). Binswanger addresses the "problems of the poetic personality," and he is "well aware of the mediations that separate the person from the work." De Man praises Binswanger for comprehending "the imagination as an act of the individual will that remains determined, in its deepest intent, by a transcendental moment that lies beyond our own volition" (47-49). The act of criticism "implies a forgetting of the personalized self for a transcendental type of self that speaks in the work." Modern literary criticism has helped establish "this crucial distinction between an empirical self and an ontological self" (50).

In *Blindness and Insight* de Man proposes a theory of "intention." Recent criticism, he writes in "The Rhetoric of Temporality" (1969), which was not originally included in *Blindness and Insight* but is contained in the 1983 republication, reveals "the possibility of a rhetoric that would no longer be normative or descriptive but that would more or less openly raise the question of the intentionality of rhetorical figures" (*BI* 188). In a previous essay he had written that "the writer's language is to some degree the product of his own action; he is both the historian and the agent of his own language"; writing "can be considered both an act and an interpretive process" (*BI* 152). He accuses the New Criticism of lacking an "awareness of the intentional structure of literary forms" and (early) structuralism of having suffered "the loss of the intentional factor . . . due to the suppression of the constitutive subject" (*BI* 27 and 32).

The notion of intention saves the intentional self, which is not the subjectivity impelled by desire that *creates* the self that we find in Lacan and Derrida. While for Derrida the self *is* language, de Man never fully merges the two. In a 1956 essay de Man says that "the ambiguity poetry speaks of is the fundamental one that prevails between the world of the spirit and the world of sentient substance" and that language does not contain or reflect experience but constitutes it (*BI* 237). That the self constitutes experience in language is, of course, not the same as language constituting the self. Over ten years later, in "The Rhetoric of Temporality," de Man's argument rests upon the self/ nature distinction. This is, obviously, to posit the Romantic self whose limitations he then describes: the Romantics establish "a relationship of the subject towards itself" (though they did not intend to do this); the self is unable to accomplish "an illusory identification with the non-self"; man's "temporal destiny" takes place "in a subject that has sought refuge" against time (*BI* 206-7). And some years later, in the well-known essay on Derrida's deconstruction of Rousseau, de Man interprets Derrida to be saying that Rousseau makes the mistake of believing that there might be the "unmediated presence of the self to its own voice" (*BI* 114). Derrida, continues de Man, deconstructs Rousseau by showing that Rousseau's theory of metaphor is founded on "the priority of the literal over the metaphorical," while Rousseau himself declares the opposite: that language is fundamentally metaphor. De Man shows that Rousseau knew this (i.e., deconstructed himself). Indeterminacy of meaning is, for de Man, a predicament of intentionality. Consequently, he finds that Rousseau and Derrida are "saying the same thing" because both intend to show that all language is like literary language (metaphorical). De Man can take this approach because, maintaining the constitutive intentional self, he treats both Derrida and Rousseau as subject-authors with opinions. Derrida, however, has always attempted to demonstrate not only that truth evades the self because language is metaphor, but also that truth cannot exist because the self *is* this metaphorical language: it is not that the self cannot be present to its own voice (the self is its voice), but that there is no external reality that can be present to the linguistically constructed self. For de Man, the author creates the text; for Derrida, there is no author, only text. For de Man, language must always mediate between self and world; for Derrida, self and world are generated by language. For de Man, language cannot state unerringly and without contradiction what it is intended to mean; truth cannot be grasped. For Derrida, truth cannot even be imagined.

None of this analysis is meant to argue that Derrida knows better than de Man and that de Man should have been a more faithful disciple of post-structuralism. On the contrary, de Man, free from the single-minded obligation felt by the French post-structuralists to discard the phenomenological (and, of course, the humanist/Cartesian) self, often achieves what might seem a judicious balance between selfhood and language in *Blindness and Insight*. "An ontology can only bypass the primacy of the cogito," says de Man, echoing Heidegger, "if the 'I' in the 'I think' is conceived in too narrow a way" (*BI* 50). Our effort here has been, of course, to examine how post-structuralism is employed in an American context, in which the self of a Romanticism reinforced by phenomenological existentialism permeates critical analysis and underlies the critical methodology, even if that methodology is presumed to be, in part, imported from foreign territory. In this context de Man can state that there is "a screen of language that constitutes a world of intricate intersubjective relationships" (*BI* 11) and that literature is "the steady fluctuation of an entity away from and toward its own mode of being" (*BI* 163). Such statements preserve the centrality of language as well as the entity of individual self.

As the influence of post-structuralism increases in the 1970s, de Man will show, in *Allegories of Reading*, more and more of its influence although his basic predisposition, albeit challenged, will remain what it was in *Blindness and Insight*. In the earlier book de Man treats critics who write of literary works, and the major issue concerns the coherence of logical propositions. That issue does not require an attentiveness to a theory about the referentiality of all language, which clearly is required if the question is raised (as it is in *Allegories of Reading*) regarding the meaning of poetry and philosophy. No longer can rhetoric be simply the cosmetics of argumentation; it takes on an analytic priority, which brings into question not only the possibility of consistency in meaning but even the properties and creative functions of language itself. There is still, in *Allegories*, an attention to conflicting meanings: the essay on Proust discloses "mutually exclusive meanings," even multiple meanings, "all of which are true and false at once" (*AR* 76). But de Man, in shifting to poetry and philosophy—both of which, significantly, he handles as intentional propositional statements—also faces the fundamental problem that if all language is ultimately rhetoric, then anything of which it speaks cannot be demonstrated to have any substance beyond its description. Analysis "explodes the myth of semantic correspondences between sign and referent" (*AR* 6), which was the primary accomplishment of structuralism from Saussure onward. If language is propositional and sign and referent are severed, we are left with propositions about something to which language cannot be directly referring. In literature, the link between figure and meaning "can always be broken"; we cannot know with certainty whether language "is about anything at all including itself, since it is precisely the *aboutness*, the referentiality, that is in question" (*AR* 161).

Yet to de Man "the notion of language entirely freed of referential constraints is properly inconceivable. Any utterance can always be read as semantically motivated" (de Man's intentionality); "from the moment understanding is involved the positing of a subject and an object is unavoidable" (*AR* 49). As for Descartes, Husserl, and Heidegger, the necessary must be the place where we start. Nevertheless, what cannot be otherwise, the logically unavoidable, is itself unsubstantiatable; substantiation would require an additional prerequisite axiomatic surety, not simply the (apparent) comparison of statement and objective reality, which can only motivate and not legitimate the axioms of a system.

Self-hood is not exempt from such a critique. In discussing the *Birth of Tragedy*, de Man reveals Nietzsche's positing of the possibility of "truth," the "immediacy" of a language that resembles, in this work, music for Nietzsche, whose subsequent writings each subvert the assumption of such immediacy. Nietzsche, de Man says, came to recognize that "the phenomenalism of consciousness" is susceptible to being deconstructed "as soon as one is made aware of its linguistic rhetorical structure" (*AR* 109). In the essay on Rilke, de Man determines that the categories of subject and object stand "in the service of the language that has produced them" (*AR* 37); and in that on Proust, the relationship between the self of the narrator (Marcel) and the narration is metaphorical. Of Rousseau we learn that, "from the point of view of truth and falsehood, the self is not a privileged metaphor" (*AR* 187).

There is a distinction, addressed by Lacan, between the self and the representation of the self in language by the use of the word "I." Like all other signifiers, "I" cannot correspond directly to the signified. When de Man discusses the self as metaphor, he is, I believe, referring to the signifier of self that is located between authorial self and reader, which leaves the ultimate nature of the self (the self itself) unknowable. This is different, in an important way, from establishing, as Lacan and Derrida attempt to do, that there is no *entity* of self at all. For example, the poetic representation of "I"—as Paul Jay perceptively addresses it in *Being in the Text*—the poet's attempt to circumvent "the artistic problems of translating a *psychological* subject into a literary one" (27; emphasis added) is not congruent with post-structuralism. De Man tries to define the "complex relationship between selfhood as metaphor and the representation of this metaphor," which he sees as a focus in Heidegger and Kant (*AR* 187). His position is basically that, as for Kant, the thing-in-itself cannot be known, because, as for Heidegger, selfhood has no manifestation outside language. Although the signifiers of self prove inadequate, the self is never entirely eroded in de Man.

The literary criticism of de Man does not require, any more than does that of Miller, the full post-structuralist epistemology. What is primarily at issue is multiplicity of interpretation, supported both by the actual discovery in texts of indeterminacy (interpretive undecidability and internal contradiction) and the logical impossibility of verifying the referentiality of language. Neither of these issues logically compels a final decision about the constitution of self. Admittedly, between *Blindness and Insight* and *Allegories of Reading* de Man undergoes significant changes of emphasis and purpose. Nevertheless, the evidence of the text indicates a retention of the self of phenomenology. We find in the later essays that the entity of self has become unknowable, not eradicated. Even a critic like Juliet MacCannell, who hopes to demonstrate that de Man was never a phenomenologist (nor a neo-Romantic) but was a deconstructor even in the early essays, remarks that de Man retains his "heroic subjectivity" although he "knew he would fail." Why he would do this, MacCannell finds "unanswerable" (MacCannell [1985] 70).

De Man himself presents his strongest statement in defense of the Derridian view of self in an essay in which he argues that, for Nietzsche, "the idea of individuation, of the human subject as a privileged viewpoint, is a mere metaphor by means of which man protects himself from his insignificance by forcing his own interpretation of the world upon the entire universe." Because "faced with the truth of its own non-existence, the self would be consumed," the self is placed in a text as if it might preserve itself by acquiring the permanence of the text, even if the purpose of the text, in Nietzsche, is to deny the self. (In speaking of Rousseau [AR 136], de Man says, the "radical negation of self is in fact its recuperation.") Yet "by asserting in the mode of truth"—that is, Nietzsche's text as declaration—"that the self is a lie, we have not escaped from deception"; the text deceptively creates the very self (in this case, Nietzsche) that it purports to deny (AR 111-12). De Man's language in this analysis combines both the self as agent and the self as language. One must ask, Just what is this self that is protecting itself? And how, if it does not exist, can it potentially be consumed by the knowledge of its non-existence? Furthermore, "individuation" and the human subject as "viewpoint" are not the same, although de Man's sentence structure makes them so. In Nietzsche, the self is a strong presence: Nietzsche is hardly—as Stanley Corngold demonstrates in *The Fate of the Self**—a post-structuralist. (Also, Werner Hamacher, who declares that for Nietzsche the being of the individual

---

*Stanley Corngold, in an admirable analysis, acknowledges that "the main tendency of the New French criticism is an attack on the self as it has been understood since German Idealism as the agent of its own development." Nietzsche and certain other German writers have been misrepresented as somehow fully supporting such an attack, when in fact, according to Corngold, Nietzsche does "reconstruct in the place of the deconstructed subject the possibility of another authentic self" (4). Admittedly, this self is a "divided *unity*" (x; emphasis added); and although "the self as self is precisely what cannot be represented in the concept" (5), it "lives as a conscious subject aiming through poetic activity to produce the self which it means to be" (10). Interestingly, Corngold admits that, while the procedure to "thematize the self" in the German writers he studies provides "*apodictic* [self-evident, in the Cartesian sense] evidence of the self," he cannot claim that it is "also *adequate* [empirical?] evidence of the self." Nevertheless, he concludes, to believe that the self is "merely a metaphor" would be "to go mad." Consequently, he strongly opposes "the proclamation of the death of the subject" (12).

is over and above "every determinable form of human life" (119), notes Nietzsche's statement that the "individual has *monstrously grand significance*.") De Man, in fact, resembles Nietzsche more than he does Derrida. He is more a rhetorician than a philosopher, more an opponent of (false notions of) truth than of self, which is perhaps why he must use the Nietzschean text to make, ostensibly, a Derridian point. Again, this is not to argue that de Man should have been more like Derrida. De Man's position, from an American point of view, is more understandable than that of Derrida, whose intention to fully deconstruct the entity of self, supported by an invented, often changing, vocabulary of non-words, may itself simply raise conundrums. And for Derrida to admit his skepticism becomes more of a tactic than a theory. De Man's maintenance of the self, which his theory of intention and authorship demands (to establish the site of insight), is not, at least from the perspective of American literary criticism, a weakness but a strength. It permits author, reader, and critic to be granted identity, even if that identity cannot be unquestionably signified.

In an early essay, "Intentional Structure of the Romantic Image," de Man posits that the language of the Romantic poets "seems to originate in the desire to draw closer and closer to the ontological status of the *object*," although language can never achieve the "absolute identity with itself that exists in the natural object" ([1960]; in *The Rhetoric of Romanticism* [1984] 6-7). The theme is repeated in "The Rhetoric of Temporality": the subject/object union, striven for by the Romantic poets, is unachievable, and the self is always prevented from fulfilling "an illusory identification with the non-self" (*BI* 207). The motivation for seeking this union with objects is that the existence of natural objects, or at least nature altogether, is not time bound, like that of a human being, who has "an authentically temporal destiny" (*BI* 206). Humankind, for whom "understanding can be called complete only when it becomes aware of its own temporal predicament" (*BI* 32), yearns to escape time, to "take refuge against the impact of time in a natural world to which, in truth [the self] . . . bears no resemblance" (*BI* 206).

The theme is prominent in Sartre's existentialism. We exist only in time, our definition and our tragedy, since time must bring with it death. The quest of poetry, as Bloom will repeat again and again, is the quest for eternity, the overcoming of death. The awareness of death is ever present in existentialism; the post-structuralists, infrequently to be sure, also must acknowledge it. "The intermediary of death," states Lacan, "can be recognized in every relation in which man comes to the life of his history" (*Ecrits* 104). Foucault refers to "Desire, Law, and Death . . . the concrete figures of finitude" (*The Order of Things* 378). Derrida speaks of "death as the concrete structure of the living present" (*Of Grammatology* 71).

In an essay on Shelley, de Man is reminded by *The Triumph of Life* that "nothing . . . ever happens in a relation, positive or negative, to anything that precedes, follows, or exists elsewhere, but only as a random event, whose power, like the power of death, is due to the randomness of its occurrence" ("Shelley Disfigured" [1979] 69). This passage, perhaps outrageous, reminds us not only of existentialism but also of Hume's critique of cause and effect, a pillar of his skepticism. We have mentioned that Derrida serves the function, in his relationship to empiricist structuralism, of a modern Hume, while at the same time his basically Kantian esthetic provides a link to the Romanticism that attracted the New Critics. The reception given to de Man's use of post-structuralism can be understood in this context.

As the optimistic outlook, following World War II, of a society based upon the achievements of science and technology began, for humanists, to be challenged, existentialism was at first received in the United States with optimism, despite the pessimism of the French sources. Individuals were free, life was self-discovery, and unavoidable death (as described in the writings of the existentialist theologians) was more a motivation than a disability. This viewpoint was quite compatible with the turn of an originally "scientific" New Criticism toward Romanticism, despite the rightist politics of its practitioners. By the mid-1970s, much of the optimism had dissipated, at least for those in the humanities who had allied themselves with a nearly millennial liberalism. In an empiricist setting this waning optimism generated skepticism, to which post-structuralism contributed. When we recognize that de Man's comments on Nietzsche, quoted above, are similar to notions of the "necessary fictions" that humans must live by—the ideas of Hans Vaihinger, Wallace Stevens, and even Hartman in his "Structuralism: The American Adventure" (and we have earlier cited Lyotard's definition of post-modernism as the disappearance of any sustaining "grand narratives")—de Man's import becomes clearer. De Man seeks to sustain courage in the face of a growing recognition that knowledge, *all* knowledge, is being undermined. It is, in part, the courage that existentialism proposes, despite the inevitability of death. Critics have commented upon de Man's "rhetoric of authority . . . the impression of having a grip on truth" (Lentricchia 284), upon his "didactically asserting what he claims is true" while he denies truth (Culler, *On Deconstruction* 274), upon his "pretending to truth . . . in the mode of error" (Corngold, "Error" [1983] 106). We see this not as an arrogance in *Blindness and Insight* (although not to minimize the authoritative demeanor of the style) but as a version of existentialist commitment in the face of the undecidable, in the face of death. But as Denis Donoghue states, "De Man's mind is so ascetic that it thrives without joy" (*Ferocious Alphabets* [1981] 184). De Man represents the search for principles in a milieu that, in the 1970s, increasingly subverted all principles, a milieu in which the lack of certainty no longer verified our freedom (as did existentialism) but threatened to impose an inescapable determinism. De Man, from France, recognized this better than did others in America. The pessimistic aspect of existentialism becomes amalgamated with the darker side of Romanticism, the pessimism of its irony. In *Allegories of Reading* there is a certain wisdom, but it is the wisdom of resignation. In *Blindness and Insight*, after all, there is "insight." Even if the "temporal act" of understanding has no completion (*BI* 32), there is an "insight" that somehow, perhaps paradoxically, transcends, emerges from, error. But such insight can only be a personal achievement of the critic (how else use the word?); a text itself cannot have insight. Post-structuralism does not, in de Man, replace existentialism, or Romanticism (Steven Melville sees de Man's work as "a continuing effort to recover Romanticism" [120]), but confirms its most pessimistic consequences, in the way that, for a humanist, a similar turn from empiricism is a turn toward the unverifiable, which courage alone cannot itself sustain—at least not in the United States, where, unlike modern France (where Marxism is the predominant intellectual force), the intellectual class customarily relies, even if unwittingly, on the support of traditional spiritual and/or religious values.

In the 1960 essay, "Intentional Structure," de Man had written, "the existence of the poetic image is itself a sign of divine absence, and the conscious use of poetic imagery an admission of this absence" (*Rhetoric of Romanticism* 6). This assertion much resembles Miller's announcement of the "disappearance of God." As this absence became for Miller more than a notable historical phenomenon, became the condition of persons in the modern world, so for de Man the poetic attempt to evade time and death, to link humankind and eternity, has proven, as it must, a failure—a failure that may leave us wiser, but nonetheless more insecure and desperate. Miller has remarked, "De Man might be called 'the master of the aporia,' though this would be an oxymoron, since the aporia, like the chasm it opens, cannot, in fact, be mastered" ("'Stevens' Rock'" 338). It seems very much the case that de Man's "mastery," his stylistic authoritativeness, is the substitution of a dominance of the text for an unachievable mastery of truth, time, and mortality.

This analysis allows us to ask why, in Miller and de Man, the literary criticism is so weighted with apparent importance, drama, even melodrama. If poems may have more than one interpretation, perhaps even innumerable interpretations, why does this call forth the language of the "abyss," the destruction of the referentiality of language, and finally the vanishing of our very selves? These would seem, at first, to be conclusions far in excess of the matter at hand, the difficulty of interpreting literary works in one way only. Yet "insight" for de Man is not unlike a spiritual attainment, a transcendence of error not through additional logic but through something that de Man does not name. His eventual alienation from this "insight"—an alienation prominent in *Allegories*, in which deconstruction arrives to beleaguer the authorship on which de Man had much depended—is an alienation, like Miller's admission that God is not here where we are, from his access not only to truth but to self. De Man's stylistic deportment, which is much to his credit (although Americans, in these matters, demand passion: Kierkegaard or Keats), does not minimize the circumstances. If selfhood vanishes, even the heroic struggle of poet or critic against death, heroic because futile, would be reduced to the inconsequential. The only symbol of eternity left is the endlessness of literary interpretation—hardly a consolation. Everything thought to be known, even that I am I, threatens to fall, for de Man, into the post-structuralist "space," which is time as well, that has gaped opened to its widest dimensions.

Geoffrey Hartman: The Critic as Seer

The attempt to establish truth on what is fundamentally undeniable has been the primary task of philosophy, whether what is fundamental is determined to be unquestionable logical propositions or the irreducible contents of consciousness, sensation and self-awareness. Language has traditionally been used both to express, to describe, the basic data and, through deduction, to build the philosophical system. But once the status of language is questioned, once it becomes uncertain that language can express, as a transparent medium, a reality external to itself, then the customary idea of truth is challenged. "Truth" may be seen as a property internal to the linguistic system, an inter-structural attribute. It becomes no more than an internal consistency, perhaps conventional. That real things may exist outside of us may not be denied, since most theorists reject solipsism. Nevertheless, perhaps all we can know is language, reality itself being beyond direct comprehension.

Such an approach, whether it is found (or thought to be) in Nietzsche, Saussure, Peirce, or Sapir and Whorf, is not equivalent to post-structuralism. It is one thing to deny that ultimate truths are knowable and another to propose—as do Lévi-Strauss and the post-structuralists—that the human self is itself nothing but language, since pure desire is contentless, and when the content of self is sought nothing is discovered but language (even sensation becomes knowable only through language). The distinction is not always kept clear. Vincent Leitch, for example, notes that "one of the more *curious* and *extreme* aspects of post-structuralist theory is the deconstruction of the self" (111; emphasis added), as if this aspect were but a quixotic application of post-structuralism, rather than its founding tenet.

That the ground of truth (God, logic, pure sensation, faith, "apodictic" certainty, a priori knowledge, mystic revelation, or whatever) should vanish is a bad enough predicament, one that many have come to live with in the past hundred years. It is a predicament that, despite the absence of certainty, can call forth commitment and courage, at least an altruism, perhaps a persistent grasping toward the unreachable, even with the threat of discouragement and despair. But that the self should be denied: Is that not a crushing blow? For even our commitments then lose their dignity, it would seem, as does our despair, and we apparently are kept going only by unquenchable desire. In the recent writings of Miller and de Man there is a recognition of the problem; and I believe they reach a steadfast resolution, a calmness that is not an optimism, mastering texts instead of truth, going as far as the deconstruction of the self as it is presented in textual form, the signifiers of the self, without yielding to the complete eradication of a self with its own ontological status, although this becomes unknowable. Despite the threat of a full-blown Derridian analysis, they retain a position in phenomenology and existentialism. Hartman and Bloom also come to assert the self, the subject, with an enthusiasm and a vigor absent in Miller and de Man—and not because they know something Miller and de Man do not. For de Man and Miller, perhaps more judiciously, deconstruction reveals the absence, the empty space, in the midst of existence, which does not permit one to say more than to disclose what one cannot know. Hartman and Bloom, also knowing this, have no qualms about continuing with confidence along the optimistic path that is the American interpretation of existentialism and Romanticism (freedom, self-definition, and spontaneity, rather than caution, absence, limitation, and self-control), even without evidence, even knowing that all belief may be fiction and error.

By his repeated assertions concerning freedom and his citation of Romantic poets as models of the creative process, Hartman consistently reaffirms his belief in the ontological status that we find granted to the self by Descartes, Coleridge, and Sartre. Derrida's post-structuralism first, for Hartman, releases critical creativity by treating language as a malleable medium of art, like the sculptor's clay, a medium that surpasses the meaning it is customarily constrained to communicate. Language has an "excess over any assigned meaning." Language is "not reducible to meaning" (Preface to Bloom et al., *Deconstruction and Criticism* viii). The word "excess" typifies Hartman's stance. To him, indeterminacy in language yields an abundance that is reason for exuberance, much unlike Miller's "abyss" and de Man's resignation to "blindness." The creativity of the critic places him in a role, elaborated in *Criticism in the Wilderness* (1980; cited hereafter as *CW*), equivalent to that of the Romantic poet, near to the sacred and prophetic. Although, as Hartman further absorbs Derrida, the nature of the poetic self is scrutinized in more detail, and creativity becomes, in *Saving the Text* (1981; cited hereafter as *ST*), a composing (inventing, defining) of the self in addition to its free expression. This marks a significant difference between the two books, published but one year apart.

The only critic "whom we must take seriously," Hartman declares, is one "who overextends his art, having decided that his role is creative as well as judicious" (*CW* 215). Such a critic will "reject previous rules of expository sparseness, pedagogical decorum, and social accommodation" (174), will reject the "neoclassical decorum that, over the space of three centuries, created . . . over-accommodated prose" (85). His work will be a "fusion of creation with criticism" (190). And creation is inseparable from freedom: "Each work of art, and each work of reading, is potentially a demonstration of freedom . . . a mode of expression that is our own" (2). If we want a rejuvenated American criticism, then we must look to "'a certain eternal tradition of abounding vitality and moral freedom'" (11; Hartman is quoting Randolph Bourne).

These assertions are reminiscent of Sartre's in *What Is Literature?*, although Hartman does not mention Sartre. The ancestry he does claim is that of Romanticism. Matthew Arnold was interpreted by the New Critics as valuing criticism "only as attached to art," subordinated to it, denying "its [criticism's] own autonomous or freelance qualities." This, for Hartman, is an overly restricted interpretation: there is a "falsification, even repression, of Romantic origins in Arnoldian and much New Critical thought" (*CW* 7 and 9). A proper rereading of modern criticism will demonstrate that criticism should not be subordinated, that it is itself a distinct creative form, creative in the way that the Romantic poems are (compare the deconstruction of Arnold in Miller's "Search for Grounds"). It is preferable, Hartman advises, to look to Emerson.

The deconstructivist perspective is found helpful, although minimally interjected here, in order to substantiate the indeterminacy of texts, which Hartman then uses to substantiate the freedom of the critic. In a much earlier essay "irony," "paradox," and the removal of "the mimetic dependence of imagination on reality" (Wordsworth is his example) were considered by Hartman to be literary techniques, part of the history of style (*Beyond Formalism* 48). Post-structuralism comes to demonstrate that such characteristics—though Hartman eventually stops calling them by their New Critical names—are necessarily present, as indeterminacy, in all literary texts. "The more pressure we put on a text . . . the more indeterminacy appears" (*CW* 202). For Hartman, whose use, here, of post-structuralism amounts to borrowing a concept rather than a methodology, indeterminacy is not, as for Miller and de Man, the end of the critical path, where the aporia is reached and the text is unraveled. Instead, indeterminacy is the beginning, the place where the critic, having broken loose from the shackles of univocal meaning, assumes his freedom, his creative license. Philosophical skepticism becomes a waiver. Indeterminacy of the text, the absence of definitive meaning, becomes allied with a rejection of philosophical determinism, with the presence of freedom, specifically the freedom to create (essentially Coleridge's "imagination"), and more specifically to create criticism (like Arnold, Emerson, and Carlyle). No such alliance can easily be found in Derrida's writings through the early 1970s, for there is in fact no necessary logical connection between the terms (critical) "indeterminacy" and (philosophical) "determinism," despite their sharing an etymology. Humans may not be free, yet linguistic meaning may be limitless.

If language is in excess of meaning and textual meaning is consequently indeterminate, then philosophy becomes a quest for truth and not a possible statement of it (recall Jaspers's comments on Kant), an expansiveness of meanings rather than a discovery of absolute meaning. Philosophy becomes like art. In this view, Derrida, no matter what he contends, does not subvert philosophy, so defined, but joins with its most significant functions (Preface to *The Fate of Reading* [1975] x). Although "no one can agree on what to name" them, a group of "recent" critics (and Hartman means the Yale critics) have crossed the line "into philosophy, theology, linguistics, sociology, and psychoanalysis" (*CW* 240; implications of this interdisciplinary movement are lauded in MacCannell and MacCannell [1982]). In Derrida, all language, even that traditionally thought to be the communication of propositions, is transformed into the Kantian art object. In Hartman, similarly (though without reference to Kant), criticism, as a form no longer subordinated to the works of which it speaks, can now become both philosophy and art. The critical essay becomes "an intellectual poem" (*CW* 190), like the "philosophic work of art" envisioned by the German Romantics, the "synthesizing criticism that would combine art and philosophy" that Schlegel foresaw (38), an example of which Hartman, in *Saving The Text*, will find in Derrida's *Glas*. Such a work of criticism, achieving "the difficult alliance . . . between speculation and close reading" (174), could become "a *sacred book*"—a that notion Hartman finds in Burke, Frye, and Augustine (strange bedfellows, it may seem to us)—"yet one created out of everyday, profane experience" (92).

Invoking the possibility of achieving the sacred is Hartman's paramount purpose in *Criticism in the Wilderness*. In his essay in *Deconstruction and Criticism*, Hartman had called the poet a "reader of a prior and sacred text" ("Words, Wish, Worth" 196). Much earlier, in *Beyond Formalism*, Hartman had asked, "Is visionary poetry a thing of the past, or can it coexist with the modern temper?" The "death of poetry" was an idea that occurred to the Romantic poets. After them "the future belonged to the analytic spirit, to irony, to prose" (310; the essay quoted was written in 1962). Implicit here is the disillusionment with science and technology, the opposite of poetry for the Romantics and for the New Critics, a disillusionment extending in America well beyond literary criticism. By the late 1970s Hartman will associate the possibility of the visionary, which seems for him to be essential to the sacred, with criticism. We are reminded of Arnold's turn from writing poetry to writing criticism in the midst of his own career.

In *Criticism in the Wilderness* Hartman exhorts critics to imitate "older, more sacred modes of commentary," to reinstitute "sacred exegesis" (*CW* 176). A reacquaintance with the Romantics, with their aspirations for a union of philosophy and criticism, will permit us "to recover from the forgetfulness of the sacred" (45). And Hartman goes even further: "criticism is a contemporary form of theology" (54).

The theology of criticism is set against empiricism and, accordingly, against science. "Criticism cannot be identified as a branch of science"; we must "renounce the ambition to master or demystify . . . by technocratic, predictive, or authoritarian formulas" (*CW* 40-41). Hartman is rejecting not only (early) structuralism, whose style he calls an "evasion" to the extent that it proposes "a scientific metalanguage," but also the formalism of the New Critics. He proposes that "only the empiricist tradition contributes to English studies" in America; "despite Coleridge and Carlyle," German idealism has never been received and incorporated in American criticism (156).

It is the effect of empiricism on language (the "over-accommodated prose") that most concerns Hartman. He characterizes as "ludicrous" (*CW* 155) "the spectacle of a polite critic dealing with an extravagant literature . . . in his own tempered language." He laments the "imperative of language purification," the idea that language and meaning can, if sufficient pains are taken, coincide, an idea whose origin he at one point finds as far back as the Renaissance "in a scientific or religious or parareligious form," although it is clearly the ramifications of this history, abetted by empiricism, for the English language that is Hartman's emphasis.

It is intriguing that Hartman also attributes a weakness in American criticism to "democratization," for (as has been discussed in Chapter Four) the premises of democracy, as of empiricism, can also be traced to Locke (the *Two Treatises on Government* of 1698), although Hartman does not make this connection. For Hartman, democratization "prevented a new mystique" from entering criticism; students have learned to extract meaning from literature without any "higher or abstruse theory" (*CW* 285). And since criticism cannot be a science, its pretense to science will cause it to relinquish more than it can gain: "we gave up one province after another, especially to the social sciences; and then stood back to mock them" (290).

In Chapter Two I argued, somewhat contrary to Hartman, that the New Critics, as they progressed, made a strenuous attempt to counteract empiricism by drifting more and more toward Romanticism, particularly toward Coleridge—a process that Hartman seems both to recognize and to underestimate. Hartman understands that empiricism has often been the adversary for modern literary critics. It was so for the New Critics (eventually) and for the phenomenologists. Early structuralism was but a momentary attempt at a criticism grounded, like the early New Criticism, in empiricism, an empiricism that the structuralists derived from Marxism. But the reaction to classic British empiricism is not simply a matter of undoing the "accommodation" of language or of method. Empiricism is an encompassing philosophy, a totalizing epistemology as well as a politics that cannot be the philosophy that will someday yield the philosophic art and criticism to which Hartman, like the German Romantics, aspires. The empiricist temperament so impermeates our cultural inheritance that all attempts to escape it have failed, often ending in disillusionment and dissatisfaction, perhaps in withdrawal. In this empiricist environment alternatives to empiricism (whether evangelicalism, the late New Criticism, a popularized existentialism, the work of Chomsky, the counterculture of the 1960s or, in all likelihood, post-structuralist deconstruction) appear unable to predominate, although Hartman, representing a minority justly proud of their membership (Shelley's "unacknowledged legislators"), is hoping this might happen, with literary criticism leading the way.

In *Criticism in the Wilderness* Hartman is not, in the Derridian sense, a post-structuralist. His deconstructivist "indeterminacy" legitimates a freedom and creativity derived from American and English sources, to which is added the ingredient of an Americanized existentialism. His poetic language is a variant of the Kantian art object and his freedom is the play of Schelling, both seen from the perspective of the Romantic poets, who set in opposition art and science. But this opposition is also contained in the New Criticism. Hartman, like the New Critics, segregates literary language from other language, as did Richards (when he contrasted emotive and propositional language), whose psychological poetics Hartman will come to emulate.

While the details of Derrida's philosophy contained in *Of Grammatology*, *Writing and Difference*, and *Margins of Philosophy* are of little concern to Hartman (even less than to Miller and de Man), the creativity of Derrida, especially in *Glas* (and we note, as well, "Fors" [1977] and "Living On" [1979]), a work much unlike its predecessors, provides Hartman with an example, more than with a theory, of poetic/philosophical achievement, an example that Hartman attempts to replicate. We have already argued that Derrida, having poeticized all language, is frequently writing poetry. "*Glas* is an art form itself" (*ST* 35).

For the Romantic theorists, the merger of philosophy and art was to yield insight into the truth. Just as Kant's "Reason" could "know" truths that logic, "understanding," could not itself substantiate, so might the esthetics of idealism provoke a poetry that constituted the truth within its own linguistic structure rather than by its reference to the objective facts of reality, facts demonstrable by other means. The poet's discovery of truth was equally his creation of it (the theme of Abrams's *The Mirror and the Lamp* [1953]). Kant had shown that what we know is inseparable from what we, as subjects, contribute to knowing. For Kant, however, the contribution of the subject is determined by the necessary and inescapable structuration that mentality imposes upon sensation, which is a different matter from the human capacity to structure or restructure perception through the intentional creation of objects of art. While Kant firmly believed in the validity of science and philosophy as sources of knowledge, of truth, the Kantian esthetic is one more of pleasure than of knowledge. The idea that poetic insight creates what is, for us, truth comes not so much from Kant's own conclusions but from a critique and reformulation of Kant. One can interpret Coleridge's "secondary imagination," which disassembles and then newly reorganizes perception, either as a psychological theory, in which case poetry affects us as if it were true even though it is not true in the same way that scientific statements are (the empiricist interpretation; Richards's view), or as an epistemology in which poetry, through symbol for example, does yield truth, since truth is what the subject projects into, rather than receives from, the world. This latter position is closer to the Romantics, and their belief that philosophy and art might join is a belief about the potential for access to truth.

Derrida does not intend to be either a Kantian or a Romantic. His poeticization of all language rests upon Kant's Third Critique but clearly excludes the First Critique. Derrida means to subvert the notion of "truth" in philosophy. Though he recognizes that humans believe some statements to be true and others not, he removes the ground for such belief. Philosophic truth is a fabrication of the logocentric tradition; all we really have is language, without access to anything beyond it. Because he relies on Derrida as his example, Hartman's version of the integration of philosophy and truth is not quite that of the Romantics to whom he refers. Philosophy, in fact, has really lost its definition. Philosophy, in Hartman, *becomes* art; but the union is achieved only by eradicating what have always been the pretensions of philosophy. "The very desire of philosophy to be itself . . . absolute knowledge is the ultimate pathos," Hartman declares, and then immediately refers to "the fullness of equivocation in texts" (*ST* 23). The goals of traditional philosophy are subverted, and Hartman asks whether we can "live in this verbal revel" or must we continue to seek to surpass it, to achieve that "metaphysical 'beyond' or 'real presence,' which has gone under so many names" (26).

Believing that philosophy and art can merge, Hartman asserts that "the religion of art, a phrase we would ordinarily associate with the Romantics . . . is about to turn into a philosophy of art" (*ST* 72). The phrase "philosophy of art" would seem to imply that there can be a philosophy of other things, that philosophy is not encompassed by art. But Hartman further refers to "the birth of philosophy out of the spirit of art" (72), which makes art, as parent, the source of philosophy. Whether or not Hartman is meticulous in his argument is not the point. Rather, the point is to understand that Hartman's (and Derrida's) fusion of philosophy and art only becomes possible once the possibility of truth is undermined, once philosophy itself forfeits its credibility, which was not the situation envisioned in the late eighteenth century. Steven Melville remarks that "philosophy has turned increasingly to criticism for an understanding of its own activity, and so has risked also its possible disappearance into it" ([1986] 115). Similarly, writing from the perspective of the Frankfurt school, Seyla Behabib "dissents" from the turning of philosophy into "literary criticism, aphorism, or poetry" ([1986] 15). Hartman's Romanticism is a truthless critical exuberance, in which artistic and critical creativity become a substitution for truth, hence also a replacement for religion and philosophy. The "sacred" of *Criticism in the Wilderness* becomes not the location of the most sanctified truths; the sacred is artistic creativity.

If this is so, what legitimates artistic activity beyond the enjoyment of it or the immediate experience of it? This is the very question that is usually put to critical formalism, including the New Criticism. And as the New Critics claimed that poetry can affect our lives, despite the absence of any truth other than the contextual, so Hartman will take a similar stance. Whether the deconstructive critics have, in fact, any contribution to make to human well-being, to personal or social change, is a topic raised by a number of critics.

That art—which here includes criticism—serves a special purpose for the *practitioner* is also a concern of Hartman's. His reading of Derrida's *Glas* "suggests a new theory of how literary works are generated by the dispersal of a name that seems to be and never is 'proper' " (*ST* 18). The author's search for his own self is his search for the meaning of his own name, the signifier of himself that is his authorial signature. Yet the direct referentiality of a signature, like that of other words, is an impossibility: language is always in excess of meaning. "The psyche may have to live in perpetual tension with its desire to be worded" (131). In Lacan's theory, the child viewing its specular image "imagines" a unified autonomous entity, which is a potentiality, at that moment, since the child is still weak and dependent. Because, afterward, the self is created by language, the language of the Other, the self is not the envisioned autonomous entity but a linguistic structuration of desire in the empty space between one human biological organism and all others. Similarly, to Hartman, "literature is the elaboration of a specular name," which is "always already a fiction." "The quest . . . becomes lifelong" (111).

The post-structuralist "space" between signifier and signified, the space in which most post-structuralist generativity (of self, "man," meaning) occurs, Hartman names a "wound." He quotes Derrida: "The signature is a wound, and there is no other origin to the work of art"

(*ST* 101). The wound is "the expectation of a self that can be defined or constituted by words, if they are direct enough," an expectation that, since it cannot be fulfilled, has "traumatic consequences" (131). For the author, his works are an attempt to create (de Man called it "recuperate") a self that will be fully named, signified, by his signature. The attempt cannot succeed; the possibility of a "proper" name fades, the "fading of the self in or into the literary work" (37).

It is notable that Hartman remarks that "the true name of a writer is not given by his signature, but is spelled out by his entire work" (*ST* 128). This passage is similar to those found in the phenomenological critics, although Hartman does not proceed very far in this direction.

The search for a self whose process of self-definition lasts lifelong is also a tenet of the existentialists: Sartre states in "Existentialism is a Humanism" (1946) that for man "existence precedes essence," which supports the position that individual self-definition is concluded only by death. Lacan's theory is likely indebted to Sartre, for the lecture in which Lacan posits the mirror stage was delivered in 1949. For Sartre, of course, as for Descartes, the self does exist, with its freedom, prior to what will be for the individual its definition—obviously not a strong argument from the vantage point of post-structuralism. But if freedom is to mean true freedom of choice, then positing a primary entity of self can hardly be avoided, for a free "agent" is needed; not to take this approach is eventually to be led to determinism, which I find post-structuralism to be. Hartman has a theoretical foot in both camps. If we ask what might be the "psyche" to which Hartman refers (*ST* 131), just as we might ask of Lacan *who* the prelingual child is that imagines an autonomous personal entity, we can understand, in thinking through possible answers, why the Anglo-American ego psychologists posited independent ego strengths distinct from primal libidinous desire (id). Freedom, presumably, requires an agent that the socially constituted self, derived from the later Marx, cannot provide. Hartman, like the majority of American theorists in the humanities (which distinguishes them from the scientific behaviorists, whom they have always opposed), wishes a freedom in its widest sense—not the freedom of Spinoza, which is an acceptance of the necessary, nor a freedom that is only a space for unconstrained desire, distinct from intellect.

Post-structuralist thinking, according to Hartman, has given a "shock to humanistic thinking"; textual indeterminacy has created a "graveyard of meanings." Nevertheless, human will survives, "specifically the *will to write*" (*ST* xvii). This perdurable will is, we assume, der... ed from Schopenhauer (through Freud) as well as from Nietzsche.

What motivates the will to write is language itself: language is "the motivating residue" (xvii). To define with philosophical precision the ontology of will is, admittedly, not Hartman's purpose, but it does need to be asked, again, what or who is being motivated. In Schopenhauer, Nietzsche, Marx, and Freud, conscious motivation is customarily determined by unconscious forces, yet in each of these writers a recognition of this can result not only in a knowledge of the process but also in an overcoming of it, whether by "genius" (Schopenhauer), by the unmasking of hypocrisy, by praxis, or by therapy, all of which require a notion of selfhood distinct from that of post-structuralism (although it is is possible, of course, for one to find post-structuralism preferable). The influence of Romanticism on Hartman persistently regenerates freedom, particularly the freedom of the artist; but if artistic freedom is possible, then, since anyone might, theoretically, become an artist, human freedom, in a general sense, becomes defensible. Freedom, if the word has any meaning at all beyond the unconstrained (that we are free to travel is not an argument that choosing to travel exhibits freedom), always preserves the self. Hartman introduces *Saving the Text* with a quotation from Adorno: "Spirit . . . will only recognize the nature of things if it does not cancel itself out. That force of resistance constitutes the sole measure of philosophy today."

We have already commented upon the use of communication theory, particularly speech-act theory, in the Anglo-American critique of post-structuralism. Such a use reintroduces "intention" (which has also been found in de Man) as a concept distinct from primary desire—although post-structuralism has no need of such a theory, since speech-act theory presupposes the very subject that post-structuralism denies. In addressing the effect of poetry on the reader, aside from the provocation of critical writing, Hartman takes a similar approach, calling attention to the "interpersonal impact" of words (*ST* 120). "The reality of the effect is inseparable, in literature, from the reality of words that conduct voice-feeling" (121); "the affective power of the word is what is enclosed by the literary work" (150).

Hartman recognizes that this is "a counter-statement to Derrida," a counter-statement that is a "restored theory of *representation*" (*ST* 121; emphasis added). What is represented are mental states (feelings, for example). The "mimetic and affectional power of words" should not be "cheapened." Those who propose "antirepresentational theories" (the structuralists and post-structuralists) should understand that, by denying representation, they indirectly affirm its relevance: they have "secretly declared what the *bad* magic is" (120). That "expressive" theories of poetry can be encompassed by the term "mimesis," since mental states are represented, has been asserted earlier in this study. That is one of the approaches of the New Critics, found in Eliot, and, more importantly for our purposes here, in Richards, whose perspective Hartman's resembles. In *Beyond Formalism* Hartman had confessed: "It is time I showed my hand. . . . Literary form is functional and . . . its function is to keep us functioning, to help us resolve certain hangups and bring life into harmony with itself," a function that might not only "reconcile or integrate" (a reference to the New Critics) but that might, in a "truly iconoclastic art," be "structure-breaking," not conservative but "rebellious" (366). In *Saving the Text* Hartman writes of "the tremendous impact words may have on psychic life" (*ST* 122). (Undoubtedly, Derrida understands that words can affect psychic life.) The psychological speculation of the early New Criticism was designed to account for the significance of experiencing poetry by separating "emotive" (poetic) statements from propositional (scientific) ones. This resulted in Brooks's notion of the dramatic propriety of poetic statement, which, because the New Criticism was more and more influenced by Romanticism, became a dual-truth theory. Although Derrida has demonstrated to Hartman that "truth" in the ordinary sense (reference to an objective reality) is a fabrication, Hartman wishes to maintain the importance of poetry, an importance which can only exist for him if there are subjects affected by poetry and something to which poetry really does refer. He needs, accordingly, to make a "counter-statement" to Derrida. The return to a rudimentary psychology, most compatible with the New Criticism (except that one finds unity and the other finds indeterminacy), in the context of referentiality is additional evidence of how empiricism is never quite dispelled in American criticism, even if the critic's strongest accomplishment is usually a rebellion against it. For Hartman, the poet is not only seer and prophet, artist and philosopher, but psychologist as well. Although he has moved some distance toward Derrida between *Criticism in the Wilderness* and *Saving the Text*, just as de Man did between *Blindness and Insight* and *Allegories of Reading*, Hartman cannot ultimately relinquish referentiality or the subject, to whom *Saving the Text* is dedicated (the dedication reads, "For the Subject"). The critic's daring has meaning only if a reality (even if "psychic") is confronted by the creativity of a free self.

In the introduction to *Saving the Text* Hartman refers to the "graveyard" of meaning; he alludes to the "mortality" of every code and to "corpses" of ideas. He asks whether what remains after the deconstruction of metaphysics might have a "tincture of immortality" (*ST* xvi and xxiv). Particularly important is his citation of Franz Rosenzweig, who has shown, in Hartman's words, that the philosopher's "wish to know the All takes off from a fear of death" (xvii).

As de Man masters texts in lieu of the impossibility of mastering time and mortality and as Miller's deconstructions bring us to the abyss opened by the disappearance of God, so Hartman, too, transports death—which we have also found in Foucault, Lacan, and Derrida— into the midst of his critical/philosophic art. The "oldest imperative of religion and philosophy is to make us "conscious to what degree one lives in the void, in an 'economy of death'" (ST 26).

The post-structuralist "space," the gap between signifier and signified, between language and meaning, has over time become an ontological emptiness, both death and the human condition in modern times, when (whether this be description or metaphor) God has disappeared, when the foundation of truth has been eroded. But while Miller comes eventually to arrive at the abyss, into which he peers, and de Man reaches an equilibrium in indeterminacy, Hartman starts out by accepting indeterminacy as a license for freedom and self-expression. Each of them comes to deconstruct the signifiers of the self in the literary text; each stops short of Derrida, who, we have seen, identifies deconstruction as a particularly American phenomenon (Davis and Schleifer 87). Miller and de Man seek clarity, with reserve; Hartman seeks creative expansiveness, with exuberance. Miller and de Man have their grounding in phenomenology, which leads to a resignation, and awe, in the face of the inexplicable. Hartman is a thoroughgoing Romantic. His response to the ontological emptiness, awesome for him too, is to fill it up with creativity (which brings honor, if not healing, to the "wound" that is the authorial signature), with the language of literature.

Discussing the beliefs of Schiller, Murray Krieger states that "human response takes no higher form than his aesthetic creations, which . . . are his emblems of that capacity for freedom, expressing himself as an independent authority, separate from nature as a source of value." He turns then to Nietzsche, who, says Krieger, viewed "man's potential Apollonian grace as a necessary usurpation of what had been the power of the Gods" (Krieger, Theory of Criticism [1976] 113).

For the Romantics it is not only that God has withdrawn but that man has fallen. As a consequence, the presence of God and religious salvation is replaced by the aspirations of man and his potential for bringing about his own salvation (which Abrams describes in Natural Supernaturalism). From the perspective of a twentieth-century Romantic, with his own disillusionments and perhaps unfounded hopes, the quest for truth has become the art of configuring the world so that it might be somewhat explicable and perhaps even manageable, at least a suitable place to continue our discussions with one another, perhaps for mortals a god-like act. If there is no truth, we can at least be truthful. There may, at the least, Hartman says, be "trust," for "one breaks words with the other as one breaks bread," though we live in an age where "imposture is rife" (*ST* 137). And as for other Romantics, who also, like Coleridge, assume a congruence between human and divine creativity, so for Hartman. Whether there be a deity or not, creativity is always the saving grace.

Harold Bloom: Poetry and Anxiety

Bloom's critical method is not that of Miller, de Man, or Hartman. He does not perform "deconstructions," and he attacks the French post-structuralists. Accordingly, one might acknowledge the affiliation between Bloom and his three Yale colleagues but not analyze his criticism. Nevertheless, certain issues that he raises, usually sporadically and with little of philosophy (although there is a philosophical context in Bloom, which Jean-Pierre Milieur explores), are those raised by post-structuralism, particularly as these concern the self and creativity. He develops a theory both of "intertextuality" and of indeterminacy that relies upon the consideration of the poem as human action. Intertextuality and indeterminacy become psycho-linguistic terms, attributes of the dynamics of human interaction through language, rather than attributes of language, or of a single text, itself.

Bloom proposes to prove that poets write in response to the major poets who have preceded them. Every poem incorporates, appropriates, certain of its predecessors. "There are no texts"—if by texts we mean the autonomous, self-enclosed poetic objects of the New Critics— "but only relationships *between* texts" (*A Map of Misreading* [1975] 3; cited hereafter as *MM*). Having to follow in time those poets whose achievement has already been verified by their inclusion in the accepted canon, a new poet feels the anxiety of his belatedness, of his coming afterward, of his desire for his own poetic fame and accomplishment in the face of the poetry of a precursor who serves as the highest standard and yet who must be, if the poet is to be granted an equivalent stature, matched or surpassed. The anxiety of the poet-to-be, Bloom's "ephebe," evokes his rebellion "against being spoken to by a dead man (the precursor) outrageously more alive than himself" (*MM* 19), more alive because recognition and homage through historical time bequeath a form of immortality, which the new poet may crave but surely cannot count on. To create his own work, the new poet, in what is a combination of rebellion, anxiety, envy, repression, and aspiration, "misreads" his precursor, revises him, incorporates and denies him, suppresses and depends upon him, reveres and discounts him. (Barbara Johnson, noting all the male pronouns in Bloom, calls the filiation "patriarchal" ["Gender Theory" 105].) "Poetic influence . . . always proceeds by a misreading of the prior poet, an act of creative correction that is actually and necessarily a misinterpretation" (*The Anxiety of Influence* 30; cited hereafter as *AI*). This "blindness" toward the predecessor is transformed into the "revisionary insights" of the new poet's own poems (*AI* 10). Bloom presents six "revisionary ratios" that trace the process of influence.

Elaborating this theory is Bloom's major task during the 1970s and into the 1980s. Much of his criticism is a discussion of it, which consists of patterns of interaction much resembling those of the Freudian Oedipus complex, intermixed with metaphors of "influence" derived from Greek thought and from theories of the creation of man and the universe traceable to Gnosticism and to the Kaballah. All of these are aggregated in a unique and compelling way, replete with quotations and analyses of an extraordinary range of literature, sacred and profane, organized and often subsumed within Bloom's arcane and flamboyant (Donoghue, in *Ferocious Alphabets*, finds it "regrettable and nearly useless" [139]) technical vocabulary. For our purposes here, however, we are interested in Bloom's responses to the post-structuralist concept of self, and in his views, as they are relevant to deconstruction, of the function of criticism.

Bloom has a clear understanding that the predominant issue in poststructuralism is the nature and function of the human self. He refers to "the larger subject of which the study of poetic influence is only a part." "Who speaks," he asks, "most grandly, for the isolate selfhood?" (*MM* 63). Bloom cites Emerson, whom he calls the "father of the American Romantic Selfhood," particularly because of his "sense of one's own divinity" (*MM* 64). Bloom recognizes that the French post-structuralists have sought to subvert the notion of "self" by describing (inventing) the self as a linguistic structure, and nothing else but this—which leads, claims Bloom, to the positions of Foucault and Derrida "that language by itself writes the poems and thinks." (The extent to which Bloom does or does not misread or caricature the post-structuralists should, during this discussion, be evident from our previous chapters.) Bloom's rejoinder to this "humanistic loss" is that "the human writes, the human thinks" (*MM* 60).

"At issue is the evaluation of consciousness" (*MM* 86). Consciousness is not simply a "mask." While admittedly the ego may be

deconstructed, which we find in Nietzsche, the result of such a procedure need not be to "demystify" meaning, to consign meaning to
obsolescence, for the act of *interpretation*—demonstrated by Blake, Bal-
zac, and Browning, who, says Bloom, also deconstructed the ego—can
be done "in the mode of recollecting" meaning. For Bloom, deconstruction of the ego is, it seems, a technique, not a demonstration, a
strategy rather than a proof; meaning can be regathered, re-collected,
and consciousness can be rescued from being conceived of as an epi-
phenomenon or solely what has been referred to in an earlier chapter
as a dependent variable. Consciousness and self-consciousness are not
distinguishable in Bloom (they r:.iy in any case be inseparable). Consciousness and self are likewise inseparable, although obviously not
synonymous, since that would quickly yield the constituted post-structuralist self. Not that Bloom explicates these matters in a thorough and
punctilious way, for the large majority of his interests are generally
elsewhere, outside the scope of this study.

Much of the function of the self in Bloom, or at least the function
most central to his poetics, is to recognize a danger to itself and to
counteract it, through "defences" (as Freud used the term), among
which are poetic tropes, which specifically defend against the anxiety
of influence, the anxiety caused by the poet's dependence upon the
precursor and his need to excel that precursor. Poems are a form of
"divination," which is "seeking to foretell dangers to the self" (*AI* 59).
The paramount threat to the self is, of course, death; in avoiding this
the poet searches for his own voice, his own individuality, his own
immortality, and his own name.

Bloom credits Hartman with noting that "in a poem the identity
quest always is something of a deception" (*AI* 65). This deception does
not entail that the self is a linguistic fabrication. On the contrary, the
quest, as a "formal device" of poetry, is always incomplete: that is
"part of the maker's agony" (*AI* 65), which emphasizes the dilemma
of self not obviates it. The poet first discovers that poetry is both "external and internal" to himself: his "profoundest yearnings" find their
definition in the works of other selves, "great poems outside him," yet
the poem, his own poem, poetry, is *"within* him" (*AI* 25-26).

If the self defines itself only through time, through deeds, through
acts, including the act of writing, then, as we have seen, the ontological
status of the entity that is engaged in the self-definition is called into
question. What can that entity be (it might be asked of Sartre) whose
existence precedes its essence, its definition, that originally definition-
less entity endowed with freedom? The post-structuralists, having no
need for a primary freedom, can reject this Sartrean (and Cartesian)

entity altogether. The American critics we have been discussing cannot do this; they retain a primary selfhood. Their deconstruction, as they attempt to integrate Derrida into their works, is, like Nietzsche's, usually performed upon, limited to, the *signifiers* of that self as it is found in poetry. Bloom comes to take a similar approach. By 1982 he is willing to say that "my own quarrel is not with the deconstruction of the psyche. . . . I am now more than prepared to see that reduced to the trace of a trace" (*The Breaking of the Vessels* [1982] 31). There is some humorous irony here, since the last phrase is a parody of Derrida. What Bloom is in fact willing to acknowledge is "the image or lie of voice" in the poem, "where 'voice' is neither self nor language" (4), neither the author as he is in himself nor language alone, as the post-structuralists would have it, but something perhaps in between (perhaps, we might guess, that to which others have attached the term "persona"). Bloom's interest is in "the figure that a poet makes, not so much in or by his poem, but as his poem relates to other poems" (7). He is trying both to admit into his system a poetic voice that is not the self and that shows the generative influence of other poetic voices and to preserve, somewhere, the self of the poet (the poem is *his* poem) and of the reader. "When you read you confront either yourself or another" (13). The deconstructible "psyche," an ambiguous term, seems inserted between voice and self in order to include a term that represents the constantly evolving self-definition as well as the name sought by and created by the author throughout his work.

Bloom is customarily unclear about these matters, although, since he does not pretend to write philosophy, he should not be faulted. He resolves for himself, or at least contrives to manage, the dilemma of what the "true" fundamental entity of the self might be by turning first to the Kaballah (through the writings of Gershom Scholem) and then to Gnosticism. His need for this resolution, given the prominence of post-structuralism and deconstruction, explains this move, a most ingenious one in the early 1980s, since Bloom certainly cannot refute the post-structuralist critique on philosophical grounds. In the "deep" reading of a poem, writes Bloom as Gnostic, what one comes to know is "a realization of events in the history of your own spark or *pneuma*," which is the "Gnostic spark or spirit or inmost self" (*Agon* [1982] 8). The knowledge, in Gnosticism, is of one's self. This *pneuma* "lurks beneath the *psyche*" (9). The Kaballah as well has proven to be compatible with the selfhood that Bloom demands. In *Kaballah and Criticism* (1975; cited hereafter as *KC*), we learn that the Kaballah addresses "the enigmatic joining of soul and body" (*KC* 44). The soul is clearly an entity since, according to Isaac Luria, upon whom Bloom heavily relies, it can transmigrate.

Interpretation of the Kaballah, which allows for the maintenance of selfhood—a concept that in Bloom unites mystical essences, Bergsonian vitalism, Cartesian consciousness, and "mind" (Ryle's ghost in the machine)—provides, in addition, both a paradigm for the theory of influence, a comparative paradigm that Bloom develops at some length, and an alternative metaphorical schematic to post-structuralism. Kaballah is "essentially a vision of belatedness" (KC 17). The sefirot, the "attributes of God emanating out from an infinite center to every possible finite circumference" (23), are "primarily language" (25); the emphasis in Kaballah is always upon "interpretation" (33). Most significant is Bloom's treatment of Luria's version of the "breaking of the vessels." To Bloom, the ramification of this cataclysmic shattering, as he describes it in Agon, is that "meaning gets started by a catastrophe" (43). An exceptionally compelling analogy can be made (though Bloom does not do so) between the breaking of the vessels and the splitting apart of signifier and signified in post-structuralism, represented, in Lacan, by the bar (which becomes a wedge) in the fraction S/s. From Saussure's "difference" to Derrida's différance, meaning flows (pours out) not from terms (words) but from the spaces between them, a space that post-structuralist theory has burst open by shattering, in its own view, all of Western philosophy. The modern "catastrophe," the breaking apart of language and reference, is what Foucault describes.

Bloom, whose dominant motivation for turning to esoteric sources is, we believe, the preservation of the self so threatened in modern times, does not proceed in this direction. That those in the Kaballistic tradition had as their own motivation the desire for an "end to exile" (KC 52), an end to the Diaspora, allows Bloom to return to an earlier theme, which he equates with the theme of exile, that of "all poetry . . . defending against death" (KC 52).

We have included in the analysis of each of the deconstructivist critics the theme of a literary criticism that, when addressing the self, calls forth the prospect of death and the human attempt to confront it, to understand its meaning, to master and commit to a life's work despite, or perhaps because of, this threat.

The theme is a central and powerful one in Bloom, frequently repeated. "Poems are refusals of mortality" (MM 19); "every poet begins . . . by rebelling . . . against the consciousness of death's necessity" (AI 10); there is a "deep hidden identity between all psychic defence and the fear of dying" (KC 84).

The subject of death is generally absent from Freud's works until the later writings. Because the infant cannot know of death (the id has no knowledge of it), death cannot be a motivation. In the later works (e.g., *Beyond the Pleasure Principle*) Freud proposes a death (thanatoptic) instinct or urge (drive), a desire to return to an earlier state, the anxiety-less and conflict-free state of pre-organic quiescence. This premise has become the least acceptable of the Freudian hypotheses in Anglo-American psychoanalytic theory. With references to the later Freud, Bloom also equates death with a state existing prior to an individual's life, rather than (only) an event, a conclusion, that comes at the end of it. In Bloom's speculations on poetic language, the prior state, death, is associated with language as it exists before the individual is born into it. We can relate this to the *langue* of Saussure, to which the structuralists and post-structuralists assign the constitution of the self for the very reason that the self is composed of a language that preexists the user of it. Bloom, while he preserves selfhood, designates "literal" meaning "as a kind of death," since "if death ultimately represents the earlier state of things, than it also represents the earlier state of meaning, or pure anteriority" (*MM* 91). Since the poet writes to defend against death, he must reject, to the extent that this is possible, linguistic meanings as they would exist without him. The poet defends himself "against the deathly dangers of literal meaning" (*MM* 94).

To have identified the theme of death in the four Yale critics, particularly as it is associated with time and absence (the post-structuralist "space"), is not meant to reveal the discovery in American deconstruction of a single motivating concern. After all, the topic of death is a ubiquitous one, hardly avoidable in the discussion of any literature whatsoever. But the analysis of the *manner* in which the subject is treated in the American critics helps substantiate that the elimination of a fundamental entity of self (the basic proposition of the structuralists and post-structuralists) is avoided by the American critics, who, unlike their colleagues in France, refrain from moving into a linguistic determinism grounded in a fully constituted linguistic self. Bloom rejects post-structuralism because he clearly recognizes the underlying suppositions. In Miller, de Man, and Hartman the self of phenomenology, existentialism, and Romanticism (in quite different proportions in each critic) endures. If self and freedom are retained, death is configured quite differently than in a theory that does not posit them: this is a major difference between existentialism and post-structuralism. The American critics more resemble the former than the latter, for reasons that involve the cultural environment in America—the religious heritage, the ambivalence toward an irremediable empiricism, the values of self-discovery and personal striving, the belief in freedom (as a philosophy and a politics), the disaffection with philosophy and meta-physics, and so on—topics repeatedly addressed here. Bloom asserts that "writing" in Derrida, in the "spirit of the great Kabbalist inter-preters," is a trope designed to "keep us from the void" (*MM* 48). From our perspective, however, post-structuralism has also created a void and placed it in the midst of philosophy. It is a void that, when post-structuralism is imported, becomes allied in America with ontological emptiness, death, alienation from Being, religious doubt and Romantic disillusionment; yet at the same time it is the site of freedom, self-determination, creativity, and individualism.

Poetry, for Bloom, is an act of the human self: "a poem is . . . act," he states in *The Breaking of the Vessels,* "or else we need not read it a second time" (40). And in *The Anxiety of Influence* he asserts that "poems are written by men" (43). Because a poet must misread his predecessors if he is to achieve his own best poetry, as (for similar reasons) critics must misread the texts they analyze, and because these misreadings are, through influence, part of the meaning of any poem, all poems are intertextually related. "Let us give up the failed enterprise," pre-sumably that of the New Critics, "of seeking to 'understand' any single poem as an entity in itself" (*AI* 43). Our knowledge of a text is our reading of a text, a reading that also creates a new text. A reading is never objective, never free from our own psychic needs. There is only misreading, which does *not* imply, as Culler believes it does, that there is "the possibility of a correct reading" (Culler, *On Deconstruction* 115). In poetry, "every poem is a misinterpretation of a parent poem"; in criticism, "there are no interpretations but only misinterpretations, and so all criticism is prose poetry" (*AI* 95). In criticism, we learn elsewhere, "the reader is to the poem what the poet is to his precursor" (*KC* 97). That critics and poets share their mission as well as their methodology is a bond between Hartman and Bloom, for whom the language of poetry and the language of criticism "cannot differ, in more than de-gree" (*BV* 29; in *Agon* 16, Bloom finds in the two languages "no dif-ferences, in kind or in degree"). Both poets and critics are creative misreaders.

It is the theory of misreading that encourages Bloom to claim, in *A Map of Misreading,* that poetic meaning is "radically indeterminate" (*MM* 69). Bloom's "indeterminacy" is a link to his Yale colleagues, and it suggests similar problems. It is not certain in de Man whether "blind-ness" is a psychological characteristic of the critic or a circumstance imposed by language (which we believe it to be in Miller and in Hart-man); even if language is indeterminate, why cannot the critic under stand, and himself reveal, his own blindness? (The compromise is to allow especially good writers to deconstruct themselves.) In Bloom, similarly, it is uncertain whether indeterminacy is within the language of the poem, or all poems taken together, or in the psyche of those who must interpret the poem from a biased position of self-interest. Bloom's "indeterminacy" seems, like the New Critical "paradox," another psycho-linguistic term ("old ambiguity and irony writ large," says an unappreciative Grafi in *Literature against Itself* 145). Yet he does not seem to want to make a final commitment here. In his contribution to *Deconstruction and Criticism* Bloom writes, "When I observe that there are *no* texts, but only interpretations, I am not yielding to extreme subjectivism, nor am I necessarily expounding any particular theory of textuality" ("Breaking of Form" 7). Despite Bloom's evasiveness, which is understandable since he makes no claim to a philosophically rigorous poetics, his theory certainly appears to be more of a psychology than a study of language itself. Bloom's "indeterminacy" is, in any case, certainly not in the deconstructive mode derived from Derrida.

In fact, says Bloom, responding to post-structuralism, "meaning . . . is excessively impoverished by a Nietzsche-inspired deconstruction, however scrupulous" (*MM* 85). The French post-structuralists with "all their invocations of semiology or the archaeology of discourse conceal a few simple defensive tropes, and they are at least as guilty of reifying their own metaphors as any American bourgeois formalist has been" (*KC* 105). (Derrida's reifications were addressed in Chapter Eight.) For Bloom, the "so-called linguistic model" has merely set up a "demiurgical entity named 'Language' "; he does not find "this trope any more persuasive than the traditional trope of the Imagination," since it cannot account for how meaning "ever got started anyway" (*Agon* 43). The "problematics of deconstruction" in France are the "death throes of German Romantic philosophy" (*Agon* 30). And Bloom goes much farther, accusing the post-structuralists of having an "obsession" with "language," which in their usage is no more than "a defensive trope" (*KC* 105). In *The Anxiety of Influence* he refers to the "dreariness of all those developments in European criticism that have yet to demonstrate that they can aid in reading any one poem by any poet whatsoever" (13).

Bloom's attack on post-structuralism can hardly be convincing, although it certainly is enjoyable, because it is based on no real argumentation. It is an outright rejection, not a rebuttal. I have been emphasizing that the structuralist and post-structuralist subversion and elimination of the autonomous, free entity of self (the self as it is found in Locke, Descartes, or Kant) cannot be duplicated by American critics, for whom the constituted consciousness of Marxist theory is of little theoretical consequence. While Miller, de Man and Hartman all avow Derridian allegiances, their deconstructive criticism ultimately retains the self, especially as it is defined in either phenomenology, including existentialism, or Romanticism. Bloom's discarding of post-structuralism, which nevertheless has influenced him, is the most blatant example of this preservation of selfhood, a fundamental critical purpose in Bloom, accounting for his own probing into venerable mystical disciplines, which is his own "defense" of the beleaguered self.

The Romantic poets and theorists, German and English, sought truths of a universal validity. They intended themselves to be "representative" of a humanity functioning at its best, with insight and creativity. Their poetry, philosophy, and esthetics were to reflect the human condition and human potential in its most encompassing definition. The poet, in the writings of Bloom, has a more personal and self-centered mission: to ward off dangers to the self, to surpass predecessors, to establish a personalized literary identity and immortality. (This is viewed by Lentricchia as Romanticism misunderstood [329].) In Hartman the poet-philosopher is seer; in Bloom he is egoist. The theory of influence is one of a self-absorbed competitiveness, a competitiveness that bears a resemblance to the ambition of an American self-made man forging his own success, a self-interest partially justified by Freud and also saturated with an egocentricity that, in Bloom's unique recipe for achievement, contains the residue of a modernized reconception of the personality of the nineteenth-century artist: egoist and genius, tormented and struggling, the "isolate selfhood" in what is for Bloom its most compelling manifestation.

CHAPTER TEN

Deconstruction:
The Critical Setting

The similarities among the four Yale critics consist of certain themes to which they are attentive, rather than of directly corresponding critical practices. While all four critics rely upon concepts of indeterminacy, of the excess of language over any single meaning or aggregation of meanings, and of the creative function of the critic as distinct from an explanatory duplication or clarification of the text, Miller and de Man most frequently treat the isolated text as an enclosed linguistic system, while Hartman and Bloom usually treat the text as the crossroads where many texts intermingle. Despite their differences, however, and for reasons that the previous chapter has addressed, the four critics customarily have been classified into a "school" of criticism, called "deconstruction," by those who either follow or disparage the approach.

Our review of the entry of deconstruction, treated as if it were a coherent theory, into the critical milieu has raised many general issues, some of which were prominent during the time when the New Critical outlook was pervasive. Of particular importance here are: whether literary criticism is a science, is like a science, or is in some way an interpretive discipline quite different from a science; whether the fundamental empiricist predilections of Anglo-American theory are confirmed or challenged by deconstruction; and whether the connection of deconstruction to French post-structuralism is of more or less significance than the links to elements within the American cultural environment, including some additional recent Anglo-American viewpoints on critical theory. Now that the theory of deconstructive criticism has been reviewed, we must again address the issues in psychology and politics that arose during our earlier discussion of structuralism.

Derrida has admitted to some surprise at the explosion of the American deconstructive enterprise: deconstruction, after all, "was far from being either the first or the last word" and "was not intended to be a password for everything that was to follow" ("All Ears," discussed by Llewelyn [63]). That deconstruction is not simply a replication of post-structuralism has already been demonstrated.

Deconstruction, the New Criticism, and Romanticism

Because deconstructive critics read a literary work as closely as the New Critics did, the similarity of method may suggest that the two critical practices are analogous. William Cain remarks that "anyone versed in the techniques of the New Criticism" can readily acquire the deconstructive method, even if deconstruction relies on philosophical theories for which the New Critics had no need. Despite the theories, which appear to some critics as "foolish and extravagant," the critical methodology has not much changed ([1984] 114). To Peter Brooks, post-structuralism in the United States seems, for the most part, "simply the indulgence, under a new guise, of the traditional American penchant for exegesis and interpretation" ([1981] xvii). And Eagleton asks whether the recent treatment of the literary text as a linguistic system is "really much different from the New Critical treatment of it" (*Literary Theory* 111).

Since a critical methodology may be used within almost any theoretical context (a Jungian psychologist and a biographer might also be close readers), the comparison of deconstruction and the New Criticism at this level has limited usefulness. Nevertheless, some critics sense a resemblance between the two critical practices, and their impression merits some support. Language is not "referential" for the structuralist and post-structuralist, but neither is it necessarily so for the New Critic, if "referential" is defined as the function of language to reproduce (describe) that which exists independent of it. If the referentiality of the language is at issue, says Walter Benn Michaels, "we might all claim to have been deconstructors some twenty years *avant la lettre*" ("The Interpreter's Self" [1980] 185). There is a difference, however. For the New Critic, it was poetic language only, distinct from propositional uses of it, that had a "contextual" rather than a referential meaning. Poetry was, in fact, often defined in the New Criticism by what it was not: it was not scientific language. Its statements were not verifiable by any objective tests of truth and falsity. But referential language had to be presupposed in order to know how poetry was a special, a unique, use of language. The New Critics did not consider, as do the post-structuralists, that perhaps *no* language is directly representational (although Frye considered this at the end of his *Anatomy*), that no language can directly present or re-present a reality external to the mind. What has occurred in post-structuralism, from the American perspective, is that all language has now become like poetic language had been for the New Critics. The New Critical domain of poetry has been expanded. Deconstruction might be seen as an imperialistic form of the New Criticism: the opponent's territory has been colonized. This has been, for the deconstructors, legitimated by what we have seen as Derrida's transformation of all language into the art-object derived from Kantian esthetics, the same place that is the ultimate source, filtered through the post-Kantians and Coleridge, of the New Critics' art-object.

But if *all* language is contextual, the possibility of "truth" is eradicated: to know the truth, we must be able to identify falsity. The New Critics, unlike the deconstructionists, would not relinquish the possibility of truth. The rudimentary psychology of Richards, with its pseudo-truths that have a psychologically adaptive function, eventually became inadequate, and pseudo-truth theory became dual-truth theory (truths of poetry, truths of science) in order to preserve truth in poetry. Insofar as the content of mentality was represented, New Critical poetic truth maintained a form of mimesis, although it was a major step to assert (by the time of Brooks's *Well Wrought Urn* [1947] and Krieger's *New Apologists* [1956]) that the content of the poem does not simply reproduce a pre-existing mental content but that both are created simultaneously as the poem is written. The complete subversion of referentiality may be seen as a logical possibility inherent in the New Criticism, rather than as an aim of it.

Dual-truth theory was a version of Locke's belief in two sources of knowledge, perception and reflection. But it was also the Romantic distinction between science and art, which empiricism can, pushed far enough, allow for—as can German idealism. And what pushes it far enough is not only the recognition that reflection is a source of knowledge but also the possibility in empiricism of Humean skepticism. Empiricism supports both the access to truth (e.g., scientific method) and the impossibility of truth. The New Critical turn to Romanticism is, we have said, a reaction against the consequences of empiricism (determinism, materialism, science and technology), legitimated by skepticism; the deconstructive turn to indeterminacy is also legitimated by skepticism, that of Derrida, perhaps influenced by his own studies in the United States as a young scholar at Harvard in the 1950s. Deconstruction does not *require* any philosophical substantiation through German philosophy, neither from Kant, Nietzsche, nor Heidegger. Empiricist skepticism, however, is not sufficient by itself to justify a Romantic poetics. It does, as a first step, allow an escape from the assumption that the mimetic referentiality of all statement is verifiable. Romanticism, in which reflection is granted a creative (not merely an associational) function, then becomes an option. Deconstruction in America has, in effect, continued on the path into Romanticism along which we followed the New Critics; it has attained the point where all language is like poetry, specifically Romantic poetry.

In poetry the New Critics found a balance of opposites; the deconstructive critics deny the balance. Nevertheless, that there are opposites, propositional irreconcilables, in the literary work is conceded by both sides. In Europe, "contradiction" had been placed in a Hegelian and Marxist context; contradiction, which was a universally generative force, could never vanish, for contradiction was a process, not simply a "synchronic" state of affairs, as it is in New Critical interpretation. Post-structuralism maintains the Marxist conflict without, however, allowing for intermediary syntheses. Criticism in the United States, at the time of the New Critics, had no need of Marxist dialectic, for a "balance" of disparates could be found in Coleridge. That disparate elements cannot be reconciled in deconstruction follows not unnaturally in the American tradition (sociology underwent the same change, from theories of harmony and balance to theories of conflict and group interest) because it can result not only from the influence of post-structuralism but also from a skeptical reading of Coleridge. From this point of view, deconstruction is a skeptical New Criticism.

The methodology of deconstruction assumes, in fact, that literature might have propositional meaning and then shows that it does not. De Man and Miller analyze poetry as if it attempts to say what they prove it cannot say, which is to some extent to set up a straw man. The abyss of indeterminacy is created by the shock of discovering indeterminacy where "univocal" determination may have been supposed to be; but the shock only occurs if the determinacy has been anticipated in the first place. While the New Critics professed that the meaning of a poem can be determined, this meaning was ambiguous, paradoxical, and ironic, held together through the "organic" unity of the poem. But the abyss, the limitlessness, the indeterminacy in the poem is no less a function of its structure as an entity than is balance, harmony, and determinacy, even if one discards the term "organic." That the poem is held together by the meaning-generating strategies of its own rhetoric is an assertion both of deconstruction and of the New Criticism. It is a principle that can be affirmed without the support of post-structuralism, German philosophy, French existentialism, and

Marxist theory. There is continuity, not schism, between the New Criticism and deconstruction.

Derrida's writings can, in fact, themselves be explicated by a New Critical methodology. The disparate elements he both opposes and reconciles are logocentric philosophy and his rejection of it, a rejection that he admits can be accomplished only within the language of logocentrism—an approach itself at the far reaches of irony and paradox, as well as of skepticism. Derrida is not, obviously, intending to write a poem suitable for New Critical analysis; but from an American perspective this possibility is precisely what makes him so attractive. He can be read, as Hartman reads him, as poetry, poetry holding the irreconcilable in a perpetual multiplicity but in balance, too, the balance *inside* Derrida's individual works, in which the crucial terms change from essay to essay, functioning as poetic terms, since Derrida claims no referential value for them.

If Derrida's philosophy is read as poetry, then a literary criticism based on it can be granted the status of poetry. The deconstructors have done this, not all to the same degree, whether criticism is a form of poetry, as for Hartman and Bloom, or a close relative, as for Miller and de Man. This helps account for the rapid proliferation in the United States of the "criticism of criticism," the "theory" of criticism, in which works of criticism are "interpreted." And if this analysis is applicable to criticism, which was previously thought to resemble a science, an empiricist study, it might, with some imagination, be applicable to all language, to all disciplines of investigation, science included, for these are all interpretive. Deconstruction and the New Criticism here part company, for the New Critics always maintained that criticism, unlike poetry, was an empiricist, science-like, enterprise. Early structuralism did not challenge this idea. Post-structuralism rejects it. This rejection accounts for the disappearance of that form of empiricism promoted by the early reception of structuralism. The discussion of "semiotics" wanes. The attention to Frye as a transitional "structuralist" and to Chomsky as a structuralist ally vanishes in the theory of deconstruction. While the New critics sought in poetry an alternative to an empiricism that included literary criticism, the deconstructionists believe they might vanquish empiricism by subsuming all language in poetry, which subverts the notion of verifiable propositional truth.

It has been said that deconstruction "threatens" criticism because it removes the possibility of claiming verifiability in interpretation, which the New Critics certainly did seem to believe they might achieve. But asserting that the truth cannot be known for certain is different from claiming that there is no such thing as truth. The latter position is inherent in Derrida's post-structuralism, and we do not believe that such an approach can survive in an empiricist setting. Although deconstruction seems to head in this direction, its position on the nature of truth is ambiguous, or unformed, because the critics are not philosophers and the discussion is generally limited to matters concerning literary interpretation. In an empiricist environment, the limitations on human knowledge are conceded but truth is not forsaken. This position is represented by E. D. Hirsch, who believes that "knowledge is possible even in textual interpretation" but that we can never know if "that knowledge has in fact been achieved . . . for we cannot know *that* we know" (*Aims of Interpretation* 12). The threat to validity in interpretation is not a threat but a widespread admission; and the possibility of numerous interpretations is what motivates the profession of criticism in the first place.

A further threat to traditional criticism, it can be argued, comes from the undermining of the *unity* of the literary work. Since the notion of the art-object as entity is not affected whether opposites are reconciled or forever unreconciled, whether there is a harmony of meaning or an abyss of meaning, whether there is a single meaning or an infinity of meanings, this threat is superficial.

On the other hand, I have argued that deconstruction in America is ultimately author centered because indeterminacy comes to function as a property of *communication*. De Man addresses the "blindness" of individuals; Hartman's philosopher/poet is our modern seer and prophet; Bloom's poet is an Oedipalized personality. Perhaps a significant threat to literary criticism is that, as the New Critics recognized, if the focus is given to criticism as creativity, which includes reader-reception theory, then criticism might be put in the position of forfeiting its autonomy (as Richards once thought it should) to the disciplines of individual or social psychology.

The relationship between deconstruction and the New Criticism deserves an extensive study in which the much-abused notion of "Romanticism" would play a large part. It might even be asserted that the multitudinous interpretations given to the word "Romanticism" is, for American criticism, the primary example of indeterminacy at work. What Romanticism might be, what that signifier might signify, is a fundamental critical puzzle, the basic "aporia." Perhaps much of the indeterminacy that the deconstructive critics find in Romantic poetry is a result of trying to determine what the encompassing message of Romanticism is, as if each individual poet is an incarnation of it.

Earlier, it was mentioned that Todorov and Scholes link structuralism and Romanticism. The same issues arise in assessments of post-structuralism and deconstruction. Graff contends that the impulses in Romanticism and deconstruction are the same; he finds in both a "paradoxical double attitude of a near nihilism coupled with the most fervent yearning for the conquest of nihilism" ("Deconstruction as Dogma" [1980] 408). Norris, on the other hand, believes that deconstruction is "a resolute critique of the central motivating impulse in Romantic poetics," the impulse to form an "indissoluble fusion between language and reality." He admits, however, that pressing language and logic "up against their limits," which deconstruction does, also "paradoxically validates the 'rhetoric of Romanticism'" (*Deconstructive Turn* 129-31). Both critics refer to a paradox, which is to identify the problem of relating deconstruction and Romanticism, but not to go very far toward solving it. Critics who discuss deconstruction commonly refer to Romanticism to show either that deconstruction is different, new, and innovative or that it is derivative and nothing new: their motivations are usually easier to recognize than is their evidence.

I have maintained the position that in America deconstruction—a concept that Derrida develops during a refashioning of phenomenology—progresses further in the same direction traveled by the New Critics. In this way, a bond is formed between all of them, and a good name for this bond may well be Romanticism.

Tracing the theoretical lineages does not, of course, explain the phenomena, which I have tried to do in earlier chapters. The continuing motivations in modern American criticism evolve from the larger cultural environment. There is the intent to counteract classic empiricism as the only form of valid knowledge, particularly as this knowledge yields science and technology; to reject determinism, particularly as this takes the form of a scientific behaviorism; to verify "creativity"; to establish the legitimacy of poetic statement, even if non-propositional or even non-referential; and, most importantly, to preserve certain notions of self. These have been related to the politics of the "left" and to the social movements of the 1960s and 1970s in the United States. In handling each of these topics, as in the treatment of the esthetics of literary criticism, the concept of Romanticism has proved relevant.

Science and Literary Interpretation

Marian Hobson points out that, in French, the word "empiricism" has mostly negative connotations. It is defined in the *Dictionnaire Robert* as that which "'n'a rien de rationel ni de systematique,'" and one of its antonyms is "scientifique" (290). In France, the heritage of Germanic philosophy remains inescapable: "empiricism" connotes naive, inadequately interpreted sense perception. In the Anglo-American environment, empiricism, defined according to its English uses (the sense in which we have been using it throughout this study) has always been the dominant and most-respected tradition. Frequently, its synonym is "scientific."

This distinction assists the clarification of differences between deconstruction in America and post-structuralism in France. In an Anglo-American empiricist setting, the result, for literary critics, of the interaction between a Humean skepticism that logically results from Locke's empiricism and an imported phenomenology (whether existentialism or post-structuralism) yields an empiricist critical methodology much like the New Criticism (close reading) in which what is discovered is philosophic indeterminism and literary indeterminacy. In America, empiricism provides method; phenomenology provides freedom. We have argued that in France there also has been a movement resembling that from Locke to Hume; this is the movement from the "empiricism" of the later Marx, which is the empiricism of linguistic structuralism, to the "skepticism" of Derrida. In a setting where German philosophy, from Kant to Heidegger, is most influential, the result of the confrontation of an "empiricism" turned to skepticism and phenomenology, in post-structuralism, has been a phenomenology attempting to integrate an empiricist "linguistic model," a determinism that subverts phenomenology's claim to knowledge. In France, phenomenology provides method; empiricism provides determinism.

In Anglo-American literary criticism it is empiricism that yields the methodology, so the question of the relationship between criticism and science remains important. While science cannot explain the existence of meaning (as has been argued in Chapter Seven), which is an irreducible concept, it can address the function of meaning, how it operates. This is also a central task of literary criticism. If the existence of meaning is a given, then we need to inquire *how* meaning, a specific meaning, comes to be obtained by the reader of a literary text. The responses to this inquiry may be that the meaning is contained in the words and structure of the text and the reader has the ability to extract it, replicate it in his mind; or that the meaning is created in the mind of the reader by the act of reading, and the text provokes this emergence of a meaning it does not itself contain. All of the other responses fall between these two, attempting to combine them, attempting to locate a level at which the alternatives can (if the critic has a need to do this) be held simultaneously valid.

The New Critics believed that meaning resides in the text and that this meaning may be disclosed by a specific methodology. Hirsch also affirms that "verbal meaning is determinate"; for him "the philological effort to find out what an author meant" is "the only proper foundation of criticism" (*Validity in Interpretation* 57). Geoffrey Thurley declares that "we are justified in speaking of a 'real' meaning" since, even if ambiguities and contradictions are discovered, they nevertheless "constitute a whole" and "co-exist in meaningful inter-commentary" (156-57). Some critics find that certain meanings reside in the text even though the author may not have intended them: psychoanalytic criticism serves as an example of this related approach. In still another context, Wellek rebukes Grant Webster for his assertions in *The Republic of Letters* (1979) that critical theory is historically relative (based on Kuhn's "paradigm" theory). He does so because of his conviction that there is a valid theory and technique for discovering the meaning that the text itself contains: "Acceptance of Mr. Webster's scheme would mean the end of all rational discussion" ("An End to Criticism" 188). Raman Selden, in *Criticism and Objectivity* (1984), admits into his theory the ascertainment of authorial intention, "the explicit marking out of meaning which consists in limiting the connotations" (93). De Man also discovers what meaning the author intended to place in his work. For Miller the aporia is within the text itself.

At the other end of the spectrum is the belief that the process of reading creates the meaning of the text, that even what is called authorial intention is produced by reading. Fish and Bloom have the most radical of such theories. Chapter Six has already shown that the early history of reader-reception theories is the development of the idea that texts have gaps or spaces that only the reader can fill. The meaning of the text requires the contribution of the reader, who "concretizes" the text (Ingarden), or views it from, or on, a historical "horizon" (Gadamer). Hans Robert Jauss accepts Gadamer's notion of the "horizon," the reader's expectations and prejudices that determine how a text will be normatively understood in the reader's social setting. The literary work can, however, provoke a change in horizon, "can break through the expectations of its readers and at the same time confront them with a question"; art can "confront the reader with a new, 'opaque' reality that no longer allows itself to be understood from a pregiven horizon of expectations" (from a 1970 essay, translated in Jauss, *Toward an Aesthetic of Reception* [1982] 44). The emphasis in Wolfgang Iser is more upon the individual text (as in Ingarden and the New Critics) than upon the historical process. The production of a text "implies" an idealized reader of it. That implication is built into the structure of the text, which, in a way, is created in anticipation of its reception. There is a convergence of reader expectation and the content of a text. Any given reader actualizes the text in his own way, of course, by striving in the reading process to create order, consistency, meaning, and esthetic unity in the work, which unfolds for the reader sequentially and has points of indeterminacy. "The convergence of text and reader brings the literary work into existence, and this convergence can never be precisely pinpointed, but must always remain virtual, as it is not to be identified either with the reality of the text or with the individual disposition of the reader" (Iser, *The Implied Reader* [1974] 275). In *Reception Theory* (1984) Robert Holub describes a group of researchers in Germany who, through data gathering, record, measure, and classify reader response.

Stanley Fish goes much further. To him, even what seem to be the textual structures that define, delimit, or constrain the scope of possible interpretation are the result of the makeup of the reader—even Iser's points of "indeterminacy" are imposed, not simply located, by the analysis of the reader. Fish rejects the notion that a substratum of objectively discoverable meaning inherent in the text might preexist the reading process—an opposing view, obviously, to the New Critics and to critics who look for at least a foundation of objectively knowable meaning in authorial intent (most prominently, E. D. Hirsch). The meaning of an utterance "is not a function of the value its words have in a linguistic system that is independent of context"; "it is because the words are heard as already embedded in a context that they have a meaning" (Fish, *Is There a Text in This Class?* [1980] 309). The existence of the properties of a text—of all properties—is bestowed upon the text by the reader. Such a position, by the way, is not meant to lead either to "solipsism" or to a simple "relativism" since the "assumptions and opinions" of the reader are not originated by him but are social constructs "available" to him (320).

In *Language Crafted* (1984), Timothy Austin suggests that what, in fact, the reading community shares is a "set of rule-governed . . . syntactic processes," the customary (normal) syntax of the language that relates "sound to meaning" (11). On the other hand, equally "non-linguistic" (i.e., non-syntactical) "completely independent" "aesthetic" factors (94)—applied in a manner related to the literary competence model described by Culler—determine the interpretation of a literary work.

Furthermore, Norman Holland, who has had readers record their responses, has attempted to show in *5 Readers Reading* (1975) that the psychological profile of the reader, his personality, determines what meaning will be found in the text. If poetry has the function of yielding for the reader a psychological adaption, which Richards, Hartman, and Bloom have professed, such a conclusion may seem quite feasible. Whatever differences there are among reading theorists consists of the apportionment of meaning between the text and the reader.

Both approaches to the interpretation of meaning—meaning found in the text, or meaning found in the reader—can be compatible with the scientific method (though, as in the work of Hartman, they need not be made compatible). Both have therefore been treated favorably in the Anglo-American empiricist setting. In most critics the approaches are intermingled. The scientific method requires that method be explicit and results be verifiable. Verification, in empiricism, results not from a feeling of rapport or agreement with a statement but from the belief that a valid method, the application of logic to perception, has produced it. That poems may have innumerable meanings does not prevent criticism from being "scientific"; all that is required is that the derivation of assertions be demonstrable.

For example, there is a clear relationship in de Man and Miller between the method, the objective evidence, and the conclusions. Their "deconstruction" can become a reproducible empiricist technique, which their followers can apply. Since the technical procedure of analysis can be abstracted and shared, the form, the configuration, of interpretation (distinct from the interpretation itself) is predictable, a circumstance that some find as unfortunate in deconstruction as others once did in the New Criticism. This cannot be said of the recent criticism of Hartman and Bloom. In between their method and their conclusions is not precisely "evidence" but a "material" that cannot be objectified as empirical evidence; there is a purpose and a style that can be imitated, but no empiricist method that can be formulated as a procedure.

To the extent that a text is an object with definable properties, the critic must be an empiricist, which in literary criticism is often called "formalism." If the properties include meaning (they need not), the critic empirically determines that meaning, as the New Critics did. Criticism, including interpretation, becomes science-like: an interpretation becomes, at some level, verifiable, confirmable, even if there may be many different interpretations. To the extent that meaning is wholly or partly the contribution of the reader, criticism cannot be, at the level of the single interpretation itself, an empiricism; but as a consequence (which is what has happened in recent years), the criticism of criticism becomes an empiricism. What becomes verifiable or confirmable is the consistency, even the accuracy, of critical theory and of application. An interpretation becomes explicable rather than defensible.

These distinctions still apply whether meaning is referential (directly representational) or not. The critic can believe that language is referential and in his method be an empiricist, like the New Critics, the Marxists, the neo-classicists, Arnold, or the reader-reception theorists—or not be an empiricist, like Pater, Shelley, or Emerson.

The critic can, on the other hand, claim that language is not referential and be an empiricist, like the structuralists (Lévi-Strauss, Jakobson, Todorov), Foucault, Lacan, de Man, and Miller. But this position is self-contradictory, and at some level referentiality must eventually be introduced (linguistics, archaeology, psychology, textuality) in order to be able to assert that there is some thing about which the critic is speaking. This position, like reader-reception theory, creates a critical meta-language; it is a criticism of criticism, a methodology applied to methodologies.

Or the critic can claim, like Derrida and Hartman, that language is not referential and that he is not an empiricist. This latter position is impossible to defend if any possibility of knowledge is posited. (Even Hartman needs to introduce "representation" in his "counter-statement" to Derrida.) Only Derrida consistently holds this position, through the most extreme of skepticisms, supported by an invented terminology that revokes what it asserts, and it is hard to say where this can lead beyond a modern solipsism.

If all language is non-referential, then there is no distinction, beyond the formalities of organization and a distinctive communicative function, between literary language and other language. This is the post-structuralist position. If, on the other hand, all language is referential, then poetry is referential, too; it refers either to an external reality (nature, human nature, the transcendent) or to an internal one (feelings, emotions, hopes, dreams).

Some recent theory has been based on the conciliatory assumption that some uses of language are referential and others not, a consolidation that is perhaps what Anglo-American common sense and level-headedness suggests, more than does philosophy. We have mentioned the approaches of Brooks and Krieger, in which the meaning of the poem is brought into being by its composition; it refers to itself (which is self-reflexivity, not referentiality).

In this duality lies, also, the significance for criticism of the speech-act theory proposed by J. L. Austin and those who follow him. The basic theory, since it admits referentiality, is a referential one, with modifications based on certain specific categories of utterance, such as promises, commands, and requests; these categories allow a distinction between "meaning" (reference) and what one "means" (intention). In speech-act theory, intention and a mental predisposition (conventions) in any situation determine what meaning will be obtained. For example, Mary Pratt has based a speech-act theory of literary meaning on the meaning that a text has specifically for the reader who has assumed the socially determined role of an "audience" prepared to acknowledge and receive certain utterances as "literature" (*Toward a Speech Act Theory* [1977]). That the referentiality of literature depends upon the social conventions assumed by author and reader is an aspect of the theories of Culler, Fish, John Ellis, and Steven Mailloux (Mailloux, in *Interpretive Conventions* [1982], has a comprehensive analysis of American reader-reception theory): literature is defined not by its own inherent attributes but by what the reader expects of a text. For Charles Altieri, who attempts to replace the notion of "conventional" understanding with "dramatic" understanding (meaning derived through the interpretation of action, not statement), texts have their "properties" because we "construe them as specific [types of] performances" (*Act & Quality* [1981] 235). Since all of these theories admit that the *causes* of any specific interpretation can objectively be determined, they are clearly empiricist; they are criticisms of criticisms, which serve as theory. Even Fish mandates the avoidance of solipsism, which can certainly follow logically from his views, by proposing an objectively knowable interpretive "community." Finally, that these theories are empiricisms, science-like, helps explain why they came to prominence at the same time that structuralism did and why they were often mistaken (in the way that Culler uses reading theory) for structuralism.

In the empiricist Anglo-American setting, then, if the act of criticism is to yield knowledge, criticism will consistently be purported to be grounded in empiricism to legitimate its findings. This is because metaphysics, revelation, inspiration, and esthetic empathy have been generally excluded from the legitimation of knowledge in the settings where "research" occurs. Even the deconstructors seek to validate formalist assertions. At the same time, numerous critics generally wish to locate not only a meaning but also some form of truth in literature, pleasure alone being insufficient for them to justify reading. Since that truth is, presumably, not like that of science, there is as well a reaction against empiricism—which has been a theme throughout this study— a reaction provoked in part by the disillusionment with science and technology, particularly as these issue in various psychological and sociological determinisms.

The science/poetry duality remains a prominent issue in Anglo-American critical theory. Selden speculates that the dichotomy "became the dominant critical paradigm of English criticism" following the polarization of science and poetry (thought and feeling) by John Stuart Mill (19). Graff, in *Literature against Itself*, attributes the unfortunate polarization to the Romantics. Walter Benn Michaels attributes a similar severance to the yielding of late nineteenth-century "i. ealism" in England (Bradley, for example) to a new "realism" (Russell, Moore). That "realism" placed in an ambivalent position the notion of "belief," which can be thought of either as requiring validation or as being a substitute for it. In literary criticism, the poem became an "object" of investigation, yet its content became unverifiable. While for Michaels's term "realism" we would use "empiricism," we have also found that the result of the severance is, at least in literary studies, skepticism: "for the skeptical realist, the truth is finally unknowable" ("Saving the Text" 790). "Empiricism," writes Marian Hobson, "may collapse into the contradictions of the skeptics" (295). Although each of these approaches is different, each helps to substantiate that the science/poetry duality arises in an empiricist setting from the fundamentally irresolvable issues of empiricism, which have been treated at some length. Empiricism deconstructs itself.

That empiricism has its own aporia we have seen as a basic factor in four transitions: from Locke to Hume, from the early to the later New Criticism, from structuralism to post-structuralism, and from the New Criticism to deconstruction.

When structuralism first made its appearance in the United States, the expectation again arose that criticism would be provided with a scientific legitimation, the "science" of linguistics. Structuralist thought was allied with the work of Frye and Chomsky to substantiate this expectation. This project was momentary and short lived. The results of the later New Criticism, their "Romanticism"—from my view, a critique of empiricism—remained a strong force, and the transition from structuralism to deconstruction occurred quickly. In England, where empiricism has been strengthened by positivism in philosophy and, in the 1960s and 1970s, by the influence of Marxism, which has been of comparatively little importance in the United States (although see Jameson, *Political Unconscious*; Ryan, *Marxism and Deconstruction*; Andrew Parker, "Between Dialectics"; and the essays in Nelson and Grossberg, eds.), a significant amount of criticism attempts to reconcile (a Marxist) empiricism and post-structuralism without yielding to the extremes of a deconstructive skepticism. Peter Widdowson declares that in England "Marxist criticism now means 'critical theory' " (5);

and the works of Eagleton, Butler, and Coward and Ellis illustrate the attempted reconciliation, which usually involves a theory of ideology. In America (Marxism aside), the inherent duality within the New Criticism seems to have split into two separate approaches to criticism: the "Romanticism" has been extended by deconstruction; the "empiricism" has been extended by what has become almost a new discipline, the criticism of criticism, not uncommonly influenced by reader-reception theory.

Yet even the criticism of criticism has not resulted in the elimination of dualities, although they may not always be expressed as an incongruence between science and poetry. Critics often open up the possibilities of two separate types of criticism. Hirsch, for example, throughout *Aims of Interpretation*, distinguishes between the "meaning" of a literary text, which is objectively (for example, historically) verifiable, and the "significance" of the text, which varies, subjectively, from reader to reader. For Robert Weimann, in *Structure and Society in Literary History*, "mimetic" and "expressive" knowledge require familiarity with the author's "world"; understanding the "affective" and "moral" effect require knowledge of the receiving audience (53). There is duality in Fish, which he minimizes in *Is There a Text?*, between the subjectivity of the reader and the observable interpretive "community." Denis Donoghue, in *Ferocious Alphabets* (1981), distinguishes between "epireading" and "graphireading." In the first, the reader seeks to learn the meaning in the text communicated by the author, who comes in this way to be known and understood; in the second, the reader seeks his own creative responses to the text of another. "Epireaders say to poems: I want to hear you. Graphireaders say: I want to see what I can do, stimulated by our insignia" (152). Krieger, in his *Theory of Criticism* (1976), asks that we treat the text as an object with organic unity and coherence, as the New Critics did, but that we have as well a "self-conscious sense of the fiction" of this notion, recognizing "organicism and our forming power to be a fond dream, realized for now without lulling our skepticism" (224). Elsewhere, Krieger advises that "we need the healthy skepticism . . . but the culture's need to have [authoritative, "empirical"] claims made . . . is not thereby eliminated" (*Arts on the Level* 42). Rodolphe Gasché finds that there is an "inside" and an "outside" to the text and refers both to the "infinite as well as the finitude of the text's signification" ("Deconstruction as Criticism" [1979] 209). Raman Selden, in England, believes in "the possibility of the objective knowledge of the historical determinants of literary texts" (2); at the same time, because the historical determinants to which the critic is himself subjected change over time, "the critic cannot finally interpret texts, because they are necessarily decentered" (157). William Ray, also in England, distinguishes in *Literary Meaning* (1984) between "meaning as a subjective event (the particular implications a reader draws from the text) and meaning as a grounding structure (the identity theme or shared type idea)." He sees the tension between the two, between meaning as historically bound act and meaning as a permanent textual fact, as fundamental to recent critical practice (105).

These critics are not cited together because their theories can be equated with one another. It would be possible to show similar dualities in the work of Hayden White (*Metahistory* [1973]) on metaphorical language in the writing of history (for a discussion see Dominick LaCapra). Richard Rorty (*Consequences of Pragmatism* [1982]) writes on the contextual nature—the context of manipulation and control—of supposedly "objective" scientific language; his position is attacked by Christopher Norris, who rejects the idea that "*all* theory is a species of sublimated narrative" (*Contest of Faculties* [1985] 23; also, on Rorty, see Alexander Nehamas). Gregory Jay and David Miller refer to critics who follow "a double itinerary that both inhabits a given framework and transgresses its limits" (*After Strange Texts* [1985] 9). My point is that the critical format is a breaking of the field of study into two parts, with the hope of allowing for the ascertainment of the properties of the text, which includes the conveyance of meaning, and the responses of the reader, which includes the creation of meaning. These two parts correspond, at different levels, to objectivity and subjectivity, to the study of cause and the study of effect, to meaning as received communication and meaning as created response, and to Romanticism and empiricism. Each of these dualities, which have come to replace (and then to serve the function of) the dual-truth theory of the New Critics, are understandable in terms of the dilemma of empiricism—the duality of knowledge as perception and knowledge as reflection. This dilemma cannot, in the Anglo-American environment, be resolved by what is usually an unappealing German or French metaphysics or an equally unappealing critique of metaphysics. A not unusual approach for those American critics influenced by post-structuralism is to leave the issue unresolved, justified by what is thought to be a healthy abstention from the metaphysical narcotic. In the Anglo-American setting, literary criticism needs an empiricist foundation; but that foundation always proves inadequate, customarily resulting in dualities of one sort or another. Those dualities may have many advantages for the practitioner of criticism, but, since they often serve more as guidelines than as theory, they are hardly sufficient to serve as a theory complex enough to satisfy the demands (to whatever extent in America there are such demands) of either scientific or philosophic thought.

There has been the intriguing suggestion that there is a relationship between post-structuralism and the most advanced modern scientific theory. For some time scientists have not perceived the universe as an assemblage of isolated solid objects moving through space and time in a way describable by a mechanics based on the Newtonian concepts of mass and gravity. In a booklength study Floyd Merrell describes certain recent theories in which the universe is portrayed as "holistic," as an infinite "seamless web," perhaps ultimately inexplicable, a unity beyond which there is nothing. Such a model bears a striking resemblance to structuralist linguistics and to the post-structuralism of Derrida, in which language is often described in a quite similar way (*Deconstruction Reframed* [1985]).

Furthermore, Heisenberg's demonstration that the position and velocity of the electron cannot *both* be determined for a given instant has raised paradoxes concerning both the indeterminacy of measurement and the effect on the outcome of measurement by the tools of measurement themselves. Such considerations resemble those of the literary critics for whom textual meaning cannot be finally determined and for whom the process of examination itself determines the results, the basic premise of reading theory. Gödel's proof that any complex deductive mathematical system contains a proposition that is true within that system but cannot be *proven* to be so leaves a "gap" in any system of propositions that seems, we are told, to subvert the possibility of an encompassing coherence of truth. The "truth" that has been subverted in the "natural" language system has been subverted in mathematical systems as well. Both Heisenberg and Gödel are quite often cited, for such partisan purposes, by non-scientists.

Physicists have been seeking a "unified field theory" that would encompass the phenomena of both small particle physics and cosmological physics, a theory that could integrate quantum physics and theories of astrophysics. The approach to language in structuralism and post-structuralism was likewise intended (and perhaps still may be so) to be a unified field theory, which some have argued would subsume research in a wide variety of fields, such as history, law, psychology, and other disciplines, through a general theory to which the name "semiotics" has been attached. In the preface to his *Introducing Semiotic* (1982), John Deely forecasts that "semiotics . . . is bound to rewrite the entire history of culture and philosophy": it will establish the "new conditions of a common framework" (xv).

A number of other possible areas of inquiry arise. It might be noted that the concepts of holism in science resemble notions of organic unity in poetry; the universe as a whole is somehow, it appears, envisioned as the Romantics envisioned it. Whether the "linguistic model" can be more than a metaphor in fields other than linguistics is discussed in Chapter Six. And quite interesting questions of influence might be raised: Hjelmslev's version of structuralism came from Copenhagen, the home of the foremost model of quantum physics; Gödel is referred to by Derrida in the introduction to his 1962 translation of Husserl's work on geometry in order to assert that there can be no set of logical axioms from which an internally consistent and complete system of truths can be derived; Gregory Ulmer suggests that the challenge to Euclidian geometry in nineteenth-century mathematics can be related to the concept of the "equivocity" of language in post-structuralism ("Op Writing" [1983]). Holistic theory in the non-physical sciences, such as the "gestalt" psychology initiated by Wolfgang Köhler, also seems pertinent to recent critical theory, as does the theory of codes and the transmission of messages in the theory of genetics. Recent "information theory," based on the work of Claude Shannon in the 1940s and used in solving problems of sending messages electronically, addresses how the ambiguity of messages is caused and how it can be reduced, how the "noise" between sender and receiver can be overcome (see Jeremy Campbell, *Grammatical Man* [1982]); this approach, too, may be brought to bear on literary theories of communication and interpretation.

Such speculation is enticing although it cannot be pursued here. Were we to pursue these topics, I would guess that each science in its turn will yield results that seem of immediate importance, followed, as always, by the satisfying discovery of literary critics that, once again, "literature"—for whatever reasons involving either theory or, more likely, their own temperaments and predilections—escapes the scientific laboratory.

Self, Psychology, Religion

We have briefly traced, in an earlier chapter, some of the history of psychology in America, emphasizing the polarization of a science of behavior (behaviorism) and a science of introspection (American "phenomenology"), the former having come to dominate the field of psychology.

The majority of those involved in the study of literature rejected the behaviorism that threatened the humanist concept of self, for it is necessary to maintain such a concept if "creativity" is to have a meaning that will satisfy the literary scholar. The work of Chomsky helped in the critique and rejection of behaviorism by attacking the theory of Skinner at its weakest point, accounting for language acquisition. Chomsky served to defend both the Cartesian self as well as the freedom required by Frye and implicit in the New Criticism. Phenomenology, grounded on introspection and therefore at the furthest distance from behaviorism, would seem at first to provide support, as it does in existentialism, for the Cartesian self. However, it is most significant that at the extremity of phenomenology arises a theory, poststructuralism, in which the study of language is the strongest point; yet this theory also discards the very same concept of self that behaviorism attacked. At both extremes, the autonomous, free, entity of self is abandoned; at both extremes, also, resides determinism.

From this perspective American literary criticism is caught in the middle. Both the New Critics and the deconstructors favor the self of Romanticism and a conservative phenomenology, including its derivative existentialism. The result of this not always conscious defense of selfhood has been the creation of technical terms that I have called quasi-psychological, terms that are put forth as if they were properties of the text but that are in fact inexplicable without some underlying psychology, terms like "irony," "ambiguity," "paradox," "indeterminacy," "abyss," "blindness," and "aporia." Some theories (those of Bloom and Hartman for example) are ultimately dependent upon psychological presuppositions. Speech-act theory and reader-reception theory are coherent only to the extent that they can, if they can, be validated by psychological assumptions, assumptions that in these cases may not be incompatible with a psychological determinism.

In the Anglo-American setting neither psychology, aside from an intentionally "humanist" psychology (e.g., Maslow, Perls), nor the pervasive philosophical tradition from empiricism to analytic positivism, nor the importations of structuralism and post-structuralism are designed to offer any support to traditional, perhaps naive, notions of self. The literary critic therefore finds himself persistently in the awkward position of seeking an alliance with those very disciplines whose suppositions challenge the beliefs that often, as a motivation, make the study of literature rewarding.

Yet the search for that alliance is a necessary one in an environment where empiricism reigns. The critics, from the New Criticism to deconstruction, go as far as they can go in the direction of the scientific method, or what they take to be the scientific method—as if, for example, a scientific linguistics can be used to support post-structuralism—only then to recognize the implications that are inharmonious with their intentions, at which point they look elsewhere for allies. This process will likely continue. It is a process within empiricism. For example, there have recently developed strategies in philosophy to link Derridian post-structuralism with the work of Frege (Norris, *Contest of Faculties*) and of Wittgenstein (see Staten), who has himself been set in opposition to Descartes (Cottingham 45-46). And since it is a process within empiricism, there is, consequently, little need of the Kantian and post-Kantian Continental European philosophic heritage, except as this can be interpreted in the context of psychological theory rather than in the original metaphysical context of idealism.

A valuable approach to this dilemma would be an analysis of how religious trends and influences in America relate to and conflict with scientific ones. We have our Emersons and our Edisons. Certainly, in America the customary notion of self is derived as much from the religious concept of "soul" as from any science or philosophy.

Eugene Goodheart, in *The Skeptical Disposition* (1984), views structuralist and post-structuralist skepticism as a threat to the religious-based humanistic values he upholds. He sees these movements, with their subversion of the possibility of truth, as an encroaching secularization. "Cut off from religion, literature becomes a thing of the world like an object of scientific study" (26). Yet, he continues, "one has to have some kind of belief in values that inhere in literary experience, and those values have their source in religious thought" (28). Goodheart argues that the "dissolution of the self" in post-structuralism is self-contradictory. On the other hand, with similar evidence, Douglas Atkins maintains in *Reading Deconstruction* (1983) that post-structuralism fits well with a modern theology. While much theology is based on a "hellenistic rationality"—within which God is knowable, the universe is founded on logos, truth is revealed, and man is purposeful—modern theologians, such as the existentialists, acknowledge a universe that cannot be totally reduced to logical understanding, to the order of words. Post-structuralism, especially in the notion of "freeplay," is compatible with "the dehellenization of theology. The result is similar: *freedom*, notably the *freedom* to make" (47; emphasis added). For Atkins, a dehellenized theology is close to the biblical outlook, an outlook he finds in Hartman and Miller. Robert Scharlemann, going even further, declares that deconstruction "opens thought to deity existing not as a transtemporal or metaphysical entity but as an actuality in life and history" (107).

The relationship of post-structuralism to the biblical outlook, particularly to the functioning of the "word" in the Old Testament, is of much interest. De Man has written on a related theme, declaring that "the monotheistic moment . . . is essentially verbal," and that the name of God, in this tradition, functions "symbolically, yielding knowledge and discourse" ("Hegel on the Sublime" 145). Susan Handelman amalgamates Judaism and the theories of Derrida in an essay that proposes that "the home of the Jews is a sacred text in the middle of commentaries" and for them "the text not only precedes speech but precedes the entire natural world" because "language . . . constitutes the essence of reality" ("Derrida and the Heretic Hermeneutic" 99 and 103-4). T. J. J. Altizer finds Derrida to be, like Arnold Schoenberg and Franz Kafka, "a uniquely twentieth century Jewish witness" (151). James Hans asserts that Derrida has rewritten the "ontotheologic" system in terms "of absence, in terms of death, only *disguised* as writing" (818). The use of the Kaballah in Bloom has already been reviewed; and he has an essay on the Jews as a people of the text in *Agon*. Hartman's belief in the critic as prophet and Miller's analysis in *The Disappearance of God* also have previously been discussed. Finally, it is interesting to note (especially in light of Miller) Carl Raschke's view that "deconstruction is the death of God put into writing."

A number of books on modern scientific theories propose an apparent equivalence between such theories and the Buddhist or Taoist philosophy. There are various popular works on the subject, such as Fritjof Capra's *The Tao of Physics* (1975) and Gary Zukav's *The Dancing Wu Li Masters* (1979). I have referred repeatedly to the transformation of "difference" in the linguistics of structuralism to the ontological "space" of post-structuralism. This space has been related to the "void" in the philosophy of the Eastern religions. Merrell finds, in *Deconstruction Reframed*, that the infinite possibility of interpretation in post-structuralism resembles the Buddhist view that supreme order and supreme chaos can exist simultaneously, with the sum of mutually cancelling truths totaling the Buddhist "One." He refers to the "unthinkable" void, which is no-thing, in the Sanskrit Sunyata, and compares this both with modern physics and with the writings of Derrida. Robert Magnolia also discovers a similarity between the thought of Derrida and the Buddhist concept of the void. Coming to the void results from Derrida's analysis of the vain search for a "center," for a "transcendental signified." Magnolia's particular interest is in Nargajunist Buddhism: "Nargajuna takes as his specific task the deconstruction of the principle of identity," and he "employs the same logical strategy . . . as Derrida." In his synthesis, Magnolia asserts that even the "mystery of the [Christian] triune God can be apprehended anew," can be supported, in terms of Nargajunist thought and Derridian "deconstruction," "erasure," and "alterity" (*Derrida on the Mend* [1984] 89 and 134).

Each of these writings provides evidence that there is likely much to say about the religious or spiritual environment in which literary criticism is produced, a topic to which we cannot give adequate attention here. Jean-Pierre Mileur speculates that in modern times poetry has been used to isolate (Christian/Judeo) "transcendence" in a limited sphere (literary studies, particularly with a focus on Romantic "self-consciousness") so that "rational humanism" can continue its work unimpeded. Yet that an effort is being made to unify science and religion (perhaps the New Critical reconciliation of disparates at the highest level)—a synthesis sought in the Anglo-American environment since the time of Lyell's *Geology* and Darwin's *Origins*—exemplifies the enigma of dual-truth theories, found in Western thought as early as the attempts of Aquinas and Averroes to integrate Aristotelian logic and religious belief. We may recall that the Faustian bargain is that the price for whatever may be gained is the relinquishing of the "soul," perhaps the basis for an interesting allegory concerning modern "knowledge" and the forfeiting of "self." Be that as it may, explorations into the most complex regions of spirituality and religion—whether at the levels of history, influence, resemblance, or personal commitment—may yield compelling, even if speculative and unverifiable, insights into the setting of literary criticism, even though such approaches are usually far removed from the everyday concerns of the practitioner.

The Feminist Self

Epistemological conceptions of the self have applicability and pertinence to theoretical approaches used by and applied to the analyses of feminist criticism, both social criticism and literary criticism. While a variety of theories underlying interpretations of culture may ultimately lead to conclusions harmonious with one another—for example, that changes need to occur in the expectations of both men and women concerning social roles and access to these roles—even an apparent consensus about a social or political agenda is not equivalent to a shared philosophical perspective.

The same distinction has been drawn in regard to literary critical theory. The same methodology (e.g., formalism) may be based upon different theories that are, like the New Criticism and post-structuralism, incompatible at the level of epistemology. Similarly, a feminist critique based on the sociological methods most common in the United States and one based upon Marxist theory or structuralist theory may yield related strategies, although underlying assumptions concerning the contents of consciousness and the formation of self may be different. This is not to argue, of course, that such underlying theoretical issues need to be addressed in every instance; clearly there are issues of immediate social concern to which one may, with reasonable cause, assign a predominance. Since issues of selfhood and critical theory have been, however, a primary focus of this study, it is necessary here to abstract that level of analysis, without losing sight of the larger issues relating to the social environment.

These issues have for some years been interwoven with literary studies. "There is a fundamental transformation of consciousness taking place at this time in history," Josephine Donovan writes, "and the women's movement is a, if not *the*, critical part of this change" (*Feminist Literary Criticism* [1975] 75). For literary studies in particular, Cary Nelson concludes that the analyses of the modern feminist movement regarding "the gendered construction of knowledge are having a more powerful impact on the profession than any other contemporary body of theory has had" (3). Lillian Robinson has pointed to the "apparently systematic neglect of women's experience in the literary canon" (106); and Nina Baym asserts that even theoretical approaches to American fiction are male oriented, so that such fiction may be, from a limited theoretical view, classified as if it were all "a melodrama of beset manhood" (79). For Elaine Showalter, women writers have been isolated within the literary canon through the assumption of a specifically "female literary tradition" ("Feminist Criticism in the Wilderness" 185). Other studies address feminism and reader reception theory (e.g., those in Flynn and Schweickart, eds., *Gender and Reading*), and still others illustrate how women are treated in as limited or distorted a way in literature (Ferguson) as they are in pictorial art (O'Kelly).

Feminist theory may be based upon the assumptions of a humanist sociology that presumes the empiricist outlook: objective data can be gathered scientifically from the world by the investigator, who looks objectively out upon it. Society can, in this way, be isolated as the object of scientific study. Similarly, a psychology based upon empiricist principles assumes a fundamentally Lockean self, a self capable of receiving "pure" sensations as well of reflecting as an observer upon its own mentality. Studies from this perspective (the one to which most American analysts are accustomed) demonstrate, for example, that cultural images "constitute much of the input into our socialization process" (Ferguson 57). Carol Gilligan has addressed how the moral positions and attitudes of women are outcomes of their socialization; and Frances Boudreau points to research that shows how "the child not only learns the proper names for things but also the proper attitude to take toward that which is named" (66), including the appropriate attitude toward one's own gender identity.

This sociological approach customarily assumes that human beings are socially malleable and that, consequently, social structures may be intentionally modified. Basic presuppositions concerning selfhood are usually not raised. There is, nevertheless, a difference between this sociology and the approach of Marxism, from which structuralism and post-structuralism have been derived. First, the sociological approach often contains the assumption that society is basically well structured, or at least that its structure is apparent (public), although it could be better and more equitably managed. The Marxist approach is based upon the assumption that the structure of modern society has as a primary function the suppression of its fundamental motivations and inescapable inequities. "The contemporary state attempts to contain the subversive content of liberal feminist demands, which have the capacity to recognize the sexual-class oppression of women" (Eisenstein 220). Second, in both approaches the assumption may be made that human behavior and even thought is a response to societal influence, that there is no invariable human "nature" (innate mental content) that ineluctably causes behavior. But there is a difference between an interior coherent entity of self open to innumerable possibilities, some perhaps primarily influenced by its own determination, and a self that is a consciousness that is not an entity but a constituted (a continually being-constituted) structure. In the first case, a fundamental selfhood might be given (through social influence) or could take (through personal initiative) various roles and attitudes; consciousness would be an attribute of self. In the second case, constituted consciousness *is* self, not a property of it; roles are definitive of self, not acquisitions or accomplishments of it.

These matters have already been discussed at some length, repeatedly, but their applicability to feminist criticism is most germane to literary critical theory, insofar as such theory is obliged to integrate the feminist critique. It makes a difference (at least theoretically) whether, for example, the notion of "consciousness raising" is seen as "rooted in Marxist premises" (Donovan, *Feminist Theory* 65) or whether it is seen as founded in the premises of psychology, perhaps nurtured in the psychology-based "self-awareness" movement. Similarly, the attack upon traditional literary studies may be made from either the humanist perspective, which feminism may seek to transform or rehabilitate while sharing certain fundamental values, or from the viewpoint that "in the academies, feminist critics could ally themselves with

Marxist critics in attacks on the class-bound elitism of the traditional literature syllabuses" (Ruthven 22), a viewpoint in which the Marxist category of "class" (and, consequently, class struggle) takes precedence.

Donovan, quoting from Derrida's "Purveyor of Truth," speaks about the "collusion" of phallocentrism with logocentrism that "unites feminism and deconstruction" (*Feminist Theory* 114). Michael Ryan, in his chapter on socialist feminism in *Marxism and Deconstruction*, states that "deconstruction must be articulated" with the feminist movement (and others) "because the elimination of domination . . . cannot occur completely without the transformation of the thought categories and the processes that sustain and promote domination" (212). The relationship of Lacanian theory to feminism is discussed by Ellie Ragland-Sullivan, who writes that "Lacan shows . . . that, in a given culture and family, sexual role possibilities await a neonate on whom to impose preexisting identity functions and actually precede an infant's biological conception" (268; lectures by Lacan and members of his "school" on femininity are collected in Mitchell and Rose, eds., *Feminine Sexuality*). The relevance of post-structuralist theory to feminist theory should to some degree be clear from the earlier analyses in this study, since what pertains to a theory of selfhood encompasses selfhood of any kind. Post-structuralism, as an explanation (or an attempt at one) of how selfhood is constituted—through language—could, obviously, serve as an epistemological foundation for a feminist literary criticism if it can be made to serve as such a foundation for *all* criticism. (Already such a transition has been made in a substantial area of film criticism.) Carolyn Heilbrun and Margaret Higonnet see feminist literary criticism including not only new literary and historical evidence, which challenges customary categories, but manifesting "a shift in focus from discrete images to structural and semiotic analysis" (xiii). It is interesting to note that the speculations of George Herbert Mead, which Boudreau uses to show that "individuals form their conceptions of themselves in response to others' actions towards them" (66), can certainly be read, and perhaps modified, in the light of Lacan's notion of the Other, even though the underlying assumptions are far apart—since Lacan is speaking of the formation of self, and Mead of the self's acquisition of its own self-image.

Post-structuralist deconstruction may, in fact, allow for an analysis of the self from a feminist perspective that questions even the very biological distinctions between female and male. For example, Ragland-Sullivan states that "Lacan saw the effect of the Oedipal nexus as that which decides the assignment of sex, where sex is correlated with identity rather than gender" (268). This is to say that one has

gender (one is, biologically, male or female) regardless of identity formation or identification. But Rosalind Coward, in *Patriarchal Precedents*
(1983), has raised the more radical point that even to concede that
maleness and femaleness are fundamentally distinguishing human features—to concede, that is, that the biological categories reveal fundamental classificatory categories—is to adhere to "essentialism," since
the primacy of biological categories (male, female) are determined by
the social structure that engenders them no less than are what seem
to be the categories of personality (feminine, masculine). Even to ask
for a just and equitable society for both men and women is to accept
that there are irreducibly "natural" categories of men and women,
categories that Coward would have deconstructed and consequently
obviated, since the apparent (but false) "naturalness" of these categories allows society to manipulate them in the first place. "Women
are subordinated because sexual identity is taken as fundamental" (268).

Not all critics would welcome an alliance with Continental ideas.
Showalter, for example, believes that an affiliation with Marxism and
structuralism would not be advantageous for feminism because "both
Marxism and structuralism see themselves as a privileged critical science." For Showalter, "a key word in each system is 'science' " (139).
The questions that feminism asks "go beyond those that science can
answer." While such a response may be more appropriate to early
structuralism (the linguistic model based on Saussurian linguistics) than
to post-structuralism, it is of interest to see how, from at least this
American view, the issue of a persistent antagonism toward the domination of science, raised so often in this study, again comes to the
foreground.

The possible interactions between feminism, feminist literary criticism, post-structuralism, and deconstruction has been commanding
substantial attention, particularly in the environment of academic literary studies. Although the subject has been treated but briefly here,
some topics of theoretical import have been identified. There is, in this
area as in others, an American critical perspective that is not, in its
origins, equivalent to post-structuralism, which nevertheless can be,
perhaps will be, amalgamated and transformed in a new setting.

Self and Politics

During the 1960s literary criticism came to require a legitimation on
the political left, which we have reviewed in Chapter Four. Structuralism emanated from and was an extension of Marxist thought, which
encouraged a favorable reception in American literary criticism. While

post-structuralism comes from the same setting, its skepticism challenges the truths of Marxism as well as all other truths, and the allegiance of the post-structuralists (of Derrida and Althusser, for example) to an orthodox Marxism has been questioned. Some, with whom I tend to agree, see post-structuralism as condoning a withdrawal from politics, since skepticism subverts commitment: "It allows you to drive a coach and horses through everybody else's beliefs without saddling you with the inconvenience of having to adopt any yourself" (Eagleton, *Literary Theory* 147). Sturrock notes that there were "no structuralist night-clubs on the left bank," that the methodology did not entail the cohesion of a social commitment (2). (Marxist responses to structuralism and post-structuralism have been reviewed in Chapters Six, Seven, and Eight.) This political retreat may be attributed to the recognition of French intellectuals that their political power and effectiveness had been greatly diminished, illustrated, though not caused (the process can be traced back to the time of de Gaulle), by the minimal results of the uprisings in Paris in 1968, which, it can be argued, augmented a political defeatism and despair. Unable to undermine or refashion the political structure, the philosophers undermined truth and dismantled language instead. LaCapra cites White's belief that post-structuralism represents the extremity of Western self-doubt (80).

While circumstances in the United States do not center around the success or failure of Marxist politics, since the "left" is not equivalent to Marxism, there is a parallelism that has received some attention. The political optimism on the left in the late 1960s and early 1970s, the belief that a thoroughgoing social reform was near at hand, quickly waned as the political climate radically altered. Because much of the movement on the left was based in the universities, its decline eroded the belief of intellectuals on the left that they were in the forefront of social action, a belief which had greatly contributed to their sense of power, influence, and self-esteem. Disillusionment developed. A similar condition can be identified in English Romanticism: because of disappointment in the ultimate outcome of the French Revolution, there occurred, some argue (McGann; Graff in *Literature against Itself*; Abrams in *Natural Supernaturalism*), a retreat from the arena of political action and social thought into the primacy of the mind, into the potentiality of artistic creativity, and into poetic speculation as a source of knowledge and achievement.

This withdrawal into the capabilities of mentality seems to characterize deconstruction; and we have seen how each of the critics endeavors mastery in the face of an encompassing powerlessness, frequently magnified (ennobled) to the powerlessness over human mortality. The power that remains is power over the text, likely an inadequate recompense. While post-structuralism is imported as a theory on the left, it is quickly partitioned from politics on the left. This separation transforms what at first seemed to be an attack on the "establishment" to a component of the establishment. Recent literary studies, Edward Said declares, "far from producing works to challenge or revise prevailing values, institutions, and definitions, have in fact gone a very long way to confirming them" ("Reflections on American 'Left' " [1979] 20). Michaels sees in the "new formalism" an escape from avowing beliefs and, accordingly, from political effectiveness ("Saving the Text"). It is possible, of course, to discover some political implications in deconstruction: for Evan Watkins, indeterminacy in interpretation counteracts the "totalitarianism" of critics who believe themselves to have privileged access to correct and final interpretive judgments. But this is surely a weak argument. Jonathan Arac's position is a more accurate one: deconstruction has had "in the American academy . . . a conservative effect." The essays in the volume he has edited with Wlad Godzich and Wallace Martin support the view, Arac concludes, that the Yale critics are "conservatives" (178-79). Paul Bové, in the same volume, demonstrates that deconstruction was a "perfect institutional response" during a "crisis" of "economic and methodological changes, and epistemological and evaluative doubts" (6): despite the purported doubt and despair, the new methodology perpetuated traditional academic "text-production" (17). Eagleton accuses deconstruction of a "complicity with liberal humanism": the academic can "savor the delights of textual agnosticism precisely because it is institutionally secure" (*Function of Criticism* 103). In his book devoted to the place of deconstruction in the universities, Michael Fischer argues that what seemed initially to be a rebuttal to "the academic profession fails, resulting in the assimilation of revisionist criticism by the institution that it wants to oppose" (*Does Deconstruction Make Any Difference?* [1985] 85). The methodology becomes a technical revision of the New Critical methodology.

Two themes are intermixed here: the social powerlessness of the literary critic, and the immediate sign of this in the inability even to change the setting in which the critic works. Furthermore, the apparent unimportance of literary criticism in what might be called the general scheme of things can be linked to the apparent decline in the prospects for the profession—to the decline in student enrollments, for example, or to the difficulties that younger teachers have, with their vigor and avowed iconoclasm, in obtaining satisfactory employment. (And those who have such employment find their status diminishing and their income falling behind the pace of inflation.) Yet the deconstructive critics, and often those who respond to them, not uncommonly write as if the destiny of civilization were at stake in literary interpretation. That there is no truth, that all that can be known are the operations of language (which is not knowledge at all, but only a conviction immersed in skepticism) is certainly a momentous conclusion. Nevertheless, the effects of such thinking, the impact upon the world around us, is undoubtedly negligible.

There is, then, a political aspect to preserving the autonomous, creative, free entity of self in American literary criticism. This act of preservation is a perpetual tactic, regardless of what seems to be—and I use this qualification, since the last word on these subjects has hardly been spoken—the disheartening evidence either from modern science or from recent philosophy. Raymond Williams writes of the Romantics that, at a time when the poet had little political or social influence (Shelley's "legislators" are "unacknowledged"), he began to describe himself as "a specially endowed person, the guiding light of common life" (*Culture and Society* 36). The reaction, in literary theory, against the empiricism that attracts it (the essence of all courtship) has come also to serve as a way of insisting upon the prominence, the effectiveness, the importance, and the dignity of the selves of those very critics who are themselves engaged in the discipline. This is not a dishonorable motive. Like the Romantic poets, literary critics seek their wisdom in their own speculations; the world at large seems not to occasion it. The preservation by literary critics of the self derived from Romanticism and an imported existentialist phenomenology may be, for a while at least, that self's only academic haven.

That literary criticism aspire to a politically important role is one of the four criteria I have earlier offered as necessary for an American literary critical theory to prove inclusive and satisfying. The other three are the ability to account for language in general, the acquisition of a legitimation in some form of science, and the integration of a theory that preserves the paramount significance of mentality and the creative self. A number of candidates have been willing to serve as the consensus of opinion—structuralism and post-structuralism have been addressed with these criteria in mind. Each of the parties is currently guarding their votes, however, with reader-reception theory likely holding, in the era of the "consumer," the largest number. So far they have declined to form any ruling coalition.

Bibliography

Abrams, M. H. *The Mirror and the Lamp: Romantic Theory and the Critical Tradition*. New York: Oxford UP, 1953.

———. *Natural Supernaturalism*. New York: Norton, 1971.

Adams, Hazard, ed. *Critical Theory since Plato*. New York: Harcourt, 1971.

Adams, Robert M. "Literary Studies: The Last Fifty Years." *The American Scholar* 51 (1982): 205-17.

Allison, Henry E. "Locke's Theory of Personal Identity." *Locke on Human Understanding*. Ed. I. C. Tipton. Oxford: Oxford UP, 1977. 105-22.

Althusser, Louis. *Lenin and Philosophy*. Trans. B. Brewster. New York: Monthly Review, 1971.

Altieri, Charles. *Act and Quality*. Amherst: U of Massachusetts P, 1981.

Altizer, T. J. J., et al., eds. *Deconstruction and Theology*. New York: Crossroad, 1982.

Anderson, Perry. *In the Tracks of Historical Materialism*. Chicago: U of Chicago P, 1984.

Angenot, Marc. "Structuralism and Syncretism: Institutional Distortions of Saussure." Fekete 150-63.

Arac, Jonathan. Afterword. Arac, Godzich, and Martin 176-202.

———, ed. *Postmodernism and Politics*. Minneapolis: U of Minnesota P, 1986.

———, Wlad Godzich, and Wallace Martin, eds. *The Yale Critics: Deconstruction in America*. Minneapolis: U of Minnesota P, 1983.

Arnold, Matthew. "The Function of Criticism at the Present Time." Hazard Adams 533-95.

Aronowitz, Stanley. "The Production of Scientific Knowledge: Science, Ideology, Marxism." Nelson and Grossberg 519-37.

Atkins, G. Douglas. *Quests of Différance: Reading Pope's Poems*. Lexington: UP of Kentucky, 1986.

———. *Reading Deconstruction / Deconstructive Reading*. Lexington: UP of Kentucky, 1983.

Austin, J. L. *How to Do Things with Words*. Cambridge: Harvard UP, 1975.

Austin, Timothy. *Language Crafted: A Linguistic Theory of Poetic Syntax*. Bloomington: Indiana UP, 1984.

Ayer, A. J. *Language, Truth, and Logic*. New York: Dover, 1952.

———. *Philosophy in the Twentieth Century*. New York: Random House, 1982.

Bagwell, J. Timothy. *American Formalism and the Problem of Interpretation*. Houston: Rice UP, 1985.

Barfield, Owen. *What Coleridge Thought*. Middletown, Conn.: Wesleyan UP, 1971.

Barrett, William. *Irrational Man*. New York: Anchor-Doubleday, 1962.

Barthes, Roland. *Critique et vérité*. Paris: Seuil, 1966.

———. *Elements of Semiology*. Trans. A. Lavers and C. Smith. New York: Hill and Wang, 1968.

———. *Image, Music, Text*. Trans. S. Heath. New York: Hill and Wang, 1977.

———. *Mythologies*. Trans. A. Lavers. England: Paladin, 1973.

———. *New Critical Essays*. Trans. R. Howard. New York: Hill and Wang, 1980.

———. *On Racine*. Trans. R. Howard. New York: Hill and Wang, 1964.

———. *The Pleasure of the Text*. Trans. R. Miller. New York: Hill and Wang, 1973.

———. "The Structuralist Activity." DeGeorge and DeGeorge 117-42.

———. *Systeme de la mode*. Paris: Seuil, 1967.

———. *S/Z*. Trans. R. Miller. New York: Hill and Wang, 1974.

———. "To Write: An Intransitive Verb?" Macksey and Donato 134-44.

———. *Writing Degree Zero*. Trans. A. Lavers and C. Smith. New York: Hill and Wang, 1967.

Barzun, Jacques. *Classic, Romantic and Modern*. New York: Anchor-Doubleday, 1961.

Baym, Nina. "Melodramas of Beset Manhood: How Theories of American Fiction Exclude Women Authors." Showalter 63-80.

Behabib, Seyla. *Critique, Norm, and Utopia: A Study of the Foundations of Critical Theory*. New York: Columbia UP, 1986.

Belsey, Catherine. *Critical Practice*. New York: Methuen, 1980.

Benamou, Michel. "Notes on the Technological Imagination." De Lauretis et al. 65-75.

Bennett, Tony. *Formalism and Marxism*. London: Methuen, 1979.

Benoist, Jean-Marie. "The End of Structuralism." *20th Century Studies* 3 (1970): 31-54.

———. *The Structural Revolution*. New York: St. Martin's, 1978.

Benveniste, Emile. *Problèmes de linguistique générale*. Paris: Gallimard, 1966.

Bergson, Henri. *Time and Free Will: An Essay on the Immediate Data of Consciousness*. Trans. F. C. Pogson. New York: Macmillan, 1921.

Berkeley, George. *A Treatise Concerning the Principles of Human Knowledge*. Vol. 2 of *The Works of George Berkeley*. Ed. A. A. Luce and T. E. Jessop. 4 vols. London: Nelson, 1948-57.

Bloom, Harold. *Agon: Towards a Theory of Revisionism*. New York: Oxford UP, 1982.

——. *The Anxiety of Influence.* New York: Oxford UP, 1973.

——. "The Breaking of Form." Bloom, et al. 1-38.

——. *The Breaking of the Vessels.* Chicago: U of Chicago P, 1982.

——. *Kaballah and Criticism.* New York: Seabury, 1975.

——. *A Map of Misreading.* New York: Oxford UP, 1975.

——, et al. *Deconstruction and Criticism.* New York: Continuum, 1979.

Bloomfield, Leonard. *Language.* 1914; 1935. New York: Holt, 1966.

Boorstin, Daniel. *The Republic of Technology.* New York: Harper and Row, 1978.

Booth, Wayne. *The Rhetoric of Fiction.* Chicago: U of Chicago P, 1961.

Bostetter, Edward. *The Romantic Ventriloquists.* Seattle: U of Washington P, 1963.

Boudreau, Frances. "Sex Roles, Identity, and Socialization." Boudreau, ed. 63-83.

——, ed. *Sex Roles and Social Patterns.* New York: Praeger, 1986

Bourne, Randolph. *History of a Literary Radical and Other Essays.* Ed. Van Wyck Brooks. New York: Huebsch, 1920.

Bové, Paul. "Variations on Authority: Some Deconstructive Transformations of the New Criticism." Arac, Godzich, and Martin 3-19.

Bowie, Malcolm. "Jacques Lacan." Sturrock 116-53.

Braun, Ernst. *Wayward Technology.* Westport, Conn.: Greenwood 1984.

Brecht, Bertolt. *Brecht on Theatre.* Trans. J. Willett. New York: Hill and Wang, 1964.

Bremond, Claude. "La logique des possibles narratifs." *Communications* 8 (1966): 60-76.

——. *Logique du récit.* Paris: Seuil, 1973.

Brooker, Peter. "Post-Structuralism, Reading, and the Crisis in English." Widdowson 73-85.

Brooks, Cleanth. "Irony as a Principle of Structure." 1949. Hazard Adams 1041-48.

——. *Modern Poetry and the Tradition.* Chapel Hill: U of North Carolina P, 1939.

——. "The New Criticism." *Sewanee Review* 87 (1979): 592-607.

——. *The Well Wrought Urn.* 1947. New York: Harvest-Harcourt, 1975.

——, and Robert Penn Warren. *Understanding Poetry.* 1938. New York: Holt, 1952.

Brooks, Peter. Introduction. *Introduction to Poetics.* By Tzvetan Todorov. Minneapolis: U of Minnesota P, 1981. vii-xix.

Butler, Christopher. *Interpretation, Deconstruction, and Ideology.* London: Oxford UP, 1984.

Cain, William. *Crisis in Criticism.* Baltimore: Johns Hopkins UP, 1984.

Calder, Nigel. *Technopolis: Social Control and the Uses of Science.* New York: Simon and Schuster, 1970.

Campbell, Jeremy. *Grammatical Man.* New York: Simon and Schuster, 1982.

Camus, Albert. *The Myth of Sisyphus.* Trans. J. O'Brien. New York: Vintage-Random House, 1960.

——. *The Plague.* Trans. S. Gilbert. New York: Knopf, 1948.

―――. *The Stranger*. Trans. S. Gilbert. New York: Vintage-Random House, 1960.

Capra, Fritjof. *The Tao of Physics*. Boulder: Shambhala, 1975.

Cattingham, John. *Descartes*. London: Blackwell, 1986.

Caws, Peter. "What Is Structuralism?" *Partisan Review* 35 (1968): 75-91.

Chappell, V. C., ed. *The Philosophy of Mind*. New York: Dover, 1981.

Chatman, Seymour, ed. *Approaches to Poetics*. New York: Columbia UP, 1973.

Chisolm, William, Jr. *Elements of English Linguistics*. New York: Longman, 1981.

Chomsky, Noam. *American Power and the New Mandarins*. New York: Pantheon, 1969.

―――. *Cartesian Linguistics*. New York: Harper and Row, 1966.

―――. *Language and Mind*. New York: Harcourt, 1968.

―――. *Problems of Knowledge and Freedom*. New York: Pantheon, 1971.

―――. *Reflections on Language*. New York: Pantheon, 1975.

―――. Review of *Verbal Behavior*, by B. F. Skinner. *Language* 35 (1959): 26-58.

―――. *Syntactic Structures*. The Hague: Mouton, 1957.

Cohen, Ralph. "The Rationale of Hume's Literary Inquiries." *David Hume*. Ed. K. R. Merrill and R. Shanan. Norman: U of Oklahoma P, 1976. 97-116.

Coleridge, Samuel Taylor. *Biographia Literaria*. 1817. New York: Dutton, 1960.

Collingridge, David. *The Social Control of Technology*. New York: St. Martin's, 1980.

Cooper, Barry. *Michel Foucault: An Introduction to the Study of His Thought*. New York: Mellen, 1982.

Copleston, Frederick. *A History of Philosophy. Vol. V: Hobbes to Hume*. Westminster: Newman, 1961.

Corngold, Stanley. "Error in Paul de Man." Arac, Godzich, and Martin 90-108.

―――. *The Fate of the Self: German Writers and French Theory*. New York: Columbia UP, 1986.

Coward, Rosalind. *Patriarchal Precedents: Sexuality and Social Relations*. London: Routledge, 1983.

Coward, Rosalind, and John Ellis. *Language and Materialism*. London: Routledge, 1977.

Crane, R. S. "Cleanth Brooks: or, the Bankruptcy of Critical Monism." *Modern Philology* 45 (1948): 226-45.

Crawford, Donald. *Kant's Aesthetic Theory*. Madison: U of Wisconsin P, 1974.

Croce, Benedetto. *Aesthetic as Science of Expression and General Linguistic*. Trans. D. Ainslie. New York: Farrar, 1909.

Culler, Jonathan. "Jacques Derrida." Sturrock 154-180.

―――. *On Deconstruction*. Ithaca: Cornell UP, 1982.

―――. *The Pursuit of Signs*. Ithaca: Cornell UP, 1981.

―――. *Roland Barthes*. New York: Oxford UP, 1983.

―――. *Structuralist Poetics*. Ithaca: Cornell UP, 1975.

Daiches, David. "The New Criticism." *A Time of Harvest*. Ed. R. Spiller. New York: Hill and Wang, 1962.

D'Amico, Robert. "Text and Context: Derrida and Foucault on Descartes." Fekete 164-82.

Davidson, Hugh. "Sign, Sense, and Barthes." Chatman 29-50.

Davis, Robert Con. "Error at Yale: Geoffrey Hartman, Psycho-Analysis, and Deconstruction." Davis and Schleifer 135-56.

——, ed. *The Fictional Father: Lacanian Readings of the Text.* Amherst: U of Massachusetts P, 1981.

——, and Ronald Schleifer, eds. *Rhetoric and Form: Deconstruction at Yale.* Norman: U of Oklahoma P, 1985.

Deely, John. *Introducing Semiotic: Its History and Doctrine.* Bloomington: Indiana UP, 1982.

DeGeorge, Richard, and Fernande DeGeorge, eds. *The Structuralists from Marx to Lévi-Strauss.* Garden City, N.Y.: Anchor-Doubleday, 1972.

De Lauretis, Teresa, Andreas Huyssen, and Kathleen Woodward, eds. *The Technological Imagination: Theories and Fictions.* Madison: Coda, 1980.

De Man, Paul. *Allegories of Reading: Figural Language in Rousseau, Nietzsche, Rilke, and Proust.* New Haven: Yale UP, 1979.

——. *Blindness and Insight: Essays in the Rhetoric of Contemporary Fiction.* New York: Oxford UP, 1971. New edition, Minneapolis: U of Minnesota P, 1983.

——. "Hegel on the Sublime." Krupnick 139-53.

——. *The Rhetoric of Romanticism.* New York: Columbia UP, 1984.

——. "Shelley Disfigured." Bloom et al. 39-74.

Derrida, Jacques. "All Ears: Nietzsche's Otobiography." Trans. A. Ronell. *Yale French Studies* 63 (1982): 245-50.

——. *De la grammatologie.* Paris: Minuit, 1967.

——. "Economimesis." *Diacritics* 11:2 (1981): 3-24.

——. "Fors." *Georgia Review* 31 (1977): 64-116.

——. *Glas.* Paris: Galilee, 1974.

——. *Glas.* Trans. J. P. Leavy and R. Rand. Lincoln: U of Nebraska P, 1986.

——. "Living On: Border Lines." Bloom et al. 75-176.

——. *Margins of Philosophy.* Trans. A. Bass. Chicago: U of Chicago P, 1982.

——. *Of Grammatology.* Trans. G. C. Spivak. Baltimore: Johns Hopkins UP, 1976.

——. Introduction. *L'Origine de la geometrie.* By Edmund Husserl. Trans. J. Derrida. Paris: Presses Universitaire de France, 1962.

——. *Positions.* Trans. A. Bass. Chicago: U of Chicago P, 1981.

——. *Speech and Phenomena.* Trans. D. Allison. Evanston: Northwestern UP, 1973.

——. "Structure, Sign, and Play in the Discourse of the Human Sciences." Macksey and Donato 247-64.

——. *Writing and Difference.* Trans. A. Bass. Chicago: U of Chicago P, 1978.

Descartes, Rene. "Meditations on the First Philosophy." *Descartes: Selections.* Ed. R. Eaton. New York: Scribner's, 1955.

Descombes, Vincent. *Modern French Philosophy.* Trans. L. Scott-Fox and J. M. Harding. Cambridge: Cambridge UP, 1980.

Dewey, John. *The Philosophy of John Dewey.* Ed. J. McDermott. New York: Putnam, 1973.

Ditta, Joseph. *Natural and Conceptual Design: Radical Confusion in Critical Theory.* New York: Lang, 1984.

Donato, Eugene. "Historical Imagination and the Idioms of Criticism." *Boundary 2* 8 (1979): 39-55.

——. "Of Structuralism and Literature." *MLN* 85 (1967): 549-84.

——. "The Two Languages of Criticism." Macksey and Donato 89-97.

Donoghue, Denis. "Deconstructing Deconstruction." *New York Review of Books* 27.10 (1980): 37-41.

——. *Ferocious Alphabets.* New York: Columbia UP, 1984.

Donovan, Josephine. *Feminist Theory: The Intellectual Traditions of American Feminism.* New York: Ungar, 1985.

——, ed. *Feminist Literary Criticism: Explorations in Theory.* Lexington: UP of Kentucky, 1975.

Dowling, William. *Jameson, Althusser, Marx.* Ithaca: Cornell UP, 1984.

Dreyfus, Hubert, and Paul Rabinow. *Michel Foucault: Beyond Structuralism and Hermeneutics.* 2nd ed. Chicago: U of Chicago P, 1983.

Eagleton, Terry. *The Function of Criticism from "The Spectator" to Post-Structuralism.* London: Verso, 1984.

——. *Literary Theory: An Introduction.* Minneapolis: U of Minnesota P, 1983.

——. *Marxism and Literary Criticism.* Berkeley: U of California P, 1976.

Eccles, J. C. *The Human Psyche.* New York: Springer, 1980.

Eco, Umberto. *A Theory of Semiotics.* Bloomington: Indiana UP, 1979.

Ehrmann, Jacques, ed. *Structuralism.* Garden City, N.Y.: Anchor-Doubleday, 1970.

Eisenstein, Zillah. *The Radical Future of Liberal Feminism.* New York: Longman, 1981.

Eliot, T. S. "Hamlet and His Problems." *The Sacred Wood.* London: Methuen, 1928.

——. "The Metaphysical Poets." *Selected Essays, 1917-1932.* London: Faber, 1932.

——. "Tradition and the Individual Talent." *The Sacred Wood.*

Ellis, John. *The Theory of Literary Criticism: A Logical Analysis.* Los Angeles: U of California P, 1974.

Empson, William. *Seven Types of Ambiguity.* 1930. Harmondsworth: Penguin, 1961.

Erikson, Erik. *Childhood and Society.* New York: Norton, 1963.

Erlich, Victor. "Roman Jakobson: Grammar of Poetry and Poetry of Grammar." Chatman 1-28.

——. *Russian Formalism.* 1955. New Haven: Yale UP, 1965.

Fekete, John. "Modernity in the Literary Institution." Fekete 228-247.

——, ed. *The Structural Allegory.* Minneapolis: U of Minnesota P, 1984.

Ferguson, Mary Ann. *Images of Women in Literature.* Boston: Houghton Mifflin, 1973.

Ferkiss, Victor. *The Future of Technological Civilization.* New York: Braziller, 1974.

——. *Technological Man.* New York: Braziller, 1969.

Feuer, Lewis, ed. *Marx and Engels: Basic Writings on Politics and Philosophy.* Garden City, N.Y.: Anchor-Doubleday, 1959.

Fischer, Michael. *Does Deconstruction Make Any Difference?* Bloomington: Indiana UP, 1985.

Fish, Stanley. *Is There a Text in This Class?* Cambridge: Harvard UP, 1980.

———. "What Is Stylistics and Why Are They Saying Such Terrible Things about It?" Chatman 109-52.

Flanagan, Owen. *The Science of the Mind.* Cambridge: MIT P, 1984.

Fleming, Donald, and Bernard Bailyn. *The Intellectual Migration: Europe and America 1930-1960.* Cambridge: Harvard UP, 1969.

Flynn, Elizabeth, and Patrocinio Schweickart, eds. *Gender and Reading: Essays on Readers, Texts, and Contexts.* Baltimore: Johns Hopkins UP, 1986.

Fokkema, D. W., and E. Kunne-Ibsch. *Theories of Literature in the Twentieth Century.* New York: St. Martin's, 1977.

Foster, Richard. *The New Romantics.* Bloomington: Indiana UP, 1962.

Foucault, Michel. *The Archaeology of Knowledge.* Trans. A. M. Sheridan Smith. New York: Pantheon 1972.

———. *The Birth of the Clinic.* Trans. A. M. Sheridan Smith. New York: Pantheon, 1973.

———. *Discipline and Punish.* Trans. A. Sheridan. New York: Pantheon, 1977.

———. *The History of Sexuality.* Vol. 1. Trans. R. Hurley. New York: Pantheon, 1978.

———. *Madness and Civilization.* Trans. R. Howard. New York: Pantheon, 1965.

———. *The Order of Things: An Archaeology of the Human Sciences.* New York: Vintage-Random House, 1973.

———. *Raymond Roussel.* Paris: Gallimard, 1963.

Fowler, Roger. *Linguistic Criticism,* Oxford: Oxford UP, 1986.

Freud, Sigmund. *The Standard Edition of the Complete Works of Sigmund Freud.* Ed. J. Strachey. London: Hogarth, 1962-74.

Fromm, Erich. *Marx's Concept of Man.* New York: Ungar, 1966.

Frow, John. *Marxism and Literary History.* London: Blackwell, 1986.

Frye, Northrop. *Anatomy of Criticism.* 1957. Princeton: Princeton UP, 1973.

———. *The Critical Path.* Bloomington: Indiana UP, 1973.

Gabel, Joseph. *False Consciousness.* Trans. M. Thompson. New York: Torchbooks-Harper, 1975.

Gadamer, Hans-Georg. *Truth and Method.* New York: Continuum, 1975.

Gasché, Rodolphe. "Deconstruction as Criticism." *Glyph* 6 (1979): 178-209.

Genette, Gérard. *Figures of Literary Discourse.* Trans. A. Sheridan. New York: Columbia UP, 1982.

Gilbert, James B. *Writers and Partisans: A History of Literary Radicalism in America.* New York: Wiley, 1968.

Gilligan, Carol. *In a Different Voice: Psychological Theory and Women's Development.* Cambridge: Harvard UP, 1982.

Girard, Rene. *Deceit, Desire, and the Novel.* Baltimore: Johns Hopkins UP, 1965.

Goldmann, Lucien. *The Hidden God.* Trans. P. Thody. London: Routledge, 1964.

———. "Structure: Human Reality and Methodological Concept." Macksey and Donato 98-124.

Goldsmith, Arnold. *American Literary Criticism: 1905-1965.* Boston: Hall, 1979.

Goodheart, Eugene. *The Cult of the Ego: The Self in Modern Literature.* Chicago: U of Chicago P, 1968.

———. *The Skeptic Disposition in Contemporary Criticism.* Princeton: Princeton UP, 1984.

Gould, Eric. "Deconstruction and Its Discontents." *Denver Quarterly* 15 (1980): 90-106.

Graff, Gerald. "Deconstruction as Dogma." *Georgia Review* 34 (1980): 404-21.

———. *Literature against Itself.* Chicago: U of Chicago P, 1979.

———. *Poetic Statement and Critical Dogma.* Chicago: U of Chicago P, 1970.

Greimas, A. J. *Sémantique structurale.* Paris: Larousse, 1966.

Grene, Marjorie. "Life, Death, and Language: Some Thoughts on Derrida and Wittgenstein." *Partisan Review* 43 (1976): 265-79.

———. *Philosophy In and Out of Europe.* Los Angeles: U of California P, 1976.

Grossmann, Reinhards. *Phenomenology and Existentialism.* London: Routledge, 1984.

Hamacher, Werner. "Disintegration of the Will: Nietzsche on the Individual and Individuality." *Reconstructing Individuality: Autonomy, Individuality, and the Self in Western Thought.* Ed. T. C. Heller, M. Sosna, D. E. Wellbery. Stanford: Stanford UP 1986.

Handelman, Susan. "Jacques Derrida and the Heretic Hermeneutic." Krupnick 98-129.

Handy, William J. *Kant and the Southern New Critics.* Austin: U of Texas P, 1963.

Hans, James. "Derrida and Freeplay." *MLN* 94 (1979): 809-26.

Hardison, O. B., Jr. *Entering the Maze: Identity and Change in Modern Culture.* New York: Oxford UP, 1981.

Harman, Gilbert, ed. *On Noam Chomsky: Critical Essays.* Garden City, N.Y.: Anchor-Doubleday, 1974.

Hartman, Geoffrey. *Beyond Formalism: Literary Essays, 1958-1970.* New Haven: Yale UP, 1970.

———. *Criticism in the Wilderness: The Study of Literature Today.* New Haven: Yale UP, 1980.

———. *The Fate of Reading and Other Essays.* Chicago: U of Chicago P, 1975.

———. *Saving the Text: Literature / Derrida / Philosophy.* Baltimore: Johns Hopkins UP, 1981.

———. "Structuralism: The Anglo-American Adventure." Ehrmann 137-57.

———. "Words, Wish, Worth: Wordsworth." Bloom et al. 177-216.

Harvey, Irene. *Derrida and the Economy of Différance.* Bloomington: Indiana UP, 1986.

Hawkes, Terence. *Structuralism and Semiotics.* Los Angeles: U of California P, 1977.

———. *That Shakespeherian Rag: Essays on a Critical Process.* London: Methuen, 1986.

Head, Morrell. "Technology in American Culture." *American Character and Culture.* Ed. J. Hague. Florida: Edwards, 1984. 116-30.

Hegel, G. W. F. *The Phenomenology of Mind.* Trans. J. B. Baillie. New York: Colophon-Harper, 1967.

Heidegger, Martin. *Being and Time.* Trans. J. Macquarrie and E. Robinson. New York: Harper and Row, 1962.

———. *On the Way to Language.* Trans. P. Hertz. New York: Harper and Row, 1982.

———. *Poetry, Language, Thought.* Trans. A. Hofstadter. New York: Colophon-Harper, 1975.

Heilbrun, Carolyn, and Margaret Higonnet, eds. *The Representation of Women in Fiction.* Baltimore: Johns Hopkins UP, 1981.

Heilman, Robert. "Cleanth Brooks and the Well Wrought Urn." *Sewanee Review* 91 (1983): 322-34.

Held, David. *Introduction to Critical Theory.* Berkeley: U of California P, 1980.

Hirsch, E. D., Jr. *The Aims of Interpretation.* Chicago: U of Chicago P, 1976.

———. *Validity in Interpretation.* New Haven: Yale UP, 1967.

Hjelmslev, Louis. *Prolegomena to a Theory of Language.* Trans. F. Whitfield. Madison: U of Wisconsin P, 1961.

Hobbes, Thomas. "Answer to Davenant's Preface to *Gondibert.*" Hazard Adams 212-17.

———. "Concerning Body." Citations in Copleston, 1961, who translates from *Hobbes: Opera philosophica quae latine scripsit.* Ed. W. Molesworth. London: Bohn, 1839-45.

———. "Human Nature." Ed. W. Molesworth. *Body, Man, and Citizen.* Ed. R. S. Peters. New York: Collier, 1962.

———. *Leviathan.* 1651. New York: Dutton, 1947.

———. "Objections to Descartes." Citations in Copleston, 1961, who translates from *Hobbes: Opera philosophica quae latine scripsit.*

Hobson, Marian. "Deconstruction, Empiricism, and the Postal Services." *French Studies* 36 (1982): 290-314.

Hofstader, Richard. *Anti-Intellectualism in American Life.* New York: Knopf, 1963.

Holland, Norman. *5 Readers Reading.* New Haven: Yale UP, 1975.

Holub, Robert. *Reception Theory: A Critical Introduction.* London: Methuen, 1984.

Hook, Sidney. *The Hero in History.* Boston: Beacon, 1966.

Hughes, H. Stuart. *The Sea Change. The Migration of Social Thought 1930-1965.* New York: Harper and Row, 1975.

Hulme, T. E. "Bergson's Theory of Art." Hazard Adams 774-82.

———. "Romanticism and Classicism." Hazard Adams 767-74.

Hume, David. *An Enquiry Concerning Human Understanding.* 1751. *Enquiries concerning the human understanding and concerning the principles of morals.* Ed. L. A. Selby-Bigge. Oxford: Clarendon, 1927.

———. "Life of the Author, by Himself." *The Philosophical Works of David Hume.* Vol. 1. Boston: Little Brown, 1854.

———. "Of the Rise and Progress of the Arts and Sciences." *The Philosophical Works of David Hume.* Vol. III. Boston: Little Brown, 1854.

———. "Of the Standard of Taste." Mourant and Freund 476-89.

———. "Of Tragedy." *Four Dissertations*. New York: Garland, 1970.

———. *A Treatise of Human Nature*. 1737. Ed. L. A. Selby-Bigge. Oxford: Clarendon, 1958.

Husserl, Edmund. *Cartesian Meditations*. Trans. D. Cairns. The Hague: Nijhoff, 1960.

———. *Ideas: General Introduction to Pure Phenomenology*. Trans. W. R. Boyce Gibson. New York: Collier, 1962.

Hyman, Stanley Edgar. *The Armed Vision*. New York: Knopf, 1948.

Hymes, Dell. "Review of *Noam Chomsky*." *On Noam Chomsky: Critical Essays*. Ed. G. Harman. Garden City, N.Y.: Anchor-Doubleday, 1974. 316-34.

———, and John Fought. *American Structuralism*. The Hague: Mouton, 1981.

Ingarden, Roman. *The Literary Work of Art*. Trans. G. Grabowicz. Evanston: Northwestern UP, 1973.

Irwin, John. *Doubling and Incest/Repetition and Revenge: A Speculative Reading of Faulkner*. Baltimore: Johns Hopkins UP, 1975.

Iser, Wolfgang. *The Act of Reading: A Theory of Aesthetic Response*. Baltimore: Johns Hopkins UP, 1978.

———. *The Implied Reader*. Baltimore: Johns Hopkins UP, 1974.

Jakobson, Roman. "Linguistics and Poetics." DeGeorge and DeGeorge 85-122.

———, and M. Halle. *Fundamentals of Language*. The Hague: Mouton, 1956.

Jakobson, Roman, and Claude Lévi-Strauss. "Charles Baudelaire's 'Les Chats.' " DeGeorge and DeGeorge 124-46.

Jameson, Fredric. *The Political Unconscious*. Ithaca: Cornell UP, 1981.

———. *The Prison-House of Language*. Princeton: Princeton UP, 1972.

Jaspers, Karl. *Kant*. Trans. R. Manheim. New York: Harcourt, 1977.

———. *Way to Wisdom*. Trans. R. Manheim. New Haven: Yale UP, 1964.

Jauss, Hans Robert. *Toward an Aesthetic of Reception*. Trans. T. Bahti. Minneapolis: U of Minnesota P, 1982.

Jay, Gregory S., and David L. Miller, eds. *After Strange Texts: The Role of Theory in the Study of Literature*. Alabama: U of Alabama P, 1985.

Jay, Paul. *Being in the Text: Self-Representation from Wordsworth to Roland Barthes*. Ithaca: Cornell UP, 1984.

Johnson, Barbara. *The Critical Difference*. Baltimore: Johns Hopkins UP, 1980.

———. "Gender Theory and the Yale School." Davis and Schleifer 101-12.

Johnston, M. "Philology in the Epoch of the Cogito." *Criticism* 25.2 (1983): 109-122.

Kampf, Louis. "Culture without Criticism." *Massachusetts Review* 9 (1970): 624-44.

Kant, Immanuel. *Critique of Judgment*. Trans. J. C. Meredith. Oxford: Clarendon, 1952.

———. *Critique of Pure Reason*. Trans. N. K. Smith. London: Macmillan, 1929.

Kaufmann, Walter. *Existentialism from Dostoevsky to Sartre*. New York: Meridian, 1957.

Kendler, Howard. *Psychology: A Science in Conflict.* New York: Oxford UP, 1981.

Kermode, Frank. *Romantic Image.* New York: Random, 1964.

Kierkegaard, Søren. *Fear and Trembling / The Sickness Unto Death.* Trans. W. Lowrie. New York: Anchor-Doubleday, 1954.

Korner, S. *Kant.* London: Penguin, 1955.

Kretzmann, Norman. "The Main Thesis of Locke's Semantic Theory." *Locke on Human Understanding.* Ed. I. C. Tipton. Oxford: Oxford UP, 1977. 123-140.

Krieger, Murray. *Arts on the Level.* Knoxville: U of Tennessee P, 1981.

———. "The Existential Basis of Contextual Criticism." Hazard Adams 1224-30.

———. *The New Apologists for Poetry.* Minneapolis: U of Minnesota P, 1956.

———. *Theory of Criticism.* Baltimore: Johns Hopkins UP, 1976.

Kristeva, Julia. "The Ruin of a Poetics." *Russian Formalism.* Ed. S. Bann and J. Boult. Edinburgh: Scottish Academic, 1973. 102-21.

———. *Semiotikè.* Paris: Seuil, 1969.

Krupnick, Mark, ed. *Displacement: Derrida and After.* Bloomington: Indiana UP, 1983.

Kuhn, Thomas. *The Structure of Scientific Revolutions.* 2nd ed. Chicago: U of Chicago P, 1970.

Kurzweil, Edith. *The Age of Structuralism: Lévi-Strauss to Foucault.* New York: Columbia UP, 1980.

Lacan, Jacques. "Desire and the Interpretation of Desire in *Hamlet.*" *Literature and Psychoanalysis.* Ed. S. Felman. Baltimore: Johns Hopkins UP, 1982. 11-52.

———. *Ecrits: A Selection.* Trans. A. Sheridan. New York: Norton, 1977.

———. *The Four Fundamental Concepts of Psycho-Analysis.* Trans. A. Sheridan. New York: Norton, 1981.

———. "Of Structure as an Inmixing of Otherness Prerequisite to Any Subject Whatsoever." Macksey and Donato 186-94.

———. "Seminar on 'The Purloined Letter.' " *Yale French Studies* 40 (1972): 38-72.

LaCapra, Dominick. *Rethinking Intellectual History.* Ithaca: Cornell UP, 1983.

Lane, Michael, ed. *Structuralism: A Reader.* London: Cape, 1970.

Lawall, Sarah. *Critics of Consciousness.* Cambridge: Harvard UP, 1963.

Leach, Edmund. "The Legitimacy of Solomon." Lane 248-92.

Leahey, Thomas. *A History of Psychology.* Englewood Cliffs, N.J.: Prentice-Hall, 1980.

Leavis, F. R. *A Selection from Scrutiny.* London: Cambridge UP, 1968.

Lefevre, Henri. *The Survival of Capitalism.* Trans. F. Bryant. New York: St. Martin's, 1976.

Lehmann, Winfred P. "Linguistics." *Introduction to Scholarship in Modern Languages and Literatures.* Ed. J. Gibaldi. New York: MLA, 1981. 1-28.

Leitch, Vincent. *Deconstructive Criticism: An Advanced Introduction.* New York: Columbia UP, 1983.

Lemaire, Anika. *Jacques Lacan.* Trans. D. Macey. London: Routledge, 1977.

Lemon, Lee. *The Partial Critics.* New York: Oxford UP, 1965.

———, and Marion Reis, eds. *Russian Formalist Criticism.* Lincoln: U of Nebraska P, 1965.

Lentricchia, Frank. *After the New Criticism.* Chicago: U of Chicago P, 1980.

Lerner, Max. *America as a Civilization.* New York: Simon, 1957.

Lévi-Strauss, Claude. "Overture to *le Cru et le cuit.*" Ehrmann 31-55.

———. *The Savage Mind.* Chicago: U of Chicago P, 1966.

———. *Structural Anthropology.* Trans. C. Jacobson and B. Grundfest. New York: Basic, 1963.

Lipking, Lawrence. "Literary Criticism." *Scholarship in Modern Languages and Literatures.* Ed. Joseph Gibaldi. New York: MLA, 1961. 79-97.

Llewelyn, John. *Derrida on the Threshold of Sense.* New York: Macmillan, 1986.

Locke, John. *An Essay Concerning Human Understanding.* 1690. Ed. J. W. Yolton. New York: Dutton, 1978.

———. *Two Treatises of Government.* 1698. Cambridge: Cambridge UP, 1960.

Lovejoy, Arthur. *The Great Chain of Being.* Cambridge: Harvard UP, 1936.

Lukacs, György. *The Historical Novel.* Trans. H. Mitchell and S. Mitchell. London: Merlin, 1962.

———. *The Theory of the Novel.* Trans. A. Bostock. Cambridge: MIT Press, 1971.

Lyons, John. *Language and Linguistics.* Cambridge: Cambridge UP, 1981.

Lyotard, Jean-François. *The Post-Modern Condition: A Report on Knowledge.* Minneapolis: U of Minnesota P, 1984.

MacCannell, Dean, and Juliet Flower MacCannell. *The Time of the Sign.* Bloomington: Indiana UP, 1982.

MacCannell, Juliet Flower. "Portrait: de Man." Davis and Schleifer 51-74.

Macherey, Pierre. *A Theory of Literary Production.* Trans. G. Wall. London: Routledge, 1978.

Mackenzie, Brian. *Behaviorism and the Limits of the Scientific Method.* London: Routledge, 1971.

Macksey, Richard. "Lions and Squares: Opening Remarks." Macksey and Donato 1-14.

———, and Eugenio Donato, eds. *The Structuralist Controversy.* Baltimore: Johns Hopkins UP, 1970.

Magnolia, Robert. *Derrida on the Mend.* West Lafayette, Ind.: Purdue UP, 1984.

Mailloux, Steven. *Interpretive Conventions: The Reader in the Study of American Fiction.* Ithaca: Cornell UP, 1982.

Marcuse, Herbert. *Eros and Civilization.* New York: Vintage-Random House, 1962.

Markus, Gyorgy. "The Paradigm of Language: Wittgenstein, Lévi-Strauss, Gadamer." Fekete 104-29.

Marx, Karl. *Capital.* Ed. F. Engels. Trans. S. Moore and E. Aveling. Chicago: Encyclopædia Britannica, 1952.

———. *Economic and Philosophical Manuscripts.* Trans. T. Bottomore. In E. Fromm. *Marx's Concept of Man.* New York: Ungar, 1961.

———. "The Eighteenth Brumaire of Louis Bonaparte." *Marx and Engels: Basic Writings*. Ed. L. Feuer. New York: Doubleday, 1959. 318-48.

———. *The German Ideology*. New York: International, 1947.

———, and Frederick Engels. *The German Ideology*. New York: International, 1947.

Marx, Leo. "Alienation and Technology." *Technology and Social Change in America*. Ed. E. Layton. New York: Harper and Row, 1973. 121-30.

———. *The Machine in the Garden*. New York: Oxford UP, 1964.

Matthiessen, Francis O. *The Responsibilities of the Critic*. New York: Oxford UP, 1952.

McGann, Jerome. *The Romantic Ideology*. Chicago: U of Chicago P, 1983.

McLeish, John. *The Development of Modern Behavioral Psychology*. Calgary: Detselig, 1981.

McMurtry, John. *The Structure of Marx's World View*. Princeton: Princeton UP, 1978.

Melville, Steven. *Philosophy beside Itself: On Deconstruction and Modernism*. Minneapolis: U of Minnesota P, 1986.

Merquior, J. G. *Foucault*. London: Fontana/Collins, 1985.

Merrell, Floyd. *Deconstruction Reframed*. West Lafayette, Ind.: Purdue UP, 1985.

Michaels, Walter Benn. "The Interpreter's Self: Peirce on the Cartesian Subject." *Reader-Response Criticism*. Ed. J. Tompkins. Baltimore: Johns Hopkins UP, 1980. 185-200.

———. "Saving the Text: Reference and Belief." *MLN* 93 (1978): 771-93.

Mileur, Jean-Paul. *Literary Revisionism and the Burden of Modernity*. Berkeley: U of California P, 1985.

Milic, Louis. "Unconscious Ordering in the Prose of Swift." *The Computer and Literary Style*. Ed. J. Leed. Kent: Kent State UP, 1966.

Miller, G. A., E. H. Galantner, and K. Pribram. *Plans and the Structure of Behavior*. New York: Holt, 1960.

Miller, J. Hillis. "Ariachne's Broken Woof." *Georgia Review* 31 (1977): 44-60.

———. "Ariadne's Thread: Repetition and the Narrative Line." *Critical Inquiry* 3 (1976): 44-60.

———. "A 'Buchstabliches' Reading of *The Elective Affinities*." *Glyph* 6 (1979): 1-23.

———. "The Critic as Host." Bloom et al. 217-53.

———. "Deconstructing the Deconstructers." Rev. of *The Inverted Bell*, by Joseph Riddel. *Diacritics* 5.2 (1975): 24-31.

———. *The Disappearance of God*. Cambridge: Harvard UP, 1963.

———. *Fiction and Repetition: Seven English Novels*. Cambridge: Harvard UP, 1982.

———. "The Search for Grounds in Literary Study." Davis and Schleifer 19-36.

———. "Stevens' Rock and Criticism as Cure." *Georgia Review* 30 (1976): 5-31, 330-48.

———. "Theory and Practice: Response to Vincent Leitch." *Critical Inquiry* 6 (1980): 609-14.

———. "Tradition and Difference." Rev. of *Natural Supernaturalism*, by M. H. Abrams. *Diacritics* 2.4 (1972): 6-13.

Mitchell, Juliet, and Jacqueline Rose, eds. *Feminine Sexuality: Jacques Lacan and the Ecole Freudienne*. Trans. J. Rose. New York: Norton, 1982.

Moraze, Charles. "Literary Invention." Macksey and Donato 22-35.

Mouffe, Chantal. "Hegemony and New Political Subjects: Toward a New Concept of Democracy." Nelson and Grossberg 89-101.

Mourant, John, and E. H. Freund, eds. *Problems of Philosophy*. New York: Macmillan, 1964.

Muller, Herbert. "Human Values and Modern Technology." *Technology and Social Change in America*. Ed. E. Layton. New York: Harper and Row, 1973. 157-76.

Mumford, Lewis. *The Myth of the Machine: The Pentagon of Power*. New York: Harcourt, 1970.

Nehamas, Alexander. "Can We Ever Quite Change the Subject?" *Boundary 2* 10 (1982): 395-413.

Nelson, Cary. "Against English: Theory and the Limits of the Discipline." *ADE Bulletin* 85 (1986): 1-6.

———, and Lawrence Grossberg, eds. *Marxism and the Interpretation of Culture*. Urbana: U of Illinois P, 1988.

Nietzsche, Friedrich. *The Birth of Tragedy*. In *Basic Writings of Nietzsche*. Trans. W. Kaufmann. New York: Modern Library-Random House, 1968.

Norris, Christopher. *The Contest of Faculties: Philosophy and Theory after Deconstruction*. New York: Methuen, 1985.

———. *Deconstruction: Theory and Practice*. New York: Methuen, 1982.

———. *The Deconstructive Turn*. New York: Methuen, 1983.

O'Connor, William Van. *An Age of Criticism: 1900-1950*. Chicago: U of Chicago P, 1956.

Ohmann, Richard. "Literature as Act." Chatman 81-108.

O'Kelly, Charlotte. "The Nature versus Nurture Debate." Boudreau 23-62.

Parker, Andrew. "Between Dialectics and Deconstruction: Derrida and the Reading of Marx." Jay and Miller 146-68.

Peckham, Morse. "On Romanticism: Introduction." *Studies in Romanticism* 9 (1970): 3-26.

Peirce, Charles. *The Essential Writings*. Ed. E. C. Moore. New York: Harper and Row, 1972.

Pettit, Philip. *The Concept of Structuralism*. Berkeley: U of California P, 1977.

Piaget, Jean. *Structuralism*. Trans. C. Maschler. New York: Basic, 1970.

Piper, William. "Immaterialist Aesthetics: An Extrapolation from the Empiricism of Hume." *Western Humanities Review* 37 (1983): 283-305.

Plato. *Ion*. Trans. B. Jowett. Hazard Adams 12-18.

———. *The Republic*. Trans. A. D. Lindsay. New York: Dutton, 1950.

Poulet, Georges. "Criticism and the Experience of Interiority." Macksey and Donato 56-88.

Pratt, Mary Louise. *Toward a Speech Act Theory of Literary Discourse.* Bloomington: Indiana UP, 1977.

Pritchard, John Paul. *Criticism in America.* Norman: U of Oklahoma P, 1956.

Propp, Vladimir. *Morphology of the Folktale.* Trans. S. Pirkova-Jakobson. Bloomington: Indiana Research Center in Anthropology, 1958.

Pursell, Carroll. "The American Ideal of a Democratic Technology." De Lauretis et al. 11-26.

Ragland-Sullivan, Ellie. *Jacques Lacan and the Philosophy of Psychoanalysis.* Urbana: U of Illinois P, 1986.

Rajchman, John. *Michel Foucault: The Freedom of Philosophy.* New York: Columbia UP, 1985.

Ransom, John Crowe. *God without Thunder.* New York: Harcourt, 1930.

——. *The New Criticism.* Norfolk, Conn.: New Directions, 1941.

——. *The World's Body.* 1938. Baton Rouge: Louisiana State UP, 1968.

Raschke, Carl. "The Deconstruction of God." Altizer et al. 1-33.

Ray, William. *Literary Meaning: From Phenomenology to Deconstruction.* Oxford: Blackwell, 1984.

Reiss, Timothy. *The Discourse of Modernism.* Ithaca: Cornell UP, 1982.

Richards, I. A. *The Philosophy of Rhetoric.* London: Oxford UP, 1936.

——. *Practical Criticism.* 1929. New York: Harvest-Harcourt, n.d.

——. *Principles of Literary Criticism.* 1925. New York: Harvest-Harcourt, n.d.

——. *Science and Poetry.* New York: Norton, 1926.

Richards, I. A., C. K. Ogden, and James Wood. *Foundations of Aesthetics.* London: Allen and Unwin, 1925.

Ricoeur, Paul. "Symbole et temporalité." *Archivio di Filosofia* (Rome) 1 and 2 (1963).

Riddel, Joseph. *The Inverted Bell: Modernism and the Counter Poetics of William Carlos Williams.* Baton Rouge: Louisiana State UP, 1974.

Riffaterre, Michael. "Describing Poetic Structures: Two Approaches to Baudelaire's *Les Chats.*" Ehrmann 188-229.

Robinson, Lillian. "Treason Our Text: Feminist Challenges to the Literary Canon." Showalter 105-22.

Rorty, Richard. *Consequences of Pragmatism.* Minneapolis: U of Minnesota P, 1982.

Ross, Andrew. "The New Sentence and the Commodity Form: Recent American Writing." Nelson and Grossberg 361-80.

Russell, Bertrand, and A. N. Whitehead. *Principia Mathematica.* 1910. Cambridge: Cambridge UP, 1970.

Ruthven, K. K. *Feminist Literary Studies: An Introduction.* New York: Cambridge UP, 1984.

Ryan, Michael. "Deconstruction and Social Theory." Krupnick 154-68.

——. *Marxism and Deconstruction.* Baltimore: Johns Hopkins UP, 1982.

Ryle, Gilbert. *The Concept of Mind.* 1949. New York: Barnes and Noble, 1959.

Said, Edward. *Beginnings.* New York: Columbia UP, 1985.

——. "Reflections on American 'Left' Literary Criticism." *Boundary 2* 8.1 (1979): 11-30.

——. *The World, the Text, and the Critic.* Cambridge: Harvard UP, 1983.

Sartre, Jean-Paul. *Being and Nothingness.* Trans. H. Barnes. New York: Washington Square, 1966.

——. "Existentialism Is a Humanism." *Existentialism from Dostoevsky to Sartre.* Ed. W. Kaufmann. New York: Meridian, 1957. 287-311.

——. *Nausea.* Trans. L. Alexander. Norfolk, Conn.: New Directions, 1955.

——. *What Is Literature?* Trans. B. Frechtman. Gloucester, Mass: Smith, 1978.

Saussure, Ferdinand de. *Course in General Linguistics.* Trans. Roy Harris. London: Duckworth, 1983.

Schaff, Adam. *Structuralism and Marxism.* New York: Pergamon, 1978.

Scharlemann, Robert. "The Being of God When God Is Not Being God." Altizer et al. 79-108.

Scheffler, Howard. "Structuralism in Anthropology." Ehrmann 56-78.

Schelling, F. W. von. "On the Relation of the Plastic Arts to Nature." Hazard Adams 446-58.

Schiller, Friedrich. *On the Aesthetic Education of Man.* Oxford: Clarendon, 1967.

Scholem, Gershom. *Major Trends in Jewish Mysticism.* 1941. New York: Schocken, 1973.

Scholes, Robert. *Structuralism in Literature.* New Haven: Yale UP, 1974.

Scruton, Roger. *From Descartes to Wittgenstein.* New York: Colophon-Harper, 1982.

Searle, John. "Chomsky's Revolution in Linguistics." *On Noam Chomsky: Critical Essays.* Ed. G. Harman. Garden City, N.Y.: Anchor-Doubleday, 1974. 2-33.

——. "Reiterating the Differences: A Reply to Derrida." *Glyph* 1 (1977): 198-208.

——. *Speech Acts: An Essay in the Philosophy of Language.* Cambridge: Cambridge UP, 1969.

Sebeok, Thomas, ed. *Style in Language.* Cambridge: MIT P, 1960.

Selden, Raman. *Criticism and Objectivity.* London: Allen, 1984.

Shelley, Percy. "A Defense of Poetry." Hazard Adams 499-513.

Showalter, Elaine. "Feminist Criticism in the Wilderness." *Critical Inquiry* 8 (1981): 179-205.

——, ed. *The New Feminist Criticism: Essays on Women, Literature, and Theory.* New York: Pantheon, 1985.

Skinner, B. F. *Beyond Freedom and Dignity.* New York: Knopf, 1971.

——. *Science and Human Behavior.* New York: Macmillan, 1953.

——. *Verbal Behavior.* New York: Appleton, 1957.

——. *Walden Two.* New York: Macmillan, 1948.

Slade, Joseph. "American Writers and American Inventions." De Lauretis et al. 27-48.

Smith, Barbara Herrnstein. *On the Margins of Discourse.* Chicago: U of Chicago P, 1978.

Smith, Niel, and Deirdre Wilson. *Modern Linguistics.* Bloomington: Indiana UP, 1980.

Snow, C. P. *The Two Cultures.* Cambridge: Cambridge UP, 1964.

Spinoza, Baruch. *Ethics*. New York: Everyman's Library, 1959.

Spivak, Gayatri. Translator's Preface. *Of Grammatology*. By Jacques Derrida. Baltimore: Johns Hopkins UP, 1976. ix-lxxxvii.

Staten, Henry. *Wittgenstein and Derrida*. Lincoln: U of Nebraska P, 1984.

Steiner, Peter. *Russian Formalism: A Metapoetics*. Ithaca: Cornell UP, 1984.

Stephen, Leslie. *Hobbes*. Ann Arbor: U of Michigan P, 1961.

Strickland, Geoffrey. *Structuralism or Criticism?* London: Cambridge UP, 1981.

Sturrock, J., ed. *Structuralism and Since*. New York: Oxford UP, 1979.

Tate, Allen. *On the Limits of Poetry*. New York: Swallow, 1948.

———. *Reactionary Essays on Poetry and Ideas*. 1936. Freeport, N.Y.: Books for Libraries, 1968.

———. *Reason in Madness*. New York: Putnam's, 1941.

Taylor, Mark, ed. *Deconstruction in Context: Literature and Philosophy*. Chicago: U of Chicago P, 1986.

Thody, Philip. *Roland Barthes: A Conservative Estimate*. Chicago: U of Chicago P, 1983.

Thompson, Ewa. *Russian Formalism and Anglo-American New Criticism: A Comparative Study*. The Hague: Mouton, 1971.

Thurley, Geoffrey. *Counter-Modernism in Current Critical Theory*. London: Macmillan, 1983.

Tillich, Paul. *The Courage to Be*. 1952. New Haven: Yale UP, 1959.

Titchener, E. B. *An Outline of Psychology*. New York: Macmillan, 1897.

Todorov, Tzvetan. *Grammaire du Decameron*. The Hague: Mouton, 1969.

———. *Introduction to Poetics*. Trans. R. Howard. Minneapolis: U of Minnesota P, 1981.

———. "Language and Literature." Macksey and Donato 125-33.

———. *The Poetics of Prose*. Trans. R. Howard. Ithaca: Cornell UP, 1977.

———. "Structuralism and Literature." Chatman 153-68.

Trotsky, Leon. *Literature and Revolution*. Trans. R. Strunsky. Ann Arbor: U of Michigan P, 1971.

Turkle, Sherry. *Psychoanalytic Politics*. New York: Basic Books, 1978.

Ulmer, Gregory. "Op Writing: Derrida's Solicitation of Theoria." Krupnick 29-58.

Velan, Yves. "Barthes." *Modern French Criticism*. Ed. J. Simon. Chicago: U of Chicago P, 1972. 311-40.

Warren, Robert Penn. "Pure and Impure Poetry." Hazard Adams 981-92.

Watkins, Evan. "The Politics of Literary Criticism." *Boundary 2* 8 (1979): 31-37.

Watson, George. "Old Furniture and 'Nouvelle Critique.' " *Encounter* 44 (1975): 48-54.

Watson, J. B. *Behaviorism*. New York: Norton, 1924.

Watson, Robert. *The Great Psychologists*. 4th ed. New York: Lippincott, 1978.

Webster, Grant. *The Republic of Letters*. Baltimore: Johns Hopkins UP, 1979.

Weimann, Robert. *Structure and Society in Literary History*. Baltimore: Johns Hopkins UP, 1984.

Wellek, René. *Concepts of Criticism*. New Haven: Yale UP, 1963.

——. "An End to Criticism." *Georgia Review* 34 (1980): 182-88.

——. *Four Critics*. Seattle: U of Washington P, 1981.

——, and Austin Warren. *Theory of Literature*. 1942. New York: Harvest-Harcourt, n.d.

West, Cornel. "Ethics and Action in Fredric Jameson's Marxist Hermeneutics." *Arac* 123-44.

White, Hayden. *Metahistory: The Historical Imagination in Nineteenth-Century Europe*. Baltimore: Johns Hopkins UP, 1973.

——. "Michel Foucault." Sturrock 81-115.

Whorf, Benjamin. *Language, Thought, and Reality: Selected Writings*. Ed. S. Chase. Cambridge: MIT P, 1969.

Widdowson, Peter, ed. *Re-Reading English*. London: Methuen, 1982.

Wilden, Anthony. *The Language of the Self*. New York: Delta-Dell, 1968.

Williams, Raymond. "Base and Superstructure in Marxist Critical Theory." *Problems in Materialism and Culture*. London: Verso, 1980.

——. *Culture and Society: 1790-1850*. New York: Harper, 1966.

——. *Marxism and Literature*. New York: Oxford UP, 1977.

Wimsatt, W. K., Jr., with Monroe C. Beardsley. *The Verbal Icon*. Lexington: U of Kentucky P, 1954.

Wimsatt, W. K., Jr., and Cleanth Brooks. *Literary Criticism: A Short History*. 1957. Chicago: Midway-U of Chicago P, 1983.

Winters, Yvor. *Anatomy of Nonsense*. Norfolk, Conn.: New Directions, 1943. Also contained in Winters, *In Defense of Reason*.

——. *In Defense of Reason*. Denver: Swallow, 1947.

——. *Maule's Curse*. Norfolk, Conn.: New Directions, 1938. Also contained in Winters, *In Defense of Reason*.

Wittgenstein, Ludwig. *Philosophical Investigations*. Trans. G. E. M. Anscombe. New York: Macmillan, 1953.

Woodward, Kathleen. Introduction. De Lauretis et al. 3-10.

Wordsworth, William. "Preface to the Second Edition of *Lyrical Ballads*." Hazard Adams 433-43.

Yalom, Irvin. *Existential Psychotherapy*. New York: Basic, 1980.

Zukav, Gary. *The Dancing Wu Li Masters: An Overview of the New Physics*. New York: Bantam, 1979.

Index

A Note on the Author

ART BERMAN is associate professor of language, literature, and communication at the Rochester Institute of Technology.